THIRD EDITION

DEPOSIT OPERATIONS

David H. Friedman

AMERICAN
BANKERS
ASSOCIATION

1120 Connecticut Avenue, N.W.
Washington, D.C. 20036

Friedman, David H., 1942-

    Deposit operations / David H. Friedman. — 3rd ed.
        p. cm.
    Includes bibliographical references and index.
     ISBN 0-89982-333-5
     1. Deposit banking—United States. 2. Electronic funds transfers
United States. I. Title.
HG1660.U5F75 1992   92-977
332.1'752—dc20   CIP

This publication is designed to provide accurate and authoritative information in regard to the subject matter covered. It is sold with the understanding that the publisher is not engaged in rendering legal, accounting, or other professional service. If legal advice or other expert assistance is required, the services of a competent professional person should be sought.

From a Declaration of Principles jointly adopted by a Committee of the American Bar Association and a Committee of Publishers and Associations.

Contents

Exhibits

About the Author

David H. Friedman is an economist, author, and banking instructor. He received a BA and an MA in economics from Brooklyn College and has completed coursework and examinations for a PhD in economics at the New School for Social Research. Mr. Friedman has been with the Federal Reserve Bank of New York since 1967 and is currently serving as special assistant in the bank's planning department.

Mr. Friedman created the *Essentials of Banking* seminar for the American Institute of Banking and the General Banking curriculum for the Professional Development Program of the American Bankers Association. He is the author of *Money & Banking*, other works on economics and banking, and several segments of *The Money Encyclopedia*. Mr. Friedman has been on the faculty of the American Institute of Banking in New York since 1974 and has been an Assistant Professor of Economics at Brooklyn College since 1965. He has conducted seminars and training programs on banking operations, the U.S. payments mechanism, and a broad range of economics and management subjects for both the American Institute of Banking and the Bank Administration Institute. Mr. Friedman has also taught at the Iowa School of Banking, the New York Bankers Association Management School for Career Development, the American Bankers Association Business of Banking School, and New York University Graduate School.

Mr. Friedman lives in East Brunswick, New Jersey, with his wife Alice, daughter Lynne, and son Paul, whose collective support and encouragement were essential in writing *Deposit Operations*.

Preface

This third edition of *Deposit Operations* is a revision of the text published in 1987. New check endorsement standards, return-item-processing procedures, and new rules limiting the holds banks can place on the use of deposited check funds have all contributed to profound changes in deposit operations since that time. Other changes have included the entry of nonbank institutions into the credit card business, the expansion of regional ATM networks, changes in reserve requirements, and new regulations to reduce the risks in using interbank electronic payments. Eroding profitability of the nation's large banks, the S&L crisis, the creation of the Resolution Trust Corporation, and the national debate over reform of the federal deposit insurance system have provided a dramatic backdrop for banks' deposit operations in the early 1990s. The third edition of *Deposit Operations* reflects these changes.

The primary focus of the text has remained the same—an examination of how banks operate in the context of the U.S. payments mechanism, banking law and regulation, and industry practices. However, new material updates and expands the text's discussion of technological, regulatory, competitive, and managerial changes that have affected banking operations in the late 1980s and early 1990s, and the major issues confronting banks. New material on the role of the Federal Reserve in the payments mechanism and on 1989's Financial Institutions Reform, Recovery and Enforcement Act have been added and the glossary of terms used in the text has been expanded. The chapters on deposits and depositories, the regulatory structure, sources and uses of bank funds, and the evolving banking system have been totally re-structured to reflect the most recent changes.

Deposit Operations is designed for bankers who are new to the profession, as well as experienced bankers who would like current information on bank operations. The needs of both groups were considered in presenting the content material and establishing the text's objectives, which are to

❖ examine the U.S. payments mechanism, the changing nature and composition of deposits, the role of the nation's depositories, and the changing legal and regulatory environment in which banks operate

❖ generate an understanding of the check collection process, the rules and practices that govern banks' activities in effecting paper payments, and the risks banks incur in processing checks

❖ acquaint bankers with the range of cash management services banks offer

❖ discuss where banking may be headed over the next two decades and the need for banks to increase their productivity to remain competitive and profitable in the 1990s and beyond

Deposit Operations is organized for instructors as well as students. Each chapter begins with learning objectives followed by an introduction that sets the stage for the chapter's subject matter. Each chapter ends with a summary of the concepts presented and a series of discussion questions for use in the classroom or in examinations.

The introductory chapter examines the way payments are made and the form in which individuals and businesses hold and spend their money. This discussion is presented in the context of the general environment in which banks conduct their deposit operations and the major payments-related issues confronting banks.

Chapter 2 focuses on depositories and the major deposit products they provide. Chapter 3 discusses the regulations that establish the framework for much of banking's operations and current issues in bank regulation. These chapters emphasize the changing role of banks, financial intermediaries, and the Federal Reserve in the payments mechanism, the different payment services that depositories offer, and the important changes initiated by the Monetary Control Act of 1980.

The importance of check collection in bank operations, the techniques and procedures banks use to collect checks, and the body of rules and practices that govern the collection process are the subjects of chapter 4. Chapters 5 and 6 examine the broad range of electronic payment services in retail banking and the important role EFT systems play in interbank transactions. These chapters review and discuss the major issues and factors that have impeded progress in electronic retail banking and the critical risk issues that banks face when transferring funds over the interbank EFT systems.

Chapter 7 examines how banks create deposits and how the Federal Reserve regulates this process. This chapter provides a conceptual perspective of deposit operations and a foundation for understanding why banks operate the way they do.

Chapter 8's review of deposit management focuses on checks, particularly exception items, why checks have to be examined, and the bookkeeping procedures and systems banks have developed to manage deposits. The chapter also looks at the rules and regulations governing delayed funds availability and the key strategies banks employ in marketing their payment services to customers.

Chapter 9 focuses on how and why bank strategies changed in the 1970s and 1980s, examines funds management strategies banks employ, and reviews the major sources and uses of bank funds. Chapter 10 discusses the various cash management services banks offer to corporate customers and the importance of lockbox arrangements, controlled disbursement, and balance reporting as sources of earnings to many banks.

The concluding chapter of *Deposit Operations* focuses on where banking and the payments mechanism have come from and where both may be heading over the next two decades. It also reviews the strategies banks have instituted to reduce the costs of deposit operations, increase income generated from payments and related services, and strengthen profitability of banking in the 1990s.

I would like to express my gratitude to my reviewers. They provided invaluable help in critically reviewing revised chapters and making suggestions for a more effective text. These are highly knowledgeable and dedicated bankers:

Joel R. Johnson
Operations Officer
Richfield Bank and Trust Company
Richfield, Minnesota

Charles A. Walwyn, Jr.
Chairman
C. Y. King Associates
New York, New York

John Rotellini
Assistant Vice President & Loan Officer
Key Bank of Wyoming
Sheridan, Wyoming

Donie Hodge
Assistant Vice President and Cashier
Citizens Fidelity Bank and Trust Company
 Hardin County
Elizabethtown, Kentucky

Bob Multari
Director of Grants Management
New York Dept. of Transportation
New York, New York

Dan Leeth
Vice President and Cashier
Republic National Bank
Englewood, Colorado

Shirley A. McGee
Senior Vice President
MetroBank
Houston, Texas

David H. Friedman
March 1992

THE U.S. PAYMENTS MECHANISM

Objectives

After successfully completing this chapter, you will be able to

- ❖ discuss the relative importance and role of different payment devices and institutions in the U.S. payments mechanism

- ❖ define key payment-related banking terms—credit card, debit systems, ACH, check truncation, POS terminals, and ATM networks

- ❖ identify the major shortcomings in America's early payments system

- ❖ explain the Federal Reserve's role in the U.S. payments mechanism

- ❖ identify the retail electronic funds transfer (EFT) systems that are most likely to shape the nation's future payments mechanism

- ❖ cite the major unresolved issues related to the development of EFT in the United States

Introduction

This chapter presents an overview of the U.S. payments mechanism and profiles the major payment devices used in the U.S. economy—coin, currency, demand deposits, and electronic funds transfers—and their relative importance.

A payments mechanism is the system a nation uses to transfer money, make payments, and settle debts. In the United States, the payments mechanism is based on paper currency and checks for most personal and commercial transactions and on electronic funds transfers for transactions involving large sums of money. The concept of payments mechanism also includes the relationship among commercial banks, other financial institutions, and the central bank (the Federal Reserve) in transferring, processing, and settling money balances.

Money is a nation's medium of exchange—that is, anything that is generally accepted in exchange for goods, services, or settlement of debt.

Money serves two other important functions. It serves as a standard for comparing the relative value of goods and services and as a store of value, which is a means of accumulating and holding future purchasing power.

Coin, paper currency, and checking accounts (demand deposits and interest-bearing transaction accounts) have come to be accepted as the three items that make up the medium of exchange in the United States.

However, most of the country's financial wealth is not held in the form of coin, currency, or checking accounts, but in near monies—assets that may be good stores of value or good standards of value but are not generally accepted as money. Only a fraction of Americans' financial wealth, about $900 billion, is in the form of money. (See exhibit 1.1.) Several trillion dollars are held in the form of financial assets such as stocks, bonds, life insurance policies, pension funds, money market funds, and various types of interest-earning time and savings accounts in banks and thrift institutions. The American public holds more than $2.6 trillion in time and savings deposits in the nation's commercial banks, savings and loan associations, savings banks, and credit unions.

Payment Instruments

Coin, used mainly by individuals for day-to-day convenience transactions, comprises only about 3 percent of money in the United States. Paper currency, the primary medium of exchange for small retail transactions, comprises about 30 percent of the nation's money. Once the centerpiece of the U.S. payments mechanism, cash plays a relatively small role in the payments system today.

Exhibit 1.1 *Money Held by the Public for Transactions Purposes (billions of dollars)*

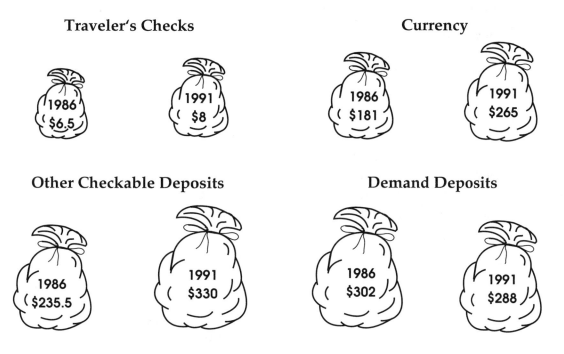

Traveler's Checks
- 1986 $6.5
- 1991 $8

Currency
- 1986 $181
- 1991 $265

Other Checkable Deposits
- 1986 $235.5
- 1991 $330

Demand Deposits
- 1986 $302
- 1991 $288

1986 total, $725 billion; 1991 total, $891 billion

Source: Federal Reserve *Bulletin*, January 1991, and Federal Reserve *Statistical Release H. 6(508)*, December 12, 1991.

Demand and transaction deposits comprise about 70 percent of the nation's money and account for more than 90 percent of the dollar value of all commercial and personal payments made in the United States. Furthermore, the volume of check usage has been growing at a rate of about 5 percent per year since the 1950s. Although check usage increased at a lower rate in the 1980s, checks are likely to remain the predominant medium of exchange for decades to come. In 1991, there were 125 million checking accounts in the United States. It is estimated that Americans wrote about 57 billion checks against those accounts, transferring more than $40 trillion. (See exhibit 1.2.)

Only a small number of payments in the United States are made by other than cash or check. However, electronic funds transfers (EFT) are commonly made among banks, between banks and the Federal Reserve, and between corporations and financial institutions. The dollar volume of these electronic financial payments can be staggering.

As exhibit 1.3 shows, electronic funds transfers play a major role in moving the dollar value of U.S. payments. The pie charts include financial transactions, such as banks' daily buying and selling of federal funds, as well as personal and commercial payments.

While credit cards and electronic funds transfers have made inroads into personal and commercial payments practices, the U.S. payments system largely revolves around checking accounts and the depository institutions that provide checking account services.

Checks

In the U.S. payments system, consumers predominantly use checks. More than four out of five families maintain checking accounts; many families have more than one account. About half of all the checks written in the United States are drawn by individuals (about 30 billion checks were written by individuals in 1991); more than half those checks are written for amounts less than $50. The average consumer writes about 20 to 30 checks each month.

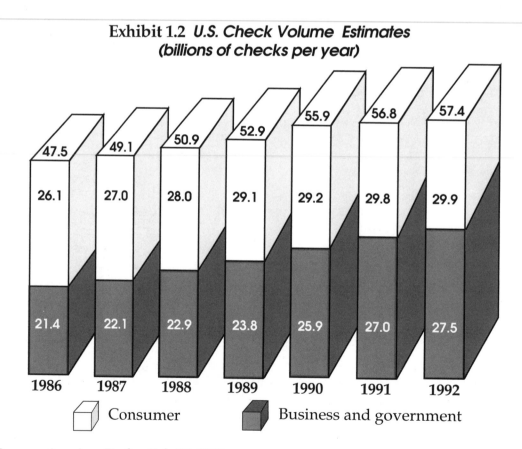

Exhibit 1.2 *U.S. Check Volume Estimates*
(billions of checks per year)

	1986	1987	1988	1989	1990	1991	1992
Total	47.5	49.1	50.9	52.9	55.9	56.8	57.4
Consumer	26.1	27.0	28.0	29.1	29.2	29.8	29.9
Business and government	21.4	22.1	22.9	23.8	25.9	27.0	27.5

☐ Consumer   ■ Business and government

Source: *American Banker*, Feb. 22, 1989

Chapter 1

Exhibit 1.3 *U.S. Payments Transactions*

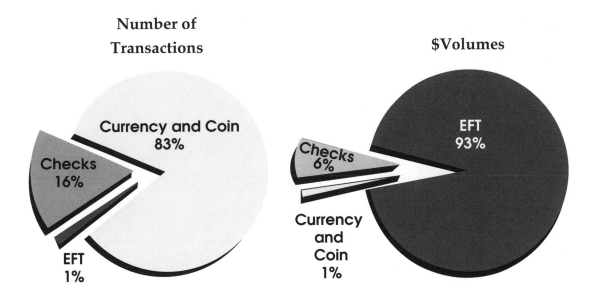

Number of Transactions

Currency and Coin 83%

Checks 16%

EFT 1%

$Volumes

EFT 93%

Checks 6%

Currency and Coin 1%

Source: Federal Reserve Bank of Kansas City, *Economic Review,*
September/October 1989.

Businesses write about 45 percent of all checks drawn—about 25 billion checks in 1991. (By contrast, government entities wrote only about 5 percent of all checks, or 2 billion checks in 1991.) Almost all business checks are written for amounts between $75 and $500 and business firms also draw nearly all the checks over $500. About two-thirds of all business checks are payroll checks. Businesses also receive about 65 percent of all checks written, most of which come from consumers.

These statistics show the central role checks play in our payments system. Individuals write checks to pay bills and buy goods and services, and they receive payroll checks from businesses as the source of money against which they write their own checks. Exhibit 1.4 lists the reasons people write personal checks.

Exhibit 1.4 *Why People Write Personal Checks*

Motive	Percentage of Total Checks Written
To obtain cash	8
To pay for over-the-counter retail purchases	32
To pay bills:	50
recurring bills—utility, insurance, rent (19%)	
bills for goods purchased previously (16%)	
nonrecurring bills—car repairs, doctor bills (15%)	
To transfer funds or make other payments, such as gifts and charitable contributions	10
Total	**100**

Credit Cards

More than half of all American families use credit cards—on average, about 10 transactions each month with an average transaction value of about $60. Credit cards are not money items; they are deferred payment devices that allow consumers to buy now and pay later. In effect, credit cards are prearranged loans.

Credit cards can be either bilateral or multilateral arrangements. In bilateral credit card arrangements (such as those made by department stores and gasoline companies), the credit card user can buy goods and services on credit only from the issuing institution, merchant, or chain.

In multilateral credit card arrangements (such as those made by national credit card and national travel and entertainment companies), consumers can buy goods and services on credit from thousands of different merchants that participate with banking institutions in these predetermined loan arrangements. Most multilateral credit cards, in fact, allow the user to draw cash on credit from depositories participating in the arrangements. Credit cards generally carry a credit line that limits the dollar amount that may be charged to the credit card. Credit lines, like most consumer loans, are typically based on such factors as income, financial assets, outstanding debt, and debt repayment history.

About one-third of all families use bilateral credit cards, primarily gasoline credit cards, and about 40 percent have more than one bank credit card. In 1992, Americans held a total of more than 280 million credit cards, averaging more than three credit cards for every adult. Some consumers use their credit cards as an alternative to checks or cash at the time of purchase—perhaps as many as one-third of all cardholders. About one-third pay off their outstanding balance within the grace period (usually 25 days) before interest charges are assessed on their loans. Others use the cards for their revolving credit feature.

The popularity of bank cards in the 1980s and 1990s has been matched by their profitability for banks. On average, banks earn a higher return on credit cards than on most other bank loans, in part because credit cards are unsecured loans that carry a higher risk of nonpayment than other kinds of loans. The sources of that higher return are

❖ interest income on credit card balances

About 75 percent of a bank's revenue from credit cards comes from interest income. In 1992, three-quarters of all bank cards carried fixed interest rates. For a standard Visa card or Mastercard, the interest rate on outstanding balances averaged 18.86 percent. Cardholders who use the revolving credit feature of their bank cards—about two-thirds of all users—kept average monthly balances of about $1,500 in 1990 and paid close to $300 in annual finance charges. They held these balances despite the high interest rates charged for the credit and the loss of tax deductibility for interest paid. In 1986, Congress enacted a five-year phaseout of the federal tax deduction for interest on most consumer loans. Many bankers expected that the tax change would motivate consumers to quickly pay off their outstanding credit card balances, thereby reducing the substantial interest income generated for banks from these balances. However, that expectation has proved groundless. The tax change had little effect on the behavior of bank card users; they held $140 billion in outstanding card balances in 1990.

❖ annual fees

Most card-issuing banks assess an annual user fee on cardholders (roughly $20 in 1992).

❖ interchange fees

An interchange fee is the payment that a merchant's bank pays to a card-issuing bank each time a card is used at the merchant's store. The interchange fee compensates the card-issuing bank for administrative costs and the risk of losses that would be incurred if the cardholder fails to pay. Merchants' banks typically pass on these fees to the merchant through discount charges.

❖ merchant discount charges

Banks that receive credit card sales slips from merchants charge them a discount fee, which is a percentage of the credit card sale—usually 2 to 5 percent. For example, if the merchant is subject to a 2 percent discount charge and deposits a $100 credit card sales slip at the bank, the merchant's account is debited by $2 at the end of the month. In effect, the merchant nets only $98 for the deposit.

❖ late payment fees

About 60 percent of card-issuing banks assess fees to cardholders who fail to make the minimum monthly payment within 15 to 30 days of the date due. These fees ranged from $10 to $15 per month in 1992.

❖ charges for exceeding the card's limit

About 40 percent of card-issuing banks assess cardholders a fee for exceeding their credit lines. The fee compensates the card-issuing bank for the extra risk of payment default. These risks (and accompanying losses) soared in the late 1980s and early 1990s as more than 2 million consumers, overburdened by debt, declared personal bankruptcy. Many bankers see rising credit card losses from personal bankruptcies leading to stricter credit card issuance, lower credit card limits, and possibly higher annual fees and service charges on cardholders by the mid-1990s.

In the late 1980s, competition for bank card customers intensified with the entry of Sears (Discover card) and American Express (Centurion) as major credit card issuers. In 1990, credit card competition became more intense as American Telephone and Telegraph Co. issued its AT&T Universal Card. (See exhibit 1.5.) To meet this competition, banks have sought to differentiate their cards. Some banks have established affinity cards— issuing cards in conjunction with a sports team, frequent-flier program, or service organization whose name and identifying symbols appear on the card. These cards are designed to establish a common association or affinity between the card-issuing bank and card users. Other banks have substantially lowered annual fees, while some large banks—400 in 1991—waived fees for new customers and high-balance, extensive-use customers. The strategy adopted by most major bank card issuers, however, has been to enhance the value of their cards by linking special benefits or features to the cards' use. (Examples of these benefits are listed in exhibit 1.6.) In 1990, the Federal Reserve ruled that large banks that issue their credit cards through subsidiaries could link their cards directly to services provided by the bank, such as checking accounts. Industry analysts expect that major bank card issuers will begin to take advantage of this ruling in the 1990s, increasingly packaging their cards with other retail banking services and charging customers one overall fee.

Exhibit 1.5 *The 10 Largest Bank Credit Card Issuers in the U.S. in 1990*

Bank	Outstanding Credit Card Balances (in billions of dollars)	Number of Accounts (in millions)
Citicorp	$ 31.5	22.0
Greenwood Trust (Discover)	11.5	18.3
Chase Manhattan	8.5	9.0
First Chicago	6.5	6.2
BankAmerica	6.0	6.5
Centurion (American Express)	7.0	6.1
MBNA	5.5	4.2
Bank of New York	3.3	2.5
Banc One	3.2	4.0
Manufacturers Hanover	2.8	2.4

Note: AT&T issued its Universal credit card in 1990. More than 7.6 million cardholders held outstanding balances of $1.7 billion on the AT&T card in 1991, making AT&T the largest nonbank issuer of credit cards in the U.S. Sears had issued its Discover card to 38 million households by 1991.

Sources: *Fortune Magazine*, **July 2, 1990, and** *American Banker*, **January 23, 1991, and October 31, 1991.**

Product differentiation is a relatively new concept in banking but is an established marketing strategy in America's manufacturing industries. Similar products, such as soap, toothpaste, and cigarettes, are routinely supplied by different producers. Through brand names, special packaging, or differences in the quality of the product, each producer seeks to distinguish its product from similar products of other manufacturers. In doing this, the differentiating producer seeks to retain or expand its share of the market and/or command a premium price for its products.

Card-issuing banks also are seeking to increase credit card use in the 1990s. America's fast-food restaurants and movie theaters, where consumers make millions of quick, small dollar-value transactions, are seen as major targets. Some targets have already been hit: the Wendy's fast-food chain in central Florida accepts credit cards. However, many bankers contend that to expand

Exhibit 1.6 *Benefits Offered by Major Credit Card Issuers in 1991 to Users of Their Standard or Premium (Gold) Cards*

❏ 3-month purchase insurance against loss or theft

❏ $100,000-$250,000 travel accident insurance

❏ 10% off long-distance telephone calls

❏ guaranteed hotel reservations

❏ referrals for medical and legal aid; emergency transportation; and funds advanced for treatment

❏ 24-hour tow truck referral service

❏ credit card registration; instant credit on disputed charges and investigation of consumer complaints

❏ lowest price guarantee for purchases

❏ warranties doubled up to one year

❏ rental car insurance

❏ discounts on car rentals

❏ cash advances

❏ $500,000 flight insurance

❏ seating for theatrical or sporting events

❏ cash rebate of up to 1% of amount charged

❏ year-end statement summarizing charges for business/tax-related purposes

into this market on a nationwide basis, simple, low-cost bank card use procedures and systems will first have to be developed so that transaction time at checkout counters and registers is not slowed. Without such procedures and systems it is unlikely that most fast-food restaurant and movie theater owners would accept bank cards.

Several major banks have examined the feasibility of introducing "smart" cards to consumers and merchants to expand credit card use. Smart cards are based on a credit card technology pioneered by the French banking industry in the early 1980s. A smart card looks like a typical MasterCard or VISA card but is embedded with a microprocessor (chip) that gives the card computational power and data storage capabilities. For example, the cardholder's personal identification number (PIN) and available credit line can be stored in the chip. Proponents of the smart card see it as a more secure and less costly bank credit card because cardholder identification can be handled at the point of use, eliminating the need to send verification data over phone lines. When the card is used, the cardholder enters the PIN at a terminal, which verifies that the PIN matches the number stored in the card's chip.

Debit Systems

Electronic funds transfer systems are not widely used by American consumers or business firms, but are widely used in most European payment systems. They are commonly called giro systems (pronounced Jye-ro) from the Latin word for transfer, gyrus. Typically, giro systems can make payments for anyone, even those without any type of deposit account, and giro has become the principal payments mechanism most European consumers use.

In a typical giro transfer—which can be either paper-based or electronic—payers authorize transfers of funds from their accounts to creditors' accounts. If the payer has no account with the giro system, he or she can present cash at the bank, post office, or other intermediary participating in the giro system, and the transfer is made.

In electronic giro systems, recipients receive confirmation that payment has been made through computer terminal hookups. In paper-based systems, the giro intermediary performs the function of check writing, mailing, or even hand delivery of cash.

In a giro system, payment is not made unless the payer's account has sufficient funds or cash is presented at the point of origination. By contrast, if a check is used for payment, the status of funds is uncertain until the check is collected on behalf of the depositor. For this reason, giro systems are often called debit systems and are more similar to a wire transfer of funds than to U.S. checks.

While there are some private, bank-run giro systems in Europe, the European postal giro systems provide the competitive standard for this type of service. These postal giro systems were established by the government as an adjunct to the existing post office; they use the postal infrastructure of offices and transport. For example, Germany has an extensive postal giro system, and Britain established a national postal giro in 1968. Sweden has a sophisticated postal giro that provides consumers with account statements after each transaction. Most other countries' giro systems provide account statements monthly.

The National Commission on Electronic Funds Transfers was established by the U.S. government in the 1970s to study the impact of electronic funds on the U.S. payments system. In its 1977 report, the commission cited the European giro systems as models for providing electronic funds transfer service to low-income U.S. consumers, who typically do not have checking accounts.

Characteristics of the U.S. Payments Mechanism

How a nation pays its bills and how that practice evolved are rooted in historical, cultural, and economic developments often unique to each nation. In the United States, four features differentiate the payments system from the mechanism found in most other industrial countries:

- ❖ numerous independent depository institutions
- ❖ an extensive central bank role
- ❖ check clearance involving two to three different banks
- ❖ large numbers of payment transactions among financial institutions

Independent Depository Institutions

The U.S. financial system is characterized by a large number of independent depository institutions that, historically, have been prevented by state and federal law from offering deposit and payments services outside a given community or state.[1] Today, there are approximately 12,200 commercial banks with more than 50,000 banking offices, about 2,650 savings and loan associations and savings banks, and about 14,500 credit unions—a total of about 30,000 separate, independent financial institutions that receive deposits and make payments for themselves and their depositors. (See exhibit 1.7.) Until the establishment of the Federal Reserve in 1913, there was no uniformity in payments practices among depository institutions across the country and no efficient way that funds could be transferred nationally.

Central Bank Role

The central bank plays an important, ongoing role in the U.S. payments system. The Federal Reserve is often referred to as a bank for banks because it provides for banks what banks provide for their depositors—payments services ranging from check collection and electronic transfer of funds to the safekeeping of securities and the provision of coin and currency.

The 12 Federal Reserve banks and their 25 branches are the centers for distributing currency and coin to the banking system. About 35 percent of all checks written in the United States are cleared and collected through the Federal Reserve banks and branches and the Reserve's 11 major regional check-processing centers. The Federal Reserve operates an automated clearing house (ACH) for banks that send and receive electronic payroll deposits and preauthorized bill payments. It also operates a wire transfer system over which money and government securities can be transferred instantaneously. This system, known as FedWire, is the primary mechanism through which the major banks do most of their interbanking business. Reserve banks also store

---

Exhibit 1.7 *U.S. Depository Institutions*

Depository Institution	Number of Institutions	1991 Asset Size (billions of dollars)
Commercial banks	12,200	$3,000
Thrift institutions		
Savings and loan associations	2,250[1]	1,000[1]
Savings banks	400	500
Credit unions	14,500	200

1. Includes 600 S&Ls with total assets of nearly $350 billion that were identified by the Resolution Trust Corporation (RTC) in 1990 as insolvent or operating with persistent losses and thus likely to be taken over by the RTC in the early 1990s. The RTC is the federal agency that was established by Congress in 1989 to take over insolvent S&Ls.

Source: Federal Reserve Bank of Chicago *Fed Letter*, December 1990, No. 40; Federal Reserve *Bulletin*, May 1991; and *Wall Street Journal*, December 12, 1991.

physical securities that cannot be maintained on the FedWire system. Through a central banking practice known as net settlement, the Federal Reserve is, effectively, behind the final and binding transfer of virtually all bookkeeping and electronic money exchanged nationally in the United States.

Check Clearance Among Banks

About one-third of all checks written in the United States are cleared internally—that is, deposited into the banks on which the checks were drawn, so that demand deposit balances are transferred on the bank's internal books. These checks are referred to as *on-us* checks.

Some 20 percent of all checks are cleared through local clearing arrangements in which checks are exchanged among several regional banks that typically receive as deposits large volumes of checks drawn on one another. About one-quarter of all checks are cleared through correspondent banks. And about 35 percent of the nation's checks are cleared through the Federal Reserve. (Some checks are cleared through more than one system. For example, checks sent to correspondent banks are frequently processed by these banks and forwarded to the Federal Reserve for collection.)

Because the Federal Reserve's check collection services were, until 1980, limited to banks that were members of the Federal Reserve System, a two-tier check collection mechanism evolved. The Federal Reserve—the first tier—effectively provided check collection services mainly to the nation's large correspondent banks. They, in turn, provided similar services to their smaller respondent banks—the second tier.[2]

Correspondent banks that receive checks from their respondent banks use local clearing arrangements and the Federal Reserve to collect most of these checks. About 12 percent of the nation's checks are collected as on-us items by correspondents or as direct sends by correspondents to the banks on which the checks are drawn.

Transactions Among Financial Institutions

A considerable volume of the money transactions in the United States occurs between financial institutions, mainly because the nation's depositories have been and continue to be fragmented into many different, usually small, self-contained units. Most of these money transactions are made electronically through the Federal Reserve's wire transfer network. They involve the buying and selling of financial assets by banks and the extension of interbank credit. Before the Federal Reserve was established, interbank transfers of money typically involved physical transfers of gold and cash, a practice that led to major shortcomings in the U.S. payments system.

The Early U.S. Payments System

The early payments system experienced shortcomings that were directly related to the check collection process and the transfer of interbank balances. Local checks could be collected by presenting them over the counter to the banks on which they were drawn, or going through local clearing arrangements. However, collecting checks drawn on banks located in different parts of the country caused problems, including exchange charges, circuitous routing, nonpar checking, uncollected funds used as reserves, and fragmented reserve deposits.

Exchange Charges

Banks on which checks were drawn imposed an exchange charge on checks presented for payment by out-of-town banks. The charge covered the costs banks incurred in shipping gold or cash to pay for the checks, the banking practice before the creation of the Federal Reserve.

Circuitous Routing

To avoid exchange charges, banks frequently sent checks on long, circuitous collection routes across the country. Circuitous routing increased the chance that checks would not be properly forwarded or would be lost in transit. Final payment took an excessively long time, and banks had no way of returning dishonored items. The cross-country collection process was costly to the banking system as well as to the public.

Nonpar Checking

Exchange charges for nonlocal checks effectively meant that checks were credited to depositors' accounts at less than par (face value). Because of this practice, nonlocal checks were often not accepted in commercial dealings. Businesses required that bills be paid either in currency or with a local check.

Uncollected Funds Used as Reserves

Correspondent banks that received deposits of checks would credit their respondents' accounts immediately, even though the checks could not be collected for several days. Since these accounts made up a substantial portion of the legal reserves of the nation's banks, the practice resulted in reserves—which were designed to ensure bank safety and liquidity—being held in uncollected funds.

Fragmented Reserve Deposits

In an attempt to receive full face value for deposited checks, banks often fragmented their correspondent balances across the country, in the form of correspondent accounts in banks in different banking regions. This practice damaged banks' liquidity and became very costly as the use of checks became more popular.

The Federal Reserve's Role

The 1913 Federal Reserve Act, which established the central bank, did not explicitly address these weaknesses in the nation's payments system, although clearing house powers were written into the act during its legislative development (in sections 13 and 16). However, once there was a banking system in which bank reserves were centralized at Federal Reserve banks, it was apparent that a nationwide clearing and settlement mechanism could be established. This mechanism would improve the nation's system for making payments.

Initially, it was felt that the Federal Reserve's collection system would become the only one, to the exclusion of private regional and local clearing arrangements. Carter Glass, Chairman of the House Banking Committee and one of the major congressional architects of the 1913 Federal Reserve Act, expected that the Federal Reserve would end "the amazing wastefulness [of] many independent collection organizations by substituting one compact collection system."[3] The 1915 Board of Governors of the Federal Reserve agreed. From their perspective, member bank reserve balances, and not the balances at correspondent banks, would "serve as the basis for a system of clearing and collecting the exchanges of the country."[4]

The Federal Reserve believed that it had a congressional mandate to establish a universal, par value check collection system. However, this idea was abandoned when a Supreme Court decision in the 1920s expressly stated that the Federal Reserve was not "an agency for universal clearance." Nonetheless, over the decades, the Federal Reserve has structured its check collection rules and practices in a way that would, even without universality of collection, promote a more efficient national payments system. Express mandate or not, it helped correct the shortcomings in the nation's check collection system.

Correcting the Shortcomings

The centralization of reserves at the 12 Federal Reserve banks provided the banking system, for the first time, with an efficient mechanism for clearing checks between the nation's regional money centers.

By the 1920s, the Federal Reserve had also developed a nationwide wire transfer and book-entry settlement system to effect interregional collections, without requiring the physical transfer of gold or currency. In addition, the Federal Reserve would accept checks and make funds transfers only at face value. This refusal to accept nonpar items, coupled with the elimination of charges for transferring funds for interregional settlement, virtually ended exchange charges for all checks by the early 1920s.[5] By effectively ending the practice of nonpar checking in the United States and, in the process, eliminating circuitous routing, the Federal Reserve introduced a degree of standardization in check payment practices.

The Federal Reserve took several other steps to standardize and expedite the check-handling process. The establishment of a deferred availability schedule for checks helped increase the likelihood that they would be collected quickly. In the 1950s and 1960s, the Federal Reserve prompted the banking industry into large-scale automation of check processing by encouraging the standardization of magnetic ink character recognition (MICR) for all checks. And, in the 1970s, it modified Federal Reserve Regulation J to require same-day payment for checks presented by member banks. This action helped accelerate check payment schedules throughout the industry.

By the 1970s, the growth of check usage began to tax the Federal Reserve's ability to process and collect efficiently all the checks deposited with it. To speed the collection process, the Federal Reserve modified its collection procedures, took actions to promote greater bank and public use of automated clearing houses (ACHs) and wire transfers of funds, and established a network of regional check-processing centers (RCPCs) to clear checks rapidly. Today, the Federal Reserve operates 46 RCPCs, 35 of which are located at a Reserve bank or branch site. The other 11 operate in suburban areas of key Federal Reserve cities, where reduction in transportation time between depositing banks and Federal Reserve offices has hastened the collection process.

In the early 1980s, the Federal Reserve's congressional mandate to eliminate Federal Reserve float[6] caused the central bank again to modify its check collection procedures and speed up collection times. The Federal Reserve also established interdistrict airline transportation to move checks more rapidly in the collection process from one part of the country to another, introduced a centralized check-return notification service for large dollar-value checks, and encouraged industry check truncation initiatives.

In the late 1980s, the Federal Reserve was given another congressional mandate —in the Expedited Funds Availability Act of 1987—to assist banks in speeding up the granting of credit to consumers on deposited check funds. Through Regulation CC, the Federal Reserve introduced automated procedures that enable banks to rapidly process and return dishonored checks and reduced check-return charges for banks that follow the new procedures. They also began testing high speed image-processing systems that transmit electronic images of checks between banks.

The Federal Reserve has maintained a wire communications network since 1918. Today, all Reserve banks and branches, the U.S. Treasury, and about 7,000 commercial banks are interconnected by terminal or computer through a computerized communications and funds transfer network. About 5,000 other banks access the wire transfer network through telephone calls to their local Reserve office. This system allows for nationwide movement of funds among banks within minutes, which aids in the efficient handling of reserve balances. In addition to transfers of account balances, the network also handles transfers of U.S. government securities.

Issues related to the Federal Reserve's role in the U.S. payments system are cited several times in this publication, most notably in discussing the future of the U.S. payments mechanism in chapter 1, in reviewing the pricing of Federal Reserve services in chapter 4, and in examining electronic funds transfer systems and services in chapter 5. The following section outlines the ways in which the Federal Reserve sees its own role in the U.S. payments system.

In 1990, the Federal Reserve issued a policy paper that presented its own views on the central bank's role in the U.S. payments system:

The Federal Reserve views its role in the U.S. payments system as

❑ promoting the system's integrity and efficiency

❑ ensuring that payment services are provided to all depository institutions on an equitable basis

The Federal Reserve contends that this role has been validated by 75 years of active involvement in safeguarding the nation's payments mechanism.

❑ Congress gave the Federal Reserve a dual role in the U.S. payments system as both an operator and a regulator, as evidenced by the authority given the Federal Reserve in the

- Federal Reserve Act of 1913

- Monetary Control Act of 1980

- Expedited Funds Availability Act of 1987

❑ Over the decades, the Federal Reserve's participation in the payments mechanism has become extensive, including

- processing checks

- providing a nationwide network for collecting financial instruments that are ineligible for processing through normal check collection channels, such as matured bonds and bankers' acceptances (draft)

- providing a nationwide electronic ACH network

- providing a nationwide electronic funds transfer system (FedWire)

- operating a book-entry securities service for the electronic safekeeping and transfer of U.S. Treasury and agency securities

- providing settlement services for private clearing arrangements

❑ This central bank involvement in payments processing since 1914 has been integral to the development of the U.S. financial system and has generated public confidence in checks and other payment devices.

The rationale for the Federal Reserve's ongoing operational presence is based on public policy considerations.

❑ Maintaining the integrity of the payments system is seen as a necessary prerequisite for financial stability and economic growth.

❑ History shows that a fragile payments system can generate economic instability. Early in this century—during the Bank Panic of 1907—the U.S. payments system broke down. In recent decades—such as during the 1974 failure of the German financial institution, Bankhouse I.D., Herstatt, the U.S. payments system was disrupted, but the system continued to function, largely because of the presence of the Federal Reserve.

❑ The Federal Reserve's direct and ongoing participation in the payments system provides strength to the system. One example of how this is done involves FedWire. Because FedWire funds transfers are final and irrevocable, the risk that one bank's failure could be transmitted—through the payments system—to another bank is sharply reduced. Another example involves the willingness of the Federal Reserve banks to provide payment services to troubled depositories that correspondent banks may not be willing to service. This practice helps ensure that the inability of a commercial bank or thrift to process payments will not trigger its insolvency.

❑ Improving the efficiency of the payments system is seen as generating benefits and cost savings for both providers and users of payment services.

   • The Federal Reserve contends that it can play a unique role in stimulating banks and thrifts to improve the payments system's efficiency because it has the expertise to contribute to technical advances in payments processing. The Fed's size and scope enable it to promote new payments technology throughout the banking industry. In fact, the Federal Reserve is publicly committed to promoting the use of electronics in providing payment services whenever it can be demonstrated that EFT technology will enhance payments system efficiency.

   • The Fed can facilitate cooperation among banks on payments system innovations, such as in the 1950s when MICR encoding of checks was adopted as a banking industry standard. Banks have been willing to accept the Federal Reserve as a facilitator because it is generally perceived by bankers as a trusted intermediary, not a competitor.

   • The Monetary Control Act of 1980 required the Federal Reserve to compete with correspondent bank providers of payment services. The Fed maintains that this competition is not inconsistent with its public policy of providing services and has actually improved the quality and efficiency of today's payments services.

❑ Ensuring equitable access to the payments mechanism for all depositories assures fair competition between banks in their provision of payment services to depositors.

   • The Federal Reserve provides payment services to small banks and thrifts in remote areas that correspondent banks might choose not to serve, thus ensuring the same payment services that depositors in major urban areas obtain.

❑ The Federal Reserve's criteria for evaluating whether to change any of its payment services is based on public policy rationale for its ongoing presence.

❑ The Federal Reserve establishes annual cost-recovery objectives for each service. If a service is not expected to generate enough revenue to recover its costs, the service will be ended, subject to the following public policy considerations:

   • The need to provide equitable access to the service for all depositories.

- The adequacy of that service nationwide. For example, in the mid-1980s several Reserve banks stopped providing cash transportation service in areas where an adequate level of service was provided by the private sector.
- Whether benefits from the service justify the shortfall in revenue.

❐ In introducing new payment services the Federal Reserve must meet all the following criteria:

- The new service must recover its costs over the long run.
- The new service must generate a clear public benefit, such as
  - promoting the integrity of the payments system
  - improving the effectiveness of financial markets
  - reducing the risk associated with payment and securities transfer services
  - improving the efficiency of the payments system
  - ensuring that an adequate level of service is provided nation-wide
- Whether private sector providers can (or will) provide the service with reasonable timeliness, cost-effectiveness, and fairness.

❐ Even if the above criteria are met, the Federal Reserve would conduct a competitive impact analysis to determine whether introduction of any new service would adversely affect the ability of other providers to fairly compete. Such an adverse impact could arise because of

- legal differences that favor the Reserve banks
- market differences that provide the Federal Reserve with a dominant market position

❐ If such a determination is made, the Federal Reserve would judge whether the public benefits outweigh the adverse effects on private sector competition.

Foreign Central Banks' Role in Payments Systems

The role of a foreign central bank in its nation's payments system varies considerably. Currency issuance and settlement may well be the only payments services all central banks provide.

Bank of England

The Bank of England's role in the English payments mechanism is limited to

- ❖ participating in check and electronic transfer systems with institutions that have accounts with it
- ❖ serving as the ultimate settlement bank

Most checks in England are exchanged between banks at the Banker's Clearinghouse in London. The Bank of England participates in these exchanges and also acts as the settlement bank, but it does not control the clearing operations. All nonclearing banks must have a correspondent-type arrangement with a member of the clearing house to gain access to the exchanges. Clearing banks in England have extensive, computerized branch networks, which enable them to make interbank transfers, including transfers for their correspondent banks. Banks settle these accounts on the books of the Bank of England.

The Bank of England is also responsible for currency issuance. Clearing banks typically draw the notes they need from the Bank of England's head office or one of its seven branches. Clearing banks distribute the cash to their branches through cash distribution centers.

Bundesbank (Central Bank of Germany)

The role of the Bundesbank in Germany's payments mechanism is prescribed by law: to ensure the efficiency of bank payments and to provide clearing facilities for interbank exchanges.

With more than 200 branches, clearing offices, and computer centers, the Bundesbank is the hub that links the giro system of the German banking industry and the giro system of the post office, the two systems through which most of Germany's domestic payments are made.

Check payments, as well as credit and debit transfers, are made primarily through the Bundesbank's clearing facilities. However, the Bundesbank does not directly process all transfers. The post office maintains accounts with almost all banks in Germany and transmits credit transfers to them directly without using the services of the central bank. Many thrift institutions also tend to use their own giro systems for interbank transfers.

Besides its clearing function, Germany's central bank acts as a fiscal agent for the government and handles its payments. The Bundesbank is also responsible for issuing currency. Notes and coins enter into circulation at the branches of the Bundesbank through giro account holders—primarily banks, post offices, and major businesses that pay for currency by debiting their accounts.

Bank of Japan

The Bank of Japan is the ultimate settlement bank for the Japanese government and for virtually all major financial institutions in Japan. The bank also issues currency.

The bank makes payments and settlements among client financial institutions through account transfers on its books. Net credit or debit balances resulting from the clearing of checks at local clearing houses are also settled by account transfers at the Bank of Japan's head office or one of its 34 branches. Japan has about 170 local clearing houses. In regions where the Bank of Japan has no branch, banks select a representative bank and hold an account with that bank for clearing purposes.

Net balances from wire transfers through the Zengin system—Japan's private wire transfer system—are settled through an account with the Bank of Japan. Almost all Japanese financial institutions participate in Japan's Zengin system, which is centrally managed by the Bankers Association of Tokyo in collaboration with the Telegraph and Telephone Public Corporation.

A significant volume of payments is made in Japan through postal transfer accounts. The Japanese Postal Administration has its own online telecommunications system for postal transfers.

Bank of France

The Bank of France issues currency and supplies cash through its 234 branches to commercial banks and post offices. The bank also manages France's regional clearing houses and ACHs, and it is the ultimate settlement bank for interbank transfers.

Most check payments in France are cleared either bilaterally at the local level or multilaterally through the Paris clearing house and a network of central bank-operated regional clearing houses. Nine major banks in France have their own arrangement, exchanging checks in Paris regardless of where the checks are drawn. The Bank of France operates ACHs in several major French cities. The interbank transactions are handled on magnetic tape.

The Bank of France also functions as a major collecting entity. It holds accounts for public utilities and the national railway, and often collects checks in localities where these account holders have no representation.

Bank of Canada

The role of the Bank of Canada in the Canadian payments mechanism is extremely limited; the bank does not directly provide commercial banks with most payments system services. It acts as the government's fiscal agent and assists in the final settlement of balances for Canada's privately operated check-clearing system. The bank, which is also responsible for issuing currency and coin, assists commercial banks in exchanging coin among surplus and deficit banks.

Canada's check-clearing system is operated by its commercial banks. Any depository without direct access to the clearing system must establish a correspondent arrangement with a commercial bank, which will process the depository's checks and represent it in clearings. The Canadian Bankers

Association is empowered by law to establish clearing houses and to make rules and regulations for their operations, subject to approval by the Canadian Treasury.

The Bank of Canada provides a settlement service for the clearing system by adjusting balances of member commercial banks. Preauthorized debit and credit payments and bank credit card payments are processed, cleared, and settled in the same way as checks. However, the legal framework for these electronic payments systems, unlike that for checks, is based on a series of relationships and rules developed entirely by the private sector.

The Future

Technological developments in banking—particularly in computer processing, communication, and financial data and funds transfer—are rapidly changing the way people and businesses make payments and use banks in the United States. However, some bankers feel that changes in banking law and regulation, in the attitudes of bank management, and, most important, in the preferences of bank customers must occur first before any electronic payments technology significantly alters the practices and patterns of American consumers and businesses.

The banking industry's experience with EFT systems in the 1970s and 1980s has caused bankers to examine more closely the prospects of change in the payments system, specifically in services and technology.

Services

EFT systems in the 1990s will likely have more influence on the way banks perform traditional deposit-related services than on providing new services. The application of EFT technology to reduce or eliminate the handling of paper checks and other routine functions performed by bank tellers is of great interest to bankers.

Technology

There is no longer any doubt that technology can provide customers with quick, efficient, and sophisticated electronic banking services. Among the most promising technological developments in banking are automated clearing houses, point-of-sale terminals, and automated teller machines. However, the widespread use of electronic payments and EFT systems is being hampered by many legal, economic, and attitudinal factors that are, for the most part, beyond a bank's individual control.

Automated Clearing Houses

Automated clearing houses operate like paper check collection systems, but they replace paper checks with computer tapes or disks. About 35,000 bank and thrift offices currently participate in regional ACHs. Since 1978, about 30 regional organizations have been linked into a National Automated Clearing House Association. To date, however, the functions that ACHs perform have been limited, and ACH use has fallen short of expectations. In 1990, only about 1.2 billion ACH transactions were made—primarily low dollar-value corporate and government transactions, such as direct deposit of payroll and Social Security payments, and preauthorized debiting of consumer accounts for insurance and other recurring bill payments—compared with 56 billion check transactions. About 80 percent of 1990's ACH transactions had a dollar value of $1,000 or less.

The most important private sector service has been the handling and processing of recurring payments, such as payrolls. Employers deliver to their banks computer tapes or disks containing payroll information. Without a single check being processed, funds are withdrawn from the employer's account and deposited into the employees' accounts at various banks in the clearinghouse association. The federal government is the largest user of ACHs, directly depositing Social Security payments and other federal disbursements, which account for about 40 percent of ACH volume. ACH processing reduces not only the number of checks in the banking system but also the risk of having checks lost or stolen.

ACH proponents believe volume will soar when the ACH is used to process point-of-sale payments made by consumers in retail stores, and when corporations begin to see the cost-saving and recordkeeping advantages of using ACH transactions instead of checks to pay invoices. However, serious questions about the benefits of ACH services, the lack of electronic links between banks and ACHs, and the lack of adequate promotion have kept consumer and business acceptance low.

Check Truncation

Check truncation is considered to be a technological adjunct to the ACH. In a check truncation system, the first bank to receive a check holds it and electronically forwards the information on the check to the bank on which the check is drawn. Several means of forwarding this information have been developed, including transmission of the entire image of the check over telephone wire. The benefits of check truncation lie in its ability to reduce the volume of checks flowing through the banking system. However, before this procedure becomes widespread in U.S. banking, commercial law has to change to allow checks to transfer money without physical inspection and consumers have to be willing to give up their preference for canceled checks.

Point-of-Sale (POS)

Point-of-sale (POS) terminals are machines that allow funds to be transferred between accounts as soon as a purchase is made. Located in stores and super-markets, these terminals are online to a bank's computer. By using a debit card, a customer can instantly pay for goods. The customer also may use a credit card and make payment through the extension of credit by the bank. POS terminals also can be used to verify a customer's check.

Some POS terminals have enjoyed regional success, particularly in the Midwest, where a number of grocery chains, convenience stores, and gasoline stations have established well-received POS networks. However, in 1991, only about 2,000 online (electronically linked) POS terminals were being used in the United States for retail purchases. A number of other POS systems were being used off-line in conjunction with ACHs. These systems do not initiate instan-taneous transfers between accounts at the point of purchase. Rather, transac-tions are accumulated and processed in a batch at the end of the day, and cleared through an ACH, a practice that removes any guarantee that sufficient funds are on account to make payment.

One feature of POS transactions that discourages public acceptance is the immediate debit to the customer's account; this eliminates the consumer float[7] associated with check payments. As a result, most POS systems now used by merchants provide only authorization, verification, or check guarantee data; many POS terminals have been discontinued because of lack of public interest. In 1991, only about 70 million payment transactions—with an average dollar value of about $25 per transaction—were made through POS terminals.

Nonetheless, the prospects for POS systems are promising. These termi-nals can, in theory, provide the infrastructure for nationwide retail EFT ser-vices by permitting bank customers in one part of the country to make pur-chases from participating merchants anywhere in the United States and pay for those purchases instantly through electronic debits and credits to customer and merchant bank accounts.

Automated Teller Machines (ATMs)

Automated teller machines (ATMs) can perform many of the routine tasks bank tellers perform, and they are typically on duty 24 hours a day. Many ATMs are linked online to bank computers. ATM users can obtain cash from these machines, transfer funds from one account to another, repay loans, and request information on the status of their bank accounts.

Several legal and economic problems inhibited the growth of ATMs in the 1970s, and ATM use did not expand as rapidly as most bankers envisioned. Some states defined both ATMs and POS terminals as bank branches and imposed the same geographic restrictions on their deployment as on brick-and-mortar branches. However, deployment and use of ATMs speeded up in the 1980s as more banks linked their ATM systems into shared network arrangements[8], and more actively marketed the ATMs' speed and convenience. By 1990, there were more than 87,000 ATMs in use in the United States, as exhibit 1.8 shows, and about 140 million ATM cardholders. About half of American households hold at least one ATM card and more than half of these cardholders are using their cards at least once each month. Most ATMs are used as teller adjuncts, primarily in the outer walls and lobbies of bank buildings. However, an increasing number of banks are placing ATMs in shopping malls. In addition, there are more than 100 shared regional networks and 2 major national ATM networks.

ATM Networking

ATM networking allows customers of any member of the network to use the ATMs of any other member to obtain cash and account information, even if the ATMs are in another state.

In 1986, the U.S. Supreme Court upheld a federal appeals court ruling that ATM networking within a state or across state lines does not violate federal or state prohibitions on bank branching. The appeals court had held that ATMs not owned or leased by a bank but simply linked to the bank as part of a network, do not constitute branches of the bank. This ruling gave further impetus to new and expanded ATM networking among banks, particularly across state lines.

Exhibit 1.8 *Growth of ATMs*

	Number of ATMs	Number of Transactions per ATM
1984	57,900	4,750
1985	61,200	4,900
1986	69,200	4,700
1987	76,000	4,950
1988	81,700	5,150
1989	87,100	5,600

Source: *American Banker*, December 5, 1989.

In 1980, less than 20 percent of the nation's ATMs were linked to shared networks. By 1990, about 90 percent of banks' ATMs were being shared with at least one other bank. Indeed, about one-third of banks that belonged to networks in 1990 belonged to two or more of these networks. ATM networks have been particularly well received by ATM users. In 1990, banks reported that 30 percent of their customers' ATM transactions were being made at other banks' ATMs.

Is the Electronic Payments Revolution Inevitable?

The resolution of major legal, regulatory, economic, and attitudinal issues in the 1990s will largely determine the pace of change in the U.S. payments system in the early decades of the next century. Of the questions facing the electronic payments system, the most important is consumer and banker acceptance.

Consumer and Banker Acceptance

The largest obstacle to the EFT revolution has been the public's reluctance to accept electronic banking services. Most EFT systems have certain features that are undesirable either to bankers or to bank customers.

To the banker, a subtle advantage of a paper check system is that checks can be returned if funds to cover the checks are not in the accounts. Bankers have a sense of confidence in the records management and control of paper checks. They also know that handling large volumes of retail EFTs would require a massive and costly change in the way banks process payments—from batch processing at the end of the day to continuous processing as transactions are made throughout the day.

To consumers, electronic payment systems involve a loss of check float—the extra use of funds check writers have because of time delays in the processing or collecting of checks. The major sources of these delays are

- ❖ mail float—the time it takes for the check writer's mailed check to be delivered to the recipient

- ❖ administrative or creditor-processing float—the time it takes for the recipient to book the check writer's payment and deposit the check for collection

- ❖ check-processing or bank float—the time it takes the collecting bank to process and present the check to the check writer's bank

It is estimated that consumers and businesses obtain the benefit of an extra $200 billion each day from mail, administrative, and check-processing float.

This benefit is seen as a powerful incentive for consumers and business firms to rely on checks as their primary means of payment.

Bankers and consumers have had little economic incentive to give up checks in favor of electronic funds. Neither party has been required to pay the total costs of operating the payments system. The costs of using checks, until the 1980s, have been relatively low and the check-related services provided by banks have increasingly improved. In 1987, Congress passed the Expedited Funds Availability Act, which specifically required banks and the Federal Reserve to further improve the nation's check system. The act mandated that banks make deposited check funds more quickly available for depositors' use and encouraged the Federal Reserve and the banking industry to find more efficient and less costly ways to return dishonored checks. Over the long run, rising check service charges and account maintenance fees could encourage greater use of EFT, but there were no signs in 1992 that such a trend had begun to emerge.

Checks are familiar payment devices that have been widely used in the United States for more than 130 years. Electronic payments are unfamiliar to most consumers, having been used in this country for only the last 30 years or so. Although banks provide consumers with electronic payment services through ACHs, POS terminals, telephones, and personal computers, each of these services tends to emphasize a different method of payment and uses a different set of procedures. Many bankers feel that the diversity and complexity of EFT use procedures, compared with the ease of writing checks, have tended to restrain many consumers from more extensive use of electronic payments.

Also, consumers appear to like the characteristics of the check, such as convenience and safety. Payment by check requires a unique signature to activate the transfer or payment of funds. Thus, funds on deposit are safe if an unsigned check is lost or stolen. Other features include the stop payment order, which allows for the correction of errors, and the returned canceled check, which provides the writer with a legal receipt and physical proof of payment. These features, coupled with the privacy and control over payments that check writers enjoy when paying by check, have proven to be popular payment characteristics for more than a century. Consumers do not view electronic payments as having these advantages.

Other Questions

There are many unanswered questions concerning the use of EFT systems—questions that will be answered only over time and as need and use dictate. These questions fall into five general areas:

- ❖ sharing and development of networks

- privacy and security
- consumer rights
- uncertainty
- government involvement

Sharing and Development of Networks

Should depositories be required to share EFT systems? Should operators of communications lines, processing systems, and switching devices be allowed to establish national networks that connect terminals of different institutions with regional and interregional clearing houses? Who should own and control these systems?

Would nationwide ATM network arrangements violate government antitrust regulations?

About half the states have mandatory ATM network-sharing laws. Under these laws, a bank that has off-premise ATMs is required to share them with any bank in the state that wants access to the terminals for its own customers. However, a bank that obtains access under a sharing law must pay a fee to the ATM-owning bank for that privilege.

Proponents of mandatory sharing argue that shared networks benefit both banks and ATM users. They contend that as new banks join a shared network, the potential number of ATM users increases and the geographic area within which one bank's customers can obtain ATM services expands. Both of these conditions are likely to drive down ATM transactions costs, particularly if banks that join a network have few ATMs of their own. Proponents further contend that mandatory sharing enables small rural and suburban banks that may not be able to afford their own ATMs to provide their customers with ATM services.

Opponents of mandatory sharing argue that sharing eliminates competition between banks and in so doing eliminates banks' incentives to innovate in their provision of ATM services. They also contend that mandatory sharing is unfair to ATM-owning banks in that it allows other banks to access a network without adequately compensating the ATM-owning banks for their risk and investment.

Privacy and Security

How will the security of information in EFT systems be safeguarded? Can the public be assured that the traditional confidentiality associated with personal financial transactions is secure with EFT systems?

Consumer Rights

What should consumer rights be in EFT systems? Should consumers have access rights to all EFT systems and services?

Uncertainty

Should EFT technology suppliers and bank management wait for full resolution of the outstanding issues, or should they move ahead to develop still newer and more sophisticated technology that can be quite costly?

Government Involvement

Should the government and/or Federal Reserve have an operational presence in the electronic payments mechanism, or should it be allowed to develop without government involvement? Given the considerable costs of EFT technology, should the government regulate EFT pricing to prevent bank charges and transaction fees from moving EFT services beyond the reach of most consumers?

Should the government and/or Federal Reserve determine and enforce rules for EFT operations?

As the payments mechanism becomes increasingly more electronic, the pace and volume of transactions will likely increase. This will cause a corresponding increase in risks to the banking system, including fraud and computer hardware and software failures. Does this heightened risk mandate a need for government or Federal Reserve regulatory oversight of the payments mechanism to ensure the safety and soundness of banking?

Summary

A nation's payments mechanism consists of the instruments used to transfer money and make payments and the institutions and processes used to facilitate money transactions.

American consumers and businesses rely essentially on checks as their primary means of spending and receiving money. American banks and other financial institutions rely extensively on electronic funds transfers. In the United States, the central bank (the Federal Reserve) plays a major operational role in the payments mechanism; it clears most of the nation's interregional checks and operates a nationwide bank-to-bank electronic funds and government securities transfer system. The Federal Reserve helped correct major shortcomings in this country's early check collection system, such as exchange charges, circuitous routing of checks, and nonpar checking. On balance, the role the Federal Reserve plays is far more extensive than that of most foreign central banks in their nations' payments systems.

In the future, the American public is likely to shift increasingly to greater use of electronic payments and EFT systems. However, the pace and exact nature of that shift are uncertain. ATMs, point-of-sale terminals, and ACHs offer great promise, but basic questions related to consumer and banker acceptance of these electronic payment services have yet to be fully addressed.

Questions

1. What are the major characteristics that differentiate the U.S. payments mechanism from that of most other industrial countries?

2. What were the five basic shortcomings in the U.S. check collection system before the establishment of the Federal Reserve?

3. Is the electronic payments revolution in U.S. retail banking inevitable? Explain your answer.

4. What three features of ATM and/or POS systems do consumers not like? Why?

Endnotes

1. In the 1980s, 46 states altered their laws to permit banks from other states to establish branch offices within their boundaries. Most laws had clauses that permitted branching between states only in a given geographic region in the 1980s, but permitted full interstate reciprocity in the early 1990s. The establishment of these reciprocal branching agreements was upheld by the Supreme Court in 1986.

2. The Monetary Control Act of 1980 required the Federal Reserve to offer its check collection services, at set prices, to all depositories and to compete with correspondent banks in providing services to respondent banks.

3. 51 Congressional Record, part 17, p. 563

4. *Annual Report* (Federal Reserve Board, 1915).

5. Because most banks were not members of the Federal Reserve and did not clear checks through the Reserve banks, not all exchange charges ended in the 1920s. Some banks in the Midwest imposed exchange charges until the late 1950s.

6. Federal Reserve float is the extra use of funds that banks obtain because the Federal Reserve credits banks for deposited checks before it receives payment from the banks on which the checks are drawn.

7. Consumer float is the extra use of money a check writer obtains from checking account balances because of the time lapses between making a payment with a check and the debiting of funds from the account.

8. A shared ATM network enables a group of banks to share some or all of their ATMs with one another's customers. A proprietary ATM network is owned by one bank and all its ATMs are for the exclusive use of that bank's customers.

DEPOSITS AND DEPOSITORIES: CHANGING DEFINITIONS AND ROLES

Objectives

After successfully completing this chapter, you will be able to

* ❖ identify the banking innovations, changes in banking law and regulations, and competitive factors of the 1980s that have altered the structure of the depository industry

* ❖ explain the differences between NOW accounts, money market deposit accounts, demand deposits, time deposits, and savings deposits

* ❖ identify significant shifts that have occurred in the 1990s in the public's deposit holdings at banks and thrifts

Introduction

The depository industry is in the midst of significant change—change brought about by banking innovations, new competition, and changes in banking law and regulations.

In the 1980s, Congress removed the legal limits on the interest rates banks and thrift institutions could pay on time deposits and ended banks' monopoly as the nation's sole providers of demand deposits. Congress authorized savings banks and savings and loan associations to offer checking accounts to customers and permitted credit unions to offer share drafts. All depositories were granted the authority to offer new types of interest-earning deposits on which checks could be drawn—NOW (negotiable order of withdrawal) and ATS (automatic transfer service) accounts in 1980 and money market deposit accounts in 1982. Thrift institutions were also given broad new deposit-taking, lending, and investing powers. The 1980s saw the entry of money market funds, credit card companies, brokerage firms and other nonbank institutions into the payments system as major competitors of banks and thrifts in the provision of payment devices and deposit products.

Changes such as these, along with high-deposit interest rates for most of the decade, induced consumers and business firms to transfer noninterest-earning demand deposit money at banks into new interest-earning near monies at banks, thrifts, and nonbank institutions. The interest-earning deposits were relied upon as payment or transaction devices. The traditional use of noninterest demand deposits was altered greatly by transferring demand deposits into NOW accounts and money market deposit accounts, by establishing accounts in money market funds and at brokerage firms from which checks could be drawn, and by using bank innovations such as overdraft accounts and telephone transfers from savings to checking accounts to cover payments.

Some major changes in the payments mechanism occurred in the 1980s and 1990s. The deposit structure and the roles of the nation's depositories have changed, leading to a redefinition of the terms demand deposit, savings deposit, and time deposit altering bankers' and economists' notions about money, bank deposits, and the role of different types of financial institutions in the U.S. payments system.

New Payment Accounts

A tidal wave of payments system innovations swept through the financial industry in the 1980s. Among the major payment innovations were NOW accounts, ATS accounts, preauthorized third-party telephone transfers, money market deposit accounts (MMDAs), and Super NOW accounts.

NOW Accounts

NOW accounts are savings deposits on which checks can be written.

In 1972, a Massachusetts state court decision authorized mutual savings banks in that state to offer customers interest-earning checkable deposits. Within months, New Hampshire followed. In 1974, to enable commercial banks in those states to compete with the mutual savings banks, Congress authorized all depositories in Massachusetts and New Hampshire to offer NOW accounts. During the succeeding years, Congress extended NOW account authority to all depositories in the other New England states, New York, and New Jersey. This was followed by the Monetary Control Act of 1980, which brought regulatory equity to banks and thrift institutions in other parts of the country by granting NOW account power to depositories in all states, beginning in 1981.

The Monetary Control Act classified NOW accounts in the same category as demand deposits. Starting in 1981, NOW accounts became subject to reserve requirements on transaction accounts. Reserve requirements on personal time and savings deposits were eliminated entirely by the 1980 legislation. Until 1986, when interest-rate ceilings on savings deposits were removed, the maximum interest rate banks could pay on NOW deposits was the same as that on passbook savings accounts (5¼ percent).

Initial public response to NOW accounts was cautious. Higher service charges on NOW accounts than on demand accounts and a lack of adequate promotion were partially responsible. However, stepped-up marketing efforts by banks and escalating service charges on noninterest-earning demand accounts in the 1980s saw the public increasingly shift funds into NOW accounts. In 1992, NOW account balances were nearly $225 billion, nearly equal to total savings deposits and well in excess of consumers' total demand deposits.

ATS Accounts

ATS accounts allow depositors to automatically transfer funds from an interest-earning account to a checking account. ATS accounts are substantially the same as NOW accounts or credit union share drafts. Like those two innovations, ATS accounts provide a direct substitute for demand deposits as payment devices.

In 1978, the Federal Reserve Board and the Federal Deposit Insurance Corporation (FDIC) authorized ATS accounts for commercial banks. Automatic transfers were to be used for transactions such as providing cover for an overdraft or maintaining a minimum checking account balance. However, automatic transfers allowed banks to pay interest on funds that would have been held in checking accounts. ATS accounts provided an opportunity for commercial banks in states where NOW accounts were not permitted to compete with banks in neighboring states where NOW accounts were offered.

When commercial banks introduced ATS accounts in 1978, the public initially responded by rapidly shifting demand deposits into these accounts. However, ATS accounts did not significantly affect payment practices. Lack of sufficient marketing, consumer convenience of having just one transaction account, service charges imposed on ATS transactions, and the establishment of nationwide NOW accounts and money market deposit accounts in the 1980s virtually eliminated public demand for ATS accounts.

Preauthorized Third-Party Telephone Transfers

Telephone transfers allow savings account holders to transfer funds by phone either to checking accounts or to third parties. Savings and loan associations have been permitted to offer this payment device since the 1960s. In 1975, the government allowed banks to do the same. It also allowed preauthorized payment of recurring bills directly from savings accounts.

Telephone transfers were seen as eliminating a major inconvenience for bank customers—having to go to the bank to transfer funds from a savings account to a checking account. However, the telephone transfer proved to have significant drawbacks as a payment device and had only limited appeal in the 1980s.

One disadvantage is that customers do not receive a canceled check as proof of payment when they pay bills directly from savings accounts by phone transfer. Surveys show that consumers are reluctant to forego this recordkeeping feature. Another disadvantage is that banks and thrift institutions typically impose transaction charges on savings account withdrawals made by phone. These charges can be quite large compared with those imposed on checking account transactions.

Money Market Deposit Account

Money market deposit accounts are savings deposits on which only a limited number of checks can be written each month.

The Garn-St Germain Act of 1982 authorized depositories to offer this new type of account so that banks and thrifts could offer depositors an account competitive with those offered by money market funds. The new account, called a money market deposit account (MMDA), was not subject to any interest-rate ceilings (then still in effect), but it permitted only limited checkwriting privileges.

A money market deposit account has the following characteristics:

❖ Deposits carry no minimum maturity, but banks may require seven days' notice of withdrawal.

- ❖ Depositors may make six transfers per month from the account, three of which may be by check. However, depositors are permitted unlimited withdrawals by mail or in person.

- ❖ Deposits carry no legal minimum average balance requirements. However, from December 1982 to March 1986, account holders were subject to the following rules. In 1983 and 1984, the minimum balance was $2,500. In 1985, the minimum requirement was reduced to $1,000. With the elimination of interest-rate ceilings on time and savings deposits in March 1986, all legal minimum-balance requirements ended as well. However, most banks and thrifts have continued to maintain a $1,000 or $2,500 account balance minimum to offset interest costs and to discourage low-dollar balance accounts.

- ❖ Banks can pay any interest rate on MMDA funds on deposit. In 1992, most banks were tying interest rates to average balances, paying a lower rate if account balances dropped below a stated minimum.

- ❖ Although money market deposit accounts have some characteristics of a demand deposit account, Congress authorized that MMDAs could be classified as savings accounts for reserve requirement purposes. As personal time and savings deposits are not subject to reserve requirements—which impose a cost on banks—this classification made MMDAs even more competitive with the nonreserveable accounts offered by the nation's money market funds.

Money market deposit accounts had an immediate and profound effect on the public's payments practices. Today, these accounts are the largest single deposit category on most banks' books. In 1991, banks held more than $375 billion in MMDA balances. (Thrift institutions held about $125 billion in MMDA funds.) Most deposits, however, did not come from money market fund customers, as many bankers expected. The deposits were transferred by bank customers from their traditional, lower paying demand and time and savings accounts. In December 1982, money market funds held about $185 billion in noninstitutional deposits. In December 1991, money market funds held $350 billion in deposits for individual customers.

Super NOW

The Super NOW account was authorized in January 1983 to enable banks and thrifts to provide depositors with a transaction account that would not be subject to interest-rate ceilings and would offer unlimited checkwriting privileges. At that time, NOW accounts were subject to a $5\frac{1}{4}$ percent interest-rate ceiling, and money market deposit accounts were (and still are) subject to monthly checkwriting limitations. However, the Super NOW was subject to a 12 percent reserve requirement and a $2,500 minimum-balance requirement.

Many banks, faced with a proliferation of new accounts in the early 1980s and extensive marketing commitments to the new money market deposit accounts authorized a month earlier, downplayed the Super NOW. The lack of bank promotion, coupled with the high minimum-balance requirement imposed on Super NOWs, had a significant dampening impact on these accounts. By 1986, there were relatively few Super NOW accounts on banks' and thrifts' books. The average Super NOW balance, however, stood at $12,000 in 1986, compared with $4,500 for regular NOW accounts. With such high average balances susceptible to withdrawal, few banks moved to reduce Super NOW account balance minimums when legal requirements ended in March 1986.

Fed Reserve change everything *** ***

Overview of the Monetary Control Act of 1980

The 1980 Monetary Control Act dramatically altered the regulatory and service relationship between banks and the Federal Reserve, the deposit and cost structure of banks, and the nature of banks' competition. Several of the provisions of the act were phased in during the 1980s—new reserve requirements, which became fully applicable in 1987, elimination of Regulation Q ceilings in 1986, pricing of Federal Reserve services in 1981 and 1982, and pricing of Federal Reserve float in 1984.

The Monetary Control Act of 1980 was the most significant banking law since the 1930s.

☐ It provided for a gradual phaseout of interest-rate ceilings on time and savings deposits at banks and thrifts (Regulation Q); all ceilings were removed in 1986.

☐ It authorized NOW accounts for all depository institutions nationwide.

☐ It increased FDIC and FSLIC insurance coverage to $100,000 per account.

☐ It authorized mutual savings banks to obtain a new federal charter that granted broader powers, so that savings banks could compete more effectively with commercial banks. These powers allowed savings banks to

- make business loans (up to 5 percent of assets), if those loans are made in the state or within 75 miles of the bank's home office

- accept demand deposits in connection with business loan

☐ It also authorized broader powers for federal savings and loan associations, allowing S&Ls to

- make consumer loans and invest in commercial paper and corporate debt securities (up to 20 percent of assets)

- issue credit cards

- exercise trust and fiduciary powers

- make real estate, land acquisition, development, and construction loans without regard to geographic area

A major regulatory change involved the Federal Reserve and its relationship to the banking system.

- ❏ The act subjected all depository institutions to the Federal Reserve's reserve requirements.

  - The Federal Reserve was given control over the money-creating and -lending capacity of virtually all the nation's depositories.

  - Competition between Federal Reserve member and nonmember commercial banks and between banks and thrifts was made more equitable by imposing uniform nationwide reserve requirements.

  - New reserve requirement categories were established. Reserve requirements on transaction accounts in 1992 are 3 percent on the first $42.2 million and 10 percent on amounts over $42.2 million. In 1980, a 3 percent reserve requirement was also imposed on corporate or business time deposits with maturities of less than 1½ years and Eurocurrency liabilities (primarily borrowings by U.S. banks from banking offices in other countries). These reserve requirements were eliminated in 1990. There are no reserve requirements against time and savings deposits. In addition, the Garn-St Germain Act of 1982 exempted the first $2 million of a depository's reservable liabilities from reserve requirements. This exemption is increased annually with the growth in banks' deposits. In 1992, it covers the first $3.6 million of reservable liabilities. (The Garn-St Germain Act effectively exempted from reserve requirements about 1,500 commercial banks and S&Ls and 17,000 credit unions that held about one-half of 1 percent of all deposits in the nation in 1982.)

  - A new type of reservable liability—transaction accounts—was established. Transaction accounts consist of demand deposits, NOW accounts, share draft accounts, automatic transfer system accounts, and any other accounts or deposits from which payments or transfers may be made.

  - The Federal Reserve's Board of Governors was given power to change reserve requirements and impose additional emergency reserve requirements for greater monetary policy control. The board was authorized to pay interest on emergency reserves.

- ❏ Congress allowed reserves of non-Federal Reserve member banks to be held in a pass-through arrangement—reserves held on deposit with a correspondent bank, which must redeposit the reserves at a Federal Reserve bank.

  The pass-through arrangement allowed nonmember banks to keep their reserve account relationship with the Federal Reserve indirect and to help preserve the extensive correspondent banking relationships that have traditionally linked most U.S. banks.

- ❏ The act reduced reserve requirements for commercial banks that were members of the Federal Reserve, while it raised requirements for nonmembers.

  - Member banks' reserves were phased down over a three-year period ending in 1983.

  - Nonmembers' reserves were phased up over an eight-year period ending in 1987.

  - The net effect was a reduction in total reserves held by the Federal Reserve. The Federal Reserve contends that monetary policy has improved because it controls a larger number of depository institutions than before 1980.

The reasons Congress enacted the law are as follows:

- [ ] In the mid 1970s, the Federal Reserve urged Congress to enact legislation to deal with declining commercial bank membership in the Federal Reserve System and the ensuing loss of monetary policy control.

- [ ] The Federal Reserve wanted Congress to allow Reserve banks to pay interest on bank reserves or to make reserve requirements mandatory for member and nonmember banks.

  - In the 1970s, more than 500 banks left the Federal Reserve, and the Reserve's control of the nation's bank deposits declined by 10 percent.

- [ ] The solution by Congress to the Federal Reserve's membership problem also resolved other banking issues that had emerged during the 1970s.

  - Congress legalized NOW accounts and other interest-earning transaction accounts that had been established by thrifts in the Northeast for depositories nationwide.

  - Consumer demands in the 1970s for higher interest rates on savings and time deposits were met by raising interest-rate ceilings and finally eliminating them in 1986.

  - Due to the growth of electronic funds transfers and EFT systems, thrifts and other nonmembers were pressuring for access to the Federal Reserve's payments services. The act provided open access to all depositories, but the Federal Reserve was required to charge depositories explicitly for all payments services.

  - Congress had enacted the International Banking Act of 1978, which subjected branches and agencies of foreign banks in the United States to reserve requirements and gave them access to Federal Reserve services. This was done to establish regulatory and competitive equity between branches and agencies of foreign banks and domestic banks. Uniform reserve requirements on all depository institutions were consistent with this new regulatory approach.

For the Federal Reserve, the most significant impact of the act involved the open access and pricing of Reserve bank services.

- [ ] Access to Federal Reserve loans (through the discount window) was granted to all depository institutions holding transaction accounts or nonpersonal time deposits.

  - Congress told the Federal Reserve to consider, in granting loans, the special needs of thrifts, their sensitivity to high interest rates, and disintermediation.

  - Access to the discount window was to be available only after reasonable alternative sources of funds had been tried. (This provision of the act is designed to place discount window access in context with other sources of liquidity for banks and thrifts.)

- [ ] The act required that Reserve bank services be explicitly priced and made available to all depository institutions at the same price and terms.

- [ ] The Federal Reserve established a new type of clearing account to accommodate depositories that do not maintain reserve accounts at a Reserve bank.

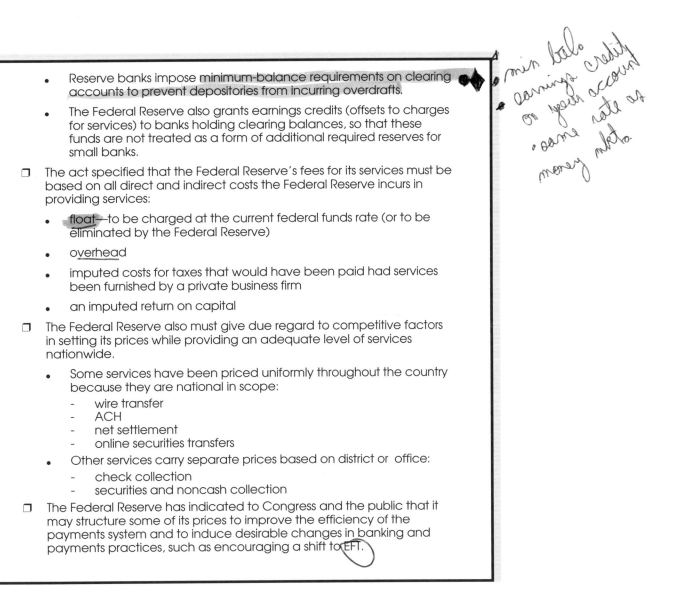

- Reserve banks impose minimum-balance requirements on clearing accounts to prevent depositories from incurring overdrafts.
- The Federal Reserve also grants earnings credits (offsets to charges for services) to banks holding clearing balances, so that these funds are not treated as a form of additional required reserves for small banks.

❑ The act specified that the Federal Reserve's fees for its services must be based on all direct and indirect costs the Federal Reserve incurs in providing services:

- float—to be charged at the current federal funds rate (or to be eliminated by the Federal Reserve)
- overhead
- imputed costs for taxes that would have been paid had services been furnished by a private business firm
- an imputed return on capital

❑ The Federal Reserve also must give due regard to competitive factors in setting its prices while providing an adequate level of services nationwide.

- Some services have been priced uniformly throughout the country because they are national in scope:
  - wire transfer
  - ACH
  - net settlement
  - online securities transfers
- Other services carry separate prices based on district or office:
  - check collection
  - securities and noncash collection

❑ The Federal Reserve has indicated to Congress and the public that it may structure some of its prices to improve the efficiency of the payments system and to induce desirable changes in banking and payments practices, such as encouraging a shift to EFT.

(handwritten note in margin: min bala earnings credit on your account · same rate as · money mkto.)

Depository Institutions

Commercial Banks

Innovations in the payments system and new payment powers granted banks and thrift institutions in the 1980s have significantly altered the business profiles of the nation's major depositories and their competitive relationships with one another.

Commercial banks provide more services, and engage in more activities over broader markets, than they did 10 years ago. In addition to their traditional services, most commercial banks now offer a wide range of time and savings deposits, rent out safe deposit boxes, exchange foreign currency, maintain ATMs, issue credit and debit cards, and sell traveler's checks. Some of the nation's larger banks also operate trust departments and sell government securities. About 6,000 bank holding companies in the nation today own or control one or more banks. Together, these companies hold more than 85 percent of commercial bank deposits. Banks that have established holding companies engage in financial activities ranging from the sale of economic information and data-processing services to brokering gold bullion and underwriting credit life, accident, and health insurance through their holding company affiliates.

Most of the 12,200 commercial banks in the United States are small, state-chartered, privately owned institutions that direct their deposit-taking and lending to the areas in which they are located. Nearly 60 percent of all the banks in this country each hold less than $50 million in deposits and employ about 25 people. Relatively few commercial banks are global corporations with hundreds of branches and thousands of employees. These banks hold a relatively large share of the banking system's total deposits and tend to be concentrated in the nation's money centers of New York, Chicago, San Francisco, and Los Angeles. In fact, the top 30 banks in the United States hold more than 30 percent of all bank deposits.

The basic business of commercial banking is still making loans and investments, activities that result in the creation of new demand deposit dollars—the nation's dominant money. A major market for banks has traditionally been the business sector, although in 1991 approximately 30 percent of loans in the commercial banking system went to business firms. In recent years, commercial banks have developed a significant consumer market. About 20 percent of the banking system's total loans are to consumers, while another 40 percent are for mortgages, many on one- and two-family residences. The relatively large share of bank loans in mortgages reflects the collapse of savings and loan associations in the 1990s, the traditional primary suppliers of residential mortgage funds. (The remainder are other loans, such as agricultural loans, loans to brokers and dealers, and loans to financial institutions.)

Time and savings deposits have now become the predominant deposit at commercial banks. In the 1960s, demand deposits dominated; but, by 1990, total time and savings deposits had climbed to nearly $2 trillion, compared with $300 billion in total demand deposits. The ownership of both time and demand deposits at commercial banks is still heavily weighted toward the business sector. Businesses own more than 60 percent of the demand deposits, and much of the banking system's time deposits consists of large-denomination certificates of deposit owned by corporations.

The business profile of commercial banks has changed significantly: commercial banks have lost their unique role. Other financial depositories now offer most of the services once provided only by commercial banks, including demand deposits and other types of transaction deposits that are used as payment devices. Not only do savings and loan associations, savings banks, and credit unions now compete directly with commercial banks, but a broad range of nondepository institutions—money market funds, insurance companies, finance companies, retail chains, brokerage firms, and credit card companies—compete as well.

Thrift Institutions   Savings Banks / Credit Unions

Savings banks, savings and loan associations (S&Ls), and credit unions are known as thrift institutions. Savings banks and S&Ls lend their deposits primarily to those who want to buy houses (in the form of mortgage loans). Credit unions lend their funds to consumers (in the form of installment loans). There are about 400 savings banks, 2,250 savings and loan associations, and 14,500 credit unions in the United States.

The 1980s saw thrift institutions virtually achieve their long-standing goal of providing a full range of financial services to depositors, thereby becoming a significant competitor to commercial banks. The Monetary Control Act of 1980 substantially equalized most of the payment and deposit-related powers of commercial banks and thrift institutions. The end of the decade, however, also witnessed a collapse of the savings and loan industry and growing public concerns over the safety of the deposit insurance programs for thrift institutions.

Savings banks

Savings banks are located primarily in the New England and Mid-Atlantic states. They were first organized in the early 1800s, before commercial banks started accepting individual savings deposits, to encourage thrift and provide a safe repository for public savings. Traditionally, the deposited funds have been used for mortgages. Until the 1980s, most savings banks were state-chartered, state-supervised, nonstockholder institutions operated by boards of trustees for the benefit of depositors. The depositors owned these mutual institutions and received profits in the form of interest on deposits.

Savings banks have traditionally obtained most of their funds from small individual deposits. Passbook deposits have typically supplied about 90 percent of savings banks' funds. Upon presentation of a passbook, the depositor can have savings deposits converted to cash, although savings banks can require the depositor to provide written notice at least seven days before withdrawal. About 60 percent of savings bank assets are in the form of mortgages; most of the remainder is invested in U.S. government and corporate bonds.

In the 1980s, Congress gave mutual savings banks new powers to offer interest-bearing checking accounts, make local business loans (up to 5 percent of the bank's assets), and to offer demand deposit accounts to business loan customers as well as to consumers. Congress also broadened savings banks' overall lending and investment powers and gave mutuals the option of converting to federal charter and becoming stockholder institutions. By issuing stock, savings banks could more readily obtain capital to expand and compete more effectively. Most mutuals converted to stock ownership.

Savings and Loan Associations (S&Ls) *trouble*

Savings and loan associations, like savings banks, are depositories that specialize in residential mortgage lending. Most savings and loan associations are small; some are owned by their members—the savers and borrowers—but most are owned by stockholders. S&Ls may be state or federally chartered.

In 1992, about 2,250 S&Ls held nearly $1 trillion in assets, more than 60 percent in the form of mortgage loans and mortgage securities. Their mortgage holdings represent about 25 percent of all outstanding residential mortgages held by all lending institutions. Offsetting these assets are time and savings deposits, which represented more than 80 percent of the savings and loan associations' liabilities.

The Monetary Control Act of 1980 equalized the residential real estate lending powers of federally chartered savings and loan associations with those of federally chartered commercial banks. Geographic restrictions and maximum loan restrictions were removed, and authority to make acquisition, development, and construction loans was extended. The Monetary Control Act also significantly broadened the investment powers of federally chartered savings and loan associations and gave them the same powers as commercial banks—to issue credit cards, offer NOW accounts, and engage in trust and fiduciary activities. The Thrift Institutions Restructuring Act of 1982 added commercial lending and still broader investment powers.

In the early 1980s, the new interest-earning transaction accounts authorized for banks and thrifts introduced a degree of instability to the operations of savings and loan associations. S&Ls saw their traditional source of funds shift from stable, low-cost, long-term passbook deposits to volatile short-term accounts sensitive to market interest rates, which were rising at that time. More important, S&Ls' income—mainly from fixed-rate mortgages—failed to keep pace with their rising cost of funds. The result was a substantial squeeze on profits.

To expand their earnings, many S&Ls drew on recently granted powers, and switched from making low-yielding residential mortgages to high-yielding—but riskier—consumer, commercial real estate, and business loans. However, a large number of S&Ls overextended themselves and suffered substantial losses when economic conditions soured and commercial real estate and business borrowers could not repay.

In 1982, about 85 percent of all S&Ls lost money and two-thirds found themselves with liabilities that exceeded the total market value of their assets. Although interest rates declined sharply in the mid-1980s, many S&Ls

continued to lose money because of bad loans, excessive operating costs—including very high interest rates paid on deposits—and fraud. By the late 1980s, a growing number of S&Ls had become insolvent (their liabilities exceeded the accounting value of their assets) and some were closed, necessitating a government payout of funds to insured depositors and raising public concerns about the overall health of the industry.

Congress moved to address these concerns in 1989 by enacting the Financial Institutions Reform, Recovery and Enforcement Act (FIRREA). The act created an Office of Thrift Supervision to oversee S&Ls and established a new savings association insurance fund (SAIF). It also created a new agency—the Resolution Trust Corporation (RTC)—to take over the insolvent S&Ls and either find buyers for them or liquidate their assets and pay off insured depositors.

By 1990, about 400 S&Ls, with total assets of about $200 billion, had been taken over by the RTC. Another 600 S&Ls, with total assets of nearly $350 billion, were also identified as either certain or likely to be taken over by the RTC in the early 1990s.

The collapse of the savings and loan industry in the 1980s wiped out the gains of 30 years of S&L deposit and loan growth. It also threatened to cripple S&Ls as major depository institution competitors in the 1990s. In 1991, only half the S&Ls that had been operating in 1980 were in existence and anxious depositors were continuing to withdraw funds from even soundly managed associations. Commercial banks were making nearly 40 percent of all U.S. residential mortgage loans while savings and loan associations accounted for only 30 percent. Industry analysts project that if this trend continues, commercial banks will become the nation's primary providers and holders of residential mortgages by 1993.

Credit unions

Credit unions are cooperatives—associations of people who have some common interest or affiliation and who want to pool savings and borrow funds from that pool. Members of credit unions purchase shares in the credit union with their savings. These shares are effectively their savings accounts; owning shares allows members to borrow from the pool of all credit union shares. Interest income from loans and other investments provides funds from which members are paid dividends on their shares.

Most of the nation's 14,500 credit unions are small operations with few, if any, full-time paid employees. Many credit unions are composed of employees from one company, with the credit union operating out of the company premises. Members may work at the credit union on a voluntary or part-time basis. The provision of rent-free space and the absence of labor costs keep overhead low and often allow small credit unions to offer more attractive lending rates than rates offered by other thrift institutions. However, some credit unions have assets that exceed those of many savings and loan associations and savings banks. About one-third of the nation's adult population are credit union members. In 1991, credit unions held more than $200 billion for 60 million depositors.

Members' savings—share accounts—represent about 85 percent of the total liabilities of credit unions. Loans to members account for more than 75 percent of total assets. Traditionally, credit union loans have been short-term loans repaid in installments. But changes in banking law and regulation in the 1970s and 1980s drastically altered the scope of credit union activities.

Credit unions now make mortgage loans of up to 30 years, offer checking account services through share draft accounts, and offer certificates of deposit through variable-rate share certificates. The Monetary Control Act of 1980 permitted credit unions to make overdraft loans on share draft accounts and to make real estate cooperative loans.

Federal regulations governing credit unions give them many competitive advantages over other types of thrift institutions and commercial banks, and in the view of many bankers, these advantages have been largely responsible for helping credit unions register the most rapid asset growth of all financial institutions in the 1980s.

As cooperatives, credit unions are considered nonprofit entities and are, therefore, not subject to taxes. Credit unions are also subject to fewer restrictive and costly-to-administer regulations than banks. These advantages have raised issues about the fairness of competition between credit unions and other depository institutions.

Broader issues related to the safety and soundness of credit unions became a concern of Congress and the public in the 1990s. About 10 percent of the nation's credit unions do not have federal deposit insurance. Rather, these credit unions—more than 1,400 with $18.6 billion in deposits—are insured by one of nine private insurance funds.

The 1991 insolvency of the private insurance fund that covered credit unions in Rhode Island necessitated a temporary state-mandated closing of Rhode Island's credit unions and triggered national concern over the safety of all credit union deposits. Most of the 20 states that permit private deposit insurance for credit unions moved quickly to bolster public confidence by requiring credit unions covered by private funds to obtain federal coverage. At the same time, legislation was introduced in Congress to impose federal insurance on all credit unions. However, no action was taken on these bills in 1991.

Nondepository Competitors

Money Market Funds

Technically, money market funds are not depository institutions, but open-ended investment companies that purchase securities on behalf of shareholders, either individuals or institutions. Typically, money market funds offer checking accounts that enable shareholders to write checks of $500 or more against their shares. Shares also can be redeemed by wire transfers or ACH transfers sent by the fund to the investor's bank account.

Most money market funds hold short-term certificates of deposit, commercial paper (short-term unsecured corporate IOUs), and U.S. Treasury bills. On occasion, they purchase other high-grade money market instruments. Some money market funds limit their investments to U.S. government securities to attract investors who are averse to risk. Other funds invest exclusively in Eurodollar certificates of deposit, tax-exempt municipal bonds, or shares of other funds.

In 1991, there were more than 700 funds, of which one-third held only investments that were free from taxes. Not all of these funds are open to individuals. Many funds are for the exclusive use of institutional investors. Other funds are sponsored by brokerage firms. Minimum initial investments for most general-purpose funds range as low as $500, and some require no minimum. Most institutional investor funds require minimum investments of $50,000 or more.

Money market funds began operation in 1972, and by 1974 were widely used. By 1978 their assets had grown to $10 billion. Today, the funds have more than 10 million shareholders with assets of nearly $450 billion. The phenomenal growth of the funds in the early 1980s—before banks could offer money market deposit accounts—was sparked by interest-rate-conscious individuals and institutions that increasingly shifted money from accounts at banks and thrift institutions into higher-yielding money market fund shares. The continued growth of the funds into the 1990s, however, has confounded many bankers.

In the mid-1980s the money market deposit account was expected to attract depositors away from the funds. A major contention of bankers was that the MMDA would emerge as the preferable deposit because it offered individuals FDIC protection, as well as a competitive interest rate. However, that preference did not materialize. The money market funds were able to keep their interest rates above those offered by banks on MMDAs because money market funds have broader latitude to invest and trade in riskier—higher paying—financial instruments, such as commercial paper. Also, cost and profitability pressures throughout the 1980s limited banks' ability to post interest rates that matched the returns of the funds. Nonetheless, most bankers believed that the value of FDIC protection on MMDAs would more than offset the higher returns paid by the funds.

Industry analysts now contend that money market fund shares and MMDAs may not be comparable or competitive products. The funds offer individual and institutional depositors investment returns and money management services that cannot be equated with the deposits and services banks offer. Moreover, they argue that money market funds and banks appeal to different markets. Most often cited is the appeal of money market funds to individuals and institutions that are willing to put their money at risk to obtain a high investment return or to shelter earnings from taxes. The experience of both banks and money market funds in the early 1990s tends to support this contention.

Most banks deemphasized deposit growth in 1991 because of limited lending opportunities in a weakened economy. They posted interest rates on their money market deposit accounts that averaged only 5.8 percent in early 1991, about 1.3 percentage points less than the average rate paid by the money market funds. Nonetheless, banks took in deposits. Anxious thrift depositors, concerned more with the safety of their deposits than interest return, transferred their deposits to banks. At the same time, deposits poured into the nation's money market funds. The flow of deposits into the funds has been attributed not to interest-rate sensitive bank depositors, but to individual and institutional investors in common stock who were concerned with protecting their returns from stock market volatility induced by the uncertainties of 1991's recession and Persian Gulf war.

Consumer Banks

In the 1980s, nondepository institutions began to compete with banks and thrifts in providing payment and other banking services. Several major insurance companies, retail chains, brokerage firms, and credit card companies acquired consumer banks, which gave them the ability to provide direct payment and banking services to individuals. (See exhibit 2.1.)

A consumer bank does not make or hold business loans. Nondepository institutions found a loophole in the Bank Holding Company Act of 1956 that enabled them to purchase commercial banks and, by divesting the banks' business lending activities, retain ownership and control of the banks. This bank ownership practice was prohibited by federal law in 1987. However, Congress permitted nondepository institutions that had entered the banking business before the prohibition to retain ownership of their consumer banks—170 in all.

Today, Sears, the nation's largest retail chain, offers banking, insurance, real estate, and brokerage services through financial service centers in many of its stores. Sears owns two consumer banks, a savings and loan association, an

Exhibit 2.1 *Major Nonbank Corporations that Operate Consumer Banks*

Name of Holding Company	Primary Business	Name of Subsidiary Consumer Bank
Advest Group, Inc. Hartford, CT	Brokerage/Mutual funds	Advest Bank, Hartford, CT
Aetna Life and Casualty, Hartford, CT	Insurance	Liberty Bank & Trust, Gibbsboro, NJ
American Express Co., New York	Travel and entertainment card	Boston Safe Deposit and Trust Co.; Advisory Bank & Trust, Minneapolis, MN; American Express Centurion Bank, Newark, DE
Bear Stearns Co., New York	Brokerage	Custodial Trust Co., Trenton, NJ
Chrysler Corp., Highland Park, MI *going out of it.*	Manufacturing/ Finance co.	Automotive Financial Services, Inc., Highland Park, MI
Dreyfus Corp., New York	Brokerage/Mutual funds	Dreyfus Consumer Bank, East Orange, NJ
General Electric Co., Stamford, CT	Manufacturing/ Finance co.	Monogram Bank, Blue Ash, OH
Home Group Inc., New York	Insurance	Premium Bank, Oceanside, CA
J.C. Penney Co., Inc., New York	Retail chain	J.C. Penney National Bank, Harrington, DE
John Hancock Subsidiaries, Inc. Boston, MA	Insurance	First Signature Bank & Trust Co., Boston, MA
Merrill Lynch & Co., New York	Brokerage	Merrill Lynch Bank & Trust Co., Plainsboro, NJ
Montgomery Ward & Co., Chicago, IL	Retail chain	Clayton Bank & Trust Co., DE
Sears, Roebuck and Co., Chicago, IL	Retail chain	Greenwood Trust Co., New Castle, DE; Hurley State Bank, Hurley, SD
Travelers Corp., Hartford, CT	Insurance	Massachusetts Co., Boston, MA

insurance company, the nation's largest real estate brokerage firm, and the fifth largest securities brokerage house in the country. Sears also offers consumer credit to more than 35 million credit cardholders.

Merrill Lynch, the world's largest securities brokerage firm, owns a consumer bank, a real estate financing company, and an insurance company. In addition to banking, brokerage, real estate, and insurance services, Merrill Lynch maintains a money market fund and allows customers to write checks against their investment in the fund. Other brokerage firms offer similar money market fund services to their customers.

The American Express Company acquired a major securities brokerage firm and three consumer banks in the 1980s. It now offers credit card payment and installment credit to millions of households and business firms (in addition to its traditional travel and entertainment card) and is one of the most popular names in traveler's checks.

The nation's finance companies also became aggressive competitors of banks and thrifts in the 1980s. Auto finance companies used below-market financing rates—from 2.9 percent down to zero—instead of price tag reductions to boost sluggish car sales. They accounted for almost three-quarters of all car loans made in the 1980s. Other finance companies increasingly began to finance not only the products of their parent manufacturing companies, but other companies' products—taking a large share of banks' general consumer installment loan market.

Evolution of Traditional Accounts

Transaction Accounts

During the 1980s, the structure of deposits and competitive relationships were not the only things that changed at depository institutions; the nomenclature of banking changed to include such concepts as transaction accounts. These accounts allow depositors to withdraw or transfer funds by check, draft, order of withdrawal, or telephone transfer. Demand deposits, NOW accounts, savings deposits subject to automatic transfer, and share draft accounts are all considered transaction accounts.

The term transaction account was created by Congress in the Monetary Control Act of 1980 as a descriptive term to encompass all deposits against which depository institutions would have to maintain reserves. The inclusion of interest-earning checking account-type deposits in the definition represented a significant change in government regulation of those deposits. Before the 1980 law, those accounts were treated as savings deposits, which carried lower reserve requirements than demand deposit accounts. The Monetary

Control Act exempted personal time and savings deposits from reserve requirements.

Transaction accounts have become exceedingly costly accounts for most banks. Not only do banks pay interest on a substantial share of their transaction deposits, but reserves have to be set aside for these funds. The costs of processing checks drawn on these accounts are enormous. To offset costs, most banks charge customers for transaction account services—a flat fee, a sliding scale of fees based on the account's average balance, or a per item charge based on the number of transactions.

Demand Deposits

Demand deposits enable the holder to withdraw cash on demand or to make payments by check. In 1933, the federal government prohibited the payment of interest on demand deposits. With the introduction of NOW accounts, automatic transfers from savings accounts, phone transfers from savings accounts, and credit union share drafts, the characteristics that differentiated a demand deposit from a time deposit all but disappeared. Today, a demand deposit is specifically defined as a deposit that is payable on demand or issued with an original maturity of less than seven days. In 1991, commercial banks held $275 billion in demand deposits for individuals and business firms but more than $200 billion in interest-earning transaction accounts (primarily NOW accounts). Thrift institutions held about $85 billion in demand and other transaction accounts.

Demand deposits were once the exclusive account of commercial banks. Since 1980, these accounts have become relatively commonplace at savings banks, savings and loan associations, and credit unions. Moreover, competition in the 1980s from interest-bearing transaction accounts has taken its toll on this core bank deposit. Most bankers expect little future growth in demand deposit accounts—either in balances or in number of accounts.

Most demand deposit balances held in banks are for commercial accounts. Personal checking account balances represent only about one-quarter of total demand deposit balances. However, personal accounts constitute 90 percent of most banks' total number of accounts.

Although the traditional checking account appears to have little growth potential, banks have continued to innovate in their demand deposit offerings. The 1980s saw increasing numbers of banks offering flat fee consumer checking accounts, overdraft checking, and check guarantee services. In the Midwest, banks also instituted free checking and premium accounts for senior citizens.

Rather than impose a variable fee based on balance levels and transaction volumes, banks actively promote checking accounts that carry fixed monthly charges, regardless of balances or transactions. Many banks have also introduced a streamlined checking account with very low service charges to provide a lifeline type of payment service to low-income individuals and senior citizens. Banks now offer customers overdraft checking, which combines a checking account and a personal line of credit that can be accessed through the checking account. Some banks also offer a check guarantee service linked to the checking account. This service guarantees to merchants and to banks that a check presented by the issuing bank's customers will be paid by the bank. The guarantee feature usually is represented by a check guarantee card that provides identification and specifies the guarantee conditions.

Time and Savings Deposits

Time and savings deposits are deposits that earn interest and technically cannot be withdrawn on demand. A savings deposit is an interest-earning deposit contract that does not require notice of withdrawal but gives the depository the right to require seven days' written notice of intent to withdraw. Deposits can be withdrawn from savings accounts without loss of interest. A time deposit cannot be withdrawn for seven days. If it is withdrawn before seven days, or before the time deposit contract matures, an interest penalty is invoked. The penalty is loss of at least seven days' interest for time deposits withdrawn within the first six days after a time deposit is made. For business time deposits with maturities of 18 months or longer, the penalty is the loss of one month's interest.

Passbook Savings Accounts

Passbook savings accounts, the staple deposit of savings banks and savings and loan associations, represent only about one-quarter of the total of all small denomination time deposits in commercial banks. Until 1975, only individuals and certain nonprofit organizations could hold these deposits. In 1975, partnerships and corporations were permitted to hold savings deposits of up to $150,000. This limitation was removed in March 1986, when interest-rate ceilings were eliminated.

Three factors have had a corrosive effect on passbook savings balances—the introduction in the 1980s of NOW accounts, other interest-earning transaction accounts, and savings certificates whose interest rates keep pace with market rates. However, the effect has not been as substantial as many industry analysts expected. In December 1982, when the MMDA was introduced, savings deposits on bank and thrift books totaled almost $360 billion. By 1992, passbook savings balances had actually increased to more than $415 billion.

Despite the relatively low interest rate on passbook accounts and the greater convenience and higher returns available on other accounts, most consumers, particularly in the East where most savings banks are located, continue to covet their passbooks. Banks and thrift institutions have found maintaining the paper-based passbook savings account system to be very costly. Maintaining passbook accounts is labor intensive; the institution must keep dual records (internal records plus the depositor passbook), which increases audit and security procedures. Tellers must manually process transaction activity, and bank management must continually deal with the problem of lost or stolen passbooks.

Some depositories have offered customers inducements to give up their passbooks in exchange for monthly or quarterly automated statements. These inducements have included slightly higher interest rates, bonuses or gifts, and more convenient and faster teller service. Banks in the western states have been successful in eliminating passbooks. However, financial institutions in most other states have been generally unsuccessful in getting depositors to alter their savings practices.

Consumers tend to favor the physical aspect of the passbook—being able to watch money grow—and the ability to add and withdraw small amounts with no maturity or penalty constraints. Long-standing public familiarity with the characteristics of passbook accounts also may be a factor in their popularity.

With the removal of interest-rate ceilings in 1986, banks were no longer limited to paying 5¼ percent on passbook accounts. However, the general decline in market interest rates in the late 1980s and early 1990s prompted many banks to lower, rather than raise, the passbook rate. Some banks also moved to convert their passbook accounts from fixed-rate to variable-rate accounts. Nonetheless, most bankers do not expect public attitudes toward passbook savings to change.

Large Denomination Certificates of Deposit (CDs)

Large denomination CDs ($100,000 or more) are sold by banks primarily to corporations. They bear fixed interest rates and are payable at maturity, which can be any date seven days or longer after deposit of the funds. Although CDs can be issued in nonnegotiable bearer form (payable only to the bearer by the issuing bank) the most popular CDs among big corporations are those that are negotiable (salable in the secondary market).

Most of the nation's large banks offer their CDs through nationwide brokerage firms as well as through their own local or regional offices. By using a brokerage firm to sell its CDs—particularly a firm with an extensive network of nationwide offices—a bank can reach a broader market than it could reach on its own. Banks generally have to pay a higher interest rate on their brokered CDs than those issued locally. However, banks have found that these higher interest rates tend to be less than the rates they would otherwise have to pay to borrow funds in the nation's money or capital markets.

The nation's largest banks have also found that they can obtain funds from out-of-town customers through brokered CDs without having to increase the interest rates they offer to local depositors. This has been particularly true for banks in the nation's money centers, such as New York City, where the proximity and competition of the large banks tends to keep deposit interest rates higher than in other parts of the country. In the early 1990s, brokered CDs enabled New York banks to attract money from areas of the country where deposit rates were lower. About 1 to 2 percent of banks' total deposits come from brokered CDs. However, for the nation's largest banks—those with assets of $10 billion or more—brokered CDs account for 3 percent of all their domestic deposits. (These banks held more than $200 billion in large denomination CDs in 1990.)

Although big business firms and institutions constitute the primary market for brokered CDs, brokerage firms sold nearly $40 billion in small denomination CDs to individuals in 1990. Some bankers contend that risk-averse individuals appear to favor brokered CDs over comparable investments because of the FDIC insurance accorded such certificates (up to $100,000). However, other bankers contend that growing public concern in the early 1990s over the safety and soundness of banks and the FDIC have largely erased the advantage that brokered deposits may have had over comparable investments in the 1980s.

The future of brokered CDs in the 1990s is doubtful because of the public examination of the reasons for the collapse of the savings and loan industry in the late 1980s and the national debate over reforming the federal deposit insurance system. In the 1980s, many S&Ls relied extensively on brokered deposits to obtain funds when they were nearly insolvent. They used the funds to expand unsound lending and investments. Although banks did not use brokered CDs to finance loan or investment expansion but to supplement traditional sources of funds, the practice itself has been called into question.

Bank regulators see some merits in the prudent use of brokered deposits. Until 1992, banks that met regulatory standards for adequate capital did not need prior approval to sell CDs through brokers. However, banks that were below nationwide capital standards had to obtain permission from the FDIC. In 1991, about 100 banks had sought and obtained such permission. The FDIC contended that the practice of attracting deposits through brokered funds benefitted undercapitalized banks because it enabled them to obtain a stable base of deposits at a lower cost than if they had to borrow funds. Congress, however, was unconvinced. Among the changes made by Congress in 1991 in the federal deposit insurance system was a limit on insurance coverage for brokered deposits. The 1991 law requires the FDIC to issue regulations in 1992 that prohibit all depositories, except those that significantly exceed all capital requirements, from accepting brokered CDs.

Savings Certificates

Savings certificates are time deposits with fixed maturities and fixed interest rates that are offered in small denominations, primarily to individuals. These certificates are usually nonnegotiable; that is, they must be presented to the bank by the original depositor for redemption. Although they can be issued in any denomination, most banks require a minimum deposit of $500 to $2,500 for their certificates, depending on maturity. Once issued, no funds may be added to or withdrawn from the certificate until it matures. In 1991, banks held about $215 billion in certificates with 6 to 12 months maturity, and nearly $170 billion in certificates with 12 to 30 months maturity. These maturity ranges were the two most popular savings certificates on banks' books. (See exhibit 2.2.)

IRAs and Other Retirement Accounts   *Mutual fund/.401 K Plans.*

Self-employed workers and workers not covered by an employer's pension plan are able to open interest-earning retirement accounts, some of which are tax-deductible. For the self-employed, these accounts are known as Keogh accounts or SEP accounts (simplified employee pension). For individuals the accounts are called IRA accounts (individual retirement accounts).

Most banks offer IRA accounts as trust or custodial time accounts. IRAs may carry a fixed or a variable interest rate over the life of the account, with withdrawals not allowed (without a 10 percent IRS tax penalty) until the depositor reaches age 59-$\frac{1}{2}$. Individuals not covered by a pension plan can deposit up to $2,000 a year in a tax-deferred IRA account. That is, funds deposited can be subtracted from total income on which taxes are paid. Individuals covered by a pension plan also can open IRA accounts on which interest is not subject to taxation until withdrawal. However, in most instances the funds deposited cannot be deducted for tax purposes.

In 1981, IRAs were made available to all employees as part of broader tax reform measures enacted by Congress. With the liberalization of eligibility rules, IRA deposit growth at banks soared. Banks, thrifts, brokerage firms and other financial institutions held about $26 billion in IRA deposits in 1981. By 1986, when Congress rescinded the liberalization, more than $350 billion in IRA deposits were being held for 20 million account holders, with commercial banks holding about one-quarter of this total.

Since 1987, IRAs have been subject to income thresholds that prevent all but low-income earners from being able to deduct IRA deposits from current taxes. Among the factors that influenced Congress in changing IRA rules was a sense that the tax deduction was being used primarily by upper-income individuals to shelter income from taxes and that the Treasury would lose about $26 billion in income tax revenue from 1987 to 1991 if the deduction was continued.

Exhibit 2.2 *Commercial Bank Business and Consumer Deposits in 1991* (billions of dollars)

Savings deposits		$240
Small denomination time deposits		754
Original maturities of:		
7 days to 3 months	50	
3 months to 6 months	162	
6 months to 1 year	215	
1 to $2\frac{1}{2}$ years	170	
$2\frac{1}{2}$ years and over	157	
Large denomination time deposits (CDs)		375
Demand deposits		290
NOW accounts		240
Money market deposit accounts		400
IRA and Keogh deposits		<u>146</u>
Total business and consumer deposits		$2,445

Source: Federal Reserve *Statistical Release H.6 (508) Special Supplementary Table,* December 1991, and Federal Reserve *Bulletin,* November 1991.

Some bankers contend that without broad tax deductibility IRAs will fade as a meaningful deposit product of the 1990s. Other bankers feel that IRAs will continue to attract substantial funds. They base this contention on the fact that one-third of IRA holders who opened accounts between 1981 and 1986 continue to qualify for the annual $2,000 maximum tax-free deduction. They also note that interest earned on all IRA accounts is tax deferred until withdrawal and that all IRA funds are protected by FDIC insurance. In 1991, banks held about $145 billion in IRA and Keogh deposits.

Summary

The traditional differences between demand deposits and time deposits, as well as the differences between banks and thrifts, were largely erased by payment system innovations and changes in banking laws in the 1980s. NOW accounts, money market deposit accounts, and IRAs have significantly altered public payment and savings practices, while demand deposits and passbook savings accounts have lost much of their luster.

The Monetary Control Act of 1980 essentially equalized most of the payment and deposit-related powers of commercial banks and thrifts. However, the public's shift into new types of time deposits and interest-earning transaction accounts—accentuated by rapidly rising interest rates in the early 1980s—had a devastating impact on the nation's savings and loan associations. Moreover, both banks and thrifts have experienced heightened and continuing competition in the 1990s from nondepository institutions for depositors' funds.

Questions

1. Cite the three basic ways the Monetary Control Act of 1980 allowed thrifts to become more like commercial banks.

2. Why did money market deposit accounts grow so rapidly in the 1980s?

3. What differentiates a demand deposit from a time deposit and a savings deposit?

4. Why have money market funds and credit unions had a competitive advantage over banks and other thrifts?

THE REGULATORY STRUCTURE AFFECTING DEPOSITS

Objectives

After successfully completing this chapter, you will be able to

- ❖ describe the regulatory philosophy that has shaped the treatment of banking in the United States
- ❖ cite major responsibilities of the bank regulatory agencies
- ❖ explain the defects in the early U.S. regulatory structure
- ❖ discuss why deposit interest rates were deregulated in the 1980s
- ❖ identify current issues related to deposits and deposit regulations

Introduction

Changes in payments practices and technology, the introduction of new banking services, and deposit innovations have paralleled some significant changes in the regulatory structure affecting deposits. Four key Federal Reserve regulations govern much of banking's deposit-related operations: Regulation D (reserve requirements), Regulation E (electronic funds transfer systems), Regulation J (check collection), and Regulation Q (interest on deposits). A fifth deposit-related regulation, Regulation CC, which governs check endorsements, funds availability and return items, is examined in chapter 8's discussion of deposit management.

The resolution of two current issues in deposit regulation and management—deposit insurance reform and the updating of bank service regulations and federal regulatory structure—will profoundly affect bank profitability and competitiveness in the years to come.

Sharing of Regulatory Power

The sharing of bank regulation responsibilities by federal and state agencies on such key matters as mergers, branching, bank holding company activities, and bank records examination has been a long-standing feature of the U.S. banking system. Today, no fewer than four separate government entities share the regulation and supervision of commercial banks—the Federal Reserve Board, Federal Deposit Insurance Corporation (FDIC), Comptroller of the Currency, and state banking agencies.

Over the years, Congress has allocated regulatory power among the government agencies and has expanded the role of the Federal Reserve in recent decades. However, the division of bank regulatory power between the central bank and other government agencies continues to be the dominant characteristic of U.S. banking regulation.

Banking regulation in the United States has been shaped essentially by the country's attitudes toward money and its control, which encompass the long-standing debate about the power and rights of the federal government relative to those of the states. With this as a background, the following characteristics unique to the U.S. banking system have evolved.

First, a banking industry has been created that is essentially composed of small banks with diffused market power. This is primarily due to laws and regulations that have severely limited branching, merging, and the geographic radius of a bank's business. Federal law effectively prohibits interstate branching; state law has been the controlling factor. The 1927 McFadden Act restricts all nationally chartered banks to the various banking laws of the states. The Douglas Amendment to the 1956 Bank Holding Company Act prohibits the acquisition of a bank in any state but a bank holding company's home state, unless authorized by state law. In the 1980s, 46 states enacted reciprocal branching agreements allowing banks in other states—usually within their region—to open branches within their borders if those states permit the same for their banks. About half the agreements allow for states outside the region to be included in the early 1990s. However, no uniform national rules cover interstate branching.

Second, a system of dual regulation has been established where the states or the federal government may charter, examine, and oversee banks. This has led to a system in which rules and directives are pervasive and examinations are frequent.

Third, the banking industry and its regulation have not followed the historical pattern of other U.S. industries and their regulation, a pattern of consolidation and concentration of small firms into industrial giants and movement toward mass national marketing. There has also been little consolidation of government oversight of banking practices.

Shortcomings in the Nation's Early Banking System

Between the end of the Civil War, when commercial banking in the United States began to grow substantially, and the beginning of World War I, when the United States began to emerge as the world's premier industrial power, a number of serious shortcomings in the nation's banking system and bank regulatory structure became glaringly apparent. Congress addressed these defects when it established the Federal Reserve in 1913. Today, the central bank has become the cornerstone of the U.S. bank regulatory structure. But before creation of the central bank, serious regulatory problems had developed.

Reserve Problems

The first problem was due to the popular practice of pyramiding reserves into a few of the nation's money center banks, leaving most banks with insufficient liquidity in times of stress.

The National Banking Act of 1863 specified a three-tier structure of reserve requirements for nationally chartered banks. Small rural banks could keep some of their reserves in vault cash, but they were required to deposit most of their reserves with larger banks in the nation's major cities (reserve city banks). Reserve city banks, in turn, had to deposit most of their reserves in still larger banks in the nation's money centers of New York City, Chicago, and St. Louis (central reserve city banks). The central reserve city banks had to keep all their reserves in vault cash.

The banking system's reserves, dispersed throughout the country, could not be transferred quickly to banks in regions that might be under liquidity pressure. And, because the central reserve city banks were the ultimate repositories of the banking system's reserves, they were particularly susceptible to cumulative pressures that often led to bank panic.

Typically, a bank panic would begin in the Midwest, when small, farmer-oriented banks found that they did not have enough currency on hand to pay out. This was usually a seasonal phenomenon that occurred when farmers were selling crops. The smaller banks would call on their reserve city correspondents for their reserves. The reserve city correspondents, now with less cash for their own needs, would, in turn, call on the central reserve city banks for their reserves.

A few central reserve city banks, hit with these cumulative demands for reserves, were unable to meet the liquidity needs of thousands of rural banks.

The Bank Panic of 1907—one of the most severe—led Congress to establish the Federal Reserve. During this panic, New York City banks could not come up with enough immediate funds to honor reserve claims, so they quickly called in loans made to brokers and dealers. Broker and dealer firms, in turn, were forced to sell stocks and bonds to raise money to repay loans.

The ensuing selling frenzy on Wall Street drove down securities prices and made it impossible for firms to repay loans. Some firms defaulted and failed, bringing banks down with them. When New Yorkers learned of the plight of brokers and banks, they panicked, withdrew their funds from fiscally sound banks, and hoarded the money. This compounded the liquidity problems of the banking system. During the 1907 panic, currency and coin became so scarce in New York City that banks, merchants, and tradesmen were issuing, accepting, and exchanging scrip[1] to stay in business.

The fundamental problem was the lack of a lender of last resort for the banking system—a source of guaranteed liquidity that all banks could tap when they needed money.

Supervision Problems

The early banking system also lacked a central supervisory body that could administer a code of regulations and law protecting bank deposits in all parts of the country.

The National Banking Act established a dual banking system in the United States, still applicable, in which banks can choose a state or national charter. The choice of charter determines the government entity and the body of regulations and law that the bank must follow.

Nationally chartered banks were subject to the stiff capital requirements and lending limits mandated in the National Banking Act, and they were subject to examination by the Comptroller of the Currency, the agency established to charter banks. National banks also were required to maintain reserves against their banks' notes and deposits.

For state-chartered banks, the myriad of state rules and regulations often resulted in inadequate bank capital, risky bank loans, and insufficient reserves against notes and deposits. With no central oversight, banking activities, such as check clearing and collection and correspondent accounts, developed privately and beyond the regulation of national policy.

The Federal Reserve's Supervisory and Regulatory Functions

The 1913 Federal Reserve Act called upon the Federal Reserve to provide the nation with a "more effective supervision of banking in the United States." Over the years, the Federal Reserve has sought to fulfill this mandate by *result of problems*

- ❖ issuing rules and regulations that outline the boundaries and procedures of acceptable banking practice
- ❖ monitoring the fiscal soundness of banks by analyzing data and information submitted directly by banks or indirectly through government agencies
- ❖ examining banks for compliance with banking laws, regulations, and procedures
- ❖ deciding in which nonbank activities bank holding companies can engage
- ❖ issuing rules for most of the consumer credit regulations implemented by the government

Unlike its monetary policy and payments mechanism roles, the central bank shares its regulatory power with other federal agencies and with agencies of state governments.

Public Policy

Banks differ from other businesses and have always been regulated differently. Banks traditionally have been the only business licensed by government to create money—demand deposits and, until 1913, paper currency. Furthermore, banks deal mainly with other people's money—deposits that are neither their own nor necessarily those of their stockholders.

Historically, government viewed banks as extenders of credit, primarily to business. Banks must operate prudently and have sufficient liquidity or access to liquidity to prevent a loss of public confidence in the banks' safety and soundness.

Government also has recognized the potential for market abuse in banks' unique power to create money. For example, banks could acquire nonbank industrial subsidiaries and drive out competition in those industries by supplying their subsidiaries with low-cost, self-created money and credit.

Scenarios such as these have led government to see banks in a public service context, more closely aligned to public utilities than to manufacturing companies.

Over time, government regulation of banking has sought to achieve four major goals:

- ❖ to maintain a safe and sound banking system
- ❖ to promote competition in banking
- ❖ to protect bank owners from management fraud and protect bank management from owners' abuse of power
- ❖ to protect consumers who use bank credit and bank services

These goals have been pursued through regulation and supervision.

Bank regulation can be broadly defined as the implementation of banking laws through government-issued rules and directives. Bank supervision can be defined as the enforcement of those rules and directives through continuous oversight—by personal inspections, off-site monitoring, and analysis of data on banking performance and practice.

Bank regulation in the United States has emphasized preventive measures to achieve its public policy goals, such as restrictions on bank branching, mergers, and acquisitions. This has been done to prevent banks from becoming big enough to wield anticompetitive market power. The government also has prohibited the payment of interest on demand deposits and regulated interest rates on time and savings deposits to reduce destructive competition.

To ensure safe and sound banking, the government has set terms and conditions under which banks can obtain and use assets and liabilities:

- ❖ insuring bank depositors against loss
- ❖ instituting capital requirements, liquidity, solvency, and profitability guidelines
- ❖ establishing a code of rights for consumers, which includes prohibiting banks from engaging in practices that are unfair or discriminatory

Primary Responsibilities of the Bank Regulators

Banking regulation is administered through a complex structure that reflects more the unplanned evolution of government attitudes toward banking than it does any grand design for public policy. The structure is difficult to follow because most of the regulators have overlapping responsibilities and jurisdictions. However, some key features can provide guideposts to understanding.

The choice of charter (state or national) determines whether a bank's primary regulator will be a state or a federal agency. Federal regulation of state-chartered banks is, for the most part, optional; they have a choice of joining the Federal Deposit Insurance Corporation (FDIC) and/or the Federal Reserve. Federal Reserve members must be insured by the FDIC, but state-chartered banks that choose to be FDIC members need not be members of the Federal Reserve. In practice, essentially all the nation's 8,000 state-chartered commercial banks are FDIC members. Thus, virtually all banks are jointly regulated by some federal or state entities.

State Banking Departments

The states charter commercial banks and, in some states, savings banks, savings and loan associations, and credit unions. For the institutions they charter, states rule on acquisition and branching applications, issue advisory opinions on acquisition applications by bank holding companies, and conduct periodic examinations.

Federal Reserve Board

The Board examines state-chartered member banks; rules on merger and branching applications of state-chartered member banks; and issues advisory opinions on merger applications submitted by national banks and FDIC-insured, state-chartered, nonmember banks. The board also rules on permissible activities for bank holding companies.

[handwritten margin note: BHC • writes most of the regulations]

FDIC

The FDIC provides deposit insurance coverage through its Bank Insurance Fund (BIF) for national banks and for those state-chartered commercial and savings banks electing insurance. Insurance is mandatory for national banks and those state-chartered banks that opt for Federal Reserve membership or are subsidiaries of bank holding companies. The FDIC also provides insurance coverage through its Savings Association Insurance Fund (SAIF) for federally chartered savings banks and for savings and loan associations that had been insured by the Federal Savings and Loan Insurance Corporation (FSLIC) until that agency's dissolution by Congress in 1989.

[handwritten margin note: • provide deposit ins]

The FDIC examines state-chartered banks that are FDIC-insured but are not members of the Federal Reserve; it rules on merger and branching applications of state-chartered banks that are FDIC-insured but are not members of the Federal Reserve; and it issues advisory opinions on merger applications of Federal Reserve member banks and FDIC-insured, state-chartered, nonmember banks. The FDIC also manages and liquidates assets of failed banks, and since 1989 has had administrative responsibility for the operations of the Resolution Trust Corporation (RTC). The FDIC's major responsibilities are outlined in exhibit 3.1.

Exhibit 3.1 *FDIC Responsibilities*

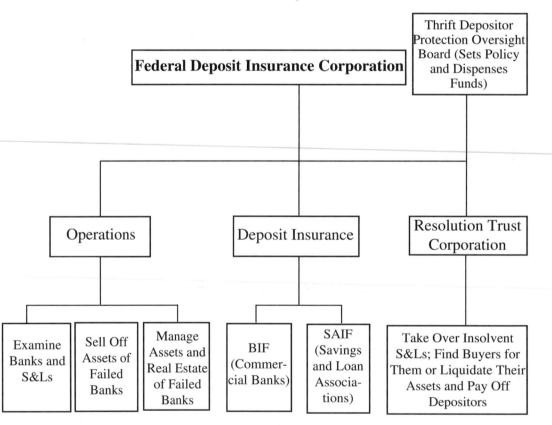

Comptroller of the Currency

The Office of the Comptroller of the Currency (OCC) charters national banks, all of which, except in U.S. territories overseas, are members of the Federal Reserve system. The OCC also examines national banks and rules on the merger and branching applications of national banks.

Office of Thrift Supervision

The Office of Thrift Supervision (OTS) was created by Congress in 1989 to assume most of the regulatory and supervisory powers of the Federal Home Loan Bank Board, which Congress disbanded that year. The OTS charters federal savings and loan associations and federal savings banks. However, these institutions are examined by the FDIC, which administers the insurance fund for S&Ls. The OTS also provides reserve credit to members of the Federal Home Loan Bank system, which it administers. Membership in that system is mandatory for savings and loan associations, and since 1989 optional for commercial banks that have more than 10 percent of their loans in residential housing.

National Credit Union Administration

The National Credit Union Administration (NCUA) charters federal credit unions, provides insurance for all federal credit unions and state-chartered credit unions that elect insurance, and examines all credit unions it insures. Through its central liquidity facility, the NCUA acts as a lender of last resort for credit unions.

Federal Financial Institutions Examination Council

Congress established the Federal Financial Institutions Examination Council in 1978 (as part of the Financial Institutions Regulatory and Interest Rate Control Act) to coordinate and standardize activities among the federal regulators of financial institutions. Since 1978, the council has developed a uniform examinations process and a uniform financial institutions rating system. The five regulatory agencies comprising the council in 1992 were the FDIC, OTS, Federal Reserve Board, OCC, and the NCUA.

The Examinations Process and Rating System

The object of examining and rating banks is to ensure that banks are complying with law and regulation and to assess each bank's financial health on a regular basis.

Rating a bank's financial health enables the regulatory agencies to identify (and monitor) banks whose poor financial condition could threaten the integrity of the banking system and erode public confidence in banks. Poorly rated banks are typically required by the regulators to take corrective actions based on recommendations and instructions from the examiners. By trying to prevent bank problems from deteriorating to the point where FDIC payouts to depositors are unavoidable, the examinations process and rating system also serve as a way for the government to protect the reserves of the federal deposit insurance fund.

Bank examiners rely on the CAMEL rating system for assessing a bank's condition. CAMEL is an acronym for five key criteria—capital, assets, management, earnings, and liquidity—that must be evaluated and scored before an overall rating can be made of a bank's financial health. Examiners rank a bank's performance against each criterion on a scale of 1 to 5, with 1 as the highest rating and 5 as the lowest. A composite rating is then derived for the bank.

A bank's **capital** represents the funds invested in the bank by its owners. These funds are intended to provide a buffer from any losses a bank might incur on its loans or investments. All banks must satisfy certain minimum capital requirements, generally expressed as a fixed percentage of capital to total assets of the bank. For most banks, the basic capital adequacy requirement in 1992 was 6 percent; for the nation's large banks involved in international banking, capital requirements were 8 percent. An international agreement between the United States and most other industrial nations in 1988 established the higher capital requirements for large banks in all countries.

In evaluating the quality of a bank's loan and investment **assets**, bank examiners must determine the expected ability of borrowers to make scheduled interest payments and repay principal. If this ability is found wanting, the examiners may categorize the loans as substandard or doubtful. They may even require a bank to charge off loans that are unlikely to be repaid. In all cases, banks are required to set aside funds as loan loss reserves to cover potential losses. Bankers generally take these funds from their current earnings. However, if earnings are insufficient, the funds must be transferred from the bank's capital.

A bank's **management** is rated on its technical competence, leadership, and administrative ability. However, in evaluating management, examiners also take into account the quality of the bank's internal controls, operating procedures, and lending and investing policies. **Earnings** are generally rated against the bank's capacity to cover potential losses and meet its capital requirement. A bank's **liquidity** refers to its ability to readily convert assets into cash to meet depositors' claims. Examiners rate this ability primarily in relation to the volatility of a bank's deposits and the bank's reliance on borrowings.

The regulatory agencies consider banks with composite CAMEL ratings of 1 or 2 to be sound banks in strong condition that are generally permitted to operate without any restrictions. A bank that receives a 3 rating is considered weaker than desired (below average) because it has been found to be deficient in at least some areas covered by the examination. These banks typically are given specific instructions on how to address their deficiencies. In some cases, however, the regulators may impose restrictions on the practices of a 3-rated bank to prevent a deterioration in its financial condition.

Banks that receive CAMEL ratings of 4 or 5 are considered to be problem banks with severe general weaknesses that could readily bring them to insolvency. These banks are placed under close surveillance, usually issued directives restricting their activities, and generally required to take immediate corrective actions to shore up their deficiencies.

Restrictions include

❖ more frequent examinations and requirements that bank management provide frequent reports on specific problem areas

   The steady flow of information enables regulatory agencies to intervene quickly if conditions worsen.

❖ a capital call requiring an undercapitalized bank to raise new funds to meet capital standards within a prescribed time period

❖ directives restricting the bank's activities, such as limiting the amount of dividends the bank can pay to its stockholders, prohibiting management from obtaining funds through the use of brokered deposits, and requiring the bank to tighten its lending standards

   Directives such as these are legally binding and usually are issued to a bank's management in the form of a memorandum of understanding, a written agreement, or a cease and desist order. These official directives are designed to prevent a bank from taking any actions that might further jeopardize its precarious financial health and to protect the deposit insurance fund from potential losses.

If a bank's financial condition deteriorates to the point where it is in imminent danger of becoming insolvent, regulators can invoke harsher restrictions. The FDIC is empowered to replace a bank's management and assume control over the daily operations of a potentially failing bank. As a last resort, the FDIC can revoke a bank's deposit insurance coverage, close the bank, and pay off insured depositors.

In 1991, Congress imposed several new requirements on the regulatory agencies designed to strengthen the importance of capital in evaluating banks' safety and to quicken regulators' response to poor banking performance. By 1993, the federal regulators must establish a five-level classification system for evaluating a bank's capital position.

Under this supplement to the CAMEL rating system, a level one designation would be assigned to the most strongly capitalized banks; a level five to the most weakly capitalized. Progressively more restrictive regulatory actions would be triggered automatically if, from one examination to the next, a bank's capital designation fell by one or more levels. By 1994, the regulators must establish additional CAMEL criteria for evaluating bank safety.

A bank's CAMEL rating is confidential and is provided to the bank's senior management only. However, in its periodic reports to Congress on the health of the U.S. banking system, the FDIC usually discloses the total number of problem banks that it is actively monitoring. In 1991, about 1,000 banks— with more than $400 billion in combined assets—had been so identified.

Overview of the Financial Institution Reform, Recovery and Enforcement Act of 1989

In 1989, Congress strengthened the FDIC's power to close potentially failing savings and loan associations as a provision of the Financial Institutions Reform, Recovery and Enforcement Act (FIRREA).

FIRREA profoundly changed the legal and regulatory environment of both banks and thrifts in the 1990s by

- providing funds for closing hundreds of insolvent savings and loan associations and giving new powers to thrift regulators to restrict risky S&L activities

- changing the laws governing federal deposit insurance to protect the government's insurance funds from the escalating claims of insolvent thrift institutions

- restricting some thrift powers while expanding others

- authorizing bank holding companies to buy healthy savings and loan associations

- imposing new stringent capital requirements on S&Ls and strengthening regulators' powers to oversee thrift activities

FIRREA was a legislative attempt to end the S&L crisis that confronted the United States in the late 1980s.

- The act established two new government deposit insurance funds under the administration of the FDIC: a Bank Insurance Fund (BIF), which had been administered by the FDIC; and a Savings Association Insurance Fund (SAIF), which replaced the fund formerly administered by the Federal Savings and Loan Insurance Corporation (FSLIC).

   The FSLIC and the Federal Home Loan Bank Board, the federal regulator of S&Ls, were disbanded. In place of these agencies, FIRREA created a new thrift regulatory agency, the Office of Thrift Supervision (OTS). Both the FDIC and the OTS were given stronger powers to enforce bank and thrift regulations.

   The FDIC was required to eliminate any differences that existed in deposit insurance coverage at banks and S&Ls. Today, both insurance funds offer the same protection to depositors. However, BIF and SAIF have different ratios of insurance fund reserves to insured deposits and assess different premiums on their member institutions.

- Under FIRREA, both BIF and SAIF must maintain reserve funds equal to 1.25 percent of the total deposits they insure. Because the SAIF ratio was well below the 1.25 percent standard in 1989, savings and loan associations are likely to pay substantially higher deposit insurance premiums than commercial banks in the early 1990s.

- In 1990, commercial banks paid 12 cents to the FDIC for every $100 in deposits they held in their domestic offices, while S&Ls paid 20.8 cents.

- The premium schedule stipulated that between August 1994 and January 1999 the insurance premium differential between banks and S&Ls would narrow. Commercial banks would pay 15 cents to the FDIC for every $100 of deposits; S&Ls 18 cents. After January 1999, the differential would end entirely, with deposit insurance premiums set at 15 cents per $100 of deposits.

- FIRREA gave the FDIC authority, beginning in January 1995, to raise insurance premiums above the statutory levels noted earlier if either the BIF or SAIF ratio of reserve funds to insured deposits threatened to fall below the 1.25 percent standard. However, a spate of bank closings and FDIC payouts in 1989 and 1990 so depleted BIF revenues that the FDIC was forced to increase banks' premiums to 23 cents per $100 of deposits in 1991. Congress also authorized the FDIC to borrow $30 billion from the U.S. Treasury to replenish its depleted reserve funds.

  The 1991 FDIC borrowing authorization law requires the FDIC to establish premiums sufficient not only to repay any borrowed funds within 15 years, but to meet FIRREA's 1.25 percent ratio of reserves-to-insured deposits standard.

❑ Congress was concerned that S&Ls could evade the high deposit insurance premiums placed on them by FIRREA by converting from thrifts to banks. Thus, FIRREA imposed a five-year moratorium (ending in August 1994) on thrift conversions.

- After the moratorium expires, S&Ls will be able to convert to banks and transfer from SAIF to BIF. However, thrifts that convert and transfer will have to pay an exit fee to SAIF and an entrance fee to BIF.

- FIRREA requires that the FDIC set the BIF entrance fee sufficiently high to prevent an erosion in BIF reserves below the 1.25 percent of insured deposits standard. This provision of the law, coupled with SAIF exit fees and the narrowing of the insurance premium differential that will take effect in August 1994, makes thrift conversions and transfers from SAIF to BIF unlikely.

FIRREA changed the mix of activities and investments that are permissible for thrifts.

❑ S&Ls were required to hold 70 percent of their assets in qualified thrift investments—essentially housing-related loans and securities. Before FIRREA, S&Ls needed to hold only 60 percent of their assets in qualified thrift investments. FIRREA also narrowed the list of loans and securities that are considered to be qualified. (In 1991, Congress reduced the 70 percent requirement to 65 percent).

❑ The OTS was empowered to prohibit undercapitalized S&Ls from soliciting brokered deposits and to impose restrictions on the asset growth of S&Ls that do not meet capital standards. (In 1991, Congress ended deposit insurance coverage for brokered deposits offered by undercapitalized banks and thrifts.)

❑ Thrifts were prohibited from investing in junk bonds (bonds that carry less than investment-grade credit ratings) and from investing in real estate. Real estate appraisal rules for loans also were tightened. S&Ls were additionally subjected to legal limits on the amount of loans they could make to any one borrower. However, FIRREA gave thrifts new power to offer checking accounts to business firms, whether related to a loan or not. Prior to FIRREA, thrifts could establish checking accounts only for firms that borrowed funds from them.

FIRREA expanded the powers of bank holding companies by amending the 1956 Bank Holding Company Act to allow the Federal Reserve to authorize bank holding companies to buy healthy thrifts. Before FIRREA, bank holding companies were prohibited from purchasing thrifts unless the thrifts were insolvent.

To bolster the capacity of S&Ls to suffer losses without becoming insolvent (a situation that creates a potential drain on federal deposit insurance fund reserves), S&Ls were subjected to three new capital requirements:

☐ FIRREA imposed a new minimum capital requirement of 3 percent on S&Ls. Under this requirement, an S&L must maintain capital (owner's equity) equal to no less than 3 percent of its total assets.

  • Thrifts were prohibited from including most types of goodwill in their measure of capital. Goodwill is the difference between the worth of a company's assets and the market value of the company itself. In essence, goodwill reflects the value of a company's name, reputation, and customer base.

☐ S&Ls also are required to hold an amount of tangible capital equal to no less than 1.5 percent of their assets. An S&L cannot count the value of supervisory goodwill as part of its capital. Supervisory goodwill is the estimated value above a troubled S&L's net worth that a potential buyer might be willing to pay for—presumably to obtain the S&L's deposit insurance coverage.

☐ FIRREA further mandated that S&Ls must meet a minimum risk-based capital requirement. Under this requirement, numerical weights (multiples) are applied to S&L assets according to the riskiness of the assets. The sum of these weighted assets determines the risk-adjusted asset base against which a minimum amount of capital must be held.

☐ Most S&L industry analysts contend that the exclusion of goodwill from capital and FIRREA's stringent capital requirements will cause some solvent thrifts to close if they cannot raise additional capital. Many other thrifts will be able to raise necessary capital only by selling off assets or by sharply curtailing their growth. In either case, analysts project that FIRREA's capital provisions will likely cause the S&L industry to shrink considerably in the early 1990s.

FIRREA eased the rules that regulators must follow when closing a failing S&L by

☐ authorizing the FDIC to assume the role of conservator or receiver for any failing S&L, whether federal or state chartered

  As a conservator, the FDIC can operate a failing S&L until it is sold. As a receiver, the FDIC is required to close the S&L, pay off insured depositors, and liquidate the S&L's remaining assets.

☐ authorizing the FDIC to end deposit insurance coverage for insolvent S&Ls

  Before FIRREA, two years was the minimum legal period required before deposit insurance coverage could be removed from a failing bank or thrift.

FIRREA established a federal agency to manage the assets of insolvent thrifts—the Resolution Trust Corporation (RTC). In 1989, Congress gave the RTC $20 billion to begin operations. Its initial holdings of failed S&L assets exceeded $100 billion. However, by late 1991, the RTC had exhausted all its funds. In November 1991, Congress gave the RTC an additional $25 billion as a stopgap measure to enable the RTC to continue asset liquidation activities into 1992 while attempts to find a long-term solution to the RTC's funding needs continued.

The act, which encompassed nearly 1,000 pages of provisions, covered more than the S&L bailout.

❏ In an effort to combat discrimination in housing lending in key urban areas, Congress authorized the regulatory agencies to make public, beginning in 1991, previously confidential ratings of bank and thrift compliance with the Community Reinvestment Act of 1977. That act requires banks and thrifts to meet the credit needs of the communities from which they accept deposits.

❏ A number of issues emerged in the legislative debate over FIRREA that could not be resolved in the framework of the act. Instead, Congress stipulated that studies on these issues be undertaken.

- Treasury was instructed to study the feasibility of changing the federal deposit insurance programs so that banks' and thrifts' deposit insurance premiums would be assessed on risk rather than on deposit size.

- A feasibility study of market value accounting for banks and thrifts also was ordered. Under current bank accounting rules, banks and thrifts carry the value of investments on their books at purchase price. Changes in the market value of these investments are not reflected on the balance sheet unless they are sold or mature. Advocates of market value accounting contend that by requiring banks and thrifts to reflect the market value of their assets on their balance sheets, depositors, stockholders, and regulators could get a more timely and accurate measure of a bank's financial condition. Opponents contend that market value accounting would provide a distorted measure of the financial condition of banks and thrifts that could prove more confusing than current balance sheets.

- Congress instructed Treasury to study the adequacy of credit unions' capital.

- The Federal Reserve was instructed to examine bank costs and banks' use of service charges and transaction fees with a view toward addressing public perception that bank service charges had become excessive.

The findings of these studies are expected to provide the foundation for more fundamental reform of banking rules and practices in the 1990s.

Key Deposit Regulations: An Overview

The regulations issued by the Federal Reserve are the means by which most federal banking law is implemented in the United States. In effect, the Federal Reserve, through its regulations, acts as an administrative arm of Congress. The following major deposit regulations apply to all depositories:

Regulation D—reserve requirements

Regulation E—protection of consumers using electronic transfer systems

Regulation J—check-processing rules and procedures

Regulation Q—interest on deposits

Regulation D

Regulation D is both a deposit regulation and a monetary policy control regulation. It establishes the reserve requirement rules that all depository institutions must follow if they hold transaction accounts. The regulation contains four major sections:

❖ defining the liabilities of depositories that are subject to reserve requirements (primarily deposits)

❖ delineating the reserve requirement percentages that must be applied to reservable liabilities

❖ specifying the type of assets that depositories can use to meet reserve requirements

❖ explaining how depositories must compute and maintain required reserves

Other significant sections of the regulation establish the procedures and rules for maintaining pass-through accounts and the penalties for reserve deficiencies.

Reserve Requirements

In 1980, all commercial banks (whether members of the Federal Reserve or not), savings banks, savings and loan associations, credit unions, Edge Act corporations (corporations established by banks that are permitted to engage only in international banking), and branches and agencies of foreign banks in the United States were brought under the reserve requirement rules issued by the Federal Reserve.

Today, only transaction accounts are subject to reserve requirements. (From 1980 to 1990, however, corporate time deposits with maturities of less than 18 months and Eurocurrency liabilities were subject to reserve requirements as well.)

Transaction accounts consist of demand deposits, NOW accounts, share draft accounts, and—with the exception of money market deposit accounts, exempted from reserve requirements in 1982—any other accounts or deposits from which payments or transfers may be made.

The reserve requirement in 1992 was 3 percent on the first $42.2 million of these liabilities, and 10 percent on amounts over $42.2 million. In calculating required reserves, banks can subtract from their total transaction accounts the amount of cash items in the process of collection and deposits of other banks on their books. Moreover, the Garn-St Germain Depository Institutions Act of 1982 exempts from reserve requirements the first $3.6 million of reservable deposits for every bank and thrift.

The reserve requirement rules of the Monetary Control Act of 1980 (and amended by the Garn-St Germain Act of 1982) call for the Federal Reserve to increase each year the amount of transaction accounts subject to reserve requirements (and subject to exemption) by 80 percent of the growth in these deposits held in the banking system. The 1992 requirements reflect the cumulative annual increases (and one decrease) since 1980.

Reserves and Computation

Depositories can use only three types of assets to meet reserve requirements— vault cash, balances maintained directly on the books of a Federal Reserve bank, and balances maintained at another institution in a pass-through account.

The Monetary Control Act established a pass-through account option for maintaining reserves for nonmember commercial banks, savings banks, savings and loan associations, and credit unions that were brought under Federal Reserve reserve requirements for the first time. These depositories had long-standing account relationships with correspondent banks or, in the case of thrift institutions, federal lending authorities such as the Federal Home Loan Banks and the NCUA.

The pass-through account option allows these banks and thrift institutions to meet the Federal Reserve's reserve requirements within the context of their existing account relationships. In a pass-through account, required reserves are deposited at Federal Reserve banks indirectly through the commingled reserve deposits of major correspondent banks, Federal Home Loan Banks, or the Credit Union Central Liquidity Facility.

Depositories that have total transaction deposits of $44.8 million or more (1992) must compute their required reserves once every two weeks, based on their daily average deposit balances beginning Thursday of the first week and ending Wednesday of the third week (see exhibit 3.2). However, depositories that have total deposits of less than $3.6 million are exempt from maintaining and reporting reserves. Depositories with total transaction deposits of less than $44.8 million have only to compute and report their required reserves to the Federal Reserve once every quarter for a one-week period during the quarter. The small depositories' exemption and quarterly computation for mid-sized depositories were efforts to reduce the reporting and management burden on smaller banks and thrifts and to relieve the processing burden on Federal Reserve banks.

Exhibit 3.2 *Federal Reserve Reporting Schedule*

Week 1	Week 2	Week 3
T W Th F S Su M	T W Th F S Su M	T W Th F S Su M

Measurement Period

Settlement Period

Regulation E

Regulation E, issued in 1980, implements the Electronic Fund Transfer Act of 1978. That act established the rights, liabilities, and responsibilities of consumers who use EFT systems and the financial institutions that offer those services.

The Electronic Fund Transfer Act is a consumer protection measure. As with other federal consumer protection legislation, the Federal Reserve was responsible for writing the rules for users and providers of EFT services. However, each institution's primary state or federal regulator is responsible for enforcement.

The Electronic Fund Transfer Act grew out of consumer concerns that dominated public debate on EFT services throughout the 1970s. Major issues included whether the privacy of EFT transactions could be ensured, whether electronic payments could be reversed, what information banks should be required to disclose about their EFT services, and who should be liable for errors and for how much.

Electronic Funds Transfers and the Consumer

An electronic funds transfer, particularly when made through a point-of-sale terminal, offers a number of institutions access to an individual's transactions data. Concerns about the growing threat EFTs posed to individual privacy were forcefully stated in the 1970s by two government commissions—the

National Privacy Protection Study Commission and the National Commission on Electronic Funds Transfers. However, law enforcement agencies maintained that their justifiable needs for access to electronic transactions data would be compromised by excessive privacy restrictions.

The National Privacy Protection Study Commission, recognizing that government entities posed the greatest potential threat to individual financial privacy, recommended that they refrain from involvement in EFT systems. Others maintained that only government involvement could ensure that individuals would be protected against privacy abuses by private financial institutions. Both commissions differed on what role the Federal Reserve should have in EFT systems.

Consumer groups generally favored more extensive protection of their rights and privileges under EFT systems, favoring an approach that would have afforded EFTs at least the same protection as check transactions. Congress essentially adopted the consumer approach in the Electronic Fund Transfer Act of 1978. Financial institutions generally wanted EFT transfers considered as cash transactions.

Provisions of Regulation E

Regulation E has four major provisions. The first limits a consumer's liability to $50 for unauthorized use of an EFT service or access device.[2]

Second, consumers must be given a written, easily understood statement of the terms and conditions of the EFT service for which they are contracting, including information on applicable service charges, rights to stop payment, and the circumstances under which the financial institution would disclose to third parties information about consumers' EFT accounts. This statement can be given at the time the consumer signs up for the service or before the consumer uses the service.

Third, the regulation specifies procedures for consumers who wish to rectify possible billing errors in their bank statements. It also establishes the principle that banks must provisionally credit accounts within 10 days of receiving a written notice of possible error while the bank investigates the complaint, unless the error can be resolved.

Fourth, the regulation requires financial institutions to provide customers with a written receipt for each transfer, either directly or through merchants if a point-of-sale terminal is involved. The regulation also requires a quarterly statement of total EFT account activity.

In 1980 and 1981, the Federal Reserve Board made several technical amendments to Regulation E. These amendments were made to reduce the cost to depository institutions of complying with sections of the regulation and to prevent a loss of service to consumers by banks that, burdened with compliance costs, might have disbanded their EFT systems. One 1981 amendment involved automatic payments to cover overdrafts under bank overdraft credit plans.

The Electronic Fund Transfer Act prohibited financial institutions from making EFTs compulsory—for example, requiring that a loan be repaid through an EFT system as a condition of obtaining the loan. However, Regulation E exempted those EFTs authorized by the consumer that occur between accounts in an institution, such as crediting interest to a savings account.

Both bankers and consumers were unclear whether overdraft account transfers were exempted by the regulation or covered by the act. Under a bank overdraft credit plan, an automatic advance is made from the bank to the consumer's account when the consumer's checking account is overdrawn. Typically, the bank debits some minimum payment from the consumer's account during the bank's routine billing cycle.

If overdraft accounts were not exempt, banks would have to provide overdraft account holders with a nonautomatic payment option. Bankers argued that the cost of maintaining two parallel payment systems for one service would be too costly, that many banks would stop overdraft services rather than incur compliance costs, and that few customers in banks with a dual system had opted for the nonautomatic service.

The Federal Reserve Board decided that automatic overdraft accounts benefited the public at a low cost precisely because the service was highly automated. The board agreed with bankers that substantial costs in complying with Regulation E could lead to higher EFT service charges, reduced levels of service, and, in the case of overdraft services, stricter qualification standards for obtaining overdraft credit or higher minimums for overdraft credit lines—all of which would adversely affect the banking public. The board allowed the overdraft account exemption and modified the regulation in other areas where compliance costs exceeded public benefits.

In 1981, the board also issued a compendium of official interpretations of Regulation E. The compendium clarified several areas of compliance that were particularly confusing to banks and offered additional legal protection to providers of EFT services. (Banks that follow the interpretations are protected against liability.)

One interpretation took the position that a home banking service—the telephone—is not an EFT terminal subject to Regulation E. This interpretation meant that banks did not have to provide a receipt of each transaction to customers who use telephone bill-paying services or authorize account transfers over the telephone.

Another interpretation determined that banks that provide full information on EFT services, rules, and charges to all customers—whether or not the customers contract for an EFT service—do not have to repeat these disclosures when customers subsequently opt for an EFT service.

In 1987, the Federal Reserve revised Regulation E to relieve retail merchants from providing periodic statements to bank customers who use ATMs and POS terminals on the merchants' premises. EFT proponents argued that the change would encourage retailers to participate in EFT systems by reducing some administrative and cost burdens of compliance and that consumers would benefit by having all transaction account information provided in one monthly statement from their bank.

Regulation J

The regulation is essentially a body of rules for banks that use the Federal Reserve to collect checks and other payment instruments, transfer funds electronically through the Federal Reserve's wire transfer network (FedWire), and settle account balances on the books of the Federal Reserve. The regulation has two major subparts. Subpart A governs check collection; subpart B governs wire transfers of funds.

Regulation J was totally restructured to cover all depositories after commercial banks, savings banks, savings and loan associations, and credit unions had obtained access to Federal Reserve bank check collection and wire transfer services under the 1980 Monetary Control Act. The new regulation now defines thrift institutions as banks.

The regulation adheres to the checking and banking provisions of the Uniform Commercial Code—the general body of business and banking law in the United States. Under section 3-506(2) of the Uniform Commercial Code, a nonbank financial institution that receives a check for payment must pay or dishonor the check before the close of business on that day. However, banks have deferred posting rights under the code. By defining savings and loan associations and credit unions as banks, the Federal Reserve has given thrift institutions the same deferred posting rights as commercial banks.

Some bankers were concerned that defining savings and loan associations and credit unions as banks could confuse the public about the differences between commercial banks and thrifts. The Federal Reserve Board acknowledged this concern by limiting the definition of banks to Regulation J.

Subpart A—Check Collection

Subpart A provides a glossary of banking terms. It defines such terms as check, bank draft, paying bank, cash items, noncash items, and nonmember clearing bank.

It authorizes Reserve banks to issue circulars explaining the procedures and practices banks must follow if they use the Federal Reserve's check collection service. The rules set forth in these circulars are binding and cover such details as Reserve bank sorting requirements and the closing times at Reserve offices for the receipt of different classes or types of collection items. Each Reserve bank issues a key circular for each of its offices, specifying the schedule when cash items received by the Reserve bank can be counted as part of the sending bank's reserves. Reserve banks can give either immediate or deferred credit in accordance with the Federal Reserve's time schedule.

Subpart A defines the limited liability of Reserve banks in check collection. A Reserve bank is essentially an agent acting on behalf of a sending bank and assumes no liability to the paying bank. Finally, subpart A dictates that Reserve banks will receive cash items and other checks only at par.

Subpart B—Wire Transfers

Subpart B of Regulation J parallels the format of subpart A, complete with an appropriate glossary of wire transfer terms. However, because most wire transfers result in near-instantaneous transfer of debit and credit balances on the books of Reserve banks, the rules and procedures that bankers must follow are not quite the same as for check collection. In effect, wire transfers processed by the Federal Reserve are more like cash transactions than check transactions.

It allows a Reserve bank to refuse a transfer request of a sending or paying bank if it believes that the bank has insufficient funds in its account to cover the transfer. A sending bank must have enough funds to cover the amount of all transfer items debited against its account. Unlike check collection, in which Reserve banks act as transfer agents with little or no liability, wire transfers processed by the Federal Reserve expose Reserve banks to liability. A wire transfer of funds is considered paid when the Reserve bank sends the transfer or advises the sender that the transfer has been made. A Reserve bank that misroutes, loses, or approves a transfer from the account of a bank with insufficient funds has to make good on the value of the transfer to the receiving bank[3].

Subpart B specifies the rules applicable to funds transfers handled by Reserve banks, but, until 1990, these rules were not necessarily compatible with rules governing funds transfers between commercial banks and private EFT systems. In fact, no uniform body of commercial law applied to private wholesale funds transfers.

In the mid-1980s, the National Conference of Commissioners on Uniform State Laws—the organization that oversees states' commercial laws—began drafting a new section of the Uniform Commercial Code to cover the rights and responsibilities of private parties involved in wholesale funds transfers. The new section, article 4A, was completed in 1989 with the assistance of bankers, lawyers, and the Federal Reserve and adopted into law by 12 states, beginning in 1991. (All other states are expected to adopt article 4A by the mid-1990s.) Subpart B provisions that were inconsistent with article 4A were revised in 1990.

Regulation Q

Regulation Q governs the payment of interest on deposits. Until 1986, it established the maximum interest rates that banks could pay on time and savings deposits. The regulation

- ❖ defines demand, time, and savings deposits
- ❖ prohibits payment of interest on demand deposits
- ❖ specifies how interest should be computed and the grace periods allowed in computing interest
- ❖ specifies procedures that banks must follow in paying out time deposits before maturity and in assessing penalties for those withdrawals of deposits
- ❖ establishes rules for advertising interest on deposits

Regulation Q and Disintermediation

Between 1981 and 1986, the maximum interest rates that banks could pay on time and savings deposits were gradually raised, then eliminated. Before 1986, interest-rate ceilings were an integral part of Regulation Q. In the 1960s and 1970s, these ceilings became an increasing source of problems for banks and thrifts as market interest rates began to rise above the deposit rate limits. Depositors withdrew their savings and redeposited the funds into money market accounts that paid higher than ceiling rates, or they bought U.S. Treasury bills, whose interest rates were not subject to Regulation Q.

Traditionally, consumers have put their savings into banks and thrifts that, in turn, have lent the funds back to other consumers. For this reason, these institutions are referred to as financial intermediaries. When depositors withdraw their funds to obtain a higher rate elsewhere, the process is called disintermediation.

Disintermediation has a devastating effect on the housing industry. When thrift institutions lose deposits, they cannot make mortgage loans. When potential home buyers cannot obtain mortgages, they cannot buy existing homes or contract for new units to be built.

The economy underwent several periods of substantial disintermediation in the 1960s and 1970s. This resulted in sharp declines in the number of new houses built and increases in unemployment in the construction trades. The impact of disintermediation on banks and thrifts, on the housing industry, and on the public's savings and deposit behavior was the principal factor that motivated Congress to gradually eliminate Regulation Q ceilings in the 1980 Monetary Control Act.

Interest-Rate Ceilings: Origins

Interest-rate ceilings originated in the 1930s. In the Banking Act of 1933, Congress prohibited banks from paying interest on demand deposits and

---

established maximum rates that banks could pay on time and savings deposits.

Economists are uncertain of the exact reasoning behind the interest-rate regulations. There was little congressional discussion of these provisions when the Banking Act was approved. However, three reasons are likely.

First, Congress believed that the payment of interest on demand deposits contributed to the liquidity problems banks experienced during the early years of the Depression, particularly because the nation's large banks used the payment of interest on demand deposits to attract the deposits of smaller banks. Many of the large New York City banks that used correspondent deposit money to make loans to stockbrokers were unable to meet the demands of their respondent banks for the deposited funds when the stock market collapsed and the broker loans could not be repaid.

Second, there was a prevailing view in the early 1930s that interest-rate ceilings and the prohibition of interest on demand deposits would prevent excessive rate competition among banks. The Regulation Q ceilings, it was thought, would prevent the unsound banking practices of the 1920s that stemmed from the intense rate competition for deposits. Today's economic historians now dispute this contention.

Third, it was felt that interest-rate restrictions would reduce bank expenses. The 1933 Banking Act required banks to pay a subscription fee to the newly established FDIC. Payments to the FDIC were expected to be offset by savings from the lowered interest rates.

Whatever the exact reasoning of Congress was, the interest-rate regulations of the 1930s had little impact on banking or the economy until the 1960s because market interest rates stayed well below the ceilings. However, as interest rates began to rise in the 1960s and banks and thrift institutions began to offer inducements to attract deposits, competition for funds began to take its toll.

Interest-Rate Ceilings: Impact

In 1966, to prevent disintermediation, the FDIC and the FHLBB—the agency that regulated thrift institutions at that time—imposed ceilings on interest rates offered by thrift institutions. Together with the Federal Reserve Board, the FDIC and the FHLBB established a differential between the maximum interest rates thrift institutions and commercial banks could pay on time and savings deposits. Thrift institutions were given a ceiling one percentage point higher than banks.

The regulation was considered a temporary measure to protect thrift institutions from competition that would erode their deposits and reduce the supply of mortgage funds. In effect, the regulation assisted the housing industry by improving the availability of mortgages.

The rationale seemed valid. The income of thrift institutions is linked to the interest-rate returns they receive on long-term fixed mortgages, some of which were made 10 to 25 years earlier. Their costs, on the other hand, are tied to the interest rates they currently have to pay to attract and maintain deposits. Without deposit-rate ceilings, thrift institutions would suffer declining profits during periods of rising interest rates.

The ceilings, however, did not prevent disintermediation. In the late 1960s and 1970s, all depository institutions lost funds to other segments of the money and capital markets where interest rates were not regulated. The Federal Reserve eliminated the Regulation Q ceiling for large, short-term negotiable certificates of deposit (CDs) in 1970, but bank and thrift institution deposits nonetheless flowed to higher-yielding Treasury bills.

In the mid-1970s, the economy once again experienced disintermediation. However, this episode was not as severe because, in 1973, the Regulation Q ceiling was eliminated for large, long-term negotiable CDs offered by thrift institutions. At the same time, ceilings on other time deposits were raised to near-market rates. In addition, financial innovation and the growing competitiveness of thrift institutions led to a progressive narrowing of the interest-rate differential from one point in 1966 to one-quarter of a point by 1973.

Throughout the 1960s and 1970s, the banking community and Congress debated whether to eliminate Regulation Q ceilings and the interest-rate prohibition on demand deposits. Despite recommendations by several presidential and congressional commissions to end the regulations, they were continued. However, sentiment began to change as interest rates continued to rise in the late 1970s, causing still another episode of disintermediation.

By 1980, it had become apparent that Regulation Q had created a market anomaly in an environment of rapidly rising interest rates. Thrift institution deposits were flowing into other forms of near money not subject to the ceilings, particularly Treasury bills, leading to a shrinkage of mortgage credit. Because Regulation Q ceilings had been eliminated for large CDs, the regulation also had the inequitable effect of preventing consumers with limited funds from obtaining a market rate comparable to the rate offered to large depositors and corporations.

Perhaps the most telling impact of Regulation Q was the fact that banks and thrift institutions, through their own ingenuity and innovation, had begun to develop new services and new near money instruments, such as NOW accounts, that effectively circumvented the regulation. It was against this background that Congress, in the Monetary Control Act of 1980, finally changed the direction of public policy on interest-rate regulation, voting to phase out Regulation Q by 1986.

Trends and Issues in Deposit Regulations

Deposit Insurance Reform

The FDIC insures depositors at banks and thrifts up to $100,000 per person. The current insurance ceiling was instituted in 1980 by the Monetary Control Act, which raised coverage from a $40,000 limit that had been established in 1974. The FDIC was created in 1933 following the failures of more than 9,100 banks from 1930 to 1933. Its major functions were to protect depositors—especially small depositors—against loss, to bolster public confidence in banks, and to prevent bank runs.

The FDIC was immediately successful; bank runs stopped, and bank failures rapidly declined and remained low for most of the next 50 years. One measure of the FDIC's success from the 1930s through the 1970s was that banks frequently received FDIC-insurance premium rebates as a result of the low level of payouts from the insurance fund to depositors at failed banks.

In the 1980s, the number of bank failures soared as banks saw the quality of their assets deteriorate and their capital levels plummet from bad loans. The FDIC, for the first time in its history, suffered major losses as it paid out funds to insured depositors at closed banks and provided financial assistance to banks purchasing the assets and liabilities of failing banks.

About 850 banks failed from 1986 to 1990. But these failures did not impair public confidence in banking or trigger widespread deposit withdrawals, in part because of federal deposit insurance protection. However, the bank failures of the late 1980s did impair the solvency of the federal deposit insurance fund. By 1990, the FDIC had paid out $23 billion from its reserves, reducing its pool of reserve funds to $8.5 billion. In 1991, the Congressional Budget Office reported to Congress a strong likelihood that the FDIC would not have sufficient funds to cover expected bank failures over the following 18 months and by 1992 the reserves could be totally depleted.

The need to fund the FDIC and hold down insurance payouts became a major priority for government and the banking industry. Among the proposals made by banker groups, the U.S. Treasury, and the FDIC were the following:

❖ Raise deposit insurance premiums.

The 1989 Financial Institutions Reform, Recovery and Enforcement Act (FIRREA) requires the FDIC to hold reserve funds equal to 1.25 percent of the total deposits it insures. FIRREA also established a schedule for banks' premiums to ensure that the FDIC's reserve ratio would be maintained. The act set bank premiums for 1990 at 12 cents for every $100 of insured deposits. In 1991, premiums were increased to 23 cents per $100 of insured deposits to replenish funds and the FDIC indicated that premiums might have to be increased to 30 cents in 1992 to provide needed reserves. In November 1991, Congress authorized the FDIC to borrow $30 billion from the Treasury to bolster the insurance fund's reserves. However, further increases in deposit insurance premiums are likely. The authorizing legislation requires the FDIC to repay its borrowings, with interest, over the next 15 years from premiums assessed on banks.

Some industry analysts contend that continuing increases in deposit insurance premiums could impose a cost burden large enough to impair many banks' profitability, which could weaken the banking system and thus increase the long-term vulnerability of the deposit insurance fund. It is estimated that for every one cent increase in premiums over 23 cents, bank's costs will increase by about $250 million.

❖ Change the way deposit insurance premiums are assessed from a fixed percentage of total domestic deposits to a variable percentage based on a bank's likelihood of failure.

The FDIC charges banks annual insurance premiums based on each bank's total domestic deposits. These premiums, plus income from investments, provide a pool of funds from which depositors are paid when banks fail. The premiums, however, are not related to the fiscal health of the paying bank. Many bankers believe that assessing deposit insurance premiums on the basis of a bank's or thrift's size is inconsistent with the principle that insurance premiums should be related to risk. Bankers maintain that the overall CAMEL rating each bank or thrift receives from its primary examiner could serve as the basis for more equitable risk-based premium assessments from the FDIC.

In 1986, the FDIC asked Congress to enact legislation to establish a risk-based deposit insurance system. In November 1991, Congress authorized the FDIC to change the way it assesses banks for deposit insurance from fixed premiums to fees linked to risk. The new premium system will take effect in January 1994. Although the FDIC estimates that only about 1,800 banks (15 percent of all banks) would have to pay additional premiums based on risk, many industry analysts remain unconvinced that this approach will provide an incentive for banks to avoid excessive risk taking.

❖ Limit deposit insurance coverage.

Deposits at banks and thrifts are insured up to $100,000 per person at each bank or thrift where a person has an account. Under FDIC rules, all accounts associated with the same Social Security number (or taxpayer identification number) at a given bank are added together in determining the $100,000 limit for deposit insurance coverage.[4] These rules provide total coverage for most depositors at banks and thrifts, although it is estimated that about one million households have some deposits that are uninsured. These depositors, half of whom are retirees, hold more than $100,000 in accounts at individual banks.

Insurance coverage can be increased at a single bank for account holders who establish an IRA or Keogh account. Retirement accounts are insured separately. Accounts established by depositors in the name and Social Security number of their spouse and/or children also are covered separately, as are joint accounts among family members or business partners. In a joint account, each combination of account holders is insured for $100,000. However, any one individual's total insurance coverage from all his or her joint accounts is limited to $100,000.

Other accounts that provide for extra deposit insurance coverage are testamentary accounts and trustee accounts. A testamentary account is an account that becomes the possession of another person—such as a spouse, children, or grandchildren—upon the owner's death. During the account owner's lifetime, the testamentary account is insured up to $100,000, and this coverage does not count toward the insurance coverage limit on the owner's own accounts. A trustee account is an account maintained by a trustee on behalf of a beneficiary. These accounts are also insured separately from any coverage accorded the trustee's own accounts. Testamentary and trustee account insurance coverage does not apply to households that establish these accounts for themselves. Such accounts are considered joint accounts and fall under the joint coverage limitations previously noted.

Among proposals made by the Treasury in 1991 to limit deposit insurance coverage was one to hold depositors to $100,000 of insurance across all depository institutions and to eliminate coverage for brokered deposits, but to leave intact the current $100,000 per person insurance limit.

The FDIC has argued that the 1980 increase in deposit insurance coverage from $40,000 to $100,000 encouraged some bankers to take excessive risks in their lending and investing, because of the near-total insurance coverage the 1980 increase provided to most corporate depositors. The FDIC has maintained that a reduction in account coverage to the pre-1980 level might induce bankers to take less risk because their actions would be open to the scrutiny of corporate depositors, most of whom would no longer be insured. Such an approach had little support in Congress or among bankers during the debate over deposit insurance reform in 1991. However, in the November 1991 legislation that bolstered the insurance fund's reserves,

Congress limited the scope of some FDIC insurance coverage. The 1991 law limits insurance coverage on brokered deposits and accounts established for employee pension plans to those offered by banks with the highest capital rating.

During 1991's deposit insurance reform deliberations in Congress, small banks contended that the FDIC's application of deposit insurance coverage rules was unequal. This inequity was embodied in the FDIC's "too big to fail" policy for large-bank depositors. Under this policy, the FDIC had pledged to back all deposits at large banks, regardless of the amounts in any given account. The policy was designed to protect financial markets and the economy from the destabilization that could be caused by the massive losses that uninsured depositors would suffer if a large bank failed.

Many bankers maintained that the too big to fail policy encouraged risk-averse depositors to maintain accounts only at large banks and did not reduce these banks' risk taking. The cost to the FDIC of paying off all depositors at large banks was invariably borne by both small and large banks through higher insurance premiums.

In 1991, Congress opted to end the too big to fail policy. Beginning in 1995, the FDIC can invoke the policy only if a large bank failure would directly threaten the stability of the financial system and only if the Federal Reserve, the Treasury, and the President approve. If such an exception is made, and the FDIC pays off both insured and uninsured depositors at the failed bank, the costs of the payout must be recovered by a special premium assessed on all banks.

❖ Supplement bank insurance premiums with funds provided to the FDIC by U.S. Treasury loans.

In November 1991, Congress authorized the FDIC to borrow $70 billion to replenish the Bank Insurance Fund (BIF) and to meet ongoing operating expenses. The authorization was made as a stopgap measure to bolster an insurance fund with reserves of only $2 billion. Congress, unable to agree on broader banking industry reform measures, passed a narrow deposit insurance reform bill while continuing into 1992 its debate on proposals to restructure banking.

The authorization bill permits the BIF to borrow $30 billion from the U.S. Treasury to cover payouts to depositors at failed banks—the FDIC's estimated payouts for 1992 and 1993—and an additional $40 billion for use as working capital. FDIC borrowings to replenish insurance fund reserves must be repaid with funds obtained from premium assessments on banks; working capital loans can be repaid from funds the FDIC receives from the sale of assets of failed banks.

As 1992 began, bankers, government officials, and Congress were divided in their views of whether the public, as well as banks, would be best served by 1991's solution to the FDIC's funding needs. At issue was whether structural changes in banking should be made that could help the insurance fund by increasing banks' profitability. Possible changes include authorizing interstate branching and allowing banks to affiliate with insurance companies and securities firms or to offer insurance and investment products.

Updating Bank Service Regulations and Federal Regulatory Structure

One of the most important questions today is, Have banks lost their competitiveness? If so, is it because regulations have unfairly prevented banks from competing with other financial institutions? If bank regulations are liberalized to allow for fairer competition, is the bank regulatory structure strong enough to support banking in the 1990s?

The entry of insurance companies, brokerage firms, finance companies, and retail chains into banking in the 1980s removed the traditional wall of separation that had long existed in the United States between banking and commerce and opened banks to a new source of competition.

However, banks were unable to compete effectively for the customers and markets of these new competitors and lost a substantial share of their own business to these firms. This happened because banking rules prohibit banks from offering a full range of brokerage, insurance, and investment services and banks lack the nationwide offices and access to customers enjoyed by most nonbank competitor firms.

Many bankers contend that the underlying issue behind banks' competitive problems is the lack of regulatory equity between banks and their nonbank competitors. They argue that increasing banks' financial services would not establish competitive equality for banks unless the finance companies, brokerage firms, and retail chains that provide banking services are regulated like banks.

In 1992, Congress considered a number of proposals to revise bank service regulations and streamline the federal regulatory structure, in part to address the problem of banks' competitiveness. Under most of these proposals, banks would be authorized to establish branches in any state. Banks would also be allowed, through their holding companies, to offer brokerage, insurance, securities underwriting, and mutual fund investment services. And to provide banks with new sources of capital for expanding into these new service lines, nonbank financial institutions and commercial companies would be allowed to own banks.

To establish regulatory equity between banks and their nonbank competitors, several proposals have called for the authorization of new corporate organizations—financial services holding companies—that could be owned by banks or industrial firms. These new holding companies would be allowed to operate separate banking, brokerage, mutual fund, underwriting, and insurance subsidiaries, each of which would be regulated by the banking, securities, or insurance agency with primary regulatory responsibility for the subsidiary's activity. Treasury has further proposed that federal regulation be consolidated to accommodate this new functional approach and to strengthen banking by ending the fragmentation of federal oversight.

Banker and congressional sentiment was divided on whether concentrating regulatory power in one or two agencies would benefit banks or the public. The appropriate division of responsibilities among the federal regulatory agencies charged with examining banks and supervising their holding companies also was a contentious issue.

Behind the debate over bank service regulations and banks' competitiveness is a broader issue. If the bank regulatory structure and the laws limiting banking activities are no longer relevant to today's deposit and payments practices, what will be the shape of banking in the 1990s in the absence of reform and revision?

Summary

The regulation and supervision of banks in the United States are shared by the Federal Reserve, FDIC, Comptroller of the Currency, and state banking departments. These regulatory agencies have common public policy goals—to maintain a sound banking system, promote competition in banking, and protect the owners and managers of banks as well as the consumers who use bank services. In furtherance of these goals the agencies conduct continuous on-site examinations to ensure that regulatory rules and directives are being followed.

The rules that most significantly affect banks' deposit operations include reserve requirements (Regulation D), the regulation limiting consumer liability on EFT services or credit cards to $50 (Regulation E), check collection (Regulation J), and interest rates (Regulation Q).

Interest-rate ceilings were the cause of significant disintermediation for banks and thrifts in the 1960s and 1970s. With the end of interest-rate ceilings in 1986, the focus of deposit regulation has shifted toward reforming the deposit insurance system, updating bank service regulations, and streamlining the federal regulatory structure.

Questions

1. What four major goals has the government sought to achieve in supervising and regulating banks? *pg. 64.*

2. What are the regulatory powers of the Federal Reserve? How do they compare with those of the FDIC?

3. Why did so many S&Ls become insolvent in the 1980s? What measures did the government take to address the S&L crisis? *FIRREA*

4. What three factors motivated Congress to enact interest-rate regulations in the 1933 Banking act?

[handwritten margin notes: • high interest rate - expense · loans were fixed income - rising cost of funds]

Endnotes

1. Scrip is a temporary document that entitles the holder to receive money or another item of value at a future date.

2. If a consumer fails to notify the financial institution within two business days after learning of the loss or theft of an EFT access device, the consumer's liability could range up to $500.

3. Reserve banks rarely have to make good on the insufficient funds guarantee. Banks that incur overdrafts cover their positions with borrowed funds.

4. Since insurance limits are based on a depositor's funds in any single bank or thrift, coverage changes if two institutions in which a depositor has accounts merge. In such an instance, deposits remain separately insured for six months from the date of the merger, then become subject to the FDIC's aggregation rule.

PAPER PAYMENTS

Objectives

After successfully completing this chapter, you will be able to

- ❖ discuss the weaknesses of the U.S. currency system before the Federal Reserve was established

- ❖ explain how new and fit currency is placed into circulation and unfit currency is removed

- ❖ identify MICR instructions and other informational data contained on a check

- ❖ identify the three basic ways that transit checks are collected in the U.S. banking system

- ❖ discuss the role the Federal Reserve plays in the check collection process

- ❖ differentiate between consumer float, bank float, and Federal Reserve float

- ❖ identify promising approaches for coping with check costs and volume in the 1990s, such as image processing and check truncation

Introduction

For much of the nation's history, the U.S. paper payments system suffered from two serious weaknesses:

- ❖ the lack of an elastic currency that could expand and contract with changing consumer and business demand
- ❖ the lack of a national clearing and settlement mechanism

Congress corrected both of these defects in 1913 when it established the Federal Reserve System. Today, all the nation's circulating paper currency consists of notes issued by the 12 Federal Reserve banks in direct response to banks seeking to meet consumer and business demand for currency. In addition, approximately 35 percent of the nation's checks move through the Federal Reserve's check collection system. This chapter examines how the paper payments system evolved, how the system changed in the 1980s under Federal Reserve pricing of check collection services, and how it works.

Currency: The Historical Experience

The United States emerged from the Revolutionary War politically independent but virtually bankrupt. To finance the Revolution, the Continental Congress issued paper currency far in excess of the colonies' capacity to produce goods and services. The result was massive inflation. By the end of the war, Continental currency had become almost worthless. By 1790, the paper notes were redeemed by the new U.S. government at the rate of one U.S. cent to one Continental dollar.

The bitter experience of colonial merchants, soldiers, tradesmen, and farmers with government-issued paper currency had a profound impact on the course of U.S. monetary history. Delegates to the Constitutional Convention voted to prohibit states from issuing paper money, granting only to Congress the exclusive constitutional power "to coin money and regulate (its) value" (U.S. Const. Art. I, §8). Congress, sensitive to the nation's disastrous experience with government-issued paper money, did not use its power to issue currency until the financial emergency generated by the Civil War, more than 70 years later. Not much U.S. currency circulated in the fledgling U.S. economy of the late 1700s. The money that did circulate in the United States—mainly Spanish and British metal coins—was hoarded or used to buy imported goods.

The small quantity of paper money that circulated in those early years consisted of notes issued by the First (1791) and Second (1816) Banks of the United States—precursors of the Federal Reserve. After the Second Bank of the United States closed in 1836, the dominant form of currency became notes issued by state-chartered commercial banks. These notes were redeemed on demand for gold or silver. It was at that point that the U.S. economy began to deal significantly with paper currency.

As state-chartered banking proliferated, so did the currency issued by those banks. Before the federal government taxed away the power to issue notes from state-chartered banks, as many as 8,000 different issues of state bank notes were in circulation. The nation did not have a uniform national currency, and the state-chartered bank note system was confusing and inefficient. Banks rarely accepted at face value notes issued by unfamiliar banks. Volumes the size of modern telephone books were circulated to help bankers recognize bogus issues and evaluate the creditworthiness of issuing banks.

National Currency

A uniform currency grew out of an ingenious plan developed by the government during the Civil War to raise money to finance the Union army. Faced with a depleted Treasury and reluctant to raise taxes on northern industries, President Lincoln reluctantly agreed to a plan by the secretary of the treasury, Salmon Chase.

The plan called for the federal government to offer a new type of banking license—a federal or national charter. Under this charter, a bank would have the power to issue a new form of currency called national bank notes. However, for each note issued, a larger dollar value of government securities would be held as collateral, as a backing requirement. The government securities would be purchased directly from the Treasury in exchange for gold and silver. Thus, the government would receive money assets—gold and silver—in return for its liabilities—government securities.

To promote the use of national bank notes and eliminate competition from state bank-issued notes, Secretary Chase also proposed a tax on state bank notes that would gradually be increased until state banks stopped issuing currency. The plan was embodied in the National Banking Act of 1863. From the mid-1860s until 1913, the nation's paper currency consisted mainly of national bank notes—currency given by the government to nationally chartered commercial banks that issued the paper as their own.

Because national bank notes had to be fully collateralized by government securities, the nation's supply of paper currency was dependent on the government's debt. The supply of currency expanded and contracted in response to changes in the value of government securities in the nation's bond markets, not in response to the needs of the economy.

When the government began repaying its Civil War debt by redeeming and retiring securities, the supply of collateral available for note issuance shrank and, with it, the money supply. Because the currency was inelastic—

people could not cash checks or obtain currency from bank tellers—there were episodes of irrational public hoarding and runs on banks. These incidents, called money panics, periodically plagued the nation until 1913, when the Federal Reserve was established.

Although state-chartered banks no longer issued currency in the post-National Banking Act era, the banks survived because demand deposits, not bank notes, were rapidly becoming the most widely used form of money and the major source of all banks' funds.

National Payments Mechanism

Before the Federal Reserve was established, the United States lacked an efficient national payments mechanism. Checkbook money could not be quickly or easily transferred from one part of the country to another because there was no nationwide check-clearing and collection system.

Banks typically had correspondent accounts and clearing arrangements with bigger banks in their localities, but few direct cross-country relationships existed. Checks drawn on banks in one part of the country but deposited for collection in another carried exchange charges. These charges could be avoided, but the checks might take three to four weeks to clear as they traversed a circuitous route from correspondent account to correspondent account.

Circuitous routing and nonpar checking made national use of checkbook money inefficient and costly. However, in the absence of a central bank, and with the number of banks growing to more than 10,000 by 1913, little could be done to make the process more efficient.

The 1913 Federal Reserve Act called on the Federal Reserve to provide the nation with an elastic currency and an efficient national payments system, tasks that have given the Federal Reserve a major role in public and banking payment practices.

The Federal Reserve's Role in Currency Distribution

The Federal Reserve is the source of the nation's coin and currency, providing cash to depository institutions in direct response to the public's changing demands. Banks experience shifts in depositors' demands as more personal and payroll checks are cashed than deposited or vice versa. Federal Reserve banks respond by sending additional cash to be charged against the banks' accounts or receiving shipments of excess cash for credit to banks' accounts.

The supply of currency is not determined by monetary policy—the public is free to decide in what form and in what proportions it wishes to hold its money. In 1992, the American people held about $270 billion in cash but used only a small part of that cash for transaction purposes. Cash holdings have expanded at a rate of almost 10 percent per year for the past two decades. The soaring growth rate of currency held by the public has confounded many economists and bankers because it seems inconsistent with the increasing use of credit cards, checks, and electronic funds transfers.

Financial analysts have two theories to explain this phenomenon. One holds that inflation and rising taxes in the 1970s and early 1980s gave life to a burgeoning underground economy in the United States. In this underground economy, cash is used as a payment device and as a savings (hoarding) instrument to avoid income and sales taxes and to mask illicit drug and other criminal activities. The other theory, which is more widely accepted, is that much of the nation's currency has been shipped overseas and is being used by foreigners who would rather deal in U.S. currency than in their own inflationary or unstable currencies. The changing denominations of currency in circulation support either theory. In 1990, about 50 percent of all outstanding cash consisted of $100 bills, a denomination consumers and businesses do not typically use in day-to-day transactions.

Before the 1980 Monetary Control Act, Reserve banks provided coin and currency solely to the 5,700 commercial banks that were members of the Federal Reserve System. Those banks, in turn, redistributed cash to nonmember banks and thrift institutions through correspondent accounts. In 1982, Federal Reserve cash services were available to all banks and thrift institutions for a fee.

Implicit in the Federal Reserve's mandate to provide an elastic currency is the need to ensure the quality of circulating currency. To do this, Reserve banks sort and count the millions of Federal Reserve notes they receive each day from depositing banks. They withdraw and destroy worn or mutilated notes and replace those notes with newly issued currency obtained from the Treasury's Bureau of Engraving and Printing.

The cost of maintaining the quality of the nation's circulating currency is high. In the 1990s, the Federal Reserve had to order about 8 billion new notes each year from the Bureau of Engraving and Printing at an annual cost of about $250 million for printing, shipping, and handling. Since this is the government's responsibility, these costs are not passed on to banks in the Federal Reserve's charges. Depositories are charged only for the Federal Reserve's costs of transporting coin and currency in response to orders for cash. Depositories do not pay for the cash itself, but exchange their deposit balances with a Federal Reserve bank for the cash received.

to improve detection of counterfeit, $50 -$100's only under a certain light.

In most Reserve districts, Reserve banks no longer provide currency shipping services (and thus impose no cash-related charges) because depositories in these districts are amply serviced by lower-cost private armored carriers. In districts where the Federal Reserve provides transportation—San Francisco and Philadelphia—the frequency of cash shipments depends on the size and location of the receiving institution.

Large banks in cities with Federal Reserve banks or branches typically receive currency and coin daily, while small banks in suburban and rural areas may receive a shipment only once every other week. Where small banks are located in remote areas not routinely serviced by armored carriers, currency is shipped by registered mail. These banks are charged for postage and insurance.

Bank Response to Cash Pricing

The Federal Reserve's fees for armored-truck deliveries of currency and coin had an impact on banks' management of depositors' currency receipts and withdrawals in the 1980s.

To hold down transportation costs associated with Federal Reserve deliveries, a number of banks and thrift institutions, particularly those with large branch networks, established their own coin and currency exchanges in the mid-1980s. Other banks opted to perform more of the cash-processing activities that the Federal Reserve previously handled.

Before the Monetary Control Act, many commercial banks used the Reserve banks for currency counting and sorting. They would ship unsorted currency deposits to Reserve banks and simultaneously order shipments of packaged, sorted, and counted currency. After shipment pricing began in 1982, many banks increased their in-house counting and sorting to cut shipping costs. New technology has enabled these banks to do the type of fitness sorting generally associated with Federal Reserve processing at a reasonable cost.

Bank Management of Vault Cash

Cash on hand, usually referred to as vault cash, can be counted by all depositories as part of the required reserves needed to meet Federal Reserve reserve requirements. In fact, most of the nation's 30,000 depositories can meet their reserve requirements solely with their working-cash balances. However, meeting reserve requirements is only one function of vault cash. More important, efficient management of vault cash can determine how profitable a bank is.

Too much cash on hand can be costly—idle cash is not an earning asset for a bank. In addition, excess cash can present bank management with day-to-day problems such as insufficient storage space and added security risks. On the other hand, excess cash deposited in a correspondent or Reserve bank account becomes a working asset. It can be used to earn a return on investment or to settle other transactions, such as check collection or wire transfers.

Too little cash also can prove costly. Frequent special deliveries from correspondent banks or the Reserve bank add to transportation costs. And it is poor customer relations to deny depositors the exact currency mix they request.

Banks additionally face a costly reporting burden when they make large cash transactions for depositors. Banks are required to file currency transaction reports (CTRs) with the Internal Revenue Service for any cash transaction of $10,000 or more made for a customer. These reports are designed to alert law enforcement agencies to possible illicit drug money being laundered through banks or unreported income associated with other illegal transactions. However, CTRs are costly to administer and prepare. From 1987 to 1990, banks filed nearly 23 million currency transaction reports with the IRS at an average cost of $14 per report. While some CTRs have provided important leads for criminal investigations, most bankers have questioned whether the benefits of the reports justify banks' annual costs of $80 million for preparing and filing them.

For large banks with automated teller machines (ATMs), the need to ensure an unbroken supply of currency for the machines presents another cash-management problem. ATMs work best when supplied with clean used (fit) currency, not new, uncirculated currency. However, currency shipped from Reserve banks is not separated into new (uncirculated) and fit (used) currency. In the mid-1980s, currency supplied by Reserve banks frequently caused ATM malfunctions. To alleviate this problem, Reserve banks raised their quality standards for recirculating fit currency, and ATM manufacturers improved the machines' ability to handle new and fit currency. Nonetheless, many bankers would like to see the Federal Reserve offer packages of specially selected currency to ATM users. This practice would be consistent, they contend, with the Federal Reserve's policy of promoting greater consumer use of EFT systems. However, the Federal Reserve counters that supplying such currency to banks with ATMs, even at a charge, would be discriminatory to small banks and their customers, who would receive a large proportion of the remaining, poor-quality currency.

In 1991, the Treasury introduced a planned change in the printing of Federal Reserve notes. To improve detection of counterfeit bills—particularly those made by using high-quality photocopy technology—Treasury began printing all new $50 and $100 bills with a plasticlike security thread stripe

---

vertically embedded in each note. The thread is imprinted with the bill's denomination and the letters USA that are visible only under certain light. An added line around the portrait on each bill reads "The United States of America" but in type so small that the line appears as a solid line except when magnified.

New smaller denomination currency will be introduced over several years to hold down annual printing costs. Thus, for a time, new security thread currency and older currency will circulate together.

Checks

A check is the predominant payment device used for retail transactions and bill payments. Bankers, however, regard a deposited check as an instruction form that tells them to

- ❖ transfer money balances from one account on their books to another
- ❖ transfer funds to an account at a different bank
- ❖ pay out cash to a depositor

Banks use virtually every piece of information on a check to effect payments for their customers. Machines process most checks today. Instructions appearing as magnetic ink character recognition (MICR) symbols allow high-speed check-sorting machines to read and sort the tens of thousands of checks received each day.

MICR Instructions

Exhibit 4.1 explains MICR encoding. MICR encoding of all checks was made an industry standard in 1956.

The first bank to receive the check in the processing chain is responsible for MICR encoding the dollar amount of the check. Banks have an incentive to MICR encode checks; without MICR encoding, credit for checks can be significantly delayed. The Federal Reserve will not treat an unencoded check as a cash item, and credit for the check will be deferred to reflect the extra time involved in manually processing it.

However, encoding can be expensive for smaller depositories and banks whose check volume does not justify the capital expenditure for encoding equipment. For this reason, many correspondent banks provide encoding as a service to respondent banks that clear checks through them.

Exhibit 4.1 *MICR Encoding*

The routing number and institutional identifier appears in the upper right corner of all checks and is used if the check has to be processed by hand or the MICR numbers verified.

$\dfrac{1\text{-}12}{210}$

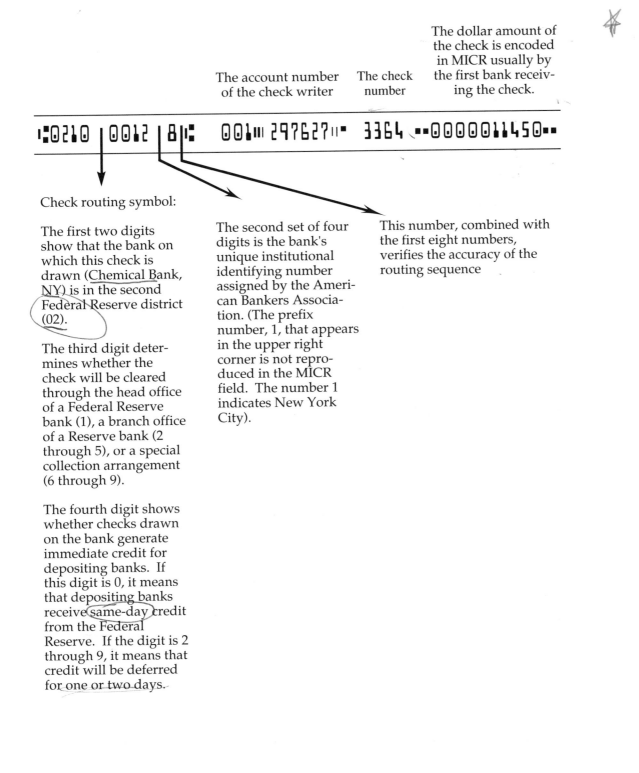

The account number of the check writer

The check number

The dollar amount of the check is encoded in MICR usually by the first bank receiving the check.

Check routing symbol:

The first two digits show that the bank on which this check is drawn (Chemical Bank, NY) is in the second Federal Reserve district (02).

The third digit determines whether the check will be cleared through the head office of a Federal Reserve bank (1), a branch office of a Reserve bank (2 through 5), or a special collection arrangement (6 through 9).

The fourth digit shows whether checks drawn on the bank generate immediate credit for depositing banks. If this digit is 0, it means that depositing banks receive same-day credit from the Federal Reserve. If the digit is 2 through 9, it means that credit will be deferred for one or two days.

The second set of four digits is the bank's unique institutional identifying number assigned by the American Bankers Association. (The prefix number, 1, that appears in the upper right corner is not reproduced in the MICR field. The number 1 indicates New York City).

This number, combined with the first eight numbers, verifies the accuracy of the routing sequence

Check Collection

Checks are cleared in the U.S. banking system in four basic ways:

- ❖ internally
- ❖ through local clearing houses or clearing arrangements
- ❖ through a correspondent bank
- ❖ through the Federal Reserve (see exhibit 4.2)

Exhibit 4.2 *Check Collection in the U.S. Banking System*

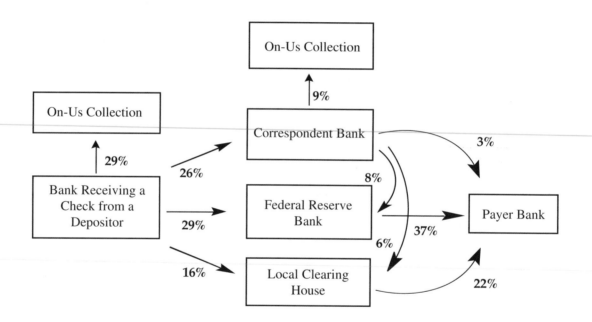

Note: Numbers represent the percentage of checks routed in this manner.

Checks Cleared Internally

Almost one-third of all checks are cleared internally. That is, they are deposited in the bank on which they are drawn, and they are collected through internal adjustments on the bank's books. These checks, called on-us items, are presented at tellers' windows by depositors who want cash for their own check or want to deposit a check to their account from another of the bank's depositors. This type of check deposit is not unusual in small towns or rural areas where one or two banks serve a large area.

Banks typically segregate on-us checks, handling them as internal credit and debit adjustments. The payer's account is reduced by the amount of the check, and the payee's account is credited with a like amount.

The remaining two-thirds of all checks, called transit or foreign items, are cleared externally through local clearing arrangements, correspondent banks, or the Federal Reserve. More than 85 percent of these checks are collected overnight.

Checks Cleared through Local Clearing Houses or Clearing Arrangements

Approximately 20 percent of all checks are cleared through local clearing houses or clearing arrangements. (See exhibit 4.3.) In a clearing arrangement, several banks in an area that receive a large number of deposited checks drawn on one another meet to exchange and collect payment for the checks.

A bank that receives a check drawn on another bank can, in theory, present it directly to that bank for payment. This type of bilateral collection would be appropriate if there were only two banks in a given region and all the checks either bank received were written by account holders of either of those banks.

Some bilateral collection does occur in the banking system. However, given the nature of U.S. banking and the local and regional markets of most banks, bilateral collection is not an efficient industrywide collection practice. It is too costly and time consuming for banks to collect from each other—banks would have to establish clearing accounts at thousands of other banks to obtain quick payment. Instead, U.S. banks have addressed multilateral collections by collecting checks through a clearing arrangement, a correspondent bank, or the Federal Reserve.

There are about 1,500 local clearing arrangements throughout the country. In a local clearing arrangement, banks present checks to a central point—a separate facility or a room in one of the participating banks. There, participants physically exchange checks, then make one net payment to the clearing house that reflects the difference between the checks presented by them and the checks presented to them by other participating banks.

Settlement for net payments to clearing houses is generally made against accounts that participating banks maintain at Federal Reserve banks.

Exhibit 4.3 *Check Collection through a Local Clearing House*

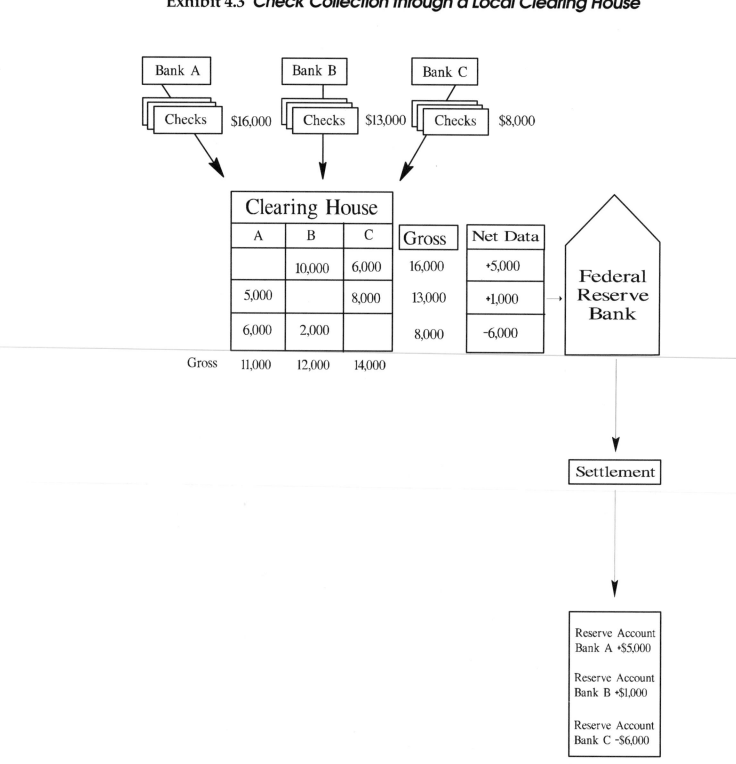

Checks Cleared through a Correspondent Bank

About one-quarter of all checks are cleared initially through correspondent banks. When a correspondent bank receives a check from a respondent bank, the check collection process can take several different routes. If the check presented by the respondent is drawn on a bank that also maintains an account with the correspondent, the correspondent transfers deposit credit from one account to another. If the check is drawn on a bank that does not have an account relationship with the correspondent, the check is credited to the respondent's account. Then it takes one of three routes:

❖ It is sent to a second correspondent bank in which the first correspondent bank and the bank on which the check is drawn both have an account.

❖ It is sent to a local clearing house.

❖ It is sent to a Reserve bank.

A significant number of checks sent to correspondents by respondent banks are, in turn, sent to Reserve banks for collection. However, small respondent banks have traditionally relied on correspondents rather than dealing directly with the Federal Reserve. There are at least two reasons for this.

Until 1980, direct access to the Federal Reserve check collection service was limited to member commercial banks. Membership in the Federal Reserve meant adherence to the central bank's reserve requirements, which were more costly than those imposed by states. For this reason most small, state-chartered banks were not members of the Federal Reserve System.

Also, correspondent banks compared favorably with Reserve banks because they offered more liberal deposit deadlines, faster credit, and sorting and encoding services. Many smaller banks that were members of the Federal Reserve used correspondents for collection services, even though that meant maintaining a clearing account or deposit balance at a correspondent as well as a noninterest-earning reserve account balance at the Federal Reserve. However, Reserve banks matched most of these favorable advantages in the early 1980s, when the Federal Reserve began to charge for its check collection services and to compete with correspondent banks.

Checks Cleared through the Federal Reserve

About one-third of the nation's checks are cleared through the Federal Reserve, although fewer than half the nation's banks and only a fraction of the nation's thrift institutions maintain direct account relationships with the Federal Reserve. Most banks do not clear their checks directly through the Federal Reserve; instead, they use correspondent banks. However, the nation's larger banks rely extensively on the Federal Reserve for check collection. Their disproportionate share of the nation's banking business is reflected in the Federal Reserve's processing volume.

The Federal Reserve collects checks by internally transferring credit balances from one account to another, in much the same way that individual banks collect on-us checks. If presenting and paying banks have accounts at two different Federal Reserve banks, an extra step is involved in the collection process. Each Reserve bank maintains an interdistrict settlement account on the books of the Interdistrict Settlement Fund, established in Washington, D.C., to handle settlements among Reserve banks. A check presented to one Reserve bank drawn on a bank in another Federal Reserve district will result in a transfer of interdistrict settlement account balances from one Reserve bank to another.

The Federal Reserve's Role in Check Processing and Collection

Rule Making

The Federal Reserve's Regulation J governs the collection of checks, checklike instruments, and noncash items by Federal Reserve banks for all participating depositories. Because the Federal Reserve has played an extensive role in national check collection since 1914, Regulation J has had a major impact on banking industry collection practices and procedures.

Processing

The 12 Federal Reserve banks, their 25 branches, and the Federal Reserve's 11 major regional check-processing centers (RCPCs) constitute a national check collection mechanism that handled about 18.5 billion of the estimated 57 billion checks written in the United States in 1991. As part of this national check collection system, the Federal Reserve charters air couriers to present checks between remote Federal Reserve districts.

Under the check collection system, a Reserve bank receives a cash letter from a depository. (See exhibit 4.4.) This is a package of checks accompanied by a list of the individual checks. The Reserve bank then sorts the checks according to the banks on which the checks are drawn and delivers them to those institutions or to their processors, which are correspondent banks or clearing houses.

Credits and debits for cash letters are usually made directly on accounts that depositories maintain on the Federal Reserve's books. However, under procedures adopted after passage of the 1980 Monetary Control Act, banks that do not maintain direct accounts with the Federal Reserve can use a correspondent's account for settlement of transactions.

The availability of credit for checks deposited with the Federal Reserve is determined by the location of the banks on which the checks are drawn and the time of day the checks are received by the processing office. (See exhibit 4.5.) Depositing banks that do their own in-house sorting have later deadlines.

Many smaller banks use the Federal Reserve's mixed or unsorted cash letter program. This program allows smaller banks to deposit all checks received from depositors—regardless of availability of credit from the Federal Reserve—in one cash letter, thereby avoiding the sorting process. Each Reserve bank has a different deposit limit for its mixed cash letter program. Limits range from 5,000 to 20,000 items per day. Banks that use the mixed cash letter program are able to collect on each check in the letter in accordance with the Federal Reserve's schedule (same day, next day, and two-day minimum availability).

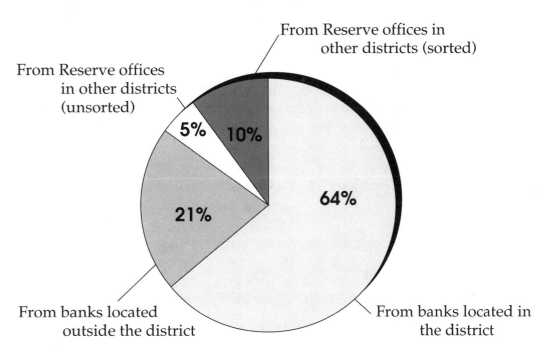

Exhibit 4.4 *Checks Received by Reserve Banks (1991)*

Settlement

Clearing a check is the process by which banks that receive deposited checks obtain payment from the banks on which they are drawn. The key element in

---

Exhibit 4.5 *Federal Reserve Basic Check Settlement Schedule*

bank credit
availability

drawer's bank

Type of Check Drawn	Time Deadline for Deposit	Credit Availability
On the U.S. government	3:00 p.m.	Same day
On a bank located in the same city as the Reserve bank	Varying times— 7:00 a.m. to 9:30 a.m.	Same day
On a bank in the same Reserve district, located near a Federal Reserve Office	Varying times— 12:01 a.m. to 5:00 a.m.	Same day
On a bank in the same Reserve district, but not near a Federal Reserve office	12:00 noon	1 day
On a bank in another Reserve district	Varying times— 10:00 p.m. to 12:01 a.m.	1 to 2 days

the clearing process is the settlement of balances (transfer of value)— either internal account balances, balances between banks when checks are settled through a correspondent or exchanged at a clearing house, or balances among banks that have accounts at Federal Reserve banks.

For many transactions, the act of payment is, itself, the settlement. For example, when cash is exchanged between two parties, settlement occurs because the change in ownership of cash represents payment for goods or services. In a similar manner, the Federal Reserve settles wire transfers through the act of transfer itself. As wire transfers are initiated between banks, the Federal Reserve immediately debits the reserve accounts of the sending banks and credits the reserve accounts of the receiving banks. This results in an immediate change in ownership. Like a cash payment, the wire transfer itself represents settlement.

A bank that deposits checks with the Federal Reserve for collection obtains settlement in the form of credit posted to its account. In this act of settlement, the Federal Reserve is responsible for processing the checks. These settlement activities typically accompany the transaction activities and are not separate services.

Net Settlement

Net settlement involves no processing activity by Federal Reserve banks other than posting accounting entries.

Net settlement is the service Reserve banks provide in effecting a payment in good or final funds when Reserve banks are not responsible for processing the items that underlie the settlement. Made through accounting entries on Reserve banks' books, the debits offset the credits, as exhibit 4.6 shows. Net settlement arrangements generally involve two or more financial institutions that have agreed to have a third party, frequently one of the institutions themselves, create entries to be posted to their accounts at one or more Reserve offices.

process somewhere else. non-local items

The Federal Reserve's net settlement service includes daily settlements for local check clearing houses and county clearing arrangements. The Federal Reserve banks also provide net settlement services for participants in regional credit card associations.

Exhibit 4.6 *Net Settlement Report*

Bank		Debits	Credits
	A		100
	B		250
	C	375	
	D	800	
	E		425
	F		500
	G	100	
		1,275	1,275

The Pricing of Federal Reserve Services

Until 1980, Federal Reserve check collection services were provided without charge to member banks only. Of course, member banks were required by the Federal Reserve to maintain noninterest-earning reserves, so these services were not actually free. The Monetary Control Act of 1980 required the Federal Reserve to impose reserve requirements on all depositories, although the requirements were lowered for many depositories. The act also mandated that the Federal Reserve charge explicit fees for its services. Congress had two objectives in requiring the Federal Reserve to price its services.

First, Congress was concerned about the amount of revenue that would be lost to the Treasury because the Monetary Control Act established lower reserve requirements. Congress saw pricing Federal Reserve services as a means of generating revenue that would partially offset the revenue losses.

How would revenue be lost? Lower reserve requirements increase banks' reserves and enable banks to lend more. To prevent banks from generating massive loans and fueling an increase in the money supply, which could cause inflation, the Federal Reserve would sell securities from its open-market account portfolio. Dealers must pay for the securities with checks drawn on banks thus depleting banks' reserves and reducing their ability to lend. Selling securities from its open-market account portfolio reduces Federal Reserve assets and earnings potential. Because net earnings of the Federal Reserve are returned to the Treasury, a reduction in Federal Reserve earnings results in a direct revenue loss to the Treasury.

Second, Congress believed that pricing for Federal Reserve services would encourage competition and ensure that services were provided at the lowest cost.

The idea of pricing Federal Reserve services did not originate with congressional deliberations on the Monetary Control Act. In 1975, the Federal Reserve proposed giving all nonmember commercial banks direct access to automated clearing house services but denying access to nonmember thrift institutions. The proposal, widely criticized by the thrift industry and the Justice Department as discriminatory, prompted a reevaluation by the Federal Reserve. It developed a broader plan to give all depository institutions access to all payments services but with explicit prices for those services.

In 1976, the Federal Reserve announced its intention to charge for payments services. However, there was substantial sentiment within the Federal Reserve that pricing should not be imposed until the Federal Reserve's problem of declining membership was resolved. By 1977, the Board of Governors decided to defer any plans to adopt a pricing schedule until an effective strategy could address the decline in Federal Reserve membership.

In 1978, Congress considered a number of bills requiring the Federal Reserve to price its payments services in conjunction with uniform reserve requirements for all depository institutions. The Board of Governors supported these bills and published for public comment a proposed schedule of prices and policies for check and ACH services. Toward the end of 1978, however, the drive toward membership and pricing legislation appeared to lose its momentum in Congress. But new bills linking mandatory reserves and pricing were introduced in the House and Senate in 1979. A bill containing a provision for pricing Federal Reserve float, as well as Reserve bank services, was also passed by the House Banking Committee. These bills became the nucleus of the Monetary Control Act of 1980.

Pricing Principles

The Monetary Control Act contained certain congressional principles for pricing Federal Reserve services. The act stipulated the following principles:

❖ Federal Reserve services must be explicitly priced.

❖ Federal Reserve services must be available to nonmember depositories on the same terms as to member banks. Since member banks obtain Federal Reserve services through direct accounts at Reserve banks, Congress recognized that nonmember banks and thrift institutions would also have to maintain accounts with balances sufficient for clearing purposes.

❖ Fees for Federal Reserve services must be based on all direct and indirect costs the Federal Reserve incurs in providing services, such as overhead, taxes it would pay, and its return on capital, as if the Federal Reserve were a private business firm.

❖ The Federal Reserve's pricing principles and practices should take into account competitive factors and the need for the Reserve banks to provide an adequate level of services nationwide.

In 1981, the Federal Reserve issued its own set of pricing principles to supplement those embodied in the Monetary Control Act. The Federal Reserve announced that its fees would be set so that revenues from major services would match costs. However, it gave notice that it might set fees for some services below cost in the interest of providing adequate service nationwide. The Federal Reserve also said that the structure of its fees and services would, over time, be designed to encourage banks to use Federal Reserve services more efficiently. They would also be designed to promote long-run improvements in the nation's payments system—principally, a shift toward electronic payments.

Price Determinants

To determine a fair price for its services, the Federal Reserve adopted two approaches.

First, it announced that prices would be set to reflect taxes and other costs the Federal Reserve would have to pay—and the return on investment it would realize—if it were a private sector firm.

Second, fees would be uniform for services having the same costs, regardless of location—generally such capital-intensive services as wire transfer, ACH services, and net settlement services. However, where there were significant differences in cost among Federal Reserve districts or offices, different price schedules would be used. This specifically applied to check processing.

The Federal Reserve arrives at its annual price markup, called the private sector adjustment factor (PSAF), by examining the returns on capital and the overhead costs of a sample of the nation's largest bank holding companies. In calculating the PSAF, the Federal Reserve makes periodic adjustments for the changing financial circumstances of bank holding companies that could, if not taken into account, lead to a higher or lower price.

In 1989, the Federal Reserve expanded the sample of bank holding companies used in PSAF calculations from 25 to 50; introduced five-year averaging of these holding companies' costs and investment returns; and adjusted its measures of bank capital to reflect the risk-based capital guidelines large banks became subject to in the late 1980s. These changes ensure that the Federal Reserve's prices in the 1990s will not be unduly affected by unusually high or low annual earnings at any one large bank, or by unusual cost factors associated with a single year.

Pricing Concerns

The initial prices that the Federal Reserve developed in 1981 were the subject of considerable controversy within the banking industry. The nation's correspondent banks depend on Reserve bank services for their wholesale banking business but compete with the Federal Reserve for retail banking services to respondent banks. Correspondent banks saw the Federal Reserve's pricing schedule as a potential threat to their respondent markets and argued that Reserve bank service prices were too low.

Conversely, the nation's smaller banks and thrift institutions claimed that Reserve bank prices were too high, or at least not low enough to offer them a meaningful competitive alternative to the services correspondent banks provide. They also contended that the Federal Reserve's rules and procedures favored large banks.

The Federal Reserve was caught in a dilemma. Imposing prices on services that it had previously supplied at no explicit charge would, in all likelihood, reduce service volume as some users switched to less costly alternatives. However, Federal Reserve services carry high fixed costs, so a reduction in service volume would raise Reserve banks' processing costs. Because the Federal Reserve's prices must by law equal costs plus markup, a drop in volume would mean still higher prices. Higher prices would, in turn, reduce volume even further. The Federal Reserve, unlike commercial banks, cannot cross-subsidize—that is, take profits from services such as wire transfer to compensate for losses caused by volume declines in services such as check processing. A major decline in service volume, therefore, could threaten the role of the Reserve banks in the nation's payments system.

In 1980, the House Banking Committee asked the General Accounting Office (GAO)—the investigative arm of Congress—to address this issue by examining whether the services provided by the Reserve banks could be better and less expensive if done by the private sector. The GAO, in a report issued in 1981, concluded that the private sector, or any government agency, could probably not provide payments services as effectively or at a lower cost than the Federal Reserve. The GAO report went on to say that it was unlikely that many payments services now performed by the Federal Reserve could or would be duplicated by the private sector if the Reserve banks ceased to perform them. The GAO report cited as examples the Federal Reserve's nationwide check-clearing and collection services. It also cited the provision of check services to geographic areas remote from major banking centers or in areas where small populations make private services uneconomical.

The Monetary Control Act requires the Federal Reserve to ensure that adequate services are provided nationwide. Congress recognized that the private sector's provision of payments services cannot necessarily ensure uniformity or adequate nationwide services nor can it protect smaller banks from market discrimination by correspondent banks on which they would otherwise be totally dependent. Check services, for example, might not be available to bank customers in small towns as quickly, efficiently, and cheaply as they are to customers in large urban banking areas. The private sector might find specific services too costly or burdensome to provide in all geographic areas.

In essence, Congress recognized the validity of the nearly 80-year commitment of the Federal Reserve to promote an efficient payments mechanism in the United States. However, the 1980s brought about a significant change in the competitive environment for interbank payments services, which has affected the role of correspondent banks, clearing houses, and the Reserve banks in the payments system.

Check Pricing

The fees that the Federal Reserve charges for check collection services depend primarily on where the checks are processed in each district (at a Reserve bank, at a branch office, at an RCPC, in the same Reserve district), the type of item being processed (mixed cash letters, other Feds), the level of presorting involved (fine sort, group sort, or nonmachinable), and, since 1991, where the checks have to be presented.

City. These checks are drawn on banks located in the same city as the Federal Reserve office. Depositing banks typically receive immediate credit.

RCPC. These checks are drawn on banks in suburban areas with a Federal Reserve office nearby. RCPC items are usually collected on the day they are presented, with the depositing banks receiving same-day credit.

Fine Sort Cash Letters. These checks are drawn on only one bank and are packaged for delivery to that institution. The presenting depository, typically a correspondent bank, does the sorting work for its respondents. Depositing banks receive immediate credit. (About 25 percent of all checks received by Reserve banks are fine sort items; 70 percent of these items are drawn on regional banks).

Group Sort Cash Letters. These checks are drawn on a group of specific banks in a geographic area. Depositories that collect large volumes of checks can obtain quicker credit availability from the Federal Reserve, and use later presentment deadlines, by sorting checks on a group basis.

Country. These checks are drawn on banks in the same Federal Reserve district, but beyond the RCPC zone. Depositing banks receive one- or two-day deferred credit.

Mixed Cash Letters. These are packages of checks containing unsorted city, RCPC, and country checks. Depositing banks receive credit for each check in the package depending on the check's same-day, one-day, or two-day deferred status.

Unencoded Mixed Cash Letters. These are packages of checks containing city, RCPC, and country checks that have not been sorted or encoded in MICR by the sending bank.

Other Feds. These packages of checks are drawn on depositories in other Federal Reserve districts.

Nonmachinable Cash Letters. These checks have been rejected by the reader-sorter equipment of the depositing banks or are physically damaged and cannot be processed by computer.

In 1991, the Federal Reserve established a tiered pricing structure for its check collection services based on where checks must be presented. Under tiered pricing, different fees are assessed for checks, not only on the basis of where the checks are processed and the type of items involved, but on whether Reserve banks have to present the checks to geographically remote banking offices that are costly to reach or to centrally located banking offices that can be reached at moderate cost. Tiered pricing enables Reserve banks to match their check prices more closely with the costs they incur in collecting checks drawn on different paying banks.

Impact of Check Pricing

The explicit pricing of Federal Reserve check-processing services had a significant impact on banking operations in the 1980s. It made all banks more aware of their operating costs—as either providers or purchasers of payment services.

Federal Reserve check pricing raised operating costs for many banks in two ways. First, Federal Reserve services that were previously free were now priced. Second, some correspondent banks instituted pass-back charges as their costs rose due to purchasing services from the Federal Reserve. Many banks sought to offset their increased operating costs by passing on to customers higher checking account service charges.

Many smaller respondent banks have sought to protect themselves and their customers from rising check-clearing costs by forming local or regional check-clearing arrangements, rather than use the collection services of the Federal Reserve or a correspondent bank. In the 1980s, hundreds of local and regional clearing houses were established across the country. Many of these clearing houses had been dismantled in the early 1970s when the Federal Reserve established its network of RCPCs. Some respondent banks have also begun to unbundle the services they buy from correspondents by using different banks for specific services, instead of relying on the traditional approach of obtaining a full-service package from one correspondent. Unbundling has enabled smaller banks to respond to price differences among correspondent banks and to hold down their costs.

In the early 1980s, many of the nation's large correspondent banks argued that the Federal Reserve had not responded to the mandate of the Monetary Control Act to promote competition. They contended that the Federal Reserve was using its regulatory powers to change payments mechanism rules to achieve a competitive advantage. A number of lawsuits were filed against the Federal Reserve.

In 1983, Congress held hearings to determine whether the Reserve banks were competing and pricing their services fairly. Both the GAO and Congress found all these allegations baseless. In fact, in its report on Federal Reserve compliance with the Monetary Control Act, Congress urged the Federal Reserve to expand its role in the payments mechanism by actively encouraging banks to use more electronic forms of payment and by stimulating the establishment of ATM networks through processing credit and debit card transactions. Nonetheless, banks' allegations that the Federal Reserve held an unfair competitive advantage continued throughout the decade.

In 1987, Congress asked the GAO to specifically address this issue by examining the Federal Reserve's check operations. The GAO found that the Federal Reserve did have an advantage over correspondent banks in providing same-day check collection services, but noted that this advantage was a result of long-standing Federal Reserve practices taken to enhance the efficiency of the check collection system.

The GAO reported that the Federal Reserve had established check collection rules that differed from state laws governing commercial banks' collection of checks. Specifically, Reserve banks require paying banks to make same-day payment on

❖ checks that Reserve Banks have not endorsed

❖ checks presented by Reserve banks up to 2:00 p.m.—a time that is later than customary within the banking industry—without imposing a presentment fee

These rules, concluded the GAO, have enabled Reserve banks to make check funds available quickly and inexpensively to commercial banks that use Reserve banks for collection. However, these rules have also made it difficult for correspondent banks to compete with the Federal Reserve in providing same-day check collection services because they cannot match the Reserve banks' collection terms.

The Federal Reserve as Competitor and Regulator

The Federal Reserve's check presentment practices differ markedly from the practices that have evolved among commercial banks. Most banks charge each other presentment fees for checks they receive directly for same-day payment. These fees discourage banks from presenting checks early in the day for immediate payment.

By discouraging banks from making early check presentments, correspondent banks are able to more efficiently manage their check-processing equipment over the course of the day. They also safeguard the controlled disbursement services they sell to corporations, which provide corporate accounts with early morning notification of the check amounts that have been presented against their accounts that day.

Same-day presentment fees increase commercial banks' check collection costs by about 30 percent. To avoid these costs, many banks rely extensively on the Federal Reserve and on local clearing houses, which do not charge same-day presentment fees. However, banks also present checks to other banks late in the day so that check payments will not be made until the next day and thus not be subject to presentment fees. This practice delays funds availability for both banks and their depositors and impairs the efficiency of the check collection system.

In the Expedited Funds Availability Act (EFAA) of 1987, Congress imposed maximum time limits on the holds banks could place on deposited checks. The act also instructed the Federal Reserve to speed up the collection of checks and gave the Federal Reserve broad new authority to regulate any aspect of the nation's check collection system. Working under the mandate of the EFAA, the Federal Reserve proposed in 1988 that presentment fees be abolished and banks be allowed to present checks to paying banks up to 2:00 p.m. for same-day payment.

This proposal was vehemently opposed by large banks and corporations. They argued that the 2:00 p.m. deadline for banks' receipt of same-day payment checks would thoroughly disrupt, if not end, controlled disbursement services by making it impossible for banks to release funds to corporations until late in the day, after all check deliveries had arrived. Early morning information on checks presented against corporate accounts gives corporations time to invest surplus funds, or borrow additional funds, while money markets are still active. A 2:00 p.m. check presentment deadline, it was argued, would make these profitable information services unworkable. The Federal Reserve responded to these concerns by withdrawing the proposal.

In 1989, the GAO issued its study on the Federal Reserve's check operations. The study recommended that the Federal Reserve should change check collection procedures to give correspondent banks the same ability to provide same-day collection services to their customers as Reserve banks. This would eliminate any perception of competitive unfairness. The Federal Reserve took this recommendation into account, as well as banks' concerns over the 2:00 p.m. presentment proposal, in issuing a new proposal in 1991.

The 1991 proposal gives banks the option of paying for checks on the day they are received—if presented by 8:00 a.m.—without charging a presentment fee, or returning these checks by the end of the day. Most large banks have responded favorably to this proposed change, anticipating that the end of presentment fees will generate substantial cost savings, while the 8:00 a.m. presentment deadline will protect controlled disbursement services. Industry analysts expect that ending presentment fees will create more competition between correspondent banks and Reserve banks in the 1990s and shift advantages from the Federal Reserve to correspondents.

Many correspondent banks contend, however, that to outcompete the Federal Reserve in the 1990s, correspondent banks will have to introduce new collection services and innovations in the paper payments mechanism. There are some valid reasons for this view. Several large money center and regional banks have established direct-send networks that offer respondent banks quicker availability on cash letters. In addition, a number of national air couriers and regional banks have instituted new collection services that offer banks overnight service on deposited checks anywhere in the country.

In the 1980s, Reserve banks modified their check services to meet commercial bank and thrift needs, made their operations more flexible, and broadened their sales efforts. However, Reserve banks are unlikely to present correspondent banks with a competitive threat to other aspects of their respondent bank service market in the 1990s. Most banking services correspondents provide to respondents are not comparable with services available from the Federal Reserve, nor are they likely to become so. Among the services correspondents provide to respondents that Reserve banks do not or cannot offer are the following:

❖ participation in loan arrangements

❖ backup lines of credit for customers

❖ dividend checks to stockholders

❖ dividend reinvestment programs for stockholders

❖ investment advice

❖ analysis of operating problems

In contrast, the following list shows banking services provided by the Federal Reserve that correspondents either do not or cannot offer:

❖ destruction of unfit currency and replacement with new currency

❖ national wire transfer, book-entry securities transfer, and net settlement services in immediately available funds

By the mid-1980s, the initial pricing-induced shifts in check-processing volume from Reserve banks to correspondent banks and clearing houses had been largely reversed. And by 1991, the market share of check-processing volume held by correspondents, local clearing houses, and the Federal Reserve had just about reverted to the prepricing levels of 1981.

Float

Consumer Float

Consumers benefit financially from delays in the check collection system in the form of consumer float. This term refers to the extra use of money that consumers obtain from their checking account balances because of the time lapse between payment by check and the time funds are debited from the account. In its broadest definition, consumer float encompasses the following:

❖ mail float—the length of time a check is in the mail to a creditor

❖ creditor processing float—the time between the receipt of a check by a creditor and its deposit in a bank

❖ bank float—the time between receipt of a check by a bank and final credit given by a correspondent or Reserve bank

Consumer float time typically ranges from about 4 days for a check presented at a bank other than the consumer's own bank to 13 days for checks sent to government agencies. Consumer float also varies for different types of check payments—4 or 5 days for most retail purchases, medical bills, and utility payments; 6 or 7 days for most credit card and insurance payments; and as much as 10 days for magazine subscription payments. During this time, checking account balances can be used to make other payments, to cash checks, or to earn interest (in the case of NOW accounts or money market deposit accounts).

Some consumers abuse the check collection system by building float into their payment practices—that is, by writing checks without sufficient funds on deposit to cover the checks. These consumers pay merchants, knowing there are no funds in their checking accounts, and that it will take at least 4 or 5 days before the check is presented to the consumer's bank for payment. Four or five days later, they deposit cash in their checking accounts to ensure that the checks are not returned by the paying bank for insufficient funds. If they fail to provide coverage in time, at worst they incur a return-item charge—an average of $20 in 1991. Banks incur the cost of handling the return item (although banks tried to pass back most handling costs to check depositors in the 1990s through higher return-item charges), and merchants become wary about accepting checks from customers.

The loss of consumer float inherent in EFT systems is often cited as a reason for consumer dislike of EFT. In its 1977 report, the National Commission on Electronic Funds Transfers concluded that consumer float is a by-product of imperfections in the nation's paper-based payments system. Consumers have no rights to float or to feel that they are owed float from banks.

Federal Reserve Float

Federal Reserve float consists of extra reserves in the banking system that occur because the Federal Reserve credits banks for checks presented for payment before the checks are collected from the banks on which they are drawn.

Federal Reserve banks collect checks for depositing banks in accordance with a deferred availability time schedule. This schedule credits the accounts of depositing banks on the day checks are presented, the next day, or a maximum of two business days later. A depositing bank receives credit in accordance with this schedule, even if the checks it presents have not yet been processed by the Reserve bank's computers or shipped to the paying bank. Once the depositing bank receives final credit, the funds become usable reserves for meeting reserve requirements, for supporting new loans, or for making investments. As long as the paying bank's account at the Reserve bank remains free from a debit by the Federal Reserve to offset the credit to the depositing bank, an extra amount of reserves will exist on the books of the banking system.

There are several components of float; each represents a reason Reserve banks often do not receive quick payment.

❖ Holdover Float. Processing delays at Federal Reserve banks can back up checks into the next day's shift. Float is created by unexpected events such as computer breakdowns, surges in check volume, or check-processing staff shortfalls.

❖ Transportation Float. Delays in physically presenting checks for payment can cause float. Bad weather or strikes that delay carriers' delivery schedules can prevent the Reserve banks from being paid on time.

❖ Rejected Items Float. Some checks are rejected by the Reserve banks' sorters because they have been damaged during the collection process. These checks require slower manual processing. Float can occur if these checks are not processed in time to meet the deferred availability schedule.

In 1991, the amount of average daily Federal Reserve float in the banking system stood at about $500 million. This was a considerable reduction from the $6.5 billion daily average that existed in 1980, before Congress mandated a change in the Federal Reserve's treatment of float.

The quick crediting of checks by Reserve banks has its origins in the Federal Reserve's mission to provide the nation with an efficient national payments mechanism. Quick credit to a depositing bank reduces that bank's uncertainty about its usable funds and promotes checks as efficient business and consumer payment devices.

The Federal Reserve's deferred availability schedule was initially based on the geographic proximity between Reserve banks and the banks on which the checks were drawn. Credit was based on the time payment was expected. The theory was that the closer the paying bank was to the receiving Reserve bank, the shorter the time it would take to collect payment on presented checks. Thus, almost immediate credit could be given for checks drawn on banks close to the Reserve bank. It would take longer to collect payment from banks remote from Federal Reserve offices, simply because of transportation time. Thus, credit for checks drawn on remote banks would be deferred until collection could be made.

In the mid-1970s, the Federal Reserve introduced a new generation of check-processing equipment that improved Reserve bank efficiency and cut float. However, the rapid growth in the volume of checks processed by the Federal Reserve in the late 1970s more than offset productivity gains, and float began to increase. In the 1970s, float increased from about $3 billion per day early in the decade to more than $6 billion per day at the end of the decade. The sharp increase in float, coupled with the rise in interest rates throughout the period, brought increasing congressional disapproval of float. To Congress, float was nothing more than an unjust and inequitable daily interest-free loan to the banking system from the Federal Reserve. This disapproval was expressed in the Monetary Control Act of 1980, which required the Federal Reserve to eliminate Federal Reserve float or charge banks for float credit at prevailing interest rates.

How Federal Reserve Float Is Created

The creation of float can be traced by using T accounts—abstracts of bank balance sheets that show changes in assets and liabilities. In the following example, three balance sheets are involved—the books of a Federal Reserve bank and two commercial banks that clear their checks through the Federal Reserve.

Federal Reserve Bank

Monday

Assets	Liabilities
Cash items in process of collection +$1 million	Commercial Bank A_____ Commercial Bank B_____ Deferred availability items +$1 million

Assume that on Monday the Federal Reserve bank receives $1 million in checks from Bank A drawn on Bank B. According to the Reserve bank's deferred availability schedule, credit is posted to Bank A's account for these checks on Tuesday, one day after presentation. On Monday, the Reserve bank records on its books that it has received $1 million in checks for credit to another bank, is in the process of collecting those checks, and is deferring credit for the checks for one day. If the Federal Reserve can sort the $1 million in checks and deliver them to Bank B on Tuesday, no float will be created and the Reserve bank's books would look like this:

Federal Reserve Bank

Tuesday

Assets		Liabilities	
Cash items in process of collection:		Commercial Bank A	+$1 million
(Monday)	+$1 million	Commercial Bank B	- $1 million
(Tuesday)	- $1 million	Deferred availability items:	
		(Monday)	+$1 million
		(Tuesday)	- $1 million

However, if the Reserve bank cannot sort and deliver the checks to Bank B on Tuesday, float will be created. Assume an unexpected snowstorm prevents carriers from delivering the processed checks to Bank B until Wednesday. In this case, the books of the Reserve bank would look like this:

Federal Reserve Bank

Wednesday

Assets		Liabilities	
Cash items in process of collection		Account of Commercial Bank A	
	+$1 million	(Tuesday)	+$1 million
		Commercial Bank B	_____
		Deferred availability items	
		(Monday)	+$1 million
		(Tuesday)	-$1 million

Bank A's account has been credited with $1 million in usable reserve assets because the deferred availability schedule called for such a credit. The reduction in the deferred availability items account reflects the end of credit deferment. However, Bank B has not yet received the checks, so they are not collected and are still carried as cash items in the process of collection on the Reserve bank's books. There is now $1 million in float in the banking system. In other words, the Federal Reserve created $1 million in reserves. In accounting terms, float is the difference between the Federal Reserve's cash items in the process of collection (assets) and its deferred availability items (liabilities).

If the checks are presented to Bank B on Wednesday, the $1 million in float will be eliminated because the Reserve bank will debit Bank B's account by $1 million and debit its own cash items account by $1 million. Federal Reserve float is continually created and destroyed in the banking system in this manner.

What is happening on the books of Banks A and B? Bank A had to wait one day until it received credit in fully collected funds from the Reserve bank, so on Monday its books showed a $1 million increase in cash items in the process of collection. This offset the $1 million in credit postings it made to depositors' accounts. Bank A carried $1 million in bank float on its books.

Bank A

Monday

Assets		Liabilities	
Cash items in process of collection	+$1 million	Demand deposit accounts	+$1 million

Bank B did not receive checks drawn on it until Wednesday. Its checkwriting depositors benefited from the $1 million in Federal Reserve float because Bank B had the use of $1 million in reserves for one day longer than it should have, and its depositors had the use of their checkbook funds for one day longer than they should have. If there had been no delay in the check collection process on Tuesday, Bank B would have paid $1 million to Bank A through an account transfer on the books of the Reserve bank. Instead, its Tuesday books carried no debits to its account at the Reserve bank or to its depositors' accounts.

Bank B

Tuesday

Assets		Liabilities	
Account at Reserve bank _____		Demand deposit accounts _____	

When Bank B received the $1 million in checks on Wednesday from the Federal Reserve's carrier, its account balance at the Reserve bank was reduced by $1 million. Bank B then had to sort the checks internally so that it could make the necessary internal debits to its depositors' accounts. If that process had been delayed because of a computer breakdown or an unexpectedly large delivery of checks, additional consumer float would have occurred.

Float Reduction in the 1980s

The Federal Reserve responded to the congressional mandate on float by shortening check-clearing schedules, speeding up presentments, and changing some deferred availability rules. These measures reduced average daily Federal Reserve float by about $6 billion between 1980 and 1986. The Federal Reserve also added an interest charge to Reserve bank check prices on the remaining float.

In 1983, the Federal Reserve began to reduce transportation float substantially by establishing its own airline transportation network to clear interregional checks more rapidly. At the same time, it instituted a uniform presentment time for presenting checks to paying banks. Reserve banks had previously presented checks for payment at times agreed upon by local clearing houses. These times had generally ranged from about 6:00 a.m. to 12:00

noon. The Federal Reserve decided that 12:00 noon would be a better standard presentment time than the earlier times. The later presentment time allowed Reserve banks to offer later deposit deadlines, reach more banks for collection, and thus reduce float. In 1984, the Federal Reserve also introduced a new check-sorting procedure aimed at speeding the collection of large dollar-value checks drawn on major regional banks.

The Federal Reserve also reduced float by changing some of its deferred availability rules. Reserve banks had given next-day credit on unsorted checks received from small banks in mixed cash letters. Some float was generated because a few checks in these letters were invariably drawn on remote banks and should have been subject to an additional day's credit deferment. To eliminate this mixed cash letter float, Reserve banks stopped crediting on the basis of a next day average and began crediting on the basis of the availability of each item in the cash letter.

Reserve banks had also followed the deferred availability schedule even when checks could not be presented to paying banks because the banks were closed. Banking hours are not uniform around the country. In Illinois, for example, some banks close on Wednesday and stay open on Saturday. In some states, banks stay open on national holidays; in others, banks close for regional holidays. Float generally increased whenever checks being collected for an open bank could not be presented to the paying bank because it was closed that day. To end this delayed presentment float, Reserve banks began adding an extra day of deferment on checks involved in a holiday presentment.

Internal Debit and Credit Checks

Not all checks processed by banks are handled the same way. Some checks receive special treatment, which can be costly. As the overall costs of maintaining the paper-based payments system rise and as banks seek to automate more check-handling procedures, the special treatment of internal debit and credit checks will come under increasing scrutiny.

Return Items

A return item is a check that is returned unpaid to a depositing bank before the collection process is completed. A check may be returned unpaid for several reasons. The checkwriter may have issued a stop payment order or the check may be

- ❖ improperly endorsed
- ❖ drawn on an account with insufficient funds and with no overdraft provisions

- ❖ a forgery or drawn on a fictitious account
- ❖ postdated

With the advent of overdraft accounts, the volume of return items in the banking system has declined significantly. However, the costs to banks of handling return items, an exceedingly labor-intensive and time-consuming process, are substantial.

Until 1988, return-item processing was costly because there was no banking industry standard indicating where on the back of a check each bank in the processing chain should stamp its endorsement. Many banks placed their endorsement directly over prior endorsements, making it difficult and time consuming for check-processing personnel to determine the sequence for rerouting the item. The lack of a standard format made return-item processing inefficient and not readily subject to automated procedures. The time allowed to return items has magnified return-item processing inefficiency. The Uniform Commercial Code permits paying banks to mail back return items as late as midnight of the day following presentment. Postal delays can add an extra four to five days to the entire return-item and chargeback process.

To reduce costs of handling return items and to speed up the overall process, Federal Reserve banks began in 1985 to act as return-item intermediaries for all depositories, even depositories that had not processed their checks through the Federal Reserve. As intermediaries, the Reserve banks accept return items of $2,500 or more from receiving banks and notify collecting banks that these checks are being returned. Banks that use the Federal Reserve's return-item notification service are charged separately for the returned checks.

Since 1988, banks' handling of return items has been governed by the Federal Reserve's Regulation CC. This regulation implemented the 1987 Expedited Funds Availability Act (EFAA). In the EFAA, Congress mandated that after September 1, 1990, banks must make funds available to depositors of local checks within two business days and to depositors of nonlocal checks within five business days.

Regulation CC established new procedures for returning checks to ensure quick processing. This would minimize the risks of bad-check losses that banks could be exposed to under the EFAA's two-day and five-day availability mandate. The regulation also introduced new endorsement standards to ensure that the endorsement sequence, which is used to determine the return route, could easily be identified.

The new return-item procedures gave banks that are returning checks to other banks an option and a price incentive to qualify their return items for automated processing at the Federal Reserve. To qualify a return check, a bank must encode the check in MICR with the routing number of the depositing bank, the dollar amount of the check, and a return-item identifier. Return items sent to the Federal Reserve in this way are assessed a substantially lower handling fee than non-qualified or raw returns.

Banks responded to Regulation CC by shifting a large volume of their return items from correspondent banks, who had traditionally handled most returns, to Reserve banks. Many banks sought to take advantage of the Federal Reserve's interdistrict check transportation system and the price incentives offered by the Federal Reserve for qualifying return items. In 1989, Reserve banks handled 20 percent of all return items in the banking system. However, because most banks were still unfamiliar with the details of Regulation CC's new procedures, a large share of the return items banks sent to the Federal Reserve were improperly endorsed and in poor physical condition. Handling these items slowed the Federal Reserve's processing equipment, required additional time, and sharply drove up Reserve banks' operating costs.

In 1990, the Federal Reserve responded to the rising cost of processing return items by sharply increasing its handling charges for qualified returns. However, the price increase did not nullify the incentive banks had been given to qualify returns. In 1991, banks were charged about 40 cents per item for most qualified returns sent to the Federal Reserve. (The exact charge depends on the location of the bank on which the check is written and the local Reserve office's deadlines.) In contrast, banks were charged about $1.20 per item for most raw returns.

Bank Checks and Certified Checks

Bank checks, often called official checks or cashier's checks, are checks written by a bank itself. Bank checks are typically issued to individuals who do not maintain a checking account with a bank, but who need to make payment with a check that assures the creditor that sufficient funds are on deposit to cover the check. Certified checks are personal or business checks that certify there are sufficient funds in the check writer's account to cover the check.

Many firms that sell goods and services, such as automobile dealers and interstate moving firms, specify that payment be made by bank check or certified check. Typically, these firms would have difficulty collecting payment if a personal or business check bounced. Banks commonly loan money and make routine business payments with bank checks.

The major difference between bank checks and certified checks is that bank checks are obligations of the bank itself. Certified checks become obligations of the bank when the bank verifies that the check writer has sufficient funds on hand to cover the check. Other differences include the inability to issue a stop-payment order on a bank check and the different treatment accorded bank checks and certified checks by the Uniform Commercial Code (UCC) in various states.

As part of the verification process, banks earmark the appropriate amount of funds from the check writer's account to ensure coverage. The check is charged to the depositor's account, transferring the funds to a separate certified checks outstanding account on the bank's books. Banks will cross out one of the MICR numbers on the check to prevent the check from being charged twice to the depositor's account when it is processed in the check collection cycle. Although banks charge for bank checks and certified checks, the issuing and handling costs, which are labor intensive and time consuming, typically exceed the charges.

Coping with Check-Processing Costs

In the 1970s, banks coped with the rising costs of processing checks by introducing new reader-sorter technology, improving operating efficiencies, and developing more sophisticated systems to manage consumer float. Corporate customers also improved their own cash management techniques. These measures caused a decline in the average number of banks involved in processing a given check, as a greater share of corporations' checks stayed in the geographic areas where their banks were located and out of national correspondent networks.

In the 1980s, banks had to cope with two new cost elements—Federal Reserve service charges and interest paid on NOW and money market deposit accounts. Banks responded by raising check transaction fees and account service charges, and by restructuring internal processing operations to improve productivity and operating efficiency. Many large banks transferred their check-processing operations offsite to locations where land, transportation, and personnel costs were lower. Some banks opted for more extensive use of part-time check-processing staff to handle the peaks and valleys in weekly check-processing volume.

Actions such as these enabled banks to cope with rising check-processing costs in the 1970s and 1980s. However, check-processing costs still account for a substantial share of most banks' overall operating expenses. Many banking industry analysts contend that banks will not be able to contain these costs and deal efficiently or profitably with the check volumes projected for the 1990s unless fundamental changes are made in the way checks are processed.

Savings Offered by Check Truncation

Many bankers and industry analysts see check truncation as the most promising way to cope with check-processing costs in the 1990s. Check truncation alters the normal flow of the check payments process so that check writers do not receive canceled checks.

Banks reduce not only the costs of labor-intensive check processing and handling, but also the costs associated with maintaining, sorting, and mailing canceled checks to depositors each month (see exhibit 4.7). Every check a bank receives has to be filed manually—either separately or in bulk— stored, then prepared for monthly mailing to checking account holders. Thirty days of canceled checks must be stored before they are mailed. The savings to banks through check truncation can be considerable, particularly if postal rates and check-handling costs continue to rise.

Although banks in the western states offer check truncation to individual customers, banks in most other areas of the country do not. They do, however, provide such services to corporate customers. About 70 percent of all banks with assets in excess of $100 million offer a check truncation program to commercial accounts.

Consumers still want to receive canceled checks. Because of this, some bankers are reluctant to introduce any truncation programs, feeling that angry depositors will shift demand accounts to banks that continue to return canceled checks. In the absence of a mandatory check truncation program at all depositories, bankers have, for the most part, been unwilling to experiment with different systems. An industrywide move to convert all check services to check truncation might be viewed as a violation of the antitrust laws and consumers' rights under the Electronic Fund Transfer Act. So the immediate prospects for check truncation for consumers are not promising.

How Check Truncation Works

Several steps are involved in a check truncation program.

❖ A bank offers its checking account holders an inducement to accept check truncation, by offering free checking accounts or lowering or eliminating minimum-balance requirements. The bank also tells customers that if they opt for check truncation, they will receive checks with attached carbon copies so they will have a replica of every check written.

❖ Records of the checks are made. When the depositor's check is received from a sending bank, it is microfilmed. The canceled check is destroyed, and the microfilm copy is kept on file. The depositor receives a monthly statement that lists, in order, each check by number, amount, and date paid. The monthly statements of national credit card companies are similar to checkless bank statements. The card companies do not send copies of receipts to card users; instead, the monthly bills contain a line-by-line description of charges—the merchant's name, date, and amount of the purchase.

❖ As part of the check truncation program, a limited number of photocopied checks are provided to customers free of charge. The photocopies can be obtained monthly or allowed to accumulate during the year until they are needed for a specific purpose. Fees would be charged for copies above a specified limit.

Truncation or not, banks now microfilm all checks they receive. Although federal law requires a record of all checks over $5,000 only, the cost of scanning every check to cull those over $5,000 exceeds the cost of simply microfilming all checks. Banks can provide depositors with a copy of a canceled check long after the original has been destroyed. In effect, banks can provide depositors with the check truncation service without absorbing additional operating costs.

Exhibit 4.7 *Check Collection Process*

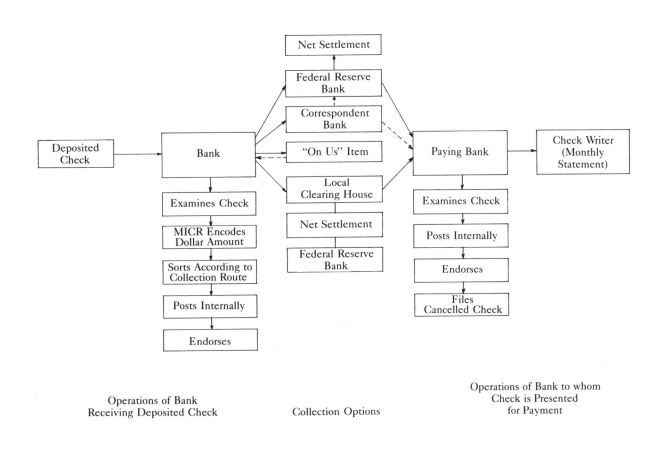

Electronic Check Presentment

Most industry analysts see electronic check presentment systems as the best way to speed up check processing, simplify the identification and handling of return items, and reduce overall check collection costs in the 1990s.

The Federal Reserve has begun to test high-speed, image-processing systems that transmit images of checks between banks, rather than the checks themselves. Several large banks also have begun to test an electronic clearing house system in which MICR data is transmitted to participating banks before actual checks are delivered.

An increasing number of banks are using check image-processing systems for dollar amount encoding of checks. These systems enable operators to view images of checks on a computer screen and enter the dollar amount of each check directly into the computer, which then encodes the check. Conventional encoding requires operators to visually scan and manually encode each check, which is more time consuming than the image process.

Electronic processing and presentment of checks is not a check truncation system, but proponents contend that it could lead to more universal adoption of check truncation programs.

In theory, in an electronic or image collection system, check data or images could be stored on computer disks by presenting banks, the Federal Reserve, or paying banks; the checks could then be destroyed, saving one or more steps in the check collection process. Some banks already are storing check images and sending monthly statements to depositors with copies of these images, rather than the canceled checks themselves.

A nationwide electronic or check image collection system could have a major beneficial impact on the banking industry, but many bankers do not see such a system on the horizon. Numerous issues relating to who would assume liability for bogus, lost, or misrouted checks and how banks would protect themselves against fraud have to be addressed. More important, the cost of current image processing and computer disk storage technology is high. Bankers and industry analysts agree that this technology is likely to become more widely applicable to banking only when its cost declines substantially.

Combining Check-Processing Operations

In 1991, several of the nation's largest banks began exploring options for reducing check-processing costs by combining their check-processing operations, such as

❖ establishing a joint business to process checks for their own banks as well as other banks

Proponents of this option contend that such a business could not only reduce owners' check-processing costs, but would provide substantial fee income to owners from the sale of processing services to other banks.

❖ designating one bank in the group to expand its operations and process checks, for a fee, for the other members of the group

Advocates of this option contend that the fee-paying banks would gain from the economy of scale of the expanded bank. That is, because of the expanded bank's new large-scale operating efficiency, check-processing costs would be less than the sum of each fee-paying bank's check costs (and less than the costs each bank would incur if they continued to do their own processing).

❖ designating a nonbank company, preferably a data-processing firm, to establish a network of large regional centers to process checks for participating banks

Proponents of this option contend that banks would benefit from lower processing and transportation costs as well as state-of-the-art computer technology from the data-processing company. In 1991, a data-processing subsidiary of General Motors announced that it was exploring such an option with a number of large banks. The check-processing network envisioned by this group for the mid-1990s would be based on image-processing technology.

Industry analysts note that many bankers may be reluctant to change well-established and proven check-processing practices, or give up managerial control of check processing by combining operations. However, analysts also note that new technologies and emerging trends in banking toward greater use of outside data-processing services, make combined operations for banks a strong possibility for the 1990s.

Future of Paper Payments

It is doubtful that we will see a cashless payments mechanism in the United States in the foreseeable future. Paper currency and checks, used extensively in the nation for almost two centuries, have become too integral a part of our personal, commercial, and banking habits to be swept aside by EFT systems. Consumer and business payment practices have responded to electronic payments technology and other innovations made by banks in the 1980s.

However, the immediate prospects for revolutionary change in national payments practices are considered small. While the importance of paper payment devices is likely to decline eventually, cash and checks will certainly remain as payment devices for decades to come. And the check payment and collection system will continue to present banks with a costly, ongoing processing burden.

Summary

Check collection is the largest, single, deposit-related activity of banks. Banks clear checks—through on-us items, a clearing house, a correspondent, or the Federal Reserve—by following long-established rules and practices. While these practices provide protection against loss, they are time consuming, labor intensive, and costly.

The Monetary Control Act required the Federal Reserve to establish explicit prices for its check collection services, which added to banks' costs in the 1980s. In the process of check collection, consumer float, bank float, and Federal Reserve float are created. Since 1980, the Federal Reserve has speeded up the check collection process and substantially reduced Federal Reserve float. However, rising check volume and processing costs have focused industry attention in the 1990s on check truncation and image-processing as some of the ways to reduce payments costs, improve the efficiency of the payments mechanism, and, ideally, shift payments practices toward electronic systems.

Questions

1. What are the three basic ways transit checks are collected in the United States?

2. What advantage does clearing house membership afford a bank?

3. What is Federal Reserve float, and how does it differ from consumer float and bank float?

4. What were the defects in the U.S. paper currency system before the establishment of the Federal Reserve?

5. What are MICR instructions, and what is their significance?

ELECTRONIC PAYMENTS: RETAIL EFT SYSTEMS

Objectives

After successfully completing this chapter, you will be able to

- ❖ list the major differences between paper-based and electronic payments

- ❖ describe how the major retail-oriented payments systems work

- ❖ discuss major advantages and drawbacks of automated clearing houses, automated teller machines, point-of-sale terminals, telephone bill payments, and home banking systems

- ❖ cite the major unresolved issues that have hindered more widespread use of electronic funds transfer systems in retail banking

Introduction

When payment is made by check, no money is actually paid or transferred until banks follow a well-defined collection procedure, acting on behalf of depositors. Over the century or so that checks and checking account funds have played a major role in the U.S. payments system, a body of industrial practices and commercial laws has developed governing the use of checks as payment devices. Electronic funds transfer (EFT) systems are only now beginning to have an impact on payments in the United States—and with them comes a new body of industrial practices and commercial law.

No uniform electronic payments system exists in the United States; rather

❖ several sophisticated electronic payments systems move almost $2 trillion of interbank funds each day

❖ several consumer-oriented systems provide retail banking services in selected regions

❖ tens of thousands of individual bank and thrift institution EFT terminals are located in or near depositories throughout the country

This multitude of electronic payments systems testifies to the many uses for EFT, and it provides some insight into the future of EFT.

Differences Between Paper-Based and Electronic Payments

The cost to banks of processing checks increased in the 1980s as rising wage and postal rates, transportation and capital costs drove up bank operating expenses. High interest rates also drove up the costs of maintaining clearing balances at correspondent banks and reserve accounts at Federal Reserve banks.

Banks spent an estimated $30 billion in 1990 on operating the check payments system—about 50 cents per check. That figure includes not only the direct costs to banks of processing checks but also the indirect costs, such as building, equipment, and administration that banks incurred in supporting the check system.

The technology and procedures of check processing do not readily lend themselves to cost cutting. Checks typically move between several depositories before returning to the check writer, and there is no centralized processing center or standardized route through which checks move.

It is against this background that the banking industry and the Federal Reserve are trying to promote EFTs. Certainly, some banks have viewed EFT systems as a means to enlarge their retail banking markets and escape the constraints of outmoded law and regulation, but the primary motivation of the industry has been to reduce the cost of retail banking.

In the 1970s, the efforts of banks and thrift institutions to promote EFT systems were not successful. In the 1980s, improvements in electronic data processing and the development of low-cost, high-speed, personal computers and terminals enabled banks and thrifts to promote a wider use of EFT by consumers. However, consumer EFTs still account for a very small portion— less than 1 percent—of all payments in the retail economy.

In essence, EFT has been difficult to promote because consumers are satisfied with the present paper-based payments system. Consumers like the security, privacy, and personal control inherent in the use of paper payments. Consumers are particularly unwilling to relinquish the recordkeeping feature of canceled checks—almost half of all consumer check writers keep canceled checks for six years or longer. To bankers, checks require a costly infrastructure of buildings, machines, and staff; are inconvenient to process; transfer value relatively slowly; and do not adapt readily to less costly modern technology. However, some major features of the paper-based payments system support its use.

❖ Checks are not money items; they can be stopped in the collection process, allowing consumers or business firms to correct errors of judgment or practice. The legal right to stop payment on a consumer or corporate check before transfer of funds has been a long-standing feature of U.S. commercial and banking law (U.C.C. § 4-402).

❖ Checks leave a paper trail through the collection and endorsement process that allows consumers and bankers to determine fairly accurately whether an error was made in processing the check and, if so, who was at fault.

❖ Checks give consumers total control over when payment will be made, to whom, and for how much. The canceled check provides physical verification that payment was made, an element of proof that can be invaluable in resolving tax or other payment disputes.

❖ A check requires a signature to begin the collection process, and additional signatures if checkbook funds are exchanged for cash or transferred to another account. The signature provides another guidepost in the paper trail and provides legal protection to the checking account holder in case a bank makes an improper payment.

The cost of using checks currently is less than the cost of using most EFT systems and services. However, if banks increase the price of check services to reflect their costs more accurately and reduce the price of EFT services, electronic payment transactions should become price competitive with checks.

Electronic payments have several arguments in their favor.

- Electronic payments eliminate float. When a payment is made, retailers, creditors, and consumers receive immediate credit for collected funds that can earn interest, be invested, or support other payments.

- Because EFTs result in instantaneous settlement, the uncertainty and risk associated with check payments—for example, stop payment orders and insufficient funds—are eliminated. Electronic funds end bad-check losses for merchants and eliminate the high cost of return-item processing for banks.

- Electronic payments are not delayed by the geographic distance separating the parties involved in the payment transaction.

- Because EFT machines are accessible 24 hours a day, bank customers can make payments, deposits, and withdrawals more conveniently than with paper-based payments systems. Many consumers place a high value on convenience and self-service in their retail transactions. The success of supermarkets, self-service gas stations, and direct-dial telephone systems demonstrates that value. EFT services that have satisfied consumers' preference for convenience have been the most widely used.

Retail-Oriented Electronic Payment Systems

There are currently five principal retail EFT systems in the United States—automated clearing houses (ACHs), automated teller machines (ATMs), point-of-sale terminals (POS), telephone bill payment, and home banking.

Automated Clearing Houses

Automated clearing houses (ACHs) are electronic counterparts to the regional check-clearing facilities operated by the Federal Reserve. They are an electronic alternative to the clearing and collection of paper checks.

The ACH concept was first developed in the early 1970s by a group of California banks that wanted to address the growing volume and increased costs of processing checks. The Federal Reserve, however, has played a major role in making ACH a national alternative to check use by absorbing much of the cost of development.

Banks use ACHs for both debit and credit transactions. An ACH debit is a preauthorized recurring or one-time payment that a bank makes on behalf of one of its depositors, such as paying a depositor's monthly insurance premium. When the payment, or transfer of funds, is made from the depositor's account, a debit is posted to the depositor's account.

Most consumers use preauthorized payments for outstanding loans, credit card payments, charitable contributions, insurance payments, and utility payments. In the 1990s, however, a growing number of corporations have begun using ACH debits to make recurring vendor payments and to consolidate daily the deposit balances held in diverse bank accounts into centralized accounts. Preauthorized debits save users, on average, about 40 cents on each ACH payment, largely through avoiding postage costs.

An ACH credit is a preauthorized receipt of funds that a bank accepts for a customer's account on a recurring basis, such as salary or Social Security payments from direct deposit programs. When a bank receives an ACH payment it makes a credit posting to the customer's account. Utility companies and business recipients of ACH credits benefit because they avoid the costs of having to handle and process thousands of monthly check payments. Also, they know the exact amount of funds that will be credited to their accounts on specific days each month.

Depository institutions using ACHs enter debit and credit items on machine-readable magnetic tapes or computer disks, then deliver the tapes or disks to the local Federal Reserve office. Or, the items can be electronically transmitted to the Federal Reserve, which then assigns the debit and credit entries to the accounts of the depositories. When the process is completed, the Federal Reserve either electronically transmits data to the receiving institutions or generates a magnetic tape of the entries, which is then delivered to the receiving institutions (see exhibit 5.1).

The Federal Reserve operates most of the nation's ACHs. The few privately operated systems, such as the New York ACH, rely on a Federal Reserve bank for delivery and settlement services (see exhibit 5.2). In 1991, nearly 30,000 commercial banks and thrift institutions were receiving payments through the nation's ACHs.

How ACHs Work

Most banks and thrifts transmit payments to ACHs on magnetic tapes or computer disks; some even use paper ledgers. ACHs, in turn, forward data to banks and thrifts the same way. Because most banks are not electronically linked to ACHs by terminal or computer, settlement of some ACH payments can take several days and return items notification can be slow. This generates risks for banks involved in ACH programs.

In 1990, only 4,000 banks and thrifts receiving ACH payments from Federal Reserve ACHs had electronic connections to Reserve banks. The nation's major private ACHs—the New York ACH and Visa—are fully electronic operations. Both these private ACHs provide services only to banks that can send and receive ACH data by terminal or computer. Unlike the Federal Reserve, these ACHs provide continuous flow processing, which enables users to send transactions data in advance for filing and subsequent forwarding to recipients. Users of Federal Reserve ACHs must submit payments data in

Exhibit 5.1 *Data Flow through an Automated Clearing House*

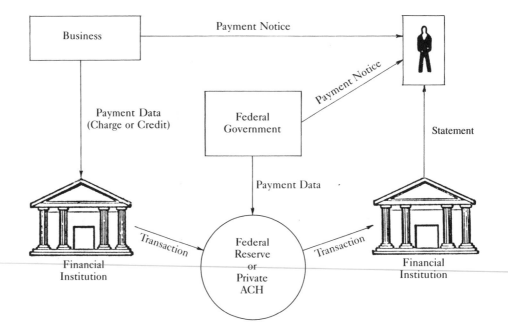

accordance with twice-a-day processing deadlines to ensure that payments will be processed on a particular day. If a sender does not meet the deadlines, payment is processed the next day.

To improve ACH efficiency and reduce risks to participating banks, the Federal Reserve proposed new ACH operating rules in 1990.

These rules require banks to establish computer or terminal links to the Federal Reserve's ACH network by 1993 and electronically send and receive all their ACH payments. A $10 penalty fee will be assessed on each nonelectronic ACH transaction for a bank that fails to establish a computer link to the ACH network by 1993. After 1993, the Federal Reserve will not process any ACH transaction sent to it on magnetic tape, computer disk, or paper ledger.

An all-electronic ACH system would limit banks' risk and improve ACH operating efficiency. Under current ACH procedures, a bank sending ACH payments data, such as a direct deposit payroll tape, must present the data to the Reserve bank ACH two days before settlement. In an all-electronic system, the banks could transmit payment on the day of settlement. Under current

Exhibit 5.2 *Federal Reserve Bank of New York Net Settlement for the New York ACH*

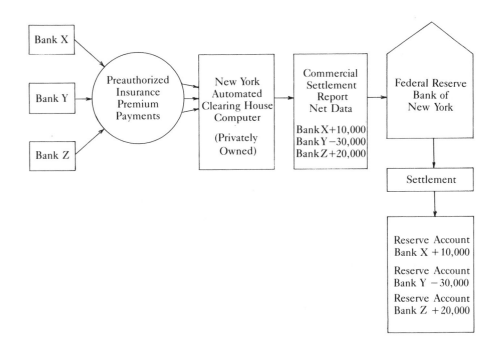

procedures, a bank sending ACH payments data for a company with insufficient funds may not receive return items notification for several days. With an all-electronic system, the Federal Reserve could substantially reduce return items notification time.

ACH Users and Uses

The number of corporations, governments, and other nonbank institutions that use ACHs has always been relatively small, and growth since the early 1970s, despite a surge in recent years, has been slow. In 1990, ACHs handled about 1.5 billion transactions, one-third federal government payments and two-thirds commercial payments made by banks and thrifts for individuals and corporations. (See exhibit 5.3.)

In the 1970s, ACH activity was dominated by government payments; as recently as 1981, government payments accounted for 85 percent of total ACH volume. In 1976, the government began an aggressive program to convert its check disbursement system to a direct deposit EFT system. Today, ACHs handle a substantial share of the government's Social Security benefits,

---

Exhibit 5.3 *Major Providers of Commercial ACH Services (1989 transactions in millions)*

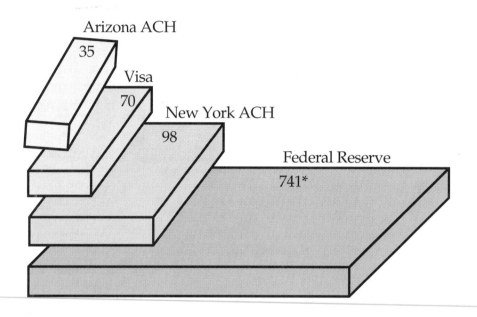

*The Federal Reserve processed more than 350 million additional transactions for the federal government in 1989. The dollar value of the 1.1 billion total ACH transactions processed by Reserve banks in 1989 was about $5.1 trillion.

Source: *American Banker*, **December 19, 1990, and** *Annual Report of the Federal Reserve Board: Budget Review 1989-90*, **Board of Governors of the Federal Reserve, February 1991.**

payroll, retirement, and revenue-sharing payments. Private sector ACH volume consists primarily of paychecks and preauthorized consumer payments for loans and other periodic bills. About 80 percent of all ACH payments have dollar values of $1,000 or less.

Bankers, in general, have not promoted ACHs because they do not feel that ACHs offer any significant marketing, competitive, or cost advantages. The Federal Reserve and the U.S. Treasury disagree. A 1981 government study found that checks deposited by mail cost banks about 60 cents to process, while a direct deposit by ACH costs banks only 7 cents to process. Nonetheless, commercial use of ACHs did not grow significantly in the 1970s. Commercial use picked up sharply in the 1980s with many banks promoting broader ACH uses to corporations, such as direct deposit of dividends to shareholders and expense account reimbursements to employees. However, bankers still doubt whether a profitable market for ACHs can be nurtured in the 1990s, in addition to several other aspects of ACH operation that trouble bankers.

Federal Reserve Role. Until 1986, the Federal Reserve's ACH service—data processing, settlement, and magnetic tape transportation—was subsidized. Prices were set well below Federal Reserve costs. Thus, few banks saw any competitive opportunities in the 1970s or early 1980s for private sector ACH initiatives. In the absence of a broad base of private ACH service providers, banks using ACHs are likely to remain subject to the Federal Reserve's rules, regulations, and standards for ACH operations.

Payrolls and Customer Float. Under the ACH system, corporations must submit payroll data to banks for processing several days before payday—a schedule many corporations cannot or will not meet. Also, many corporations are reluctant to give up the substantial float associated with paychecks. In an ACH arrangement, the entire payroll would be debited by the bank on payday. Under the paper paycheck system, checks take several days to clear, giving rise to float that corporations can use for daily investments in the money market.

Risks and Costs. In the mid-1980s, many large corporations began using ACHs to consolidate funds from regional accounts into one central account, where the funds could be invested more profitably. Typically, these corporations would issue electronic debits through an ACH every evening against their accounts in numerous banks across the country. The following morning, the funds would be credited to one account in a lead bank, where they would be invested or used to make payments. While expanded corporate use of ACHs has increased ACH transactions volume, it has generated a shift in large dollar-value payments to ACHs and raised Federal Reserve concerns about increased operational risks.

Corporations began to use ACHs to consolidate transactions because the Federal Reserve's charges for ACH debits were much lower than those imposed on wire transfers. One proposal for reducing operational risks in ACHs would require the Federal Reserve to charge higher fees for large dollar-value payments than for small dollar-value payments. By imposing significantly higher fees on large dollar-value payments—which banks would presumably pass back to their corporate originators—corporate ACH users might be motivated to switch back to using the interbank funds transfer system. This would reduce payments system risk.

Extensive corporate use of ACHs to consolidate funds has also driven up ACH float. ACH float occurs when there are processing delays. The Federal Reserve credits and debits the accounts of banks involved in ACH transactions on a fixed schedule. If an operating delay occurs and the Federal Reserve credits the account of the receiving bank before it collects payment from the paying bank, debit float is created. ACH credit float also can be generated if the Federal Reserve debits the account of the bank sending the funds but delays crediting the account of the bank expecting the funds.

Most ACH debit float occurs during evening processing because less time is available to make presentments and collect payment than during the day. The Federal Reserve recovers the cost of ACH debit float by adding a uniform surcharge to the price of each ACH debit transaction.

Employee Acceptance. To date, the major thrust of the banking industry's promotion of ACHs has been to gain corporate acceptance of direct deposit. Although public utilities, and mortgage and insurance companies have directed ACH promotional efforts toward their customers, banks have placed little emphasis on selling depositors on direct deposit or convincing customers to use preauthorized bill payment.

Although participation in direct deposit programs increased in the late 1980s, only 100,000 or so U.S. companies were offering employees a direct salary deposit option in 1990 and only 17 percent of America's workers (about 20 million people) were using this option to receive their pay.

The lack of broad-based acceptance of direct deposit appears rooted in attitudinal factors. Surveys have found that many workers refuse to participate because they do not want their spouses to know how much money they earn. Other workers live from paycheck to paycheck and either do not have a bank account or are reluctant to risk a banking error that could deny them immediate access to their pay. Some banks prevent withdrawals of directly deposited funds from ATMs on the date payroll deposits are made because the funds are not actually posted to individual accounts until late in the day. Some banks also have been slow to transfer direct deposit accounts when employees are transferred and change banks. Such actions fuel workers' reluctance to accept direct deposit.

Social Security recipients, for whom direct depositing was designed in 1976, have been particularly cautious in accepting it. Despite nearly 15 years of marketing the convenience, safety, and, often, the additional interest that can be obtained on direct deposits, the government has been able to convince only half of America's senior citizens to choose direct deposit. Industry analysts note that for many older Americans, taking a Social Security check to a bank provides an enjoyable social experience. Also, they see checks as a more familiar, certain, and tangible payment device than ACH.

Proponents of direct deposit and other ACH services note that the quicker access to deposited funds, and the convenience of not having to go to a bank to deposit checks, will increasingly attract more consumers and corporations to use direct deposit. In fact, in the late 1980s, Treasury and the Federal Reserve began transmitting Social Security, payroll, vendor, and other government payments electronically to recipients living in Canada, Great Britain, and

Western Europe. In 1990, the Federal Reserve authorized Visa, which had been operating an ACH service in California since 1987, to expand its ACH operations nationwide.

Automated Teller Machines

Automated teller machines (ATMs) are the most widely used retail EFT service banks offer today.

Most of the 87,000 ATMs in use are minicomputers placed in the lobby entrance or exterior walls of banks. ATMs provide several services:

❖ Cash Withdrawals. ATMs allow a depositor to withdraw cash against a checking or savings account. This is the most widely used ATM service. At some banks, depositors can make cash withdrawals against preauthorized lines of credit on national credit cards or an overdraft account.

❖ Deposits. ATMs accept deposits to checking and savings accounts and, in some instances, payments for utility bills and installment loan payments. Depositors usually receive a deposit receipt. The deposit itself is not normally credited to the depositor's account until it is verified by a teller, usually during the day of deposit. Some ATMs will return a limited amount of cash on an unverified check deposit.

❖ Account Balance Inquiries. About one-third of all transactions handled by ATMs are account balance inquiries, often initiated by bank customers before or after a cash withdrawal or deposit transaction.

❖ Transfer of Funds Between Accounts. Most ATMs allow users to transfer funds between checking and saving accounts, and a few ATMs can transfer funds to a third-party account maintained on the bank's books.

❖ Other Services. In 1991, the U.S. Postal Service announced a plan to dispense specially designed sheets of postage stamps through ATMs. The sheets of stamps would have the same dimensions as dollar bills and would be marketed to banks as a means of enhancing their ATM services. Several major banks will be testing the service in 1992. Banks contend that ATM service enhancements, such as selling stamps, allow them to more readily differentiate their ATM services from competitors, thereby increasing overall ATM transactions volume.

How ATMs Work

ATM minicomputers can be off-line or online. An off-line ATM is a self-contained device that reads data encoded on the magnetic stripe of the plastic card that activates the machine. An online ATM is linked directly to the bank's computer files, which contain information on the customer's account.

As each ATM transaction is processed, the bank's files are updated. The file of the day's ATM transactions is then used to update the bank's master file. After the master file is updated, a new transaction file is established for the next day's use on the online system. Only the master file requires off-line updating.

To access an ATM, a depositor must have a plastic credit or debit card and a personal identification number (PIN). Many ATM systems also permit the use of a national credit card or the bank's own debit card. In the 1980s, an increasing number of banks developed ATM networks that link their ATMs and computer systems, so depositors from any member of the network can access their accounts through the ATMs of any network bank. Today, most banks have sharing arrangements, in which one bank owns and operates the ATMs but allows other banks to use the system. About half the states require banks to share ATMs.

Shared ATM Networks

ATM use increased dramatically in the 1980s due largely to the growth of shared ATM networks. Sharing enables bank customers to obtain ATM services over a much wider geographic area than that covered by their own bank's offices or ATMs. Sharing has been particularly well received by ATM users.

Banks benefit also because sharing typically generates an increase in the number of transactions handled by network ATMs. However, to obtain these benefits, banks have to cooperate with one another by using common technical specifications for their ATMs so that other banks' customers and ATM cards can be used on their ATMs. Common ATM security standards, a common data-processing site, and common clearing and settlement procedures also are required. In 1990, about 30 percent of all ATM transactions were being made at other banks' ATMs.

Many banks introduced ATM network fees in the late 1980s, assessing charges on customers that make deposits to, and cash withdrawals from, ATMs operated by other banks in their shared networks. Today, about three-quarters of the large banks and thrifts in shared ATM networks assess such charges, which range from 75 cents to $2 per transaction. Few banks charge customers for using their own banks' ATMs, but those that do—about 15 percent of all banks—have increased their fees also (fees ranged from about 10 cents to $1 per transaction in 1991).

Most banks have resorted to fees for customers' network transactions in an attempt to offset the costs they incur when a customer uses another bank's ATM. Among these costs is an interchange fee that the bank pays to another network bank that handles one of its customer's ATM transactions; a network switch fee that the bank pays to the network for processing each of its network transactions; and other network charges to defray such operating costs as advertising and network security.

ATM use in the 1990s has shown little sensitivity to banks' imposition of transaction fees. The convenience of ATMs and the expanded number of available locations appear to be more important determinants to users than price.

The fixed costs associated with owning and operating a large ATM network are considerable. A key element is the cost of the computer switch that facilitates the electronic transfer between network members. When a transaction is made on a network ATM, the switch routes the transaction data from the ATM to the data processor of the customer's bank.

Only very large banks can generate sufficient transactions volume to profit from owning a proprietary network of geographically dispersed ATMs. Most banks find off-premises proprietary ATMs unprofitable, since these machines typically fail to generate enough transactions volume to justify their operation and maintenance.

Shared networks enable banks to spread the fixed costs of an ATM network over a larger volume of transactions than they could attract with their own ATMs. By spreading these fixed costs, banks lower overall operating costs. On balance, however, providing ATM services is still a very costly undertaking. For small banks the network interchange fees, switching fees, and network charges may exceed the benefits of offering ATM services. These benefits include potentially increasing the bank's deposit base by attracting new customers and possibly reducing teller-related transaction costs by shifting routine transactions to ATMs. The costs to large banks of maintaining proprietary networks also can be prohibitive. ATMs cost about $25,000-$30,000 each. Armored courier, maintenance services, and data-processing costs can add $200,000 to the annual operating costs of maintaining a modest proprietary ATM network.

ATMs and Expedited Funds Availability

The Expedited Funds Availability Act of 1987 (EFAA)—and the Federal Reserve's implementing regulation, Regulation CC—specifies the time periods within which check funds deposited at ATMs must be made available for withdrawal—two days for local checks and five days for nonlocal checks. However, the act established special rules for checks deposited at nonproprietary (network) ATMs, because banks do not process network deposits and therefore do not have the information necessary to apply appropriate holds to ATM-deposited checks. The act allowed banks to treat all network ATM deposits as nonlocal checks subject to the five-day maximum hold until 1990.

In 1987, when the act was passed, Congress expected that by 1990 banks would develop procedures for more efficiently processing checks deposited at nonproprietary ATMs. However, this proved more difficult than anticipated.

To comply with EFAA's 1990 deadline, deposits of nonlocal checks would be available for withdrawal several days before any bad checks could be returned unpaid. Thus, these deposits could become an attractive vehicle for check fraud. Substantial increases in operating costs or fraud losses could lead some banks to stop accepting check deposits at nonproprietary ATMs, thereby limiting a convenient banking service. Congress recognized this possibility and, in 1990, extended the special treatment of deposits at nonproprietary ATMs through 1992. In November 1991, Congress made the five-day maximum hold on nonproprietary ATM deposits permanent.

Outlook for ATMs

When ATMs were first developed, bankers felt that the innovation would enable them to lower operating costs and attract new customers. ATMs could provide 24-hour service, which would permit banks to cut back the hours they remained open, thus lowering costs. It was thought that the all-day and (in some cases) faster service ATMs offered also would prove attractive to consumers. However, ATMs were not as beneficial nor as widely used as first thought. Mistakes were made and only when these mistakes were corrected did ATM use begin to surge and banks began to reap the benefits.

Depositor familiarity with banking services is key to their acceptance, yet many banks were reluctant to launch extensive marketing campaigns to promote ATMs without some assurance that customers would use the service. Bank customers, therefore, tended not to use the unfamiliar ATMs.

Many banks made another mistake by issuing a large number of ATM access cards to ensure that the machines would be used. However, mass mailings of ATM cards proved costly, and many customers complained about receiving unsolicited cards. Providing ATM cards only to those customers who requested them proved to be less expensive and improved the chances of their being used.

Compounding these mistakes were ATM maintenance problems, which banks could not readily address. ATMs that malfunction, whether by mechanical breakdowns or user errors, often cannot be corrected immediately by onsite bank personnel. This problem can cause more inconvenience to bank customers than any other. Many banks now use outside firms that provide 24-hour ATM maintenance and repair service. Improvements in ATM technology and manufacture in the 1980s, coupled with greater public familiarity with ATMs, helped banks cope with maintenance.

Despite their popularity, ATMs still have not fulfilled banks' original expectations. Bankers have had a difficult time convincing enough of their own customers, let alone the 46 percent of the population who do not have ATM cards, to regularly use ATMs (see exhibit 5.4). Surveys of ATM users and their profiles also continue to disappoint bankers. Most ATM users tend to be younger bank customers, who, while upwardly mobile, do not like to spend much time at banks and do not yet maintain substantial deposit balances.

Exhibit 5.4 *ATM Card Use Profile*

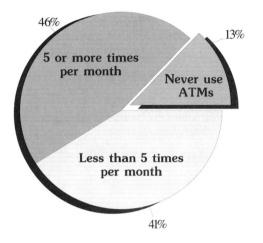

Note: Banks had issued about 150 million ATM cards by 1991 to about 54% of U.S. households

Source: *American Banker*, December 9, 1991

The surveys indicate that consumers between 18 and 24 use ATMs three times a week or more, while consumers past the age of 40 use ATMs sparingly, and those over 55 hardly ever use the machines. Moreover, cash withdrawals, which average about $40 per transaction, continue to predominate as the basic ATM use. Industry analysts maintain that changing the profile of ATM users and expanding ATM uses is the key marketing challenge that the banking industry has failed to meet in the 20 years since ATMs first appeared in the United States.

Nonetheless, ATMs represent the first significant retail EFT system in the United States that has attracted broad public use. And EFT proponents believe that ATMs can serve as an important bridge to more advanced retail electronic payments systems in the 1990s. ATMs have familiarized consumers with debit cards and remote electronic terminals.

Proponents believe that banks can build on this familiarity to market point-of-sale transactions and home banking services successfully. They also contend that ATM networking can establish the foundation for broader nationwide systems linking consumers, retailers, and banks throughout the United States.

Point-of-Sale-Terminals

A point-of-sale (POS) terminal is an electronic terminal placed by a bank at a retail site. It allows bank customers to

❖ pay for goods or services through a direct debit to their account

❖ obtain an authorization or a guarantee from the bank that a personal check drawn on their account is covered by sufficient funds

POS terminals are linked to banks' computers. A bank customer who wishes to make a purchase activates a POS terminal with a bank-issued plastic card and the customer's personal identification number. The customer's account is debited in the amount of the purchase, and a credit of the same amount is made to the merchant's account at the bank. In addition to installation charges for the POS terminal, the merchant usually pays the bank a small fee for each POS payment transaction or check authorization guarantee. Customers are usually not charged for POS transactions. In fact, they are often offered discounts to use the service. Most POS systems link merchants with only one bank but in some states, the systems are shared by several banks. This feature broadens the potential number of POS users for participating merchants.

In 1990, about 130 million payments were processed by POS systems, primarily for purchases at grocery chains, convenience stores, and national gasoline companies that use these systems. Most of these payments were for small amounts—about $25 or so—and may not have involved an immediate transfer of funds from the customer's account to the merchant's account. Some POS systems are not directly linked to banks' computers but instead require banks to make separate debit and credit postings, usually through an ACH, for payment and settlement.

Cost has been a major impediment to broader use of point-of-sale systems. Although cost is substantial, benefits are realized only through a broadly deployed system that includes a significant number of merchants and banks in a large retail market. Thus, POS systems that serve a small area and have only a few participating merchants are not cost effective.

Merchant resistance to using POS terminals has also posed problems for banks. Merchants generally have been unwilling to take the time to help customers in POS transactions that do not involve the merchant's account—such as making deposits, transferring funds, repaying loans, and paying bills.

Merchants also have complained that POS terminals take up valuable counter space at checkout sites. In the 1970s and 1980s, many terminals were removed because the volume and nature of transactions ran well below their capabilities. Banks and POS terminal manufacturers have sought to overcome merchant resistance in the 1990s by marketing terminals that combine a cash register, credit or debit card reader, and a personal identification number entry pad into one countertop machine that can handle cash, check, credit card, and payment transactions.

Loss of float has been the major barrier to consumer acceptance of POS direct debit service. However, consumers have experienced other drawbacks as well. Many POS systems do not offer immediate credit for deposits. Customers who make a deposit on Friday, for example, may be unable to draw on those funds at POS terminals until the transaction is processed and entered into the POS computer file on Monday. Also, consumers must keep records of their transactions so that they know their account balances.

POS Check Authorization/Guarantee. Most POS terminals today are used by merchants and consumers for check authorization or guarantee, which is not really an EFT service. However, many bankers see this application as an interim step toward broader acceptance of the direct debit features of POS systems for the following reasons:

❖ Merchants accept the check authorization and guarantee features of POS terminals because they can cut losses from bad checks or stolen credit cards. These features also reduce cashier time when consumers offer checks or cards as payment. Instead of having to scan a stolen credit card list or make a phone call, cashiers can get bank authorization by entering the customer's debit card number into the POS terminal. Visa offers a variation of this POS service to retailers. For a moderate fee, retailers can connect their terminals to Visa for direct bank card authorization. The J.C. Penney Co. has used this service since 1979.

❖ Consumers retain the use of float associated with check payments.

❖ In states that permit only check authorization or guarantees from POS terminals, depositories that operate POS terminals have an online EFT network in place if and when state or federal laws change.

Debit Cards

A debit card is an access device to EFT terminals, such as ATMs or POS terminals, that consumers use to make retail purchases or to pay monthly bills. The card activates the machine, which immediately transfers funds from the consumer's account to a merchant's account (in the case of a retail purchase) or to the account of a company participating in the EFT program—a utility or mortgage company, for example. In 1991, Americans made 5 billion debit transactions through ATMs and about 130 million were made through POS terminals.

A debit card is similar to a credit card—it is the same size, made of plastic, and has a magnetic stripe across the back. However, in a credit card transaction, payment is not made immediately; instead, a prearranged loan is activated. Consumers typically have up to 25 days to repay the card company or bank, and they may defer payment further by paying only a part of the bill when payment is due and carrying the outstanding amount as short-term debt. A debit card, on the other hand, immediately transfers money from the consumer's account to the seller's account.

Proponents of debit cards contend that the cards have failed to attract much consumer interest, except for use in ATMs, because banks have incorrectly promoted them as alternatives to credit cards. Consumer use of debit cards would grow, these proponents contend, if banks emphasized the benefits of debit cards relative to checks; for example,

- ❖ consumers are not inconvenienced by a tedious identification process
- ❖ debit card transactions eliminate the possibility of embarrassment and returned-check charges

The use of debit cards has been inhibited by the burden debit cards impose on consumers to keep records of account balances and by consumer reluctance to give up the float time associated with check payments and credit card transactions. Credit card transactions can generate as much as 55 days of customer float if the purchase is made the day after the statement billing date. Such a transaction would not be billed for 30 days. The customer would then have another 25 days to pay the balance in full and avoid interest charges.

Some economists argue that debit card use could be successfully promoted by building float into EFT systems through value dating. This would involve not deducting funds until an agreed date. Many bankers see value dating as negating some of the advantages inherent in EFT systems. However, a number of POS systems have built a two-day float into their debit transactions.

As an alternative, some banks are offering consumers a rebate on goods they purchase by debit card. For example, a consumer using a debit card might receive a rebate of 1 percent of the dollar amount purchased each year—in the form of a credit toward any outstanding balances owed, as a deposit to an account at the bank, or toward the purchase of merchandise at participating stores. Offering a rebate for purchases made with a debit card is similar to merchants offering discounts for cash in lieu of credit cards. However, most bankers and merchants do not consider debit card rebates as a cost-effective promotional tool.

To date, no nationwide debit networks exist. A few large national gasoline and supermarket chains have issued debit cards for use in their own outlets.

A number of major brokerage firms have issued Visa or Mastercard debit cards linked to their brokerage accounts. When these cards are used, a debit is made from either a money market account held by the user at the brokerage firm or a loan is made against securities held by the debit cardholder at the brokerage firm. These transactions, however, are not electronic. They are processed like credit card transactions or personal checks and thus entail no loss of float to the user.

Debit card issuers have found general consumer resistance to POS use and have sought to soften this resistance with strong marketing efforts coupled with deferrals of fees during an initial signup period (usually six months) and inventive promotions, such as merchandise coupons linked to the use of the debit card.

Telephone Bill Payment

Telephone bill payment allows bank customers to make EFTs at home through a direct touchtone telephone hookup to the bank's computers. After dialing a special number, a bank customer is connected directly to the bank's computer. The customer then presses the buttons on the face of the phone to indicate

❖ the account number

❖ the personal identification number

❖ the code number of the merchant or company to be paid

❖ the amount to be paid

❖ the sign-off code

Each button's unique tone provides data to the bank's computer.

The computer sorts the payments, which are directly credited to a merchant's account at the bank or, if the merchant does not have an account, mailed to the merchant in the form of a bank check. Merchants that receive a direct credit are also sent a detailed list of items comprising the credit.

Several banks also offer a telephone bill payment service to customers with rotary dial telephones. However, customers must call the bank and give a bank employee the relevant account and payment information. The bank employee, in turn, keys the information into the bank's computer.

Telephone bill payment is one of the least expensive EFT services banks can employ. The system uses the communications network and telephones provided by telephone companies. Startup costs and operating costs are relatively low. However, the costs of internal hardware and software to implement a telephone bill payment system, coupled with the necessary promotional costs, can be substantial. In addition, to be successful, the system must have the participation of many merchants and cover a broad geographic area. For this reason, most telephone bill payment systems are cooperative ventures established by groups of banks or thrift institutions in a given area.

The Seattle First National Bank introduced electronic bill paying by touchtone phone in 1973 in Seattle, Washington. However, the telephone payment service cost subscribers $6.50 per month and provided no follow-up statements or payment receipts, so it did not attract customers or merchants and was discontinued within the year. Since then, banks and thrift institutions in other states have successfully shared broadly based systems, but the overall response to telephone bill payment has been mixed. In 1990, only 500 or so banks and thrift institutions offered a telephone bill payment service; less than 10 percent of their customers used it.

The role of telephone bill payment in the electronic payments mechanism may be beyond its current applications. The major drawbacks of telephone bill payment systems are

- ❖ resistance from major utilities, credit card companies, and national retailers to accepting payment in a form that may not be compatible with their billing and remittance systems

- ❖ resistance from consumers to the loss of float provided by check payments and the lack of a canceled check as proof of payment

- ❖ reluctance on the part of merchants to establish accounts at banks specifically to receive credit for telephone bill payments

- ❖ the fact that merchants do not have immediate use of credited funds, but must wait until they are notified by mail of the bank's receipt of the telephone payment

- ❖ restrictions on telephone bill payment service in states that limit both branch banking and the deployment of POS terminals

Despite these drawbacks, many banks see in telephone banking systems an effective way to reduce customer service costs in the 1990s.

A current focus is on automated voice response systems. These systems allow customers to communicate by phone with a bank's computer by responding to options spoken by a computer-generated or taped voice. The systems are designed to allow customers to pay bills if they choose or to provide them with account balance, interest rate, or other service-related information. With these systems, many banks have been able to increase their overall level of customer service, or expand their debt collection activities without having to employ additional staff. The systems can be costly, ranging in price from $50,000 to $100,000 for a small bank system to $1 million or more for a big bank system with the capacity to simultaneously handle a large volume of customer calls.

Home Banking

Home banking enables consumers to transmit payment instructions to their banks from a personal computer or terminal in their homes. In fully automated systems, the bank acts on these payment instructions by transferring funds electronically between accounts or to other banks. In a number of partially automated systems, banks forward bank checks to merchants and other banks to fulfill payment instructions.

In the 1980s, large regional and money center banks invested heavily in developing home banking systems, but customer response was disappointing. In 1991, fewer than 50 banks were offering home banking services and only 100,000 households nationwide were using these services—just a fraction of the 28 million U.S. households that own personal computers.

Most banking industry analysts maintain that the reason home banking has been unpopular to date is that banks have not made their computer payment services more attractive to consumers than paying by check, credit card, or debit card. Analysts point to serious drawbacks in the home banking systems developed in the early 1980s. The systems take more time to use than paying by check and making payments by home computer costs considerably more than paying by check. In 1986, monthly service charges for home banking averaged about $12. Service charges on the account accessed by the home banking system added to this total, as did the cost of bank checks used to transfer funds in the partially automated systems.

Only about one in five computer owners possesses a modem—the device needed to send data by wire to the bank's computer. Consumers must purchase a modem, which can significantly increase the overall cost of the service. However, some banks have attempted to reduce costs and increase convenience by providing bank customers with computer software that reduces the amount of account-related data the bank needs.

Many bankers doubt whether the perceived benefits to consumers and banks in making and receiving payments by personal computer would justify the investment banks have to make to sustain home banking. There is also doubt about whether consumers would be willing to pay the service charges that banks would have to impose to make such investments profitable. Some bankers see home banking services for consumers as an idea that may be a generation or two ahead of its time. The home banking systems developed in the 1980s may have greater applicability to small businesses and merchants who make more payments and are generally involved in a broader range of banking transactions.

Several major regional banks believe there is a market for home banking services if customers could be provided with inexpensive, easy-to-use telephonelike devices to access services, instead of personal computers. These banks are working with telephone manufacturers to produce a telephone with a small touch screen that would allow customers to transfer funds between accounts and access other banking services over phone lines. A number of prototype devices have been test marketed.

Electronic Funds Transfers:
The Issues

EFTs have changed the way banks transact business with one another, with the Federal Reserve, and with major corporations and financial institutions. However, it is still uncertain whether EFTs will significantly change the way banks transact their retail banking business—that is, the way they provide banking services to consumers. Whether that change occurs—and, if so, how fast—will depend on the resolution of major regulatory and attitudinal issues.

The Federal Reserve's Role

One major issue that needs to be addressed concerns the role of the Federal Reserve in controlling retail-oriented EFT technology. Bankers question whether retail electronic payments systems run by the Federal Reserve would be as efficient or inexpensive as those run by private, profit-oriented financial institutions. They claim that the Federal Reserve or any government-sanctioned monopoly is often characterized by bureaucratic rules, procedures, and inefficiencies.

Bankers are also concerned about restrictions the Federal Reserve might impose if it controlled the central communications lines and switching devices connecting EFT terminals with bank computers and electronic clearing houses.

Bankers realize that competing retail electronic payments systems, each with unique terminals and communications lines, would be uneconomical for banks and unacceptable to merchants.

The most likely prospects for the successful application of POS terminals lie in the deployment of compatible terminals and common communications lines and the development of systems that can switch transfers among all participating depositories. However, this would require a central processing agent—a function that is currently performed in the check payments system by the Federal Reserve.

Some bankers question whether the Federal Reserve should run such a central switching network. Further, they question whether the Federal Reserve should mandate technical standards, procedures, and security requirements for all suppliers and providers of electronic payments terminals.

The Federal Reserve sees its emerging role as a natural extension of its settlement function, its congressional mandate to provide for an efficient payments mechanism, and its responsibility to promote EFTs. However, the question arises whether that role could eliminate competition, stifle innovation, and, by effectively centralizing the electronic payments mechanism, destroy the bank incentives to invest in new payments technology.

Sharing

Another issue is whether all depositories should be required to share the costs of EFT systems development.

The costs of retail-oriented EFT technology are substantial. ATMs and POS terminals are expensive, and installation and maintenance costs are significant. Because EFT systems carry high fixed costs, profits tend to accrue to deploying institutions only after long periods of time. The economics of EFT make deployment unprofitable for small banks and thrift institutions. Only the nation's biggest banks can afford the investment and the near-term unprofitability of EFT systems. A successful EFT venture by even the biggest depositories requires a broad base of users and merchants over a large market, a condition that applies to very few single institutions. Considering these problems, it is unlikely that banks located in sparsely populated rural areas and in low-income urban areas will invest in electronic payments technology.

Sharing EFT terminals and communications lines is seen as a means of overcoming the economics of EFT technology, avoiding costly duplication of terminals and systems, allowing smaller banks to offer EFT services, and expanding EFT access to more customers over broader market areas.

Banks and thrift institutions are already sharing EFT technology. For example, the national credit card companies and several regional banks with ATM networks have integrated their systems. Savings and loan associations in several states also share systems.

Sharing EFT services has generated many problems and has, in some cases, become a mechanism for discrimination against competitors. Fear of being denied access to EFT technology is understandable. The first ACH associations, for example, excluded thrift institutions from membership.

Any new provider of EFT services denied access to a shared system would have to deploy separate terminals and communications lines and develop a substantial base of access cardholders—all of which is costly. It is also unlikely that merchants would accept numerous independent terminals at their retail sites or be willing to establish the many account relationships necessary to maintain competing systems. Consumers, too, would be unlikely to accept a multitude of separate access cards for competing EFT systems.

One obvious solution is to make sharing mandatory because it satisfies public goals. Today, that argument is accepted in 20 states, all of which require mandatory sharing of EFT technology.

Others claim that mandatory sharing is unfair to those depositories that took the risk of investing in EFT technology. Mandatory sharing would deprive innovative depositories of a legitimate return on risk and investment and give EFT terminals and systems to depositories that took no risk.

Detractors further contend that sharing can increase the likelihood of pricing collusion, discourage innovation, and curtail market entry.

In some states, shared terminals are not legally considered bank branches. This regulatory treatment gives a competitive edge to shared systems over exclusive ones. The Justice Department has not challenged any of the state mandatory sharing laws but it has stated that mandatory sharing is uncompetitive.

The courts, however, are likely to rule in the 1990s on laws that prohibit ATM-owning banks from assessing surcharges or fees directly to customers of other banks who use their ATMs. Proponents feel this prohibition helps keep ATM fees low and prevents ATM-owning banks from overcharging customers at heavy demand no-alternative ATM sites, such as airport terminals or sports stadiums. Opponents argue that it prevents ATM-owning banks from charging fees that match the value of the service provided to ATM users at special sites, and that it discourages banks from installing additional ATMs at these sites.

In 1989, an antitrust lawsuit was filed, still pending in 1992, to nullify the surcharge prohibition. If the prohibition is revoked, many bankers contend that ATM network surcharges are likely to become commonplace in the 1990s, raising costs to ATM users, but encouraging broader deployment of ATMs by ATM-owning banks. If the prohibition is upheld, most bankers see a sharp slowdown in ATM deployment in the 1990s.

Terminals as Branches

A third issue concerns whether EFT terminals deployed by banks and thrift institutions should be subject to the same rules and regulations that are imposed on brick-and-mortar branches of those institutions.

The 1927 McFadden Act prohibits national banks from establishing branches outside their home states. Further, it requires that national banks abide by the branching laws and restrictions of their home states. For banks in states that limit branching, particularly by national banks, the issue of whether EFT terminals are branches is crucial to their business expansion plans and ability to compete with other depository institutions.

In 1974, the Comptroller of the Currency ruled that ATMs and POS terminals were not branches. In the late 1970s, however, several state courts ruled against the comptroller. The Supreme Court initially refused to review any of these state rulings, thus making EFT terminals in some states subject to the same restrictions that apply to bank branches. But in 1986, the Supreme Court ruled that ATMs are not branches if they are not owned or leased by a bank but simply connected to the bank through an ATM network arrangement. This ruling only partially clarified the terminals-as-branches issue.

In many states, national banks seeking to deploy EFT terminals are at a disadvantage in competing with thrift institutions and state-chartered banks. For national banks in states that allow deployment of EFT terminals, the comptroller has established abbreviated branch application procedures. These procedures cut red tape, but state requirements governing the capitalization of branches and the number and location of branch sites must be met. In most cases, this prevents national banks from competing with federally chartered savings and loan associations, state-chartered banks, and savings and loan associations.

The terminals-as-branches issue is as much one of economics as it is of regulatory equity. As long as EFT terminals are considered branches under the McFadden Act, national banks cannot deploy terminals without adhering to costly federal or state branching restrictions. Even in states that differentiate between branches and terminals, as long as terminal deployment is prohibited or severely restricted beyond state boundaries, banks will be reluctant to make the huge capital investment required in EFT technology.

Although state laws are rapidly changing, lack of a uniform national approach to the legal and regulatory treatment of EFT systems leaves many issues unresolved:

❖ If EFT terminals do not possess all the characteristics of branches, should they be regulated by the same rules that govern branches?

❖ Should terminals be regulated, or should the services provided by terminals be regulated?

❖ If the McFadden Act is repealed or modified to allow terminal deployment into regional markets that cross state lines, how should the sharing of EFT technology be handled?

Privacy and Security

A fourth issue is whether EFT systems pose a threat to the privacy of individuals and the security of their deposited funds.

Consumers concerned with possible violations of individual privacy contend that EFT systems will generate new and more detailed financial transactions records, which will be relatively easy to retrieve by computer. As the use of EFT systems increases, the number of people and institutions with access to transactions records will grow substantially, increasing the likelihood that individual financial privacy will be breached.

For example, information from computer files and data banks of EFT systems could provide an accurate profile of a consumer's buying, borrowing, and payment habits—even to the extent of revealing behavioral patterns, such as where the person vacations and dines, and which magazines he or she reads. This and other information could be sold to advertisers and retailers, used to determine credit standing, or used by the IRS to evaluate the accuracy of income tax statements—all actions that most consumers view as invasions of privacy.

Another threat EFT systems pose is the increased potential for illegal use or theft of deposits. Although the Electronic Fund Transfer Act of 1978 established a body of consumer rights in EFT and narrowed consumer liability in electronic funds transfer systems, unresolved questions remain.

The security of ATMs, the most widely used electronic payments system, is maintained through the use of personal identification numbers (PINs) that are typically mailed to consumers after their access card is sent. ATM users must not only insert their access card—with its magnetic encoded data—into the ATM terminal but also key in their unique PIN code to gain access to their account. However, the PIN procedure is far from foolproof. Some ATM users write their PIN on their ATM access card or keep the number on a slip of paper next to the card. Anyone finding or stealing the card could withdraw money from the account. Mail theft also can be a problem if both the access card and the PIN are sent in the same envelope.

Some banks have partially solved PIN code security problems by requiring depositors to pick up their PIN in person and to select an easily remembered number, such as a birthdate or telephone number. However, the more secure systems—fingerprint or voiceprint identification—have not been used. These identification systems are not only very costly but also can make ATM access procedures cumbersome and inconvenient. Banks must balance security concerns with user convenience. The more secure a system is, the harder it is for authorized users to gain quick access to their funds.

In the 1990s, many banks have become increasingly concerned over crime related to ATM use and the potential for lawsuits by victimized customers seeking damages. Public perceptions have also grown that off-site ATMs, such as those adjacent to bank buildings, are not safe during late evening and early morning hours. Actually, bank losses from ATM crime and resulting lawsuits have been small, and the number of outright robberies at ATM sites and the sums involved have been low. Fraud committed by customers themselves account for banks' largest losses from ATMs. Nonetheless, most banks have responded to public safety concerns by installing cameras, flood lights, and telephones at off-site ATM locations.

Another major consumer concern is the security of the EFT database. Unauthorized access to a system's database or its switching mechanism could allow the transfer of funds from a customer's account to a bogus account. Many EFT systems have safeguards built into their computer programs and transfer procedures to protect against this possibility. Examples of these safeguards include limitations on the number and amount of withdrawals permitted in a given time period, retention by the terminal of access cards that have been tampered with, and teller verification of deposits made to terminals before the funds can be used.

Efforts to improve the efficiency and lower the cost of EFT systems can pose problems for consumer privacy and account security. For example, linking regional EFT systems together so that computer processing and switching can be centralized would be a significant improvement. However, a central computer would contain information on almost every transaction made in the United States and could pose a fundamental threat to individual financial privacy. This leads to questions of whether regional EFT systems should be allowed to centralize their computer systems and data and, if so, whether this should be controlled by the private sector or the government.

Public Acceptance

The future of electronic payments in the United States will not be decided by regulatory or technological factors. Rather, it will be decided by the willingness of consumers and bank customers to accept EFT systems and electronic payments. The willingness to alter payment practices and banking behavior may ultimately depend on whether depositories or the government can make electronic payments so attractive that the advantages of using an electronic transfer system outweigh the considerable benefits provided to users of the paper check system.

That task will not be easy. The retail-oriented transfer systems do not offer consumers new banking services. Rather, they extend existing banking services to more locations and to longer hours during the day. The services these retail-oriented systems provide can be obtained by consumers through paper payment systems. Consumers will have to be convinced that EFTs are better, more convenient, and less costly than paper check payments before there is any significant shift in payment practices.

The most successful consumer-oriented electronic payments system of the past two decades has been ATMs. ATMs have offered consumers convenience, time savings, and more banking options. Because ATMs reduce waiting time at tellers' windows and provide 24-hour deposit, withdrawal, and account transfer service, depositors are willing to overlook some of the perceived drawbacks of ATMs, including the fear of irreconcilable computer error.

However, consumers did not support most of the other electronic payments systems of the 1970s and 1980s. These electronic payments systems not only offered benefits of insubstantial value, relative to check payments, but also took away desirable features associated with check payments. Check truncation, for example, eliminated the canceled check, a valued payment record. POS and telephone bill payment systems eliminated valuable float time. Preauthorized payments through ACHs eliminated consumers' control over their account balances, and debit cards offered no monetary incentive to compete with credit cards, which allow 25 days before payment.

Some bank customers who want personal service in their deposit, withdrawal, and bill-paying transactions will never opt for lower-cost EFT services. In fact, they may be willing to pay high service charges and fees for personalized services. Perhaps they distrust computers, fear errors will not be rectified, or are a product of a culture or an age that simply cannot accept entrusting money to a machine.

Some of the issues in public acceptance are as follows:

❖ Should banks promote EFT more extensively than they are now doing or wait until legal, regulatory, and attitudinal changes allow them to provide broader and more valuable services?

❖ What is the appropriate role of the Federal Reserve in helping to develop a high degree of public acceptance of EFT? To most consumers, the government is a protector against privacy abuses and loss of financial control. Should the government or the Federal Reserve involve itself in educational efforts to reassure consumers about EFT systems?

❖ Should banks use pricing more aggressively to encourage and promote EFT services—for example, by imposing check charges that more fully reflect costs?

Summary

There are five retail EFT systems in use today—ACHs, POS terminals, ATMs, telephone bill payment, and home banking through personal computers. While ATMs have succeeded in significantly altering the public's banking practices, the other retail EFT systems are not widely used. Bankers have not yet been able to provide EFT services that overcome the advantages consumers obtain when paying by check and the relatively lower costs of using checks compared with current EFT alternatives.

The electronic revolution in consumer payment practices and deposit operations that bankers envisioned 20 years ago has not occurred. Legal, attitudinal, regulatory, and economic roadblocks have prevented more widespread bank and thrift deployment and marketing of retail EFT systems. In addition, major issues face retail EFT in banking: who should control EFT technology; should EFT terminals be considered branches; will the public accept EFT; what are the relative costs and benefits of EFT?

Questions

1. What advantages do electronic money transfers have over checks as a means of payment?

2. Why have some states made sharing of EFT systems mandatory?

3. Why have consumers been unwilling to accept electronic funds transfer systems and electronic payments?

4. What are the five major unresolved issues that affect the future of EFT in U.S. retail banking?

ELECTRONIC PAYMENTS: INTERBANK WIRE TRANSFER SYSTEMS

Objectives

After successfully completing this chapter, you will be able to

- ❖ identify major characteristics of the nation's interbank EFT systems

- ❖ define key terms associated with interbank electronic funds transfer systems—online, off-line, third-party payment, store and forward capability

- ❖ discuss the benefits to banks and corporate treasurers of using EFTs instead of checks in their mutual transactions

- ❖ explain the risks that banks face in using interbank funds transfer systems

- ❖ name key measures that banks and regulatory authorities have adopted to reduce intraday overdrafts

Introduction

Electronic funds transfer systems have become indispensable to banks in conducting their own business and in providing highly profitable cash management services to their corporate customers. While individuals continue to use cash and checks to make payments, banks rely increasingly on electronic transfers to pay one another. Corporate treasurers also recognize the advantages of electronic funds in their transactions with banks.

The vast majority of electronic funds transfers made by banks to one another flow through one of two systems—FedWire (the Federal Reserve's electronic funds transfer system) or CHIPS (the Clearing House Interbank Payments System). Banks also use a payments communications network called S.W.I.F.T.—the Society for Worldwide Interbank Financial Telecommunication—to convey international payment instructions to one another.

The sharp growth in the use of interbank systems and in the dollar value of funds that move through them has caused bankers and regulators increasing concern over growing risks in the electronic payments mechanism. This chapter reviews the nature of those risks and the issues surrounding risk reduction in the 1980s and 1990s.

Bank Reliance on EFT

For banks, electronic funds transfers are safer, quicker, and more reliable than checks for large transactions. Bankers also know that funds, when transferred electronically, can be used almost immediately. The interbank funds transfer systems have given banks of all sizes the ability to adjust their reserve positions quickly. Some banks use the systems to sell excess reserves that would otherwise remain idle. Many banks purchase needed reserves from other banks through the interbank systems to avoid costly reserve deficiency penalties. Banks also use electronic systems to invest daily surplus funds, settle adverse clearing balances in the check collection process, and provide profit-generating deposit concentration and investment services to their large corporate accounts.

Under a deposit concentration service, a bank can, on a daily basis, gather corporate funds from a company's banks throughout the country into one central account for a more profitable investment in the overnight market. The funds can be transferred back into the corporation's regional and local bank accounts the next morning to cover corporate disbursements.

Each day, U.S. banks make nearly 400,000 electronic funds transfers on FedWire and CHIPS. As exhibit 6.1 shows, these two interbank systems specialize in different types of transactions. FedWire transactions are dominated by payments for U.S. Treasury securities and federal funds purchased by banks for their own accounts or for corporate and financial institution accounts. CHIPS transactions involve payments for foreign exchange purchases and the transfer of dollar funds into foreign banking offices (Eurodollar placements). The daily dollar value of all these interbank electronic funds transfers totaled $2 trillion in 1991.

The importance of interbank funds transfer systems in the nation's payments mechanism is matched only by the profitability for banks of electronic funds transfers. In the late 1980s, the nation's 20 largest money center banks were each earning more than $30 million in annual transactions fee income from their provision of interbank EFT services.

Exhibit 6.1 *Profile of Interbank EFT Transactions*

Purpose of Payment	Percentage of Transactions Made Over	
	FedWire	CHIPS
Securities purchases and redemptions	33	1
Federal funds	29	0
Commercial	18	5
Eurodollar placements	9	24
Settlement	7	5
Bank loans	3	1
Foreign exchange	1	64
Total	100	100

Source: "A Study of Large-Dollar Payment Flows through CHIPS and FedWire," Federal Reserve Bank of New York, December 1987.

The Difference Between Payment and Settlement

A wire transfer is defined as a payment. However, a payment does not necessarily mean a final and irrevocable transfer of money (called settlement) between the payer and the recipient. It is only when settlement is made that transferred funds change ownership. Such transferred funds are referred to as immediately available funds. Payments made over FedWire are in immediately available funds; payments made through CHIPS are in provisional funds—funds that are not good until settlement is made at the end of the day.

When a bank transfers funds over FedWire, the payment and settlement transactions are one and the same. Settlement occurs with the near- instantaneous transfer of deposit balances at Federal Reserve banks from the paying bank to the receiving bank. In a conceptual sense, a FedWire payment is like a cash payment—settlement occurs with the act of payment. However, when a bank transfers funds over CHIPS, a separate net settlement transaction (over FedWire) must be made by a settling bank designated to handle the final transfer of value at the end of the day. CHIPS settlement is known as a net-net settlement because the Federal Reserve's debit and credit postings are the net difference between all of a settling bank's payments to, and all of its receipts from, all other CHIPS participants.

The S.W.I.F.T. system and several proprietary systems operated by the nation's large money center banks can convey payment instructions or other financial messages only. These messages typically authorize a bank to take funds from the account of one depositor and place them in the account of another depositor. When both depositors maintain accounts at the bank receiving the message, only follow-up internal bookkeeping is required to complete the process. However, if the account to which payment is directed is at another bank, no payment can be made until a follow-up interbank payment has been initiated through FedWire or CHIPS. The ability of a participant to effect a transfer of bank balances to any other participant by a single message distinguishes a funds transfer system from a message system.

Typically, banks make wire transfers through a terminal or computer link to the EFT system—an online transfer—or through a telephone call to the system —an off-line transfer. A transfer made by a bank to another bank on its own behalf—to repay funds borrowed the day before, for example—is known as a two-party payment. A transfer made by a bank on behalf of one of its customers to an account at another bank is called a third-party payment.

Major Interbank Wire Transfer Systems

The Federal Wire System

The Federal Reserve owns and operates the FedWire system. It provides direct electronic payment services to about 7,000 banks with access to the system through in-bank terminal or computer links. It also provides EFT services to several thousand other depositories—mainly small banks and thrift institutions—that have FedWire access through telephone links. Each day, these banks make about 200,000 transfers over FedWire, transfers that redistribute about $1 trillion in deposit balances throughout the banking system. (See exhibit 6.2.)

FedWire is a packet switch EFT system. This means that funds transfers going from one Federal Reserve district to another are routed through a network of 14 processing and multiple circuit-switching centers that connect all Federal Reserve offices, key government agencies, and the U.S. Treasury. Packet switching allows each Reserve bank to forward payments to any one of three other Reserve banks, which may be either the end point for the transmission or a relay station. Normally, a Reserve bank can receive funds from another Reserve bank through one relay station only. However, during a significant power or computer outage, the packet switch network allows any Reserve bank to move the funds transfer and communications traffic of any other Reserve bank.

Funds Transfers over FedWire

The FedWire network handles three types of messages:

❖ transfers of reserve account balances (almost exclusively in large dollar amounts) from one financial institution to another

❖ transfers of U.S. government and federal agency securities in book-entry form

❖ Federal Reserve System administrative and research information

Banks transfer reserve balances as a result of borrowing funds from one another, to adjust correspondent bank balances, or to move funds to other banks on behalf of customers. Third-party payments on behalf of customers

Exhibit 6.2 *Growth of Federal Reserve Wire Transfers of Funds, 1950-1990*

Year	Number of Transfers (in millions)	Amount (in trillions)
1950	1.3	0.5
1955	2.0	1.1
1960	2.9	5.4
1965	4.4	4.5
1970	7.4	12.3
1975	17.0	31.4
1980	43.0	78.6
1985	45.0	103.0
1990	64.0	199.0

Source: *Banking and Monetary Statistics, 1941-1970.* (Washington, D.C.: Board of Governors of the Federal Reserve System); *Federal Reserve Board Annual Reports, 1973-1986; Annual Report of the Federal Reserve Board: Budget Review,* 1990-1991.

are generally for the purchase or sale of financial assets, such as U.S. Treasury securities, and for adjustments to corporate demand deposits. The Federal Reserve credits and debits only the accounts of the banks involved in the transfer. FedWire does not collect or store information related to third parties that may originate or ultimately receive the funds transferred by banks on their behalf.

Rules governing FedWire are incorporated in Federal Reserve Regulation J, which provides that a transfer is paid when it is sent by the Reserve bank. Thus, funds sent over FedWire are irrevocable and immediately available for use by recipient banks, even if the sending bank is in an overdraft position and ultimately fails to cover this position with the Reserve bank. FedWire is the only electronic funds transfer system with this feature.

Every FedWire transaction generates an immediate debit at the Federal Reserve bank to the account of the payer and an immediate credit to the account of the recipient. If both institutions maintain balances at the same Federal Reserve bank, each account balance is debited and credited immediately. If the institutions do not maintain balances at the same Federal Reserve bank, the first Federal Reserve bank debits the account of the sending bank and credits the account of the Federal Reserve bank in whose district the receiving bank is located. The latter Federal Reserve bank debits the account of the sending Federal Reserve bank and credits the account of the receiving bank. These transactions occur within minutes of the initial transmission. The Reserve banks settle among themselves through an interdistrict settlement fund arrangement.

Before 1980, banks that were not members of the Federal Reserve could access FedWire only indirectly, as customers of a correspondent member of the Federal Reserve bank. The Monetary Control Act of 1980 gave all depositories direct access to FedWire. As with check services, the Federal Reserve was required to price its funds transfer services explicitly and make them available to both member and nonmember depositories at the same price and terms.

Since 1980, the number of institutions using FedWire has increased dramatically, primarily among smaller banks and thrift institutions, because access to FedWire does not require linkage through a terminal. Although a bank can access its account by telephone, access to FedWire services requires that a depository maintain an account at a Reserve bank for funds transfer purposes.

Securities Transfers over FedWire

Through FedWire, the Federal Reserve maintains the only nationwide electronic book-entry, securities-transfer network. Banks can maintain U.S. Treasury and federal agency securities in the form of computer entries on the Federal Reserve's books, rather than in paper form. FedWire gives banks the

---

ability to access these securities instantly, for trading on their own account or for their customers. Maintaining securities in book-entry form maximizes safety for banks by eliminating the risks of storing physical securities on bank premises. Also, by reducing risk, banks save money through lower insurance costs.

The Federal Reserve's book-entry service provides automatic payment of interest and principal directly to the depositor's reserve or clearing account (or to a designated correspondent's account) on the maturity date of the obligation. This assures banks immediate access to funds from interest payments and matured book-entry securities, allowing banks to use available balances to meet reserve requirements or maximize new investment opportunities.

Reserve banks allow commercial banks and thrifts to establish separate book-entry accounts for different purposes, such as customer accounts, the banks' own investments, dealer departments, and trust accounts. This enables banks to segregate their securities to correspond with their internal records. This practice has led to more efficient portfolio management. Reserve banks also provide banks and thrifts with the option of online access to their book-entry accounts via terminals. Many of the nation's larger banks have direct computer links to the book-entry FedWire. As with online funds transfer access, transactions made via terminal are immediately acknowledged.

FedWire enables book-entry account holders to buy U.S. Treasury securities directly through original-issue auctions for their own accounts or for their customers. The nation's major money market banks typically buy or sell securities for respondent banks and for corporate and individual customers. For example, the money center banks in New York City have sophisticated systems for processing book-entry securities transactions as well as a mechanism for settling balances owed among themselves.

However, all money market banks must use FedWire for interregional transactions and for direct electronic access to the government securities market for original issues. Also, when a bank uses FedWire to buy or sell securities interregionally, a corresponding and separate funds transfer must be made over FedWire to settle the transaction. In 1990, about 11 million book-entry transfers of U.S. government and federal agency securities were made over FedWire to and from nearly 16,000 book-entry accounts maintained at Reserve banks.

The Clearing House Interbank Payments System (CHIPS)

CHIPS is the largest private electronic funds transfer system in the world and the focal point for most payments made in the world's international dollar market. It is owned and operated by the New York Clearing House Association (NYCHA) and provides payment services to about 130 participating banks.[1]

Most of these banks are headquartered in New York City and are linked to NYCHA's central computer through approximately 400 sending and receiving devices, ranging from simple terminals to large-scale computers. Each day, CHIPS participants make nearly 200,000 payments over the system for themselves or their customers, transferring about $1 trillion. (See exhibit 6.3.) It is estimated that 90 percent of the world's international interbank dollar payments are made over CHIPS. A substantial share of these payments flows through the branches and agencies of foreign banks in New York. These offices account for about two-thirds of CHIPS' participants.

CHIPS has two classes of participants—settling banks and nonsettling banks—and operates as a net-net settlement system. About 110 nonsettling banks—mainly the U.S. branches and agencies of foreign banks—settle through accounts they maintain at about 20 other banks, which settle among themselves at the close of each business day. Of these 20 or so settling banks, 13 settle only for their own accounts. The others each settle for as few as 3 or as many as 26 nonsettling banks. Net-net settlement is effected when the settling banks make FedWire transfers to and from accounts at the Federal Reserve Bank of New York. Eleven members of the New York Clearing House—the founders of CHIPS—plus 10 regional and money center banks from other parts of the country with international banking offices in New York City, are the settling banks.

Exhibit 6.3 *Growth of CHIPS Transfers of Funds*

Year	Funds Transfer Transactions (in millions)	Amount (in trillions)	Number of Participating Institutions
1970	0.5	0.5	15
1975	6.0	11.0	63
1980	13.2	37.1	100
1985	24.9	78.0	142
1990	37.3	222.0	131

Source: *Report on the Payments System* (Association of Reserve City Bankers, 1982); *American Banker (various issues); The Clearinghouse Interbank Payments System* (Federal Reserve Bank of New York, 1991).

How CHIPS Works

For the most part, international dollar payments never leave the United States but are held as deposits at money center and regional banks or at U.S. branches of foreign banks. They are transferred among accounts through CHIPS in payment for internationally traded goods, services, financial transactions, or settlement of debt.

A typical CHIPS transfer works as follows. The New York branch of a Swiss bank that participates in CHIPS receives a cable from its head office. The cable requests a funds transfer (an international dollar payment) for a Swiss corporate customer to another CHIPS participant—the New York branch of a German bank—for the account of one of the German bank's customers. The New York branch of the Swiss bank tests the cable for authenticity, then codes and keys it into the CHIPS computer through its CHIPS terminal. The central CHIPS computer confirms the transfer request, sends back any standing instructions already in the computer, and makes appropriate entries in the computer files. The computer retains the message until the Swiss foreign bank branch that originated the transaction orders it to release the transfer.

At the foreign branch, a credit officer can release payment the same day, ideally after evaluating the credit line of the account for which the transfer is being made and the total of incoming transfer requests received against that account. When the credit officer authorizes release of the payment, the central computer sends the stored transaction data to the receiving bank's terminal, where details of the transaction are typed out automatically.

This store-and-forward, same-day capability of CHIPS allows banks to enter interbank funds transfer instructions early in the day, but make the credit evaluation later in the day, when more complete information may be available. Since the CHIPS central computer files are continuously updated as transactions occur, credit officers at banks participating in CHIPS can, in theory, access the computer to determine, at any time during the day, the amount of funds held in any one of their institution's customer accounts.

However, in practice, balance inquiries mean very little because the volume of CHIPS transactions is so large and the movement of transfers is so rapid that they become outdated within seconds.

Most CHIPS payments are released immediately upon entry into the system. It is only at the close of the day that participants' final credit or debit positions are known. At that time, the CHIPS computer correlates the transfers sent and received during the day, netting out debits and credits and printing a settlement report for each participant. Since most participants settle CHIPS transfers through one of the settling banks, it is only then that the settling banks themselves know their own positions.

From Next-Day Settlement to Same-Day Settlement. From its inception in 1970 as an electronic funds transfer system to 1981, CHIPS worked on a clearing house funds or next-day funds basis. That is, CHIPS participants settled payments and receipts made through CHIPS on the business day following the transfer. In 1981, CHIPS changed its operating procedures and became a same-day settlement system. That is, settlement is made through a special clearing account on the books of the New York Federal Reserve Bank at the end of the day on which payments are made. That change was directly related to the substantial credit exposure clearing house banks had been absorbing with the rapidly rising volume of CHIPS transfers in the late 1970s.

Clearing house banks had exposed themselves to increasing risk by accepting overnight and weekend CHIPS overdrafts for participants who settled CHIPS transfers on their books. New York banks often found themselves in situations where they were making CHIPS payments against expected receipts—in effect, extending credit to respondent banks or corporate customers that did not have sufficient funds in their accounts to cover the transfer at that time. Frequently, some respondents would be in a net debit or overdraft position at the end of the day. The settling banks would have to carry these respondents overnight, with the expectation that funds would be transferred to them early the next business day when settlement was due. Since CHIPS payments were not settled until the following day, overnight or weekend overdrafts were never posted on banks' books. In effect, the books remained open until settlement was made. However, the risk incurred was real; the settling bank could be liable for funds paid the day before. The amounts involved were sometimes greater than the banks' capital.

Same-Day Settlement Procedures. Under same-day settlement, CHIPS opens at 7:00 a.m. to store and send payments and cuts off third-party payments at 4:30 p.m. CHIPS provides net-net settlement information to participants by 4:35 p.m.; at 5:00 p.m. the CHIPS settlement process begins through FedWire. All debtor settling banks must settle with the Federal Reserve Bank of New York. Then, the Federal Reserve bank (through CHIPS) sends FedWire transfers to creditor settling banks. Once the Federal Reserve sends wire transfers, payments are final and irrevocable. FedWire closes for all settlement transfers at 6:00 p.m. By keeping FedWire open well after CHIPS closes for settlement purposes, banks have ample time to borrow to cover their deficit CHIPS positions or to transfer or invest surplus funds.

Society for Worldwide Interbank Financial Telecommunication (S.W.I.F.T.)

S.W.I.F.T. is an international financial message system, headquartered in Belgium and run by a consortium of commercial banks in Europe and the United States. It links approximately 2,900 participating financial institutions in 66 countries, including about 1,500 banks. Nearly 300 banks in the United States and several major American securities firms are participants. S.W.I.F.T. rules require that participants be involved in banking-related activities and in international financial message transmission. Brokers and dealers use S.W.I.F.T. to transfer titles to securities and to communicate payment instructions on securities trades. S.W.I.F.T. does not accept nonfinancial firms as members—only as customers of members.

The S.W.I.F.T. network operates on the same store-and-forward principle as CHIPS. Banks with terminals of various types and capacities can receive and send data to one another through S.W.I.F.T. and can enter transfer messages with the network, even if a recipient's terminal is busy. All terminals of S.W.I.F.T. participants are connected by store-and-forward concentrators. These minicomputers pass messages to and from participants through a central switching center in Amsterdam or Brussels, which electronically queues and routes the messages. All messages sent over S.W.I.F.T. are retained in switching center storage files for several days so that senders or receivers can, verify transactions. More than 1.2 million messages per day—primarily funds transfer advices—are sent over S.W.I.F.T. (See exhibit 6.4.)

U.S. banks connected to S.W.I.F.T. are the largest originators of messages, followed by banks in Germany, the United Kingdom, and Italy. Given the sharp growth in S.W.I.F.T. traffic, some U.S. bankers believe that S.W.I.F.T. could become a meaningful alternative to FedWire or CHIPS, if the system could develop a settlement capability.

Exhibit 6.4 *Growth of S.W.I.F.T. Transactions, 1977-1990*

Year	Transactions (in millions)	Members	Countries
1977	7.5	350	16
1981	65.0	900	39
1985	140.0	1,700	52
1990	300.0	2,900	66

Source: *Report on the Payments System* (Association of Reserve City Bankers, 1982); *American Banker*, January 24, 1990.

S.W.I.F.T. is a message system; settlement of payment messages is made by debits or credits to the accounts that participating banks maintain with one another.

S.W.I.F.T. does not have the means to consolidate or centralize transactions between participants so that each participant's net credit or net debit position in relation to the other can be determined. Transfers sent over S.W.I.F.T. must be settled through a bilateral exchange. A U.S. bank receiving a S.W.I.F.T. transfer request debits the sending bank's account and credits the beneficiary's account. For some receiving banks that are willing to accept a credit risk, beneficiaries are allowed to draw off these credits before settling with the sending bank later in the day. If the receiving bank has to transfer funds to another bank, it does so through FedWire or CHIPS.

Established in 1977, the S.W.I.F.T. network enabled banks to send payments-related instructions to one another internationally through standard message codes transmitted by computer over private leased telephone lines. These messages cost banks a fraction of what equivalent telex or cable messages would have cost at that time. S.W.I.F.T.'s initial processing capabilities—350,000 daily transactions—quickly became strained as S.W.I.F.T. message use soared. S.W.I.F.T. began work on a replacement telecommunications network in 1981, and in 1990 began testing new technology capable of handling an unlimited volume of daily messages.

Under S.W.I.F.T.'s new network, which is expected to be fully operational in 1992, banks will send S.W.I.F.T. messages over local telephone lines to regional processors. These units will transmit the messages to a central processing network for routing. The central network will comprise separate, but interrelated processors, each one able to send and receive S.W.I.F.T. messages even during a temporary power outage or mechanical malfunction.

S.W.I.F.T.'s new network is expected to be capable of providing electronic funds transfers and other services, such as electronic data interchange, which allows corporations to exchange trade documents in electronic form. Since the early 1980s, S.W.I.F.T. has been exploring with the Federal Reserve the possibility of establishing an electronic funds transfer system in the United States that would settle on a net-net basis against the Federal Reserve accounts of U.S. bank members in S.W.I.F.T.

Banker reactions to S.W.I.F.T.'s new network and expansion plans for the 1990s have been mixed. If S.W.I.F.T.'s new network and service offerings can attract substantial new business, S.W.I.F.T. transaction costs and prices could decline, generating savings for member banks. However, because it took S.W.I.F.T. almost 10 years to replace its initial telecommunications technology, there are doubts about S.W.I.F.T.'s ability to implement its expansion plans in a timely manner.

Other Interbank Networks

There are two major regional interbank EFT systems and two major foreign systems:

- ❖ The Chicago Clearing House Association owns and operates the Clearing House Electronic Settlement System (CHESS), which provides funds transfer service to banks in the Midwest. Funds transfers made over CHESS, like those made over CHIPS, are settled at the end of each day.

- ❖ The California Bankers Clearing House Association operates an electronic funds network for banks in the western states called PRESS—Pacific Regional Electronic Settlement System. This system also transfers funds that become good at day's end.

- ❖ In Canada, the Canadian Payments Association operates a net-net settlement system through the Bank of Canada (Canada's central bank).

- ❖ In England, the Clearing House Automated Payments System (CHAPS) acts as a settling network for a key group of U.K. clearing banks. CHAPS differs from the New York CHIPS in that U.K. clearing banks are required to guarantee every payment they accept, a feature of the system that limits settlement risk. However, CHAPS does not provide uniform access to its system. Access can be made only through a clearing bank, and each U.K. clearing bank has its own access procedures. CHAPS, established in 1983, has not grown as rapidly in transfer traffic as its U.S. counterparts. It was generating only 10,000 transactions per day in 1986.

England's major clearing banks also are in the process of establishing an electronic data interchange network for corporate customers. To do so, U.K. clearing banks agreed in 1991 to standardize their individual electronic message formats and data communications procedures to provide uniform access to the new system. About 4,000 British companies already use electronic data interchange for sending and receiving intercorporate payment instructions, such as those related to invoices and letters of credit.

U.K. banks see a means of increasing revenue and improving operating efficiency by producing electronic data interchange services. These electronic services will reduce paperwork, end mailing delays, and eliminate errors inherent in manually processing records and messages. Many industry analysts see electronic data interchange becoming a major global banking service in the 1990s.

Risk Issues and Concerns

Intraday Overdrafts

The past 20 years have seen an explosive increase in the speed at which banks move funds through interbank wire transfer systems and in the amount of funds moved. The dollar volume of EFT payments grew at more than 20 percent annually from 1970 through 1990—almost three times the rate of growth of U.S. national income and output. This growth can be traced, in part, to the high level and volatility of U.S. interest rates in the 1970s and early 1980s and to the growing opportunity cost for banks and corporations of keeping transaction account balances idle during that period. The increasing use of electronic cash management services also has been a factor.

As a result of this EFT growth, the number and dollar value of daylight (intraday) overdrafts in the interbank transfer systems increased sharply, until actions were taken in the late 1980s to limit them. (These terms refer to overdrawn positions of individual banks during the day, positions that must be cleared by close of business.) Intraday overdrafts occur because banks are generally unable to match their receipt of funds with their payments and because payment practices during the day frequently generate unbalanced positions. For example, an individual bank may wire payments early in the morning on behalf of a corporate account but not receive payments due the account until the end of the day. When banks borrow from one another, they typically repay overnight loans the following morning but do not receive new borrowed funds until the afternoon.

The dollar value of daylight overdrafts generated by a single bank on a given day frequently exceeds the bank's capital. In the early 1980s, daylight overdrafts incurred by about 1,700 of the nation's largest banks on some days totaled more than $100 billion. The magnitude of these sums caused the Federal Reserve and the nation's large banks to become increasingly concerned about risk exposure to bank users of the electronic systems and to the interbank EFT systems themselves. This concern led to new regulations in the late 1980s and forced bank management to give increased attention to improving operational controls and to weighing carefully the costs and benefits of using the interbank transfer systems.

Settlement Risk

The major concern of banks that use EFT to make payments is settlement risk—the risk that one or more banks will be unable to cover (settle) payments initiated on the various payments systems during the day. The Federal Reserve bears the settlement risk for FedWire payments. Notification of payment sent by a Reserve bank to a recipient bank is an irrevocable notice that immediately available funds have been credited to the recipient's account. However, settlement risk in CHIPS is different because CHIPS' net-net settlement does not transfer money assets between participants. At day's end, each bank is in a net debit or a net credit position with respect to every other bank.

Nonsettling banks send and receive payments but pay or receive only the net balance due from or to them through one of the settling banks. Settling banks receive net credits or pay net debits attributable to their own CHIPS activity, as well as the activity of their nonsettling respondents. These net credit or net debit postings are made to a CHIPS settlement account maintained at the Federal Reserve Bank of New York.

CHIPS settlement proceeds sequentially at the end of each day. First, CHIPS reports net positions to each participant for verification. Settling banks must then confirm that their nonsettling respondents in debit positions either have sufficient funds on hand or are able to borrow a sufficient amount to cover the debit—typically through prearranged overdraft credit from the settling bank. The settling banks then indicate to CHIPS their readiness to settle. Those in debit positions send the amount they owe, in the form of a FedWire transfer, from their reserve accounts to the CHIPS settlement account at the New York Reserve Bank. When all payments are received, the funds in the settlement account are dispersed via FedWire to reserve accounts of settling banks in credit positions.

Settlement risk in CHIPS refers to several kinds of failure-to-pay possibilities:

- ❖ the inability of a nonsettling participant to cover its debit position
- ❖ the inability of a settling bank to fund its account at the Federal Reserve Bank of New York (Until 1990, CHIPS rules covered this contingency by allowing payment transactions of the participant that was unable to settle to be deleted from the overall settlement.)
- ❖ settlement failure by another participant

    Because payments made via CHIPS are provisional until settlement is completed at the end of each day, participants that make payments during the day with CHIPS receipts are exposed to the risk that the receipts will not become final. Banks that use CHIPS receipts in this way are subject to both receiver and sender risk.

Receiver Risk

Banks that have received CHIPS payments for the account of a respondent bank or corporate customer incur risk if they allow respondents to use CHIPS provisional funds before settlement. For many CHIPS participants, granting customers immediate use of CHIPS funds has become a practical and competitive necessity, given the rapidity of CHIPS transfers. However, these banks risk that the customer whose account is effectively overdrawn will not be able to cover these receipts in good funds at the end of the day.

Until 1990, CHIPS Rule 13 permitted settling banks to refuse to settle a nonsettling participant's position if that participant did not provide good funds coverage. The entire settlement would then have been unwound (reversed). While there has never been a settlement failure in CHIPS, and Rule 13 was never invoked, computer simulations of a settlement reversal indicate that the practice would have entailed serious risks for some participants, doubtful success, and the risk of a serious crisis in international financial markets.

Sender Risk

CHIPS participants incur sender risk if they pay out funds on behalf of a customer that does not have good funds in its account sufficient to cover the payment. Cover usually arrives through one of four channels—a check, FedWire, a payment instruction through S.W.I.F.T. or CHIPS. Frequently, cover arrives through CHIPS because CHIPS participants requesting that funds be transferred out do so in anticipation of CHIPS transfers coming in. Often, cover arrives from a third party. If, however, the participant's customer does not cover the payment made, the participant is at risk. Under CHIPS rules, once a payment is made by a bank, the payment is irrevocable.

Systemic Risk

The interdependence of participants in CHIPS has caused concern over systemic risk—risk that the failure of one participant to settle would lead to a domino effect and the collapse of the network itself.

Multinational corporations, foreign banks, and domestic bank participants in CHIPS have come to expect instantaneous payment when transfers are effected through CHIPS, whether or not there is sufficient funds coverage for the payments. Invariably, cover arrives by settlement deadline in the form of a FedWire transfer. Given the rapidity and volume of CHIPS transfers, however, sending banks' payments often become cover for the payments made by other participants, which in turn provide cover for still other CHIPS payments. However, the failure of a major bank to supply cover could trigger a domino effect of defaults and failures and destroy the international interbank payments system.

Operational Vulnerabilities

The extensive interrelationship of FedWire and CHIPS with the internal systems of major banks exposes these banks to operational vulnerabilities. Operational vulnerability was demonstrated on November 21, 1985, when the nation's government securities market was disrupted by severe computer problems at the Bank of New York, the major clearing agent for dealer firms that buy and sell U.S. Treasury securities daily.

Bank of New York had received large quantities of securities in book-entry form over FedWire during the day. As is customary, payment was made by automatic debit to Bank of New York's reserve account at the Federal Reserve Bank of New York. Normally, Bank of New York would have routed these securities over FedWire to other banks and received payment. However, because of a computer malfunction, Bank of New York was unable to transfer securities and receive electronic payment from other banks. As a result, Bank of New York's debits built throughout the day, pushing it into an increasingly deeper intraday overdraft position with the Federal Reserve. As the dimensions of Bank of New York's computer problem became apparent, the Federal Reserve temporarily stopped accepting securities transfers for Bank of New York's account. This stoppage caused other market participants to stop transferring securities among themselves. Other large clearing banks feared that they, too, would be plunged into overdraft, because they could not send securities to, or receive payment from, the largest clearing bank in the securities market. Faced with no option, the Federal Reserve resumed acceptance of securities transfers for Bank of New York's account and provided it with a record $22.6 billion overnight loan to cover its overdraft position.

The Federal Reserve's decision to fund Bank of New York overnight—as opposed to cutting off the bank from the FedWire system—was designed to ensure the integrity and efficiency of the nation's electronic payments system. In accomplishing that objective, the Federal Reserve's action taught bankers and regulators some important lessons about the nature of systemic risk as it relates to operational vulnerability, as well as some possible solutions.

For one, it showed that disconnecting a major participant from the FedWire system, without closing the entire system, runs the risk of generalized disruptions in the market. It also showed that electronic payments systems must be kept functioning so that settlement can be made at the end of the day. The structure of banks' internal payment and customer accounting systems requires that banks' books be closed at some point near the end of the day to allow time for accounting, reconciliation, report preparation, and delivery of account statements before the opening of business the next day. Failure to do end-of-day processing because electronic transfers have been halted or settlement postponed entails the risk of more generalized problems the next day.

The Bank of New York computer incident also underscored the efforts of banks and the Federal Reserve to ensure the operational safety and integrity of the electronic funds transfer systems. Banks using CHIPS or FedWire are required to establish back-up computer capabilities to protect themselves, and other participants, against operational problems that would prevent the receipt or payment of electronic funds. The electronic environment in banking is so interrelated that even small operational disruptions unique to one key participant can have widespread effects throughout the banking system.

CHIPS maintains a back-up computer center in New Jersey that is capable of processing CHIPS transactions within 10 minutes of a disruption to its primary and secondary New York computers. The Federal Reserve Bank of New York also operates a back-up computer contingency center in upstate New York that is also capable of processing FedWire transactions within minutes of a computer or power disruption in New York City. Both back-up centers draw on different sources of electrical power than those supplying New York City.

The need for such back-up processing was clearly demonstrated in August 1990 when an electrical utility fire in New York City blacked out most of downtown Manhattan for one week. The power outage affected several major CHIPS and FedWire participants and the New York Reserve Bank and, because of its length, strained the capabilities of the diesel power systems that these participants were using for local computer-processing backup. However, CHIPS itself was not blacked out nor was New York's connection to FedWire. The Federal Reserve Bank of New York switched its funds transfer processing operations from local diesel power backup to its upstate contingency center with no disruption to domestic or international payments.

In 1986, the Federal Reserve imposed a two-percentage-point penalty charge above the discount rate when banks are forced to borrow an exceptionally large amount from the Federal Reserve overnight because of an operating or computer problem. This was done to encourage banks to strengthen their own internal systems so they can avoid major operational problems.

Regulatory Response to Risk

Concern over intraday overdraft risk prompted the Federal Reserve in the early 1980s to begin counseling banks that consistently incurred large intraday overdrafts. Given the number of FedWire users and the daily volume of FedWire transfer traffic, Reserve banks are able to monitor the FedWire positions of only a relatively few banks on a real time (moment-by-moment), online basis. For most banks, intraday overdrafts incurred on FedWire can be detected only after account postings are examined at the end of the day. By contrast, because of their narrower user base, most CHIPS settling banks can monitor intraday overdrafts of nonsettling respondent accounts in real time.

The Federal Reserve encouraged CHIPS to implement a series of measures designed to reduce risks to participants, including

❖ bilateral credit limits—1984

❖ net debit caps—1986

❖ an arrangement for loss sharing with collateral backing to cover settlement failures—1990

Bilateral Credit Limits

CHIPS limited the net amount of payments one participant would accept from another by requiring each bank in the CHIPS network to set a bilateral credit limit for every other bank from which it might receive payments. Such limits restrict the amount that a bank pays out to each participant to a sum not to exceed payments made by the participant to the bank. CHIPS payments that might exceed any of its bilateral limits are generally blocked automatically by the sophisticated systems maintained by the money center banks.

Under CHIPS' rules, each participant must provide CHIPS with a list of its bilateral credit limits. However, participants can reduce or increase these limits at any time during the day and are free to enter into any private agreements to further limit risk or to accommodate another participant's payment needs. For example, some banks require collateral or compensating balances to obtain a higher limit from CHIPS participants considered to be risky. Other banks typically set zero limits for participants that would not be expected to make frequent multibillion dollar payments.

Net Debit Caps

Net debit caps were instituted to limit each participant's net debit position in CHIPS. The caps limit the risk exposure of all CHIPS participants collectively to any single participant and improve CHIPS' ability to settle at the end of the day. The caps are based on the bilateral credit limits set by each participant for all other participants. The net debit limit for any CHIPS member is set at 5 percent of the sum of all the bilateral credit limits extended to it by other CHIPS participants.

Net debit caps for each participant are set by CHIPS each morning at 7:00 a.m. In theory, this daily flexibility allows participants to react promptly to new risk assessments of other participants. That is, if they perceive that dealing with any other participant has become riskier they can lower their bilateral limits and in doing so reduce the next day's net debit cap for that CHIPS member. Most participants tend to keep their bilateral limits low, raise them during the day to facilitate payments, then reduce them to the starting limit later in the day.

CHIPS computers monitor all transactions against caps and bilateral limits on a real time basis. If a payment is sent that would exceed either of these limits, the transfer is blocked by the computer and stored until net positions change sufficiently to permit the payment to be made without violating the limits.

Loss Sharing and Collateral for Settlement Failures

To improve the finality (irrevocability) of CHIPS' settlement, CHIPS rules were revised to establish a procedure for completing settlement even if one or more participants fail to settle at the end of the day. The 1990s' revised rules state the following:

- ❖ Each CHIPS participant must enter into a loss-sharing agreement with CHIPS under which it pledges to provide a portion of the funds necessary to complete CHIPS settlement if one or more CHIPS participants fail to settle.

- ❖ Each participant is required to provide U.S. Treasury securities as collateral under the loss-sharing agreement. The amount is equal to 5 percent of the highest bilateral limit granted by the participant to any other CHIPS member and is held in a CHIPS collateral account at the Federal Reserve Bank of New York. In 1991, participants had deposited more than $3 billion in CHIPS collateral.

- ❖ If a CHIPS participant cannot settle its payments at the end of the day, banks must follow certain procedures. If a bank cannot cover its net debit position, it has one hour to arrange with a settling bank to cover for it. If such an arrangement can be made, CHIPS revises the day's settlement report accordingly and settles all outstanding debit and credit positions. If, however, the bank cannot find a participant that will cover for it, the bank is treated as a failed participant and its CHIPS net debit position is divided into pro-rata shares and allocated to each remaining participant. These shares, called additional settlement obligations, represent the amount each participant is obligated to pay to cover the failed participant. These payments are in addition to any net debit positions participants themselves may have to cover for their own settlement. However, in no case can a participant's additional settlement obligation be higher than 5 percent of its maximum bilateral credit limit. If a CHIPS participant cannot honor its additional settlement obligation, the New York Clearinghouse can authorize the participant's settling bank to sell the U.S. Treasury securities collateral it is required to hold at the Federal Reserve Bank of New York as part of the loss-sharing arrangement.

- ❖ In the case of several failed participants, a formula is used to allocate losses. However, the total additional settlement obligations of each remaining participant cannot exceed 5 percent of its maximum bilateral credit limit or the highest bilateral credit limit extended by the participant to the failed institutions.

Overdraft Caps

In 1986, the Federal Reserve and the nation's large money center banks adopted a program to control intraday overdrafts that built on the system of daylight overdraft limits that CHIPS participants had established among themselves. The Federal Reserve issued regulations that limit or cap daylight overdrafts to a multiple of a bank's capital. Initially, each bank's cap applied to the sum of overdrafts it could incur on FedWire and all other funds transfer systems. This consolidated cap was in addition to the existing caps that CHIPS imposed on its participants. (In 1991, the Federal Reserve removed CHIPS overdrafts from the consolidated cap because CHIPS had established settlement finality with its loss-sharing and collateral arrangement for CHIPS settlement failures.) Under the caps, banks must keep track of the intraday overdrafts they incur over all the funds transfer systems they use.

To adhere to the Federal Reserve's regulations, banks are required to rate their own creditworthiness, credit policies, and operational controls in relation to industry standards and to their peers. The banks must then combine their ratings in these three categories to determine an overall daylight overdraft limit—called a cross-system, sender net-debit cap. The cap is set at a multiple of the bank's capital. The banks with the highest ratings are allowed to generate overdrafts up to 2.25 times their capital on a single day and up to 1.5 times their capital when the daily maximums are averaged over a two-week period. Lower-rated banks are subject to smaller caps. Banks that rate themselves as unsatisfactory in any of the three categories and banks that choose not to rate themselves at all cannot incur any intraday overdrafts. The Board of Directors for each bank must approve the self-evaluation before it can be submitted to the Federal Reserve. It is also subject to review by bank examiners.

Self-Evaluation Criteria. In determining their permissible overdraft ratings, banks are required to use criteria established by the Federal Reserve. Credit policies can be rated satisfactory or unsatisfactory; operational controls can be judged strong, satisfactory, or unsatisfactory; and creditworthiness can be rated excellent, very good, adequate, or below standard. Each bank computes its overall rating using the table in exhibit 6.5.

Exhibit 6.5 *Overdraft Ratings*

Credit Policies	Operational Controls	Creditworthiness	Overall Rating
Satisfactory	Strong	Excellent	High cap
Satisfactory	Strong	Very Good	Above-average cap
Satisfactory	Strong	Adequate	Average cap
Satisfactory	Strong	Below standard	Limited cap
Satisfactory	Satisfactory	Excellent	Above-average cap
Satisfactory	Satisfactory	Very good	Above-average cap
Satisfactory	Satisfactory	Adequate	Average cap
Satisfactory	Satisfactory	Below standard	Limited cap
Satisfactory	Unsatisfactory	Any rating	No cap
Unsatisfactory	Any rating	Any rating	No cap

In determining a rating for operational controls, a bank must take two factors into consideration:

- ❖ the bank's ability to monitor its net funds transfer position across all the electronic systems it uses
- ❖ the bank's ability to monitor individual customers

To receive the highest rating (strong) in the operational controls category, a bank must be able to monitor the position of 95 percent of the dollar volume of all its wire transfers every 15 minutes. It must also be able to monitor the net position of all significant customer credits and debits, including those for cash and checks, every 15 minutes.

The overall rating determines the acceptable level of daylight overdrafts a bank can incur, as measured by multiples of the bank's primary capital. Exhibit 6.6 outlines the various caps permissible in 1991.

For example, if a bank with primary capital of $800 million gives itself an above average rating, it would be permitted to go into overdraft up to $1.5 billion on any single day. However, it could not exceed an average daily overdraft of $900 million over two weeks.

The nation's largest banks are the biggest users of electronic funds transfers and run the largest overdrafts. The Federal Reserve's cap program was designed with these banks in mind. About 2,200 of the nation's 30,000 depository institutions filed caps with the Federal Reserve in 1986 when the Federal Reserve initiated its overdraft control program—about 1,900 commercial banks, 180 thrift institutions, and 100 branches and agencies of foreign banks. These institutions accounted for about 45 percent of all overdrafts in 1986. About 3,000 other banks, most of them small, accounted for the remainder of intraday overdrafts. By not submitting a cap to the Federal Reserve, these banks opted not to incur any further overdrafts.

Exhibit 6.6 *Daylight Overdraft Caps*

Cap Category	Single-Day Cap	2-Week-Average Cap
High cap	2.25 x capital	1.5 x capital
Above-average cap	1.875 x capital	1.125 x capital
Average cap	1.125 x capital	0.75 x capital
Limited cap	0.375 x capital	0.375 x capital

Reaction to Overdraft Caps

Bankers and corporate treasurers were concerned that the overdraft caps and controls would limit both bank and corporate abilities to transfer funds. They were also concerned that banks would delay executing payments to stay under their daylight overdraft limits. However, the caps established in 1986 were set with sufficiently high ceilings to avoid any impairment to the speed or efficiency of the bank-to-bank payments systems. In addition, electronic transactions involving U.S. government securities, which account for nearly 60 percent of all FedWire overdrafts, were excluded from the initial overdraft caps.

The overdraft caps generated little adverse impact on banks' processing operations. Some banks experienced short processing delays that were not perceptible to corporate customers. Individual wire transfer payments experienced few delays.

Before the cap program was introduced in March 1986, daily overdrafts averaged about $80 billion. Shortly after the program was instituted, overdrafts fell by about 10 percent, to $70 billion per day. Toward year-end, however, overdrafts soared to new highs, prompting concerns within the Federal Reserve that the caps may have been set too high and that some banks might have misused the cap program by increasing their overdrafts up to the cap.

The Federal Reserve had initially intended to reduce the caps over time, until almost all intraday overdrafting was eliminated from the bank-to-bank payments systems. However, the increase in overdrafts in late 1986 prompted the Federal Reserve to reduce the caps by 25 percent in 1987 to current levels and to rethink its overall approach to risk reduction.

Modifying the Overdraft Cap Program

The Federal Reserve had initially excluded book-entry securities overdrafts from the caps because of concern that the government securities market might be impaired if banks limited their own government securities purchases or those made for major customers. These concerns were heightened by the recognition that four large New York banks—Bank of New York, Manufacturers Hanover, Irving Trust, and Marine Midland—clear more than half the government securities transactions made in the nation each day, and these banks alone account for two-thirds of the book-entry overdrafts made on FedWire.

These concerns lessened by the late 1980s, as banks and corporations adjusted to the caps. Overdrafts, however, were still increasing, and in 1988, the Federal Reserve imposed a $50 million limit on the size of securities transfers it would accept on FedWire. This was an interim measure to reduce book-entry transactions risk and, in 1991, the Fed brought book-entry intraday overdrafts under the cap program.

To control risk without reducing the liquidity or efficiency of the government securities market, the Federal Reserve established a collateral requirement: banks that exceed their caps frequently and substantially because of book-entry overdrafts must post collateral. Other banks can post collateral voluntarily if they want to expand their funds and securities transfer capabilities. This expansion is possible because the Federal Reserve excludes book-entry overdrafts from these banks' consolidated caps.

The Federal Reserve's requirement that collateral be posted to cover payments risk was not new. U.S. branches and agencies of foreign banks that use FedWire have long been required to maintain collateral against FedWire overdrafts. For many foreign banks, the volume of payments they make on FedWire and CHIPS through their U.S. branches exceeds by several times the level of their U.S. branch assets and their capacity to borrow funds in the United States. Because most foreign banks' assets and liabilities are located overseas, these assets are not subject to American legal claims. The Federal Reserve's collateral requirement recognizes the special payments risks associated with these institutions.

The Federal Reserve made one other modification to its cap program in the 1980s. In 1987, it exempted banks that incur small and infrequent overdrafts on the FedWire from having to undergo the self-evaluation procedures necessary to establish a cap limit. These banks are permitted to incur FedWire overdrafts up to 20 percent of their capital or $10 million, whichever sum is less. The exception recognized the disproportionate costs small banks would have to bear to complete the self-evaluation relative to the insubstantial overdrafts they might occasionally incur.

The overdraft caps were successful in containing payments risks in the late 1980s, but not in reducing them. The dollar amount of daily overdrafts on the interbank funds transfer systems continue to increase—to approximately $140 billion in 1992.

Approaches to Reducing Risk in the 1990s

The Federal Reserve has proposed that banks be required to pay interest for intraday credit on FedWire beginning in 1992. Under this plan, banks would be assessed an interest charge of one quarter of one percent per annum on daily intraday FedWire overdrafts that exceed 10 percent of their capital. Such charges, the Fed contends, would motivate FedWire participants to alter their payments practices reducing their daylight overdrafts.

The issue of charging for intraday overdrafts has divided industry analysts. Some have expressed concerns that these charges could shift payments to CHIPS and other private systems, which would reduce the Federal Reserve's exposure to risk but increase systemic risk on private systems. Other analysts contend that the Federal Reserve's proposed quarter point interest charge will not be high enough to deter overdrafting. However, many analysts maintain that the Fed's overdraft credit charges will reduce risk by inducing banks to charge corporate customers for intraday overdraft credit, develop an hourly intraday trading market for federal funds, and establish more extensive interbank payment netting arrangements.

Industry surveys indicate that about 40 percent of the nation's large banks are already considering charging customers for intraday overdrafts. However, banking analysts believe that most banks lack the technical expertise to track overdrafts accurately on a minute-by-minute basis and that they lack the technical systems to post incoming wire transfers directly to corporate accounts. Without these internal capabilities, banks would find it difficult to determine and charge for daylight overdrafts. Analysts further contend that banks' reliance on manual processing for assessing overdrafts and overdraft charges would prove unworkable. Because of the time lags involved in posting transactions manually, a corporate account could appear to be in an overdraft position when in fact the bank has not yet posted an incoming credit. Many corporate cash managers contend that if banks begin to charge for daylight overdrafts, competition will force the banks to begin providing corporate accounts with some form of compensation on the intraday funds that corporations keep on deposit in excess of stipulated amounts.

Netting is considered a highly promising approach for reducing payments risk in the 1990s. Under current market practice, if two banks owe one another money, they make separate payments to each other on FedWire or CHIPS. If, however, the two banks netted the payments and transferred only the difference between the two payment obligations, funds transfer volume—and the potential for intraday overdrafts—would be reduced. Industry analysts estimate that broader use of netting in the 1990s could reduce electronic payments system volume by as much as 40 percent and could reduce FedWire overdrafts by as much as 85 percent.

Netting has specific applicability to foreign exchange, federal funds, government securities, and Eurodollar placement transactions—transactions that dominate traffic on CHIPS and FedWire.

Risk and cost considerations have prompted a number of major clearing and settlement networks to begin converting the systems they now use to deliver paper instruments for settlement to electronic systems capable of settlement on a net basis. The Participants Trust Company's mortgage-backed securities clearing system and the Depository Trust Company's commercial paper clearing system are currently undergoing conversions to systems that will provide end-of-day net settlement either directly or indirectly over FedWire. Other examples of existing and proposed netting arrangements are the Government Securities Clearing Corporation for U.S. Treasury and federal agency securities, and FXNET and the Options Clearing Corporation for foreign exchange.

Netting systems, however, are not without payments-related risk. For example, in a net settlement system such as CHIPS, creditors of a failed bank might try to repudiate the bank's netting obligation on the day of the failure and refuse to honor the payment orders sent by the insolvent bank during the day, while keeping all funds sent to it. Although the likelihood of such a repudiation is small, if one occurred in CHIPS or any other major netting system, the flow of domestic and global payments could be seriously disrupted. To prevent such an occurrence, the New York Clearinghouse proposed in 1991 that a federal law be passed to make netting on CHIPS and other payments systems legally binding.

Many of the nation's branch banks have instituted procedures to prevent intraday overdrafts. They channel FedWire payments through one office of their multibranch system, where payments and receipts can be monitored more effectively. Other banks have switched from online to off-line access to FedWire to give management greater control over payments flows. Still other banks have focused on ways to change their funding practices and alter the way their payments flows are structured to stay within their overdraft limits.

The use of continuing payment contracts is beginning to emerge as a significant risk reduction practice. Banks have been switching from overnight borrowing from other banks—funds are returned each morning—to continuing contract arrangements (funds are returned only when no new amounts are needed). Under a continuing payment contract, banks that buy federal funds from the same bank every day do not pay and reborrow the funds daily. Instead, the federal funds contract is automatically renewed each morning. By not transferring funds back and forth on a daily basis, the potential for FedWire overdrafts is substantially reduced.

The Federal Reserve's daylight overdraft guidelines have required many banks to alter their procedures, particularly medium-sized regional banks that cannot monitor customers' transaction activity on an online, real time basis. (Most, of the nation's large money center banks have that capability.) These procedural changes have involved tighter management of corporate cash-management products and services and a delay in sending payments upon request so that the bank can determine the available funds on account. The Federal Reserve has proposed that banks be required to make more systematic procedural changes in the way they post credit and debit entries—to post ACH debits late in the day, rather than at the opening of the day as is done now, and to post checks in stages throughout the day. The Federal Reserve contends that these changes would reduce the potential for intraday overdrafts by assuring a more even pattern to the credits and debits flowing in and out of bank accounts throughout the day.

The Outlook for the Interbank Funds Transfer Systems

Over the past 20 years, large banks that handle a substantial daily volume of electronic transfers have had to commit significant and costly resources to maintain separate lines to FedWire, CHIPS, and S.W.I.F.T., as well as to regional systems. Many of the nation's money center banks also have internal telecommunications systems for their corporate accounts to support their cash management services, which have required further commitment of resources. These multiple links have magnified the potential for funds transfer routing and posting errors, and for transmission delays. This is largely because each of the bank-to-bank funds transfer or message systems has its own linkage arrangements, security protocols, message formats, account identification schemes, and operating hours. Many bankers believe that standardizing EFT payment procedures and practices would increase bank operating efficiency and reduce operating costs, often citing the handling of two-party payments over FedWire as an example.

When a bank sends a two-party payment over FedWire, it must enter instructions in the payment message that identify the sending and receiving banks and the amount being transferred. Banks have agreed to provide this information in a standardized way, so that two-party payments between banks can be processed quickly and automatically.

However, when a third-party payment is made, a bank must send additional payment instructions, indicating the receiving customer's account number and purpose of the payment. Although the American Bankers Association developed an industry standard in 1982 for the format in which to provide this information, few banks adhered to the standard. Only 10 percent or so of each day's third-party FedWire transfers in the 1980s followed the standard. This meant that banks receiving third-party payments generally had to post (credit) funds to customer accounts manually, which was time consuming, error prone, and costly.

In 1986, the banking industry endorsed a Federal Reserve proposal to mandate the use of the ABA's third-party format standard for FedWire payments. In 1990, use of the format became mandatory; the Federal Reserve automatically rejects messages that do not conform to the standard. Banking industry analysts expect that widespread use of the standard in the 1990s will reduce banks' costs and payment-processing errors by automatically crediting incoming wires to customer accounts. Other joint Federal Reserve-banking industry efforts to develop additional industrywide EFT standards are under consideration, such as standards for authenticating messages.

Looking ahead to the next decade, most bankers see bank-to-bank transfer systems as increasingly changing the way even the smallest banks operate. If the trends of the 1990s continue, costs will likely decline and greater reliance on computers will broaden opportunities for even the smallest banks, so that they can link into the bank-to-bank transfer systems and expand their services to both corporate and individual customers. Those transfer systems and expanded services are likely to encompass the buying and selling of federal funds for hourly increments—and hourly interest charges. To do so, however, the data-processing capabilities of commercial banks and Reserve banks will have to be substantially upgraded to permit storage, tracking, and pricing of funds sent and received at specified times within a 24-hour banking day. Developing the necessary computer systems and software for such intraday funds trading will take time.

Global electronic funds networks that provide 24-hour access to funds and investment markets are likely to include expanded transactions services that are now paper-based, such as bankers' acceptances and repurchase agreements.

Summary

Banks rely extensively on two interbank EFT systems—FedWire and CHIPS—when they pay one another. These systems also allow banks to provide large corporate accounts with deposit concentration and investment services. Payments made over FedWire are in final (collected) funds; payments made over CHIPS are in provisional funds that are not good until settlement is made at the end of the day.

The sharp increase in the number of transactions made each day over the interbank systems, and the dollar value of the transfers involved, have raised concerns among bankers and regulators over risks banks incur in the electronic payments mechanism. For example, some banks transfer out more funds from certain accounts during the day than they take in for those accounts, incurring intraday overdrafts. Banks that use CHIPS provisional funds during the day to make payments to others are exposed to the risk that the funds will not become good because of a settlement failure by another bank. Such a settlement failure could result in a domino effect—a series of settlement failures and collapse of the CHIPS system. FedWire's extensive interrelationship with the internal computer systems of major banks has caused concerns over its operational vulnerability.

To reduce risk in the interbank EFT systems, banks have adopted a Federal Reserve program setting daylight overdraft limits for all of their EFT customers and establishing a limit on the maximum net overdraft the banks can generate on the interbank systems. This program has helped contain intraday overdrafts and is likely to significantly change interbank payments practices.

Questions

1. What benefits do banks and corporate treasurers obtain by using EFT instead of checks when dealing with one another?

2. What are the key characteristics that differentiate the FedWire, CHIPS, and S.W.I.F.T. interbank systems?

3. Explain the difference between sender, receiver, and systemic risk in the interbank EFT systems.

4. Outline the key features of the program the Federal Reserve instituted in 1986 to reduce intraday overdrafts.

Endnotes

1. The New York Clearing House Association comprises the following twelve banks: Bank of New York, Bankers Trust, Chase, Chemical, Citibank, European American, Manufacturers Hanover, Marine Midland, Morgan Guaranty, National Westminster Bank USA, Republic National Bank, and U.S. Trust Co. (U.S.Trust is not a participant in CHIPS.)

DEPOSIT
CREATION

Objectives

After successfully completing this chapter, you will be able to

- ❖ discuss how banks create deposits

- ❖ explain the Federal Reserve's reserve requirements, discount rate, and open market operations and how they work

- ❖ identify the Treasury and public banking activities that supply or absorb bank reserves

Introduction

Banks create demand deposits by a multiple expansion process that the Federal Reserve attempts to control through three mechanisms: reserve requirement rules, the discount rate, and open market operations. In addition, the U.S. Treasury and the banking activities of the American public play a role in influencing the creation of demand deposits.

How Banks Multiply Deposits

Commercial banks create deposits when they make loans. When a bank makes a loan, it essentially monetizes a debt—that is, it accepts as an asset the debt obligation of the borrower and creates a liability on its books in the form of a demand deposit balance in the loan amount.

Loan assets are typically collateralized, either by property or other financial assets of the borrower, or by the borrower's income-earning capacity. Collateral gives the lending bank a legal claim to something of value equal—at least—to the loan amount.[1] Thus the deposits banks create when they make loans are backed by financial or property assets that collateralize the promissory note or loan agreement.

To show how deposit creation works in the banking system, this chapter will trace the T account of a single loan, following the loan as it is made and as it multiplies within the banking system. T accounts are abstracts of a bank's balance sheet, showing only the changes in a bank's assets and liabilities. For purposes of illustration only, assume that

- ❖ all of the deposits created by banks stay in the banking system
- ❖ demand deposits are the only form in which newly created funds are held
- ❖ banks lend out every available dollar

Assume that Bank A receives a cash deposit of $10,000 from a customer for credit to his or her transaction account. Under the Fed's reserve requirements, the bank must hold an amount of reserves, either vault cash or deposit balances at a Reserve bank, equal to a fixed percentage of its deposits—in this example, 10 percent.

Thus, Bank A must hold $1,000 in required reserves against its new $10,000 deposit; this leaves $9,000 in excess reserves. (See Bank A's T account before the loan.) These excess reserves can then support a new $9,000 loan. In other words, $9,000 in demand deposits can be created. (See Bank A's T account after the loan.)

Bank A
(Before the Loan)

Assets		Liabilities	
Cash assets	$10,000*	Demand deposit	$10,000
*Required reserves	$ 1,000		
Excess reserves	$ 9,000		

Bank A
(After the Loan)

Assets		Liabilities	
Cash assets	$10,000*	Demand deposit	$10,000
New loan	$ 9,000	Demand deposit	$ 9,000
		(Created for borrower)	
*Required reserves	$ 1,000		
Excess reserves	$ 9,000		

When Bank A makes the loan, its assets and its liabilities will temporarily increase to $19,000, reflecting the addition of the loan to its earning assets portfolio and the addition of the newly created demand deposit to its total liabilities. However, as soon as the borrower uses the newly created funds, Bank A's assets and liabilities will decline to their preloan level.

Assume the borrower gives the proceeds of the loan, in the form of a check payment, to a manufacturing company that has an account at Bank B. When the borrower's $9,000 check clears, Bank A will have to transfer $9,000 of its cash assets in payment for the check to Bank B, the presenting bank. Upon payment, Bank A will strike from its books the $9,000 demand deposit liability carried for the borrower.

Thus, after check clearance, Bank A has $10,000 in assets and $10,000 in liabilities. However, the composition of its assets has changed. Before the loan, it had $10,000 in cash assets; now it has $1,000 in cash assets and $9,000 in loan assets. The $1,000 in cash assets meets the 10 percent reserve requirement ratio against transaction account liabilities.

	Bank A (After Check Collection)		Bank B (Before the Loan)
Assets	Liabilities	Assets	Liabilities
Cash assets	Demand deposit	Cash Assets*	Demand deposit
$1,000	$10,000	$9,000	$9,000
Loan			
$9,000			
		*Required reserves $ 900	
		Excess reserves $ 8,100	

The $9,000 in deposit dollars created by Bank A now resides as a deposit on the books of Bank B, increasing that bank's liabilities. However, because of that deposit, Bank B also received a transfer of $9,000 in cash assets when it received payment for the check deposited by the manufacturing company. Bank B is subject to the same 10 percent reserve requirement as Bank A, so it must keep $900 against that deposit, but it can use the remaining $8,100 to support a new loan and the creation of a new $8,100 deposit.

When Bank B makes the loan, its assets and liabilities will increase initially, then decline to their preloan level when the borrower's check is collected. Assume that the borrower used that check to pay for a corporate service, and the corporation deposits the check in Bank C. Bank B's newly created $8,100 will now reside in Bank C, together with $8,100 in cash assets Bank B transferred to pay for the check.

Bank C will be able to create demand deposits equal to 90 percent of its new cash assets. If it does so, it will give still another bank the ability to create new deposits.

	Bank B (After the Loan and Check Collection)		Bank C (Before the Loan)
Assets	Liabilities	Assets	Liabilities
Cash assets	Demand deposit	Cash assets*	Demand deposit
$ 900	$9,000	$8,100	$8,100
Loan			
$8,100			
		*Required reserves $ 810	
		Excess reserves $7,290	

In theory, this process of deposit creation can continue through thousands of banks and generate, in this example, a total amount of deposits 10 times greater than the $10,000 that started the process. The total amount of deposits generated can be calculated by taking the reciprocal (the multiplier or expansion coefficient) of the reserve requirement. In this example, because the reserve requirement is 10 percent, the multiplier is 10. In reality, the reserve requirement is tiered, with different percentages applying to different amounts of liabilities. Thus, this simple multiplier is valid only in the context of this example. (See exhibit 7.1.)

$$\frac{100}{10}$$

Exhibit 7.1 *Multiple Expansion of Bank Deposits in the Banking System (10 percent reserve requirement)*

Position of Bank	New Deposits	New Loans and Investments	Reserves
Bank A	$ 10,000	$ 9,000	$1,000
Bank B	9,000	8,100	900
Bank C	8,100	7,290	810
Bank D	7,290	6,561	729
Bank E	6,561	5,904	656
Bank F	5,904	5,314	590
Bank G	5,314	4,783	531
Bank H	4,783	4,305	478
Bank I	4,305	3,874	430
Bank J	3,874	3,487	387
Sum of first 10 banks' deposit expansion[a]	$65,131	$58,618	$6,511
Sum of remaining banks' deposit expansion[a]	34,869	31,382	3,489
Total for banking system as a whole	$100,000 (Multiple Expansion)	$90,000 (Net Creation)	$10,000 (Original Deposit)

Multiple Expansion=10 Times Reserves

a. Summations inexact due to rounding.

Deposit Creation

This multiple expansion of bank-created deposits is characteristic of banking systems as a whole, but not of individual banks. No bank can create deposits in any amount greater than its excess reserves because those reserves would be insufficient as soon as the borrower's check cleared.

The multiple creation of deposits by the banking system is constantly modified by such factors as deposits flowing in and out of banks, funds moving from checking to savings accounts, and check cashing. Thus, it is difficult to determine how many deposits are being created by each bank. However, it is known that changes in the amount of reserves available to all banks lead to multiple changes in bank deposits.

The Federal Reserve's Impact on Deposit Creation

The pace at which banks can make loans, thereby creating demand deposits, is dependent on their reserves.[2] All banking is based on the principle of fractional reserves: a portion of a bank's assets must be kept in liquid form to meet demand depositors' withdrawals or depositors' checks presented for collection by other banks. Cash assets above this amount can be used to support new loans. The establishment of reserve requirements by central banks as a tool to control the money supply is based on this fundamental banking principle.

To a bank, reserves are its raw material. The more reserves it has, the greater its potential for making new loans and investments. The fewer reserves it has or, more precisely, the closer its reserves are to its liquidity margin or to its legal reserve requirements, the smaller its potential for expanding earnings. To the Fed, reserves are the means by which it controls the money supply and achieves national economic objectives.

The Federal Reserve's presence in the nation's payments mechanism and its rules and regulations as a bank supervisory agency establish the framework within which banks must operate. But the Federal Reserve's monetary policy actions, particularly those affecting reserves, determine the costs and profit potential of those operations.

Competing Goals of Commercial Banks and the Federal Reserve

The primary goal of commercial banks is to maximize profits, either by increasing the percentage return on earning assets or by capturing a larger share of the financial market. The Federal Reserve, while a profitable institution, is motivated by national goals. At times, the goals of commercial banks and the Federal Reserve coincide, and each will act to support the other.

For example, in a recession, the Federal Reserve will typically act to stimulate bank lending in the hope of sparking business and consumer spending. The Fed will buy government securities through its open market operations, an action that increases the amount of reserves in the banking system. This provides plentiful reserves to banks for expanding their loans and investments, and also provides banks with greater earnings potential. Declining interest rates, which frequently occur when loan demand is low, also tend to increase the value of securities that banks hold.

During a period of inflation, however, Federal Reserve policy may directly conflict with banks' goals. To counter inflation, the Fed will typically attempt to hold back reserves by selling government securities or slowing down its rate of purchases. When demand for bank loans is strong, interest rates rise. Banks are likely to view restraints on reserves as reducing their earnings prospects because they can no longer meet all customer loan demands, and the costs of doing business have increased. Furthermore, rising interest rates generate losses on securities that were purchased when rates were lower.

The Fed's monetary policy goal is to ensure that deposits created by the banking system are appropriate for the needs of the economy. While the Federal Reserve's focus in bank regulation and supervision may sometimes fall on individual banks, its focus in monetary policy is on the entire banking system. In implementing monetary policy, the Federal Reserve allows all banks to compete freely against one another and with other markets for deposits and loans and, most important, for the reserves that provide banks with the means to achieve their goals.

Reserve Rules

To the Federal Reserve, reserve requirements are a control device. Banks' deposit creation is directly keyed to reserve requirements. To meet reserve requirements, Federal Reserve member banks must hold reserves either as vault cash or as a deposit with the district Federal Reserve bank.

Nonmember banks must do the same or place their reserves in a pass-through deposit at a correspondent bank, which must redeposit the reserves at the Reserve bank. These reserves must equal specified percentages of certain deposit liabilities, which the Federal Reserve also determines. (See exhibit 7.2.) Banks can hold more than the required amount of reserves, but they may not hold less.

To banks, reserve requirements are a business cost. Banks incur opportunity cost (through lost earnings potential) because the reserve funds they are required to set aside—vault cash or a deposit at the Reserve bank—do not earn them an interest return.

Exhibit 7.2 *1992 Reserve Requirements*

Deposits Subject to Reserve Requirement	Reserve Requirements
Transaction accounts	0% on the first $3.6 million;
	3% on amounts over $3.6 million up to $42.2 million; and
	10% on amounts over $42.2 million

Note: Transaction accounts are deposits from which payments can be made. Time deposits, savings deposits, and money market deposit accounts are not subject to reserve requirements.

Under the Federal Reserve's 1992 rules, depository institutions with transaction deposits of $44.8 million or more must meet their reserve requirements once every two weeks. The amount to be reserved is based on a daily average of deposits held from Thursday of the first week through Wednesday of the third week. Reserves held in this two-week maintenance period are calculated based on deposits that were held in a two-week computation period that lags the maintenance period by two days. (See exhibit 7.3.) Required reserves for depositories with less than $44.8 million in transaction deposits are based on a daily average of deposits held over a two-week period ending 30 days before the end of the maintenance period.

Exhibit 7.3 *Contemporaneous Reserve Requirements*

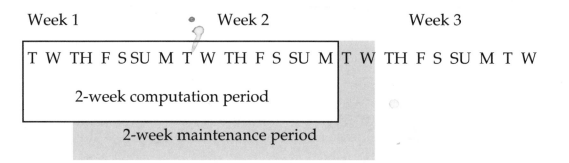

Week 1   Week 2   Week 3

T W TH F S SU M T W TH F S SU M T W TH F S SU M T W

2-week computation period

2-week maintenance period

A bank can have deep reserve deficits on any given day during the two-week maintenance period, provided it balances those deficits with reserve surpluses of like amounts on other days. The Fed's rules also allow depositories to carry a reserve deficit or surplus of up to 2 percent of required reserves into the next maintenance period. However, banks must cover a reserve deficit with a surplus of like amount in the following period if they wish to avoid a costly penalty. A period of surplus reserves should be followed by a period of reserve deficits of a like amount, since reserve carryovers can be transferred for only one period. If they are not used, they are lost.

Contemporaneous Reserve Requirements and Lagged Reserve Requirements

In 1984, the Federal Reserve instituted its present reserve rules, known as contemporaneous reserve requirements. These rules changed the procedures that had been used since 1968, which were known as lagged reserve requirements. Under lagged reserve requirements, banks could hold reserves in the present week based on deposits that were held two weeks earlier. (See exhibit 7.4.) The shift from lagged to contemporaneous reserve requirements was intended to give the Federal Reserve better control over the growth of bank reserves.

Exhibit 7.4 *Lagged Reserve Requirements*

Week 1	Week 2	Week 3
T W TH F S SU M T W	TH F S SU M T W	TH F S SU M T W
1-week computation period		1-week maintenance period

Under lagged reserve requirements, banks knew at the beginning of the banking week (Thursday) what their required reserves had to average for that week. By tracking their actual reserve balances each day against the average amount of reserves they were required to hold, banks could determine the exact amount of reserves they would need at the end of the week and the exact amount of excess reserves they had available to support new loans. By using every available dollar of excess reserves, banks' lending provided a base for strong money supply growth that supported inflationary trends. Contemporaneous reserve requirements enable the Federal Reserve to better control monetary policy. Banks are forced to be moderate in their lending because they do not know the exact amount of required reserves they will need for the current banking week.

Controlling Reserves

The Federal Reserve can alter the quantity of reserves available in the banking system by using one or a combination of three policy devices: reserve requirements, the discount rate, and open market operations. (See exhibit 7.5.)

Exhibit 7.5 *Federal Reserve Policy Tools and Their Impact on Deposit Creation*

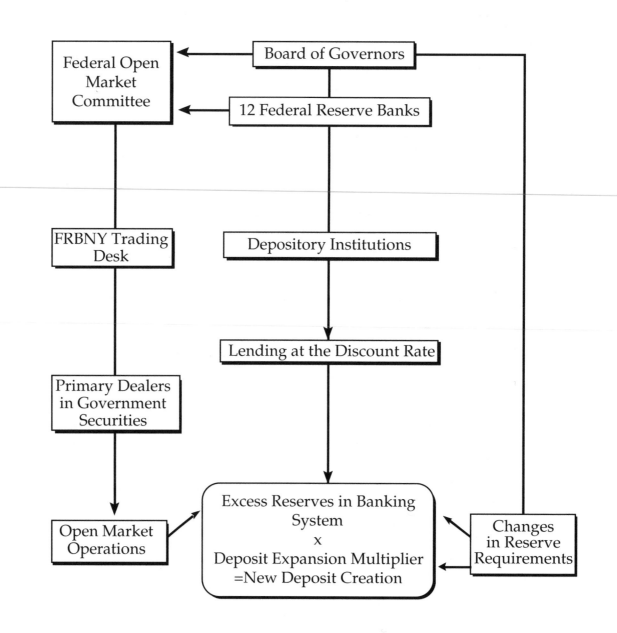

Reserve Requirements

The Federal Reserve can change the reserve requirement percentages it specifies for designated liabilities. For example, if it raises reserve requirements, banks have to come up with more required reserves. Excess reserves in the banking system would be reduced immediately as banks earmarked some or all of those reserves to meet the new requirements. The Fed also can change the rules on what constitutes legal reserves. Currently, only vault cash and deposits at Federal Reserve banks are acceptable. However, if the Fed accepted other assets, such as government securities, the total reserves available in the banking system would quickly expand. In addition, the Federal Reserve can change the base against which banks must keep reserves by including or excluding liabilities subject to reserve requirements.

Discount Rate

The Federal Reserve can raise or lower the interest rate it charges banks for borrowing reserves, depending on whether it wants to encourage or discourage this practice. It also can change the ground rules under which banks can obtain loans of reserves.

Open Market Operations

The Federal Reserve can buy or sell government securities in the open market. Whenever the Fed buys securities, bank reserves and the nation's money supply increase because the Federal Reserve pays with checks drawn on itself. When those checks are collected, banks' reserve accounts are increased, as are securities sellers' private demand accounts. Since these checks are not collected against other banks, the Federal Reserve's purchases do not redistribute reserves and money, but actually create new reserves and demand deposits.

The T account trace, outlined below, of a $1 million Federal Reserve open market purchase (after check collection) illustrates these effects.

Federal Reserve Bank of New York

Assets	Liabilities

U.S. government securities
    +$1 million
	Reserve accounts:
	Money Market Bank I
	    +$1 million

Money Market Bank I

Assets	Liabilities

Reserve account at FRBNY
 	
    +$1 million
	Demand deposit
	Securities Dealer Firm A
	    +$1 million

Securities Dealer Firm A

Assets	Liabilities
Demand deposit at	
Money Market Bank I	
+$1 million	
U.S. government securities	
-$1million	

Whenever the Federal Reserve sells securities, bank reserves and money supply decline. Securities dealers pay with checks drawn on their banks. When the Federal Reserve collects those checks, it reduces the reserve accounts of the banks on which the checks were drawn, just as banks reduce the demand deposit balances of their dealer depositors. Since these reserves and deposits are not transferred into other commercial banks but are retained by the Federal Reserve, the effect is a reduction in bank reserves and money supply.

The T account trace, outlined below, of a Federal Reserve open market sale of $1 million of U.S. government securities (after check collection) illustrates these reductions.

Federal Reserve Bank of New York

Assets	Liabilities
U.S. government	Reserve account:
securities	Money Market Bank II
-$1 million	-$1 million

Money Market Bank II

Assets	Liabilities
Reserve account at FRBNY	Demand deposit
	securities dealer firm B
-$1 million	-$1 million

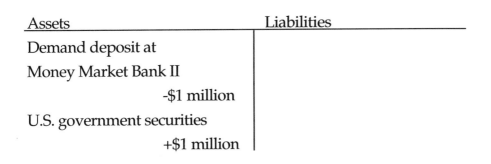

Securities Dealer Firm B

Assets	Liabilities
Demand deposit at Money Market Bank II -$1 million	
U.S. government securities +$1 million	

Effects of Federal Reserve Open Market Operations

While the Federal Reserve has the power to use all three of the preceding devices, it relies on open market operations as its basic mechanism for controlling reserves.

Open market operations are very effective in immediately increasing or decreasing bank reserves and the money supply and they have powerful secondary effects. For example, when the Federal Reserve purchases government securities, bank reserves and the money supply increase. Banks whose deposits have increased because of dealers sales of securities to the Fed find that they have a significant margin of excess reserves even though they are required to maintain a higher level of required reserves.

Banks with excess reserves will seek to turn them into income-generating assets by making loans or investing in government securities. The recipients of these bank loans or investments take their newly created money and spend it in the economy, with the funds being deposited in banks throughout the United States. These banks, in turn, invest or loan against their excess reserves, which leads to still more money in the economy. This multiple creation of bank deposits expands the nation's money supply in an amount several times greater than the amount of the Federal Reserve's initial open market purchases, which started the process.

When the Federal Reserve sells securities, the initial impact of the sale is a reduction in the excess reserves of banks whose depositors purchased the securities. Those banks with no excess reserves will be plunged into a temporary reserve deficiency as the Federal Reserve collects their depositors' checks. Banks in this predicament will try to get the reserves they need to meet reserve requirement regulations by selling secondary reserve assets (such as government securities), by borrowing from other banks or the Federal Reserve, by calling in loans, or by making some other adjustment in their assets or liabilities.

Banks that lose excess reserves may not have to make such extensive adjustments immediately. However, most banks operate under the practice of loan commitments, guaranteeing loans well in advance of the dates the loans are due to be granted. Those commitments are typically based on a bank's projection of short-term reserve and deposit growth. If the reserves do not materialize, banks must go through the same asset or liability adjustments as banks with reserve deficiencies.

An individual bank can meet a reserve deficiency in many ways. However, no combination of asset or liability adjustments will create new reserves. At best, a given bank can transfer its reserve deficiency to another bank, or a group of smaller banks can redistribute their reserve deficiencies to one or two large money market banks. But the banking system will still hold the same amount of reserves as before.

If the Federal Reserve intends, by reducing reserves, to reduce the money supply, it would indeed decline within days, as bank loans were repaid and banks made no new loans to meet their reserve requirements. It is only when the total deposit base of the banking system declines that available reserves would equal the amount needed to meet reserve requirements.

In practice, the Federal Reserve rarely uses its open market operations so drastically when it wants to restrain bank lending and money supply growth. Rather, it implements restraint gradually, by reducing the rate at which it supplies reserves, not the level.

When the Federal Reserve restricts the supply of reserves against strong demand by banks, the cost of reserves rises—specifically, federal funds. The cost of federal funds—the federal funds rate—increases because banks are competing against one another for reserves to expand their loan and investment portfolios. However, the increased cost of reserves means that banks will have to charge more on loans and command more on their investments to make the expansion in earning assets profitable. (Remember not to confuse the federal funds rate with the discount rate—which is the rate the Fed charges banks that borrow from it.)

Some banks will cut back on loans, either by a management decision or by a falloff in loan demand from customers who are unwilling to pay higher interest rates. Banks that need to restrict loans will typically allow loans to be repaid without extending new ones. They may even sell some securities to convert assets into reserves. Failing to extend new loans will reduce their deposit base and thus their need to maintain a high level of reserves. These adjustments invariably reduce the amount of demand deposits in the nation's banking system and the level of required reserves needed to support those deposits.

How the Fed Creates Reserves

In 1992, the Federal Reserve System's open market account portfolio of U.S. government and federal agency securities exceeded $260 billion. This portfolio was purchased over several decades with funds created by the Federal Reserve itself under the authority granted to it by Congress. The Federal Reserve creates money either by issuing Federal Reserve notes (currency) or by granting deposit credit. Its ability to create money is not related in any way to the required reserves that banks must deposit at Reserve banks. That is, Federal Reserve banks do not create money by investing or lending any part of the reserve balances of depositories that maintain accounts.

For example, Bank A receives as a deposit from the Colt Manufacturing Company a government check for $1 million in payment for gun barrels produced for the Department of Defense. Bank A sends the check to its Federal Reserve bank for collection, which results in a credit to Bank A's reserve account of $1 million and a charge to the Treasurer's account at the Federal Reserve bank for $1 million. Bank A has, in effect, deposited $1 million in its reserve account, which the Federal Reserve bank carries on its books as a deposit liability.

Federal Reserve Bank of New York

Assets	Liabilities
	Bank A's reserve account +$1 million
	Treasury's account -$1 million

Bank A

Assets	Liabilities
Reserve account +$1 million	Colt Co. account +$1 million

Assume that the Federal Reserve bank would like to profit from this new deposit. Bank B is short of reserves and applies for a loan at the discount window. The Federal Reserve bank advances $1 million to Bank B, simply by crediting Bank B's reserve account, not by lending Bank A's deposit. As the T account illustrates, the Reserve bank's account now shows deposit liabilities of $1 million to Bank A, $1 million to Bank B, a charge of $1 million to Treasury's account, and $1 million in new assets—Bank B's note.

Federal Reserve Bank of New York

Assets	Liabilities
	Bank A's reserve account +$1 million
	Treasury's account -$1 million
Loan to Bank B +$1 million	Bank B's reserve account +$1 million

Bank B

Assets	Liabilities
Reserve account +$1 million	Borrowings from Fed +$1 million

Assume that the Federal Reserve decides to invest Bank A's $1 million deposit. It goes to the market, buys $1 million of Treasury bills, and pays the seller with a check drawn on itself. Even in this instance, it would not be investing Bank A's deposit. Instead, it would be using its note-issuing power. The securities seller deposits the check in Bank C, which presents it for payment to the Federal Reserve bank on which it is drawn. The Federal Reserve bank credits the $1 million to Bank C's reserve account. The Federal Reserve bank now finds itself with deposit liabilities of $3 million, and it has still not used the first $1 million it received from Bank A. Also, the banks now have $2 million more in reserves than they had when the Federal Reserve bank began to look for a profitable use for Bank A's deposit.

Federal Reserve Bank of New York		Bank C	
Assets	Liabilities	Assets	Liabilities
	Bank A's reserve account +$1 million	Reserve account +$1 million	Securities seller's account +$1 million
	Treasury's account -$1 million		
Loan to Bank B +$1 million	Bank B's reserve account +$1 million		
Government securities +$1 million	Bank C's reserve account +$1 million		

In sum, the Federal Reserve does not use bank reserves to buy earning assets. Rather, every time a Federal Reserve bank lends or invests, it creates new reserves. Furthermore, those new reserves invariably support a multiple expansion of deposits. Since 1913, the Federal Reserve has provided banks with enough additional reserve balances to expand their own loans and investments to the point where the banking system's portfolio stood at more than $2.8 trillion in 1992.

Banks' Deposit Base: Reserve-Supplying Factors

Reserve Bank Credit

The Federal Reserve's open market operations and its loans to depository institutions—Reserve bank credit—provide most of the reserves to the banking system. Federal Reserve float creates some reserves but the Fed does not have a policy of using float to supply reserves to the banking system.

Rather, the Federal Reserve treats float as an unpredictable and volatile byproduct of its check-clearing process. The Fed seeks to offset this reserve effect through open market operations because float impairs the Federal Reserve's ability to predict and control the growth of bank reserves.

The Federal Reserve's purchases of foreign currency are not used to supply the banking system with reserves, but to control foreign exchange trading. The impact of foreign currency purchases is usually offset through open market operations.

U.S. Treasury Actions

Gold and Special Drawing Rights

The U.S. Treasury supplies reserves when it monetizes gold and special drawing rights (SDRs)—bookkeeping balances governments use in their international monetary transactions.

When the Treasury monetizes gold or SDRs, it issues certificates to Federal Reserve banks and receives an equivalent amount of dollars credited to its account. When these funds are spent, the amount of reserves in the banking system increases.

Today, the monetization of gold and SDRs is an almost negligible source of reserves. In the past, however, gold monetization provided the banking system with more than $11 billion in reserves. In the 1970s and 1980s, allocations from the International Monetary Fund to the U.S. SDR certificate account provided more than $10 billion in reserves to the banking system.

Treasury Currency Outstanding

Treasury currency outstanding, essentially coin, is another way that U.S. government actions supply reserves to the banking system. When the Treasury issues coin to the Federal Reserve banks for distribution to depositories, it receives an equivalent dollar value credit to its demand account at the Federal Reserve.

When banks buy coin from the Fed by paying with their reserve account deposits, total reserves are not changed, since both vault cash and deposits at the Federal Reserve are part of bank reserves. However, when Treasury spends its newly created deposit dollars, it effectively creates new reserves for those banks in which Treasury checks have been deposited. Thus, Treasury currency outstanding is a source of bank reserves.

Banks' Deposit Base:
Reserve-Absorbing Factors

Currency in Circulation

Currency in circulation is the largest single reserve-absorbing factor that affects the banking system. It accounts for almost 90 percent of the total of all reserves that flow out of the banking system. If banks receive deposits of currency from the public and then deposit the currency at their Reserve banks, their reserve accounts are credited. However, if they obtain currency in respose to depositors' demands for cash, their reserve accounts are debited.

Since 1913, when the Federal Reserve was established, banks have had to pay for more than $300 billion of Federal Reserve currency, the total amount of currency in circulation today. If no other source of reserves had been open to them, they would, by the 1990s, have exhausted their reserve deposits and would have been overdrawn by about $275 billion.

Treasury Cash Holdings and Deposits with Federal Reserve Banks

U.S. Treasury activities absorb reserves in two ways: Treasury holds deposits with Federal Reserve banks and maintains cash holdings in unspent currency or unmonetized gold.

Treasury attempts to minimize the effect of its tax collections and payments on bank reserves by maintaining accounts in most of the nation's commercial banks. In this way, tax receipts and funds received from the sale of government securities to the public do not siphon off reserves from the banking system as they would if these funds were deposited in Treasury's Federal Reserve account. However, when Treasury has to cover checks for Social Security payments and thousands of other government payments drawn against its account, these funds are transferred into Federal Reserve banks, temporarily reducing reserves.

Foreign Deposits with Federal Reserve Banks

When foreign central banks and other official institutions increase their Federal Reserve deposits, bank reserves are reduced because these deposits are generally shifted from accounts at domestic commercial banks. However, these deposits are usually very small and do not have a substantial impact on bank reserves.

Summary

When commercial banks make loans, they create demand deposits on their books. To create money in this way, banks must have excess reserves—vault cash or balances at a Reserve bank that exceed their reserve requirements. When deposits that banks create for borrowers are transferred through the check collection process into other banks, the excess reserves are transferred as well, giving other banks the ability to create new money. Through this process, the banking system can create a deposit amount several times greater than the initial loan.

Multiple expansion of bank-created deposits is constantly changed by the Federal Reserve's monetary policies, deposits flowing in and out of banks, funds moving from checking to savings accounts, and check cashing. The Federal Reserve can influence the expansion process by changing its reserve requirements, by raising or lowering the interest rate it charges depositories to borrow reserves (the discount rate), and by buying or selling government securities in the open market. The Fed uses this latter policy tool most frequently to expand or reduce bank reserves and the nation's money supply.

When the Federal Reserve buys in the open market, it pays with a check drawn on itself. When a dealer firm deposits the check in a bank, that increases bank reserves. When the Federal Reserve sells securities from its multibillion-dollar portfolio, it receives checks drawn on banks by dealers. After the checks are collected, bank reserves decline.

The U.S. Treasury also influences the amount of bank reserves by monetizing gold or SDRs, or by issuing coin. Reserves are reduced when depositors withdraw cash from banks or when Treasury or foreign governments increase their account balances at Federal Reserve banks.

Questions

1. Why is a bank's maximum amount of new loans or investments limited to the amount of its excess reserves?

2. What are the three forms in which banks that are not members of the Federal Reserve can keep their required reserves?

3. When the Federal Reserve buys or sells a government security, why are bank reserves increased or decreased by the amount of the transaction?

4. Cite the largest single reserve-absorbing and the largest single reserve-supplying factor affecting the banking system.

Endnotes

1. There is no guarantee that the collateral backing a loan will always have value at least equal to the amount of the loan. Banks typically assess the value of loan collateral at the time a loan is made. However, over the length of a loan, collateral value can change. Many banks suffered losses in the 1980s when borrowers defaulted on loans secured by commercial real estate because the market value of the properties had fallen substantially below the amount of the defaulted loans.

2. Reserves consist of a bank's deposit balance with the Federal Reserve and its cash on hand.

DEPOSIT
MANAGEMENT

Objectives

After successfully completing this chapter, you will be able to

❖ identify the reasons a bank will dishonor a check

❖ discuss the criteria that banks must apply to determine whether a check should be dishonored

❖ explain the difference between uncollected balances and available funds

❖ discuss Regulation CC's delayed availability requirements and the compliance alternatives banks face

❖ define the role of internal accounting and internal reports in bank deposit operations

❖ differentiate among the three basic pricing strategies banks can adopt in marketing their services

❖ discuss the factors banks consider in pricing their payment services

Introduction

In managing a bank's deposit operations, a disproportionate amount of time and resources must be placed on exceptions in the check collection process and on the support operations behind that process, such as bookkeeping, posting, reporting, and filing. Banks can incur losses or can be liable if they fail to adhere to commercial law and the body of rules and check-clearing practices that have developed. The Uniform Commercial Code (UCC) has specific rules for the treatment of checks and exception items—improper signatures, improper endorsements, staledates, postdates, and insufficient funds coverage. There are also important distinctions between uncollected funds and available funds.

The Uniform Commercial Code

The Uniform Commercial Code contains the body of civil law that governs the rights and obligations of all parties in the check collection process. The fundamental premise behind the UCC's treatment of checks is that all checks are good (drawn against sufficient funds) and are automatically payable on demand. Banks have the right to dishonor a check—that is, to refuse payment. However, the code makes it clear that banks can be subject to financial loss or liable for civil damages by dishonoring a good check, by failing to follow the appropriate rules and procedures governing the return of a dishonored check, and, paradoxically, by paying for a check that should have been dishonored.

Essentially, the code requires bank management to pay special attention to exceptions in the check collection process—to those 1 percent or less of checks likely to be returned. Besides adhering closely to the rules and procedures governing return items, banks often have to decide whether to pay or return a suspect check.

Banks' Rights in Honoring or Dishonoring a Check

Although banks have the right to dishonor a check, they can exercise that right only under specific circumstances. For example, if a bank does dishonor a check, it must give the check writer proper notice. If it does not, the check writer may not be held liable for failing to pay the check depositor. Banks have to be absolutely correct in dishonoring a check because the law considers a bank to be under a general contractual obligation to its checking account holders to pay their checks on demand—if there are sufficient funds in the account. If a bank improperly dishonors a check, it is liable for breach of contract. If a bank receiving a check refuses to make payment but does not return the check before midnight of the day following presentment, it becomes liable for the check.

Stop Payment Orders

Check writers have the right to notify their bank not to honor a check they wrote. This stop payment order allows checking account holders to protect themselves against a lost or stolen check or a payment too hastily made. Consumers often use stop payment orders to rescind a check after they have made payment although many bankers consider this a questionable practice. For example, assume that a consumer gives a check to a merchant for a chair and a dispute arises a day or so later because the chair arrives with a broken leg. The consumer can stop payment on the check until the dispute is resolved. This action gives the consumer considerable leverage but it is one reason many retailers and contractors require payment by certified check or bank (cashier's) check. Payment on these checks cannot be stopped unless they are lost or stolen.

Stop payment orders can be given by phone in most states or in writing in all states. In states that permit stop payment orders by phone, the order is binding on the bank for only 14 calendar days. For longer coverage, the order must be confirmed in writing within that time. A written stop payment order is effective for 6 months, unless it is renewed in writing before it expires.

The UCC stipulates that stop payment orders must give the bank enough time to act on the order. If a bank honors a check after it was properly notified to stop payment, the bank is liable to the depositor only if, in paying the check, it caused the depositor to suffer a loss.

Irregular Signatures

A bank is liable if it pays a check on which the account holder's signature has been forged or, in the case of a corporate account, the signature is not authorized or a second signature is required.

The law places on the bank the burden of knowing the signatures of all its demand depositors. That is why depositors opening a bank account are required to sign a card in the precise way in which they will sign checks. For corporations that use a machine-generated or stamped facsimile signature on their checks, a copy of the facsimile is required. The bank can then compare the signatures on file with the signature on checks presented for payment.

In many banks, the flow of checks is so rapid and so large that the costs of comparing the signature on every check received against the signature on file would exceed the potential losses the bank might incur from paying a check with a forged or unauthorized signature. Now that magnetic ink character recognition (MICR) processing of checks is commonly used, manual signature comparisons are even more time consuming and costly. Banks handling large numbers of checks may choose to run signature comparisons on selected checks only—for example, checks in excess of a designated dollar amount.

However, these banks do not expose themselves to as much risk as these practices might imply. Checking account holders must exercise reasonable care in protecting their checks against unauthorized use and must examine their bank statements and canceled checks. If a depositor fails to notify the bank of a forgery or unauthorized signature, generally within one year, the bank is not liable.

Improper Endorsements

A check's ability to transfer money freely is due to its negotiability—it can be transferred from one party to another without subjecting the recipient to legal claims that might be pending against the other party. The act of endorsement (signing or stamping one's name on the back of a check) assures a check's negotiability throughout the collection process.

A check presented to a bank for payment must be properly endorsed. Otherwise, the person presenting the check is not considered the legal holder and is not entitled to receive funds in exchange for the check.

In practice, when a bank customer deposits a check but fails to endorse it, and the teller fails to notice the lack of endorsement, many banks will endorse the check as an accommodation to the depositor. However, endorsement or not, when a teller stamps a check to indicate it was deposited for credit to an account, the bank assumes liability. An improper endorsement can include

- ❖ a forgery of the signature of the payee
- ❖ a missing endorsement
- ❖ the signature of a person other than the one to whom the check was written
- ❖ the signature of a person without proper authority, in the case of a check written to a business or institution

A bank that honors a check with an improper endorsement may be liable for reimbursing the account holder. Many banks refuse to cash double-endorsed checks because they cannot verify the legitimacy of the initial endorsement. A double-endorsed check is payable to a person other than the depositor, who has endorsed the check to the depositor. Thus the check contains two separate endorsements.

Staledates and Postdates

Banks are not obligated to honor checks presented to them that are staledated (bearing a date six months old or older) or postdated (carrying a future date). The UCC allows but does not require banks to return these misdated checks unpaid.

Many banks are specifically authorized by corporations to waive the six-month staledate on checks drawn against the corporation. These authorizations are typically from corporations that issue tens of thousands of dividend checks to stockholders but invariably find that some of the checks tend to be held for long periods of time before they are deposited. When a specific waiver is not in effect, banks often will hold the checks and "refer to maker." That is, they will contact the check issuer to obtain permission to honor the check before returning it unpaid.

Not all corporations or government entities accommodate customers that are late in depositing checks. Many checks carry the legend not good after 30 days. This advisory statement is an attempt by the issuing entity to ensure that its checks will be presented for payment quickly, which helps bookkeeping and cash-flow management.

Holds

The maximum holds banks can place on deposited checks are governed by the Federal Reserve's Regulation CC. However, banks often are required to place holds on specific accounts to keep funds from being withdrawn. When a hold of this type is in effect, checks presented against the account cannot be honored. A hold might be placed on an account when

❖ an account holder dies

The account is frozen because the checks cease to be valid. If checks are paid against the account of a deceased depositor, the bank may be liable to those with a legal claim on the funds. When notified of a depositor's death, banks sometimes impound the account until ownership of the funds is determined. In similar instances—a notice of corporate bankruptcy or declaration of a depositor's legal incompetence—banks also are required to hold all funds in the affected account. As a practical matter, most banks examine all incoming checks on a deceased person's account. If the checks were written prior to the person's death and the signature is valid, the checks are paid against the deceased person's account.

❖ the IRS issues tax levies against delinquent taxpayers

These levies bar taxpayers from withdrawing a certain amount of funds from their bank accounts. Similarly, court orders are occasionally issued to bar the use of funds by depositors who have financial judgments against them. A tax levy or a court order requires the bank to freeze a portion of the depositor's funds until the appropriate payments are made.

❖ a depositor cashes a check at a teller's window

In such cases, the check amount is entered as a hold on the account to ensure that additional checks drawn against the account do not absorb the funds already obligated. Placing a hold in the amount of a certified check is another standard bank operating procedure to ensure that funds will be in the account when the certified check clears.

Altered Checks

A check that has been fraudulently altered to increase the amount to be paid is known as a raised check. A bank that pays a raised check is liable for the falsified amount.

The law presumes that banks have ample time and opportunity to physically examine all checks. Therefore, banks are liable for failing to detect an alteration. However, they are not entirely at fault in cases where check writers are negligent and may not be liable for paying a raised check. For example, if a depositor leaves a blank space on a check so that $40 can be easily changed to $400, that depositor is solely responsible, not the bank. As with forged checks, depositors are responsible for examining their statements and canceled checks and informing the bank within a reasonable time if an error was made.

To avoid problems of liability, some banks will return all altered checks, even if the alterations appear to have been made inadvertently by the check writer—for example, crossing out one number and writing in another. Other banks will use discretion and honor checks where alterations appear to have been made with no intent to defraud.

Invalid Presentment

Banks occasionally find that checks received from a clearing house, a Federal Reserve bank, or a correspondent bank have been routed to the wrong bank. In other instances, checks received for payment may not technically be checks at all but time drafts or other instruments not subject to payment on demand. The bank must reroute all these items to avoid liability.

Uncollected and Available Funds

When a check is presented for payment, a bank must determine whether there are sufficient funds available in the account to cover the check.

Since most banks use computerized bookkeeping systems, every check received is automatically posted. It is only at the end of the day that most banks learn whether a given account has a positive or negative balance (an overdraft). A bank that chooses not to allow an overdraft when there are insufficient funds can return the check and reverse the earlier posting. Most checks returned in the U.S. payments system are returned for insufficient funds.

However, overdrafts are not always caused by depositors who cannot balance their checkbooks. Depositors enter check amounts in their checkbooks as part of their working balances, against which they write checks. But as banks first have to collect the checks deposited, these checks may not yet be usable funds.

An overdraft may occur if the sum of checks written by the depositor and presented for payment exceeds the amount of available funds on account that day. In this case, the bank is likely to return the presented checks to avoid any risk that checks being collected for the depositor will themselves be returned unpaid.

Delayed Availability

Until 1988, there was no uniform, industrywide policy among banks that specified when depositors' checks would be credited. Except in eight states—New York, California, Massachusetts, Rhode Island, Connecticut, Illinois, Maine, and New Mexico—banks' delayed availability policies were not covered by law. In 1987, however, as a result of concerns related to banks' delayed availability practices, Congress passed the Expedited Funds Availability Act (EFAA) that specifies the maximum delay in availability all banks can impose.

Before EFAA, most banks' policies were based on industry averages of the time required to collect a check in various regions of the country. Banks generally receive credit for collected checks within one to three business days. Banks would build additional time—from several days to three weeks—into their delayed availability policies to protect themselves against the risk associated with cashing a check that might be returned unpaid.

Banks in most states were free to adopt any delayed availability policy. Few banks in states not covered by an availability law routinely informed depositors of their delay policies. In some cases, bank policies were not even internally consistent. Some banks paid out funds against newly deposited checks for some customers, but required others to wait several weeks until their deposited checks cleared. These delays presented particular problems for new customers—usually new residents in an area—who wanted to draw funds against accounts in banks where they had previously lived.

Many banks also differentiated in their treatment of individual accounts and business accounts. Individual depositors had to wait for usable funds credit, but business accounts with whom banks had long-standing service relationships were given immediate access to their funds.

Deposit Management 217

Banks' delayed availability practices became an increasing source of controversy in the 1980s. Consumer groups argued that delayed availability was an unfair and deceptive business practice that the Federal Reserve or the Federal Trade Commission should regulate. The groups complained that banks and thrift institutions unfairly delayed granting usable funds credit for deposited checks so they could profit by using the funds themselves for several days or several weeks longer than justifiable. Some economists suggested that because check collection services are not profitable, earning income on delayed availability funds allowed banks to recoup some costs. Without this offset, they argued, banks would have had to sharply increase their service charges.

Bankers contended that the delays in their check-crediting schedules were justified, given the imperfections in the nation's check collection system and the UCC's clear delineation of rights and liability in the collection process. They pointed out that most banks and thrifts granted immediate credit on most checks and paid interest on checks in NOW and money market deposit accounts from the day of deposit, regardless of any delay imposed on the use of deposited check funds.

Bankers maintained that they had to treat every check, in principle, as if it were a potentially bad check. Under the U.S. check-processing system, because all checks are presumed "good," a presenting bank does not know whether a paying bank has dishonored a check unless it is notified. Before 1988, such notification was the direct responsibility of the paying bank. However, few paying banks notified presenting banks. They simply sent dishonored checks back to the presenting banks, usually by mail, which in some cases took up to three weeks.

The return-items process was slow and costly because returned checks had to be processed by hand, returned to presenting banks in accordance with strict procedures, and routed back the same way they had come. Returned checks could not be sent directly back to the presenting bank, bypassing a clearing house or the Federal Reserve, if they had been presented for collection through either of those routes. In fact, several states prohibited the direct return of dishonored checks.

Return items had to be handled manually because these checks did not contain MICR encoded information about the depositing bank that would have allowed for automated processing. In addition, banks' endorsements often were stamped on top of one another as checks moved through the collection process, so that banks returning a check often had difficulty discerning the appropriate return route. Examining multiple endorsements took time, and banks frequently misrouted returns. Misrouting errors can subject a bank to liability for the amount of the check.

Because returned checks could take up to three weeks to work their way back to the collecting bank, most banks prevented check depositors from using their funds immediately. Delayed availability credit was designed to cover the possibility that any given check would be returned unpaid, even though in practice less than 1 percent of all checks processed by banks are actually returned unpaid.

The Expedited Funds Availability Act (EFAA) of 1987 and Regulation CC

The EFAA not only specified the maximum holds banks can place on deposited checks, it also authorized the Federal Reserve to use its regulatory powers to improve check collection and return-items processing in a new way that would minimize the risks banks face because of the EFAA's short time limits on check holds.

Regulation CC, which implements the EFAA, requires banks to make funds available within two business days of deposit for local checks and within five business days of deposit for nonlocal checks. (The regulation preempts the eight state availability laws that had been in force before 1988 unless the laws require shorter holds for a category of checks than those mandated by the EFAA.)

Regulation CC defines a local check as any check drawn on a bank within the same Federal Reserve check-processing region as the bank in which the check is deposited. In effect, a nonlocal check is an interregional check. Between September 1988, when the regulation was issued, and September 1990, banks were given somewhat longer time limit holds as a transition to the two-day and five-day limits.

Banks must provide next-day availability on deposits of federal, state, and local government checks, official checks (bank checks and cashier's checks), postal money orders, electronic funds transfers, and cash. The first $100 of all nonlocal check deposits also have to be made available on the next day. The EFAA covers checks deposited into transaction accounts only; checks deposited into time accounts or money market deposit accounts are not subject to hold limits.

The EFAA emphasized banks' public disclosure of their availability policies. Regulation CC not only requires disclosure to all of a bank's transaction account holders but establishes penalties for failure to comply. These penalties range from financial sanctions by the federal regulatory agencies (such as forfeiture of fees) to possible civil or class action suits by customers. Punitive damages in a class action suit can be considerable. The EFAA allows for damages up to $500,000, or 1 percent of an offending bank's net worth, whichever is less.

The EFAA includes a number of exceptions to the delayed availability limits that address banks' risk concerns:

- ❖ Banks may place additional hold time on deposits made at network ATMs because of the difficulty banks face in verifying the composition of these deposits. Banks can treat all checks deposited at network ATMs as if they were nonlocal checks, which means that depositors' funds can be held for five days.

- ❖ Banks may place longer exception holds on check deposits over $5,000, redeposited returned checks, checks deposited into accounts that have frequently been overdrawn, and check deposits that the bank feels may be uncollectible. (In 1990, the Federal Reserve announced that these exception holds could be five days for local checks and six days for nonlocal checks.)

- ❖ Banks can exempt from the hold limits all checks deposited into newly opened accounts (accounts under 30 days).

Banks have complied with Regulation CC in several ways. Some banks have adopted the maximum two-day and five-day hold schedule. Other banks have instituted schedules that impose shorter holds. However, most banks have opted to give depositors same-day or next-day availability on all check deposits, avoiding holds entirely. This has proven to be the simplest and least costly way to comply with the regulation, although it provides banks with little protection against return-item losses and check fraud.

Some banks have chosen to assess holds on a case-by-case basis, which is acceptable under Regulation CC. For example, a bank places holds only under special circumstances, such as on checks deposited into accounts with unusually high deposit activity, or on checks that contain numerous endorsements. These holds are typically imposed at the discretion of the teller. However, banks that use a case-by-case approach must notify customers in writing on the same day a check deposit is held.

Most banks that place holds do so during account processing, when availability is computer calculated according to each check deposited. These banks do not have to notify customers at the time the hold is being placed as long as the bank's delayed availability policy has been previously disclosed to all depositors.

Return Items

Most banks had to change their procedures for handling return items under Regulation CC. The regulation created entirely new return-item-processing requirements because the EFAA's short check-hold times were not long enough time for most returned checks to be rerouted using pre-1988 methods.

Before Regulation CC, banks had until midnight on the day after receiving a check to decide whether to pay or return the item. The extra day gave account officers an opportunity to review the bank's overdraft report and decide what to do. Regulation CC, however, requires banks to return checks as quickly as they clear deposited checks.

Banks also are required to notify each other by 4:00 p.m. on the day after check presentment if they are not going to honor any check over $2,499. Notification was intended to help banks guard against customers withdrawing large amounts of cash against large dollar-value checks that might be involved in the return.

The Federal Reserve considered speeding up the notification time in 1990 but decided against the change because most banks had experienced no significant check loss problems in 1988 or 1989 in making funds available the day after deposit. Also, speedier notification might have led to an increase in the number of improperly returned checks. The Federal Reserve reasoned that with less time to make a decision on whether checks are backed by sufficient funds, banks might have returned more checks to be safe, many of which would have been good.

To cope with Regulation CC's early notification of returns requirement, many banks have instituted automatic criteria posting systems for insufficient funds checks. These systems automatically pay or return checks based on guidelines established for each customer or type of account. Automatic criteria posting reduces or eliminates the need for account officers to review overdraft reports and has allowed banks to begin the return-items process sooner.

For its part, the Federal Reserve established a separate return-item service, not just for checks processed by Reserve banks but for any checks that have to be returned. Banks can send returned checks directly to the Federal Reserve for rerouting. If they use an automated procedure, in which they MICR-encode their returns, the Fed's return-item charge is substantially less. Upon receipt of return items, the Reserve banks return the checks to presenting banks, bypassing correspondents that may have been involved in the forward collection process. Reserve banks also changed their return-items-processing schedules so that returns could be accepted from banks at night, when most check processing takes place. The schedule change speeded up return-items presentment considerably by reducing return time by about one day at each Reserve office from pre-1988 return times.

Most bankers initially opposed the federal regulation of delayed availability. They contended that the federal time limits were too short and that forced granting of faster credit on all checks would increase their bad-check losses and force them to raise service charges to offset those costs. However, bank regulators in states that enacted maximum delayed availability laws in the mid-1980s report that banks in those states did not experience significant increases in bad-check losses under the state-imposed limits. To date, there have been no reports that bad-check losses have increased under the federal limits.

Overdraft Accounts

Increasingly, banks and depositors have opted to establish overdraft checking accounts, most of them automatic, so that an overdraft becomes a formal, interest-bearing loan.

In an automatic overdraft plan, the bank's computer keeps track of the depositor's balance and credit limit and automatically advances funds to cover any overdraft. The computer also automatically debits the depositor's account according to a prearranged schedule for repaying the overdraft loan.

The automatic overdraft account is one of those rare banking services that provides valuable benefits to both depositors and banks. Depositors benefit from an overdraft account because

- ❖ it eliminates charges paid for items returned because of insufficient funds
- ❖ depositors can obtain credit in smaller increments than would ordinarily be available through a standard loan
- ❖ it minimizes the inconvenience and embarrassment of having items returned for insufficient funds
- ❖ loan repayments are made automatically, in the case of automatic overdraft accounts
- ❖ finance charges tend to be lower, since payments are always made on the due dates
- ❖ there are no late-payment charges

Banks benefit from automatic overdraft plans because

- ❖ they reduce payment delinquencies, collection costs, and time spent in processing return items
- ❖ they eliminate costs of setting up billing programs, printing payment reminders, using special encoding, processing additional paperwork, and undertaking increased collection efforts
- ❖ they give banks the option to control overdraft credit

The courts have held that a bank's coverage of an overdraft does not constitute a contract for continued overdraft coverage into the future.

Most automatic credit extensions are made in increments of $50 and, ironically, many banks with automatic overdraft account programs often honor small overdrafts on amounts of less than $25. This occurs either because the bank's computers are not programmed to extend automatic overdraft credit until the negative balance exceeds $25 or because the bank wishes to avoid generating unnecessary depositor animosity over the failure to grant overdrafts on small sums.

Examining Checks

Every check presented to a bank for payment must be examined to protect the bank from liability for mishandling a check or for honoring an improper check. When checks are examined, several criteria are applied to determine whether the check is good.

To minimize the risk of financial loss or civil damages, banks usually return unpaid any checks that fail to meet these criteria. However, banks are not legally required, in all instances, to return checks that are not good. On occasion, banks will assume a risk to accommodate a depositor.

Physical Criteria

Five physical criteria are used to determine whether a check is good or should be returned. The check must be

- ❖ a legitimate demand item drawn on a bank
- ❖ signed by the check writer, who is authorized to sign on the account
- ❖ unaltered in any way
- ❖ properly dated
- ❖ properly endorsed

Informational Criteria

A check that meets all five physical criteria may still not be good. Bank staff must draw on information not contained on each check to determine whether the check should be returned, based on one or more of the following four conditions:

- ❖ A stop payment order issued against the check.
- ❖ A full or partial hold placed on the check writer's account.
- ❖ There are insufficient funds in the check writer's account, and it is not an overdraft account.
- ❖ The check writer's account balance is not in fully available funds.

Before automation, checks were physically examined before they were posted. If a check met all the criteria applicable to a good check, it was posted. Otherwise, it was referred to a bank officer for a decision on whether it should be posted or returned unpaid.

Today, with computers at even the smallest banks, checks are examined after posting. The volume of checks is so great and the percentage returned is so small that it would not be cost effective to examine every check before computer processing. Rather, banks make provisional postings, then examine the checks. Many banks use a bulk filing process in which only a few checks are examined for date, signature, or other physical criteria. In either case, if the bank determines after the examination that a check should have been dishonored, the posting is reversed and the check is returned.

Keeping the Books

A bank's management of deposits and payments involves more than collecting checks for depositors and paying checks presented against depositors' accounts. It involves a complex process of data recording, credit and debit posting, and monthly statements to depositors.

A bank's ability to perform these bookkeeping functions accurately and in a timely fashion is the reason that many depositors remain loyal to a given bank. These bookkeeping functions also provide top bank management with the data they need to examine the deposit and payments flows that affect the structure and composition of the bank's assets and liabilities.

Just as the technology of processing payments has become increasingly automated, so has the bookkeeping for these transactions. Few banks keep the books by manually recording each day's transactions. Today, most banks have computerized accounting systems and demand deposit accounting (DDA) units that perform the basic bookkeeping functions necessary to the deposit and payments process.

The primary source of bookkeeping information that flows into a bank comes from checks taken in by tellers, checks presented for payment by a clearing house or a Federal Reserve bank, and checks received directly from other banks for payment. (See exhibit 8.1.)

A bank's DDA unit will typically

❖ examine all checks to ensure that proper account numbers and dollar amounts appear

❖ decide whether any checks should be dishonored

❖ post all debits and credits to appropriate customer accounts

❖ keep up-to-date, accurate records of the daily activity of every account and calculate a new closing balance for every account

❖ prepare monthly statements and mail them with canceled checks to depositors

❖ prepare internal reports for bank management

Exhibit 8.1 *How a Bank Processes a Check Drawn on Another Bank*

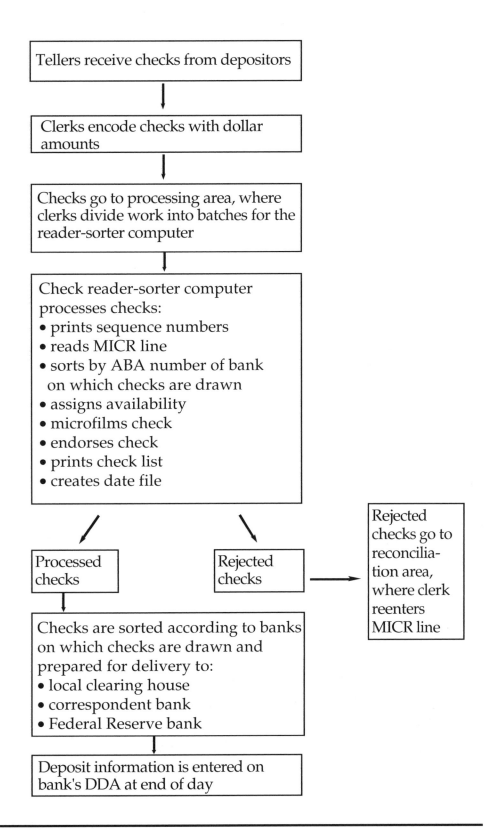

Tellers receive checks from depositors

↓

Clerks encode checks with dollar amounts

↓

Checks go to processing area, where clerks divide work into batches for the reader-sorter computer

↓

Check reader-sorter computer processes checks:
- prints sequence numbers
- reads MICR line
- sorts by ABA number of bank on which checks are drawn
- assigns availability
- microfilms check
- endorses check
- prints check list
- creates date file

Processed checks

Rejected checks → Rejected checks go to reconciliation area, where clerk reenters MICR line

Checks are sorted according to banks on which checks are drawn and prepared for delivery to:
- local clearing house
- correspondent bank
- Federal Reserve bank

↓

Deposit information is entered on bank's DDA at end of day

Banks issue monthly statements to account holders at considerable cost. In 1990, banks spent close to $2 billion in postage to send monthly statements and canceled checks to customers. Banks do this not only to accommodate customers but also to protect the bank's legal interest.

[handwritten in margin: 1 year - statements; 3 year - unauthorize endorsement]

Customers are legally obligated to examine their statements and promptly notify the bank if they find an error. The UCC gives depositors up to one year from the date of each statement and its accompanying canceled checks to discover and notify the bank of any forged or unauthorized signature or otherwise altered check, and up to three years to report unauthorized endorsements. Laws in all states parallel these provisions of the UCC.

Some of the nation's largest banks have online computer systems linked to televisionlike terminals at tellers' sites. Among the most advanced internal reporting systems in the industry, they can flash the status of any account at the teller's request.

Typically, a bank's computer-processing department or DDA unit will prepare the following items off-line:

❖ daily trial balance reports for each account that show the total credits and debits posted and the closing balance for the previous day

❖ overdraft reports for each account that indicate the dollar amount of checks paid against the dollar amount of the overdraft that would result if all postings were allowed to stand

❖ uncollected funds reports for each account that provide a breakdown of deposited funds deferred in accordance with the bank's availability schedule

❖ reports on all newly opened or closed accounts and on all accounts in which there have been exceptionally large deposits or withdrawals

❖ stop payment orders and hold reports

Bank management uses daily trial balance, overdraft, uncollected funds, and other reports to decide whether to pay or return checks. A bank with a good internal reporting system also will have a central file program that bank management can readily access to examine a broader history of any given customer's account before it determines whether to pay or return a check.

DDA reports provide the core of the internal reports most important to bank management. An immediately accessible record of inflows and outflows of major amounts is the major goal of most banks' internal reporting systems. Bank management can then determine the net funds available to invest in the money market at any moment. For example, at an interest rate of 10 percent for federal funds, a bank that leaves $1 million idle overnight loses about $270 in revenue.

Computerized Accounting

Today, most checks are processed by high-speed reader-sorter machines that determine whether the necessary MICR data have been encoded on each check. Reader-sorters not only handle an enormous volume of checks rapidly but also allow banks to computerize their DDA systems.

In such a DDA system, the bank's reader-sorters register MICR data to a computer that prepares a magnetic tape of the transactions. From this data, a list is made of each account number for which there is a transaction, the dollar amount of every transaction to be posted to each account, and a code to indicate whether the posting is a debit or a credit. Some banks produce one tape at the end of the day, while others run separate tapes as soon as checks come in from a clearing house or from in-house pickups. The number and frequency of tape runs usually depend on the bank's size and volume. Banks with multiple branches usually have to wait until late in the day to prepare one final tape containing all the day's debit and credit transactions.

The data on the tape is entered into master files and the bank's computer uses the information to update the file. A new closing balance is computed for each account, and the sum of these balances becomes the demand deposit total that appears on the bank's daily statement. The final step is the generation of a new master file for the next day's transactions.

Computerized deposit accounting has allowed banks to cope with a growing volume of checks yet reduce their costs and improve efficiency. The manual operation that most banks employed before automation was prone to human error, required costly and elaborate procedures for internal auditing, and was less efficient.

Banks' Pricing Practices

Banking is a competitive industry, with tens of thousands of competitors offering the same basic payments services and incurring the same basic costs. Laws and regulations limit markets and constrain banks' pricing options but, within the boundaries of laws and regulations, banks are free to adopt prices consistent with their individual goals.

Banks must consider a number of factors in setting prices, such as

❖ their fixed and variable operating costs

❖ fees and pricing strategies of competitors

❖ quality of service

❖ attitudes of depositors to transactions charges

❖ change in accounts and transactions volume

❖ response to a price change

❖ whether the pricing strategy conforms to the bank's objectives

Marketing Strategies

Banks can adopt several different marketing strategies, with each strategy having competitive implications.

Provide Services at the Lowest Market Price

This strategy places a premium on internal operating efficiency and maintaining substantial transactions volume so that unit costs and prices remain low. A bank that provides the lowest-priced payment services in its market should command a healthy share of that market. Such a bank is subject to competition from other banks that differentiate their payment services, perhaps by providing better quality or more customized service, even if those services are higher priced.

Still other banks can draw depositors away by directing their marketing efforts and orienting their services to a specific segment of the market, such as high-income earners, college students, or senior citizens. The lowest cost competitor is usually vulnerable to these kinds of competitive strategies because it cannot provide specialized service or devote resources to specific market segment needs without reducing operating efficiency and driving up costs.

Differentiate Services

This strategy places a premium on providing certain payment services that are better, faster, more customized, or in some way different from the same services other banks provide. Marketing, promotion, and advertising focus on these differentiating features, not on price. Banks that follow this strategy are likely to capture that share of the depositor market that recognizes the value of the differentiated service offered, even to a willingness to pay a higher price.

However, such banks are vulnerable to the appeal of low-cost services. Banks may find that in providing differentiated services, they have raised prices above what depositors are willing to pay. Also, the more competitors differentiate, the smaller the value of the services.

Banks that differentiate their services also can lose customers to banks that focus on a specific segment of the market. These banks may be able to draw away some depositors because their resources are devoted to meeting the needs of a select segment of depositors, not the needs of all potential depositors in the market.

Despite the risks, many depositories follow this pricing strategy. For example, many banks have recently tried to differentiate substantially their NOW account, money market deposit account, and credit card products from one another by creating new names for their products and linking them to debit cards, ATM access, low minimum balances, lines of overdraft credit, and other service enhancements.

Segment the Depositor Market

This strategy requires banks to focus their operations, marketing, and advertising on a select market segment. Such banks specialize in providing the services most valuable to their chosen segment, whether it includes high-income earners, senior citizens, small businesses, or college students. Banks using this market strategy tend to draw depositors who want specialized services and attention.

This strategy is not without its risks, however. Other specialized banks may choose to address the very same market segment, and banks providing differentiated or low-cost services may prove more attractive to the targeted depositors. The problems of banks targeted toward women in the late 1970s illustrate the risks of specialization. These banks eventually had to target a larger population segment and modify their competitive strategy to remain solvent, because competitor banks were able to keep their female depositors by offering similar services at lower cost.

Nonetheless, the focused market strategy is prevalent among the nation's small and medium-sized depositories. Recently, banks and thrifts have offered new services and programs specifically tailored to the needs of senior citizens, business professionals, and high-income executives.

Structuring Fees

The service charges banks impose on depositors depend on each bank's competitive objectives and marketing strategies. Although there may be several different tactical motives behind a bank's fee schedule, banks basically charge for their payment services to

❖ cover the costs incurred in providing the service

❖ generate extra income to offset expenses incurred in other areas

❖ alter depositors' payment practices—for example, imposing a substantial fee on returned items to deter depositors from writing checks against insufficient funds

At least one major court decision has supported banks that impose substantial fees on returned items. In 1981, a class action suit was brought against New York's Chemical Bank, which was charging $4 for a check returned for insufficient funds and $1.25 for a check returned for other reasons—both the maximum fees allowed under New York state banking regulations. The New York State Supreme Court, in dismissing the suit, ruled that New York banks can use an overdraft service fee as both a penalty and a deterrent. The court said that banks are free to impose low fees to accommodate depositors, but New York state banking regulations do not require them to do so.

Banks can impose charges in one of two ways: through explicit pricing—assessing a fee for a specific service or transaction or through implicit pricing—requiring depositors who use services to maintain certain minimum or average balances at all times. These balances provide the bank with a source of funds with which to generate income for the bank. Although many banks impose both minimum-balance requirements and transactions fees, the trend has been toward greater reliance on explicit pricing for services banks provide to depositors and for services correspondent banks and the Federal Reserve provide to their respondents.

Most banks have pricing systems that protect their cost structure from the impact of increasing depositor use of payment services. Banks incur certain fixed costs when they establish and maintain accounts for depositors. These costs remain the same whether the depositor makes one payment transaction or several hundred each month. Banks typically charge a fixed rate for establishing the account, a regular monthly maintenance charge, or both. The depositor is then assessed a separate fee for each check, wire transfer of funds, or other payment instrument processed through the account. In this way, depositors who use payment services pay directly for those services, while the bank is protected against increased service use.

For most EFT services, large transactions volume tends to lower the average transaction cost. For this reason, banks frequently offer volume discounts to customers to induce them to increase their use of the service.

Banks also use variations of these pricing practices in their dealings with corporate and individual depositors. Banks often present depositors with a list of available checking account services, each carrying a different pricing schedule. For example, a depositor may choose between a special checking account, a regular checking account, or an interest-earning transaction account such as a NOW or money market deposit account. Bank customers can choose the payment account and price that they consider most suitable.

Covering Costs

Most of the payment services banks provide have traditionally been priced below cost. In the late 1970s and early 1980s, however, most banks began to increase their service charges in response to the rising costs of consumer payment services. This trend has intensified in the 1990s. Explicit fees are now imposed by most banks for the following services:

❖ Overdrafts. Banks' costs for handling bounced checks averaged $12.50 per item in 1990; costs for handling other returned checks averaged about $8.50 per item. On average, customers were paying only about $11 per bounced check in 1990. Several states, such as New York, limit charges that state-chartered banks can levy on bad-check depositors; these limits were generally below banks' 1990 handling costs. New York is considering raising its bad-check charge limits to more closely match banks' costs.

- ❖ Wire transfers.

- ❖ Stop payment orders.

- ❖ Personal checking accounts. Depositors' annual costs for interest-bearing checking accounts averaged about $110 in 1990, more than 6 percent higher than 1988's average. Monthly maintenance fees and bounced check charges accounted for most of the increase.

- ❖ Cashier's checks and money orders.

- ❖ Securities transactions and collection items.

- ❖ Account balance inquiries. In 1989, about 20 percent of the nation's banks charged $1.50, on average, for providing customers with routine account balance information.

- ❖ ATM network transactions. Banks charged customers from 25 cents to $1 per transaction in 1991 for each transaction made at another bank's ATMs; some banks charged $3 per transaction at overseas ATMs.

- ❖ Credit cards.

- ❖ Miscellaneous services. Many banks charge for services that are not widely used. For example, in 1991, large money center and regional banks charged $15 to $20 for consular letters, which banks write on behalf of customers who want to sponsor immigrants seeking U.S. work permits (green cards).

Fees for these services were imposed not to increase profits or match actual costs, but to pass back some of the higher operating costs to the depositors on whose behalf those costs were incurred.

To cover costs, many large banks are closing their brick-and-mortar branches and establishing automated branches where batteries of ATMs and fewer, but more highly trained, staff deliver basic services. Many of these banks are trying to shift their retail banking activities toward machines so that employees can function more as financial service counselors or as sales staff, providing customers with investment and financial advice.

Credit Card Interest Charges and Fees

Bank credit cards lost money in the 1970s because the annual percentage rates, annual membership fees, and merchant fees did not compensate for rising bank operating costs. Not only did these costs increase with 1970s' inflation, but rising interest rates also increased the costs banks had incurred for credit to cardholders—costs that could not be recouped because of legal limits on interest rates.

The annual fees, transaction charges, and service charges that banks assessed their credit cardholders in the 1980s were aimed at the most unprofitable segment of the credit card user market—those cardholders who pay in full within 25 days and who incur no finance charge. The high interest rates of the early 1980's, and state usury laws that prohibited banks in many states from charging consumers an annual percentage rate on credit card loans close to money market rates, kept credit cards unprofitable for many banks.

Credit card profitability soared in the mid-1980s and early 1990s—as inflation slowed and interest rates plummeted. The sharp decline in interest costs to banks, however, was not matched by a reduction in the annual percentage rate most banks charged on credit card loans.

Many bankers contend that the disparity between low interest rates paid on deposits and assessed on corporate loans and the high rates charged on credit card loans is necessary to enable banks to recoup earlier credit card losses. They further contend that high administrative costs involved in credit card operations, together with high loan defaults, require substantially higher interest charges to cover these costs and provide a reasonable profit.

A number of consumer groups and members of Congress have repeatedly urged the government to legislate ceiling rates on credit card interest that would more closely match rates prevailing for most other loans or require banks to disclose their credit card rates and annual fees in advertisements.

Proponents of disclosure argue that more knowledgeable consumers would select and use credit cards only from banks offering lower rates. These actions, they argue, would help reduce overall credit card rates without federal legislation. Many industry analysts contend that disclosure is not likely to bring about a reduction in credit card rates because most credit card users do not consider the annual percentage rate when using their credit cards. Observers note that banks actively compete with one another for credit card business by offering linked products to their credit cards in the form of ATM access, generous credit limits, and discounts on merchandise. These products or features add to the card's value and thus offset some of the interest costs that consumers incur when using their cards.

Most bankers could accept disclosure but are opposed to credit card rate regulation. They argue that limiting interest rates on credit cards might cause banks to eliminate linked products and tighten credit standards, which could drive low-income consumers to even more expensive sources of installment credit for their retail purchases.

Some bankers believe that high interest rates and service charges on credit cards may generate profits in the 1990s but could lead to stronger public pressures for credit card rate regulation. Reducing bank operating costs and providing more desirable credit card services have been proposed as ways to make credit card operations profitable. Integrating all bank card systems and merchant chains into one nationwide online retail payments system is one example.

Maximizing Existing Fees

The sharpest increases in fees during the 1980s came from the nation's large banks. Small banks were less inclined to charge customers higher fees to offset rising service costs or supplement interest income. Many industry analysts see small banks (those with assets of less than $100 million) as the most likely to raise fees in the 1990s. These charges will more fully reflect operating costs or the value of services the banks provide. Existing or new services may be affected in the following ways:

- ❖ premium pricing for personal checks

- ❖ selling savings account deposit and withdrawal slips rather than providing them free of charge

- ❖ charging administrative fees for accounts that close in a certain number of days after opening

- ❖ charging customers for rolls of coin or prepackaged currency

- ❖ charging for all dormant accounts

- ❖ raising safe deposit box rental fees

- ❖ selling personal trust services

- ❖ charging for ATM transactions made at the bank's own machines

- ❖ selling securities bookkeeping and safekeeping services

- ❖ selling mutual funds and insurance, if banks are granted new powers (Under current federal regulations, banks can act as sales agents only for mutual funds and insurance companies; they cannot operate their own mutual funds or issue their own insurance products.)

Not all small banks, however, see a strategy of raising fees and service charges as consistent with their broader objectives. Many have priced NOW and money market deposit accounts below cost in an attempt to attract customers who may later take out loans, open time accounts, rent safe deposit boxes, or bring in other banking business.

Controversy over Service Charges

The increase in bank service charges in the 1980s and 1990s prompted strong concerns among some bankers, consumer groups, and Congress. Bankers are concerned that too many increases or new fees could anger customers and prompt a legislative backlash.

Recent industry surveys show growing consumer irritation at banks' service charges, particularly for basic services. A key annoyance is the complexity and packaged nature of most banks' service charge structures for checking and savings accounts. Customers say that maintenance charges, transactions charges, and levels of account balances have made bank charges difficult to understand or compare with those of competitors. In November 1991, Congress responded to this concern by enacting truth in savings legislation that requires banks to disclose—on a uniform, nationwide basis—all the terms and conditions under which interest is paid and fees are assessed on accounts. The federal regulatory agencies must have these rules in place by the beginning of 1993.

Congress and consumer groups are also concerned that banks may be pricing payments services out of reach of low-income customers. Several bills were introduced in Congress in 1991 to require banks to offer a lifeline account—a low-cost basic transaction account that everyone can afford. Although the lifeline account requirement was not enacted into law, Congress passed legislation that gives banks a financial incentive for providing lifeline accounts on their own. The deposit insurance premium rate on lifeline accounts is only half the rate applicable to other insured deposits.

Some service charges increased in the 1980s faster than the rate of inflation and bank costs. However, a 1985 Federal Reserve study found that increases in checking account fees in the early 1980s were lower than the increases banks incurred in providing interest-bearing NOW and money market deposit accounts. The study also found that most banks were providing some free services to senior citizens and minors.

In 1989, Congress requested the Federal Reserve to initiate another study of bank service charges to see if industry price and cost factors had changed.

Pricing Practices of Correspondent Banks

The prices correspondent banks charge their respondent banks for wholesale payment services include the cost of providing services plus an appropriate return on investment.

Costs and profit, however, are only two of the considerations correspondents take into account in setting prices for respondents. Often, competitive market conditions and the marketing strategy of the correspondent bank weigh heavily in pricing decisions. This results in different services carrying higher or lower profit markups than the average rate of return.

Most correspondent banks try to establish a full business relationship with respondent banks by presenting a package of payment and financial services. While most respondent banks do not use all the services correspondents offer, the ability of the correspondents to provide services that respondents may want in the future is valuable. The packaged marketing approach has worked successfully for correspondents in securing stable markets.

Pricing of Electronic Funds Transfers

The pricing of EFT services has raised particular problems for bank management. EFT systems require large initial capital outlays and a long period of operating time before they generate enough revenue to recover costs. Promotional costs are also substantial because consumers and merchants have to be sold on EFT payment practices. EFT systems are profitable only with large transactions volume, which can take years for a bank to generate because most EFT costs, like those for ATMs, are fixed. The more an EFT system is used, the more cost effective it is.

EFT services must be priced high enough to ensure that the bank has some prospect of profit but low enough to keep the services competitive. This has been difficult because more banks offer similar EFT services to similar markets. Thus, prospects for the success of a differentiated pricing strategy are bleak. Furthermore, banks and thrift institutions have helped create consumer resistance to EFT service prices by underpricing their paper payments services.

The increasing costs of check processing in the 1980s and 1990s, however, have given banks added incentive to raise their prices for paper payments. This may make EFT more attractive to both depositors and banks.

Summary

Deposit management has many facets. Exceptions in the collection process require a disproportionate share of management time and bank resources. Banks seek to eliminate risk and liability by assuring themselves that the checks they honor contain the proper signature, endorsement, and date, and are not subject to stop payment orders or holds. Until 1988, banks delayed availability on deposited checks to ensure that no loss would be incurred if they were returned unpaid. Such policies became a source of controversy in the 1980s and led to federal legislation in 1987 that sets the maximum delay banks can impose on a customer's use of deposited check funds.

Banks use computerized DDA systems to process checks. These systems have allowed banks to manage a growing volume of checks while improving their operating efficiency.

In the 1990s, banks have sought to cope with the rising costs of deposit operations by increasing their service charges, focusing on selected markets, and differentiating their products. However, banks' pricing practices and high credit card interest rates have come under congressional review.

Questions

1. Identify four common reasons a bank might be unwilling to pay a check upon presentment.

2. Since banks receive credit for checks they collect within one or two days, should banks apply this same schedule to customers in allowing them to draw against deposited checks?

3. What risk does a bank face if it allows a customer to draw against uncollected funds?

4. What three basic pricing strategies can banks follow in marketing their services?

SOURCES AND USES OF BANK FUNDS

Objectives

After successfully completing this chapter, you will be able to

❖ identify banks' key earning assets and financial liabilities

❖ discuss bank funds management change in the 1970s and 1980s, and funds management strategies banks use today

❖ explain the tactics banks use to implement a spread management strategy

❖ define key money market sources of bank funds—CDs, federal funds, repurchase agreements, and Eurodollar borrowings

Introduction

The basic sources of bank funds are deposits; the basic uses of bank funds are loans and investments. Banks generate profit primarily by positioning themselves so that they earn more on their loans and investments than they pay to attract and retain deposits. The bigger the interest rate spread between the price a bank pays for funds and the price it receives for funds, the bigger the profit return.

In managing sources and uses of funds, banks are under conflicting pressure from their markets. Depositors consistently want higher interest rate returns; borrowers want lower interest rate charges. A central problem of bank management is selecting or designing a funds management strategy that enables the bank to successfully compete in both markets while positioning the bank to increase its spread.

Chapter 7 focused on several factors that establish the boundaries of a bank's funds management strategy, primarily

- ❖ the need for excess reserves to expand loans and investments
- ❖ constraints of the Federal Reserve's reserve requirements and monetary policy on the cost and availability of reserves
- ❖ strategies other banks adopt in managing their assets and liabilities

This chapter examines how banks work within those boundaries to obtain excess reserves, and how they use the reserves. Strategies banks have long relied on—asset allocation and liability management—developed into the spread management strategies of the 1980s, and the strategies many banks use today. It also reviews key money market sources of funds (and reserves)—certificates of deposit, Eurodollar borrowings, federal funds, repurchase agreements—and banks' major uses of funds—loans and investments.

Funds Management Strategy

Until the 1960s, bank funds management was largely passive. Bankers operated under the assumption that a bank's earning assets (loans and investments) had to be financed with corporate demand deposits and consumer time deposits. That is, only by taking in additional deposits could reserves be acquired to allow for more loans and investments. Since banks had little control over the level of their deposits—their primary source of funds—sound bank management dictated that banks had to maintain substantial liquidity in the form of primary reserves (cash assets) and secondary reserves (liquid, short-term securities). Business loans were the primary use of excess funds. Bank profits equaled the difference between the stable interest rates paid on core deposits, with maximums fixed by law and regulation, and the slightly higher but equally stable lending rates banks charged. Federal law prohibited paying interest on demand deposits, and the Federal Reserve's Regulation Q established the maximum rates banks could pay on time and savings deposits.

Asset Allocation Strategy   *— loan & investment assets*

Under an asset allocation strategy, banks seek to maintain and expand earnings by continually reallocating funds between loan and investment assets. However, before any funds can be allocated, the bank must meet operating expenses and provide for the fixed assets (building and equipment) necessary to conduct business. After these provisions, funds are allocated into the following four categories in descending order of priority:

Primary reserves. The first allocation is made to vault cash and account balances with the Federal Reserve bank and/or correspondent banks to meet reserve requirements and/or day-to-day liquidity needs.

Secondary reserves. The second allocation is based on forecasted loan and deposit growth over the coming year. Funds are invested in secondary reserve assets of differing maturities—primarily U.S. Treasury securities—based on this forecast. Under an ideal asset allocation strategy, in which the bank's forecast is on target, secondary reserve assets mature at the same time the bank needs funds to meet loan demand or to cover deposit outflow.   *T-bill*

Income account. All remaining funds are used to meet loan demand. The bank's loan portfolio is its primary income-generating account.

Residual account. If there are residual funds after all loan demand has been met, these funds are invested in long-term U.S. Treasury, federal agency, and state and local securities.

The fundamental premise of asset allocation strategy is that banks buy securities when loan demand is down and interest rates low. When loan demand builds, banks sell these securities to raise funds to meet loan demand. However, rising interest rates usually accompany strong loan demand, and when interest rates rise securities prices fall. Banks that sell securities in such a market must be prepared to take capital losses on the assets sold. Capital losses make sense if they can be more than offset by interest earnings on loans made from selling the securities, or if capital losses can be used as a tax offset to shelter other income. Thus, asset allocation requires bankers to assess loan charges carefully and to be keenly aware of the bank's ongoing tax position.

banks buy sec. when loan is down & interest rates are low

Liability Management

In the 1960s and 1970s, banks revolutionized source management and funds use by focusing on liabilities—meeting demands for new loans by buying or borrowing needed funds. This approach, called liability management, requires bankers to carefully evaluate and use a balanced blend of sources of funds over which they have complete control, such as federal funds, large denomination corporate CDs, repurchase agreements and Eurodollar borrowings.

Banks also began to compete with thrift institutions, money market funds, and market instruments themselves for sources of funds by offering time deposits of different types and maturities. Under a liability management strategy, a bank's profits are largely determined by the spread between the interest rates a bank pays on money bought or borrowed and the interest rates it charges on loans or earns on investments.

Spread Management

The management of bank funds changed again in the 1980s. The Monetary Control Act restructured and simplified reserve requirements early in the decade and Regulation Q ceilings were eliminated in 1986. At the same time, the introduction of interest-bearing transaction accounts altered the public's deposit preferences, sharply increased banks' interest expense, and led to a steady narrowing of spreads. Banks could no longer rely on stable demand deposits and consumer time and savings deposits as guaranteed sources of funds.

Because banks typically take in deposits and make loans at different times, increases or decreases in interest rates can place a bank in a position where it is paying higher interest on deposits than the interest it is earning on loans and investments. When interest rate changes are gradual and predictable, banks attempt to change their sources and uses of funds to maintain or increase their interest rate spreads.

In 1979, the Federal Reserve changed its monetary policy tactics in an effort to stop the inflation that had been building in the economy throughout the 1970s. It shifted the focus of its open market operations from tight control of the federal funds rate to tight control of bank reserves and money supply growth. This resulted in sharp and unpredictable increases and decreases in short-term interest rates in the early 1980s.

In this new environment of volatile interest rates, banks' attempts to adjust their sources and uses of funds offered little assurance that the interest earned on loans and investments would exceed the interest paid to retain deposits or to borrow funds. A new defensive strategy called spread management soon emerged.

Banks that practice spread management focus on maintaining a constant difference or margin between the average interest rate they pay for funds and the average interest rate they receive on funds loaned and invested. The premise of spread management is that banks cannot forecast interest-rate changes with consistent accuracy and cannot restructure their balance sheets quickly enough to match interest-rate changes. Recognizing these limitations, spread management strategy requires banks to try to hedge against fluctuations in interest rates. That is, banks must maintain a close numerical balance between what they pay for funds and what they charge for funds. If they achieve balance, the bank's spread will be stable. As market interest rates rise, both the bank's cost of funds and its return on invested and loaned funds will increase in proportion. As market rates decline, both costs and returns will fall in tandem.

If a bank could structure itself so that its balance sheet is perfectly matched—its deposits and loan repayments perfectly match its withdrawals and new loans—then it would not have to worry about changes in interest rates because it could raise or lower the rates it charges and the rates it pays in tandem. Such structural matching, however, is not feasible. Most borrowers request loans that create a schedule of repayments that differ from the withdrawal patterns of depositors. If banks tried to force borrowers to tailor their requests to depositors' payments patterns, they would lose business. Nonetheless, tactics to implement spread management emerged in the 1980s in which bankers seek to more effectively match their banks' assets with their liabilities. These tactics include maturity matching, duration matching, and variable rate pricing of loans and deposits.

Maturity Matching

Banks developed new strategies in the 1980s to protect their interest spreads by matching the maturities of specific loan and investment assets with the maturities of specific deposit liabilities.

For example, if a bank makes $1 million in new mortgage loans, it might seek to take in $1 million in passbook savings or individual retirement account deposits because mortgage assets and passbook savings or IRA liabilities are likely to remain on the bank's books for a similar time period. Likewise, if the bank takes in $500,000 from 30-day corporate CDs, it might try to match those funds with an equal investment in 30-day Treasury bills. If interest rates increase when the CD matures and the bank has to pay more to retain the funds, it can reinvest or lend at a higher rate proceeds from the maturing Treasury bill. If the corporation withdraws its CD funds, the bank has ready funds available to meet this withdrawal from the matured Treasury bill.

A matching strategy is not easy to implement because demand for loans within specific maturity categories, such as one-year business loans, and the availability of high-return money market investments may not always match the maturities of new deposits coming into the bank. Also, economic conditions may justify holding back on making new loans or investments when growing deposits would require matching these new funds with new loans or investments.

Duration Matching

Some bankers try to match their assets and liabilities on duration—the average length of time assets and liabilities are expected to remain on the balance sheet.

For example, the average duration of a 30-year mortgage is likely to be about 5 to 6 years. Some of the bank's mortgage holders will sell their homes, others will prepay their mortgages, and others will default on their mortgage loans. If a bank carries 30-year mortgages in its loan portfolio, it need only match those assets against 5- to 6-year deposits.

A duration-matching strategy is not easy for banks to follow. Banks must continually monitor their duration positions and be prepared to realign the duration of assets to the bank's liabilities. For most banks, this can be tedious, demanding, and costly.

Variable Rate Pricing on Loans and Deposits

Many banks try to maintain their interest-rate spreads by making new loans and new deposits subject to variable interest rates—rates that change every month (or year in the case of mortgages)—to reflect changes in the bank's cost of and return on funds.

Strategies for the 1990s

By the mid-1980s, market conditions had changed. In 1982, the Federal Reserve altered its monetary policy tactics again, reverting back to tighter control of the federal funds rate. Inflation slowed dramatically and interest rates fell from the 15 to 18 percent range of the early 1980s. However, banks faced weak business and consumer loan demand, general resistance to variable rate loans, and continuing declines in profitability.

Banks' interest costs increased disproportionately to income in the 1980s because banks had to pay interest on an increasingly larger share of their total deposits. At the same time, banks incurred losses on their earning assets—securities in the early 1980s and loans throughout the decade.

Loan loss reserves, which must be set aside to cover probable but undetermined losses on loans, increased throughout the industry, particularly among banks with large portfolios of agricultural, energy, and commercial real estate loans, and loans to foreign countries.

The nation's biggest banks experienced the sharpest rise in interest costs because of their heavy reliance on interest-rate-sensitive purchased funds. These banks also experienced the largest loan losses because of the size of their foreign country loans (and loan loss provisions). Small banks saw interest costs rise because holders of checking accounts increasingly shifted their demand deposits into interest-bearing transaction accounts and holders of time deposits increasingly transferred their fixed-rate time deposits into higher yielding money market deposit accounts. Many small banks in farming states saw profits evaporate as increasing numbers of agricultural borrowers defaulted on their loans. Banks in the Southwest also were hit hard when energy producers experienced a sharp drop in earnings and in their ability to repay bank loans when world oil prices plummeted in the 1980s.

Most bankers have come to realize that there is no perfect way to manage assets and liabilities, so that banks can be assured that the interest they pay on deposits and borrowed funds always will be less than interest received on earning assets. Many banks have sought to gain greater control over interest-rate spread in the 1990s by adopting some new strategies.

In the 1990s, maintaining balanced or favorable repricing gaps in the timing of maturing assets and liabilities has become an effective strategy for some banks. For other banks, the securitization of assets has become critical to their management of funds (banks issue securities backed by expected income from such assets as mortgages and credit card loans).

Gap Management Strategy

Gap management involves selectively mismatching assets and liabilities to capitalize on expected interest-rate changes. This strategy involves grouping bank assets and liabilities into specific time periods, such as three months, six months, or one year, and identifying the gap between those assets and liabilities that have to be repriced in these periods.

For example, if a bank had more assets than liabilities subject to repricing in the next 90 days, it would be considered asset sensitive and would be exposed to the risk of falling interest rates. The bank will then obtain a lower return on all assets that are being repriced. However, the bank is still locked into paying higher interest on those liabilities that have not yet matured.

If the bank had more liabilities than assets maturing in a six-month period, it would be considered liability sensitive in that period, and it would be exposed to the risk of rising interest rates. If interest rates rise, the bank will have to pay a higher rate on all those liabilities that are being repriced. However, the bank is locked into the lower rates it receives on assets that have not yet matured.

A bank that believes interest rates will fall over the next six months would try to make its balance sheet liability sensitive for that period. If rates fall, the bank benefits because it reprices its liabilities at lower rates while it still receives higher rates on assets that have not yet matured. A fixed-rate, long-term loan locks a bank into an interest return that cannot be changed if short-term conditions increase bank costs. However, interest rates on long-term loans tend to be higher than those on short-term loans. A loan portfolio weighted toward fixed-rate, long-term maturities can generate substantial earnings if interest rates decline for an extended period after the loans are made. Indeed, as interest rates declined and then stabilized in the mid-1980s, most banks shifted toward more fixed-rate, longer-term loans and longer-term investments.

Securitization

Banks that practice securitization package their loans into securities and sell the securities to institutional investors. This strategy enables banks to obtain a new source of funds and to keep some revenue, in the form of servicing fees, from the packaged loans. At the same time, securitization can reduce banks' credit risk if the packaged loans are sold without recourse (a legal claim on the selling bank in the event of default). Loan assets securitized without recourse are no longer carried on the selling bank's balance sheet. Thus, the selling bank is not at risk if borrowers default and does not have to include the loans as assets when it calculates how much capital it must maintain for regulatory purposes.

In the 1990s, banks have been securitizing mortgages and credit card loans, and are beginning to develop markets for securitizing riskier loans, such as nonperforming loans and foreign country loans. These loans require higher capital allocations under the risk-based capital rules that large banks have been subject to since 1988.

Hedging in the Futures Market

Banks that hedge in the futures market seek to reduce the exposure of their securities investments to rising interest rates by selling some of their securities in the futures market. A futures contract for securities is a commitment to buy or sell securities at a future date at an agreed price.

If a bank that engages in hedging expects interest rates to increase, it sells securities in the futures market, locking in a current price for the securities it will deliver at a future date. When interest rates rise, securities prices fall. However, the hedged bank does not sustain a capital loss on the securities it delivers under the futures contract because it locked in the current (higher) price before interest rates rose.

A bank that expects interest rates to fall (and securities prices to increase) can hedge by buying in the futures market. Thus, when rates fall, the hedged bank receives its securities at the lower price agreed to before interest rates fell.

Other Strategies

- Banks are pricing loans so that the interest rate charged covers not only administrative costs and funding costs but also the bank's opportunity cost of committing to loans in advance. By imposing high loan commitment fees on borrowers, banks cover the opportunity cost incurred in committing to loans in advance. In the 1980s, banks' noninterest income grew faster than banks' assets, primarily because of loan commitment fees and standby letters of credit fees.

- A bank may reduce the cost of its liabilities by lowering deposit rates. Some bankers contend that this strategy is unworkable because banks that cut deposit rates will lose deposits to competitors. However, industry analysts note that banks located in the same region frequently maintain deposit-rate differences on similar accounts of as much as one to two percentage points. Analysts also cite the quality of a bank's service and the convenience of its offices or ATMs as factors that tend to offset lower deposit rates in the view of most depositors.

- Banks are seeking to reduce operating expenses and overhead costs by closing marginally profitable branches, selling product lines, cutting back on personalized customer services, and restructuring operating departments.

- Charging for services previously provided free and raising both basic and exception-item service charges is another strategy employed by banks to offset costs. Most banks incurred increased noninterest expenses in the 1980s to service a growing volume of new accounts. These banks tended to keep noninterest income and expenses in tandem by raising service fees and charges on transaction accounts to match higher operating costs.

- Banks have sought to reduce dependence on purchased funds and borrowings as sources of funds. Since the mid-1980s, the nation's money center banks have built increasingly larger bases of stable consumer time and savings deposits. This shift in funding emphasis from reliance on managed liabilities is a result of a shift in money center banks' marketing focus from corporate banking to consumer banking. In the 1990s, consumer services have become more profitable to big banks than corporate lending and reflect the movement of consumer accounts from savings and loan associations to commercial banks.

The funds management strategies that commercial banks follow are not all the same. Factors such as asset size, business orientation, market share, and number of branches and offices determine the precise strategy a bank will follow. Yet despite these and other differences, the basic products of banks—loans and investments—are essentially the same. And the principles banks must follow to obtain reserves—the raw materials needed to make those products—are similar.

Controlling Assets and Liabilities

Most banks' strategy for obtaining and using funds focuses primarily on interest-sensitive assets and liabilities that can be increased or decreased quickly. The ability to control, not simply to predict, sources and uses of funds is essential to any well-planned strategy. However, not all bank assets and liabilities are readily subject to management control.

Demand Deposits

Checking account deposits often are referred to as relationship deposits—funds flow to the bank because the depositor chooses to maintain a relationship with that specific bank, often because of the bank's location.

Although demand deposits traditionally have been considered the most stable and least expensive source of funds, they are not readily subject to short-term control by bank management. Also, because demand deposit accounts are heavy-volume transaction accounts, generally with no minimum balances, they usually have the highest operational costs and carry the largest regular monthly fees.

As a source of funds, demand deposits began to decline relative to other deposits in the 1970s. Corporations began to use more sophisticated cash management options. In the 1980s, demand deposit totals declined as consumers switched funds from noninterest-earning demand accounts into interest-earning transaction accounts—such as negotiable order of withdrawal and money market deposit accounts. In 1992, demand deposits (totaling about $290 billion) accounted for less than 10 percent of total bank liabilities (about $3 trillion).

Time Deposits

Consumer time and savings deposits at commercial banks also are viewed as relationship deposits. Until 1986, when interest-rate ceilings were entirely eliminated, consumers who maintained time and savings accounts at commercial banks gave up the opportunity to earn the higher interest rates paid by thrift institutions. Thus, consumers appeared to prefer the convenience of banking at one site. For this reason, these deposits, like demand deposits, were long considered a relatively stable source of bank funds.

Most banks involved in retail banking actively seek consumer time and savings deposits and have typically paid the maximum rates allowed to attract the funds. The liberalization of Regulation Q ceilings in the 1970s enabled banks to offer a broader range of types and maturities of time deposits and to pay higher rates, but banks lost deposits to money market funds and Treasury bills, which were not constrained by Regulation Q ceilings.

The phaseout of Regulation Q ceilings between 1980 and 1986 permitted banks to offer new consumer-oriented time deposits and to pay market interest rates. However, the elimination of interest-rate ceilings also introduced a degree of instability in time and savings deposits. Most banks were forced to compete aggressively in the 1980s with other banks, thrifts, and financial intermediaries for new types of deposits, especially for 6-month money market certificates, 30-month certificates, and money market deposit accounts. Consumers responded with remarkable sensitivity to interest-rate differences and changing rates of return. They not only demonstrated their willingness to move funds from traditional time and savings accounts into higher-yield time certificates at their banks, but also to transfer time account funds out of banks into high interest-paying Treasury bills and money market funds. Then, as market conditions changed, they were willing to transfer monies from maturing financial assets into money market deposit accounts at banks. Banks and thrift institutions experienced only moderate deposit growth, while their interest expenses soared.

Constraints on Funds Management

Before the 1960s, most banks did not have access to money market sources of funds, and they did not have enough control over their traditional sources and uses of funds to adjust quickly to changing market conditions and interest rates. Although a bank's advertising and marketing efforts could influence the future flow of consumer demand and time deposits, banks were limited in the short run by interest-rate ceilings. Bank management could forecast the flow of consumer time deposits because maturity schedules were known in advance, but they could do little to control the flow.

In addition to interest-rate ceilings on time deposits, banks were constrained by usury ceilings on consumer and real estate loans. Banks also were confronted with different reserve requirements on different types of deposits, minimum maturity and denomination requirements for certain deposits, relatively low FDIC insurance coverage on accounts, specific collateral requirements on most loans, and maximum lending limits relative to their capital and surplus. In this environment of constraints, most banks relied on an asset allocation strategy for managing sources and uses of funds.

Eliminating Constraints on Funds Management

Changes in banking regulation in the 1960s and 1970s and by the 1980 Monetary Control Act eliminated many constraints that limited banks' ability to

---

manage sources and uses of funds. The act restructured and simplified reserve requirement rules, initiated the phasing out of Regulation Q ceilings, increased FDIC insurance coverage, and authorized new accounts and market offerings. But these changes in law and regulation were prompted by a virtual revolution in the ways banks obtained and used funds.

The 1960s saw the beginning of the tight monetary policy and high interest rates that would change bank operations over the following two decades. To banks, the Federal Reserve's tight money policies, which were designed to restrain inflation, also dampened banks' ability to expand earning assets. Furthermore, high interest rates had raised the cost of holding required reserves. To reduce the amount of required reserves held, banks began to encourage customers to shift their funds from demand deposits, which carried relatively high reserve requirements, to other types of deposits that would earn interest for the depositor while carrying much lower reserve requirements. Banks soon found that financial institutions and corporations were more than willing to reduce their own holdings of demand deposits to obtain an interest return on balances that would otherwise have been held idle.

Major Sources of Managed Funds

In the 1960s and 1970s, banks began obtaining funds in new ways, such as issuing negotiable certificates of deposit, selling commercial paper through holding company affiliates, engaging in repurchase agreements, buying federal funds, and, for the nation's large money center banks, borrowing Eurodollars. The practice of managing these and other sources of funds that can be directly controlled by bankers is called liability management. (See exhibit 9.1 for a profile of large banks' sources of funds.)

The Negotiable CD

The negotiable certificate of deposit (CD), invented in 1961 by Citibank (then First National City Bank of New York), was the first step in the liability management revolution.

Regulation Q not only prohibited banks from paying interest on demand deposits but also specified that interest-earning time deposits like CDs had to have minimum maturities of 30 days.

Citibank's CD offered corporations, in effect, an interest return on their demand deposits. For Citibank and other big banks that followed its lead, the negotiable CD offered a way for high-reserve-requirement demand deposits to be converted into lower-reserve-requirement time deposits. Citibank developed a secondary market for the CDs by gaining the support of the Discount Corporation, a major government securities dealer that would buy or sell existing CDs to allow corporations to get their money back without having to wait 30 days. A corporation that had to meet a multimillion-dollar payroll on the fifteenth of the month, for example, could buy a CD on the first day of the month, then sell it in the secondary market on the fourteenth in time to cover its payroll checks.

The corporation would earn 14 days' interest, which would be reflected in the sale price; the purchaser, perhaps another corporation seeking a return on short-term funds, would earn 16 days' interest when the CD matured.

Today, large negotiable CDs account for a major share of the financial liabilities that most of the nation's large commercial banks carry. In 1991, banks with assets in excess of $1 billion held more than $200 billion in these CDs, about one-quarter of their total interest-bearing deposits and about equal to their personal and corporate demand deposits. For the banking system, negotiable CDs represent about 25 percent of total interest-bearing liabilities.

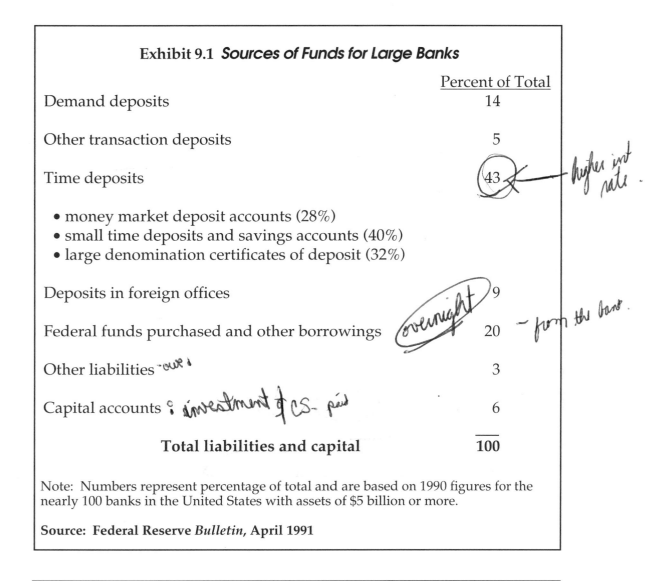

Exhibit 9.1 *Sources of Funds for Large Banks*

	Percent of Total
Demand deposits	14
Other transaction deposits	5
Time deposits	43
• money market deposit accounts (28%)	
• small time deposits and savings accounts (40%)	
• large denomination certificates of deposit (32%)	
Deposits in foreign offices	9
Federal funds purchased and other borrowings	20
Other liabilities	3
Capital accounts	6
Total liabilities and capital	**100**

Note: Numbers represent percentage of total and are based on 1990 figures for the nearly 100 banks in the United States with assets of $5 billion or more.

Source: Federal Reserve *Bulletin*, **April 1991**

Most banks find negotiable CDs very attractive as a managed source of funds because banks can negotiate on a daily basis with potential corporate depositors for CDs that match the bank's needs. Large quantities of CDs are usually available to a bank willing to bid high enough to attract those CDs that would have gone to other banks or funds that would have been invested in various money market instruments. Interest rates on negotiable CDs go up when banks need funds to meet strong loan demand because reserve funds become scarce when loan demand increases and more banks bid for a limited supply of reserves.

In the late 1960s, the nation's large banks found that their ability to use negotiable CDs to attract corporate deposits was thwarted by the Federal Reserve's Regulation Q ceilings. In 1966 and 1969, interest returns for Treasury bills and commercial paper were higher than interest rates allowed for CDs under Regulation Q. This not only made the issuance and secondary market trading of CDs unattractive but also precipitated a massive trading out of CDs as they matured. In 1970, the Federal Reserve removed Regulation Q ceilings on large-denomination, short-term CDs (the most popular corporate-oriented instrument). However, by the late 1960s, the nation's largest banks had moved on to another innovation to obtain reserves—Eurodollar borrowings.

Eurodollar Borrowings

Eurodollars are U.S. dollars deposited in banking offices outside the United States. Foreign banks and foreign branches of U.S. banks lend these dollars to U.S. banks for a reasonable price. When U.S. banks borrow these funds, they are recorded as Eurodollar borrowings (liabilities).

In the late 1960s, the nation's large banks began to borrow significant amounts of these dollars to bolster their reserve positions and offset losses of corporate CDs. As the practice escalated, primarily between the London and Paris branches of U.S. banks and their head offices in New York City, so did the concerns of bank regulators.

Mechanics of Eurodollar Borrowings

When the head office of a U.S. bank obtained Eurodollars, it borrowed from its overseas branch. Just as a corporation borrows funds and not deposits from a bank, the head office borrowed funds and not deposits acquired by its branch in the Eurodollar market. The Eurodollar deposit was handled as a liability on the books of the overseas branch. The head office could not and did not borrow the deposit liability of its own branch.

To borrow from its overseas branch, the head office of a U.S. bank would instruct the branch to bid for Eurodollar deposits. Since overseas deposits were free from Regulation Q ceilings, branch offices could pay high rates to draw funds, which generally came from institutions or corporations with accounts at U.S. banks.

When the branch obtained these funds, it instructed the owners of the dollars to have their banks in the United States pay the dollars to the branch's head office. The banks of the Eurodollar owners then issued official checks to transfer the funds to the head office. When the head office received the checks, it recorded them on the books as cash items in the process of collection. The head office listed the checks as liabilities due its foreign branch, not as deposits.

After the official checks cleared, reserves were redistributed within the U.S. banking system. While the Eurodollar transactions did not change the level of total reserves, they did change the level of required reserves.

In the late 1960s, Eurodollar liabilities due to an overseas branch by its head office were not subject to reserve requirements. The bank could use the additional reserves generated by the checks without having to hold a fraction of the funds as a required reserve against outstanding deposit liabilities.

The Effect of Eurodollar Transactions

Because liabilities to overseas branches were not technically deposits and thus not subject to reserve requirements, the banking system could carry a larger amount of liabilities for a given amount of reserves. Since banks that obtained funds from their branches typically had reserve deficiencies and tended to employ all available funds, the additional liabilities were used to meet loan commitments or reduce borrowings from other sources. The acquisition of reserves by head offices through the Eurodollar operations of their branches increased available reserves by turning some required reserves into excess reserves.

To address this problem, the Federal Reserve in 1969 imposed a special reserve requirement on Eurodollar borrowings, in an effort to reduce banks' reliance on this source of funds and to improve the Federal Reserve's monetary control. When the Monetary Control Act of 1980 restructured reserve requirements, a 3 percent reserve requirement was retained for Eurodollar borrowings. The Federal Reserve eliminated the requirement in 1990 in an effort to stimulate bank lending by providing banks with a ready supply of excess reserves.

To borrow Eurodollars, a bank has to have access to an overseas bank. Thus competition for Eurodollars is not as strong as for domestic market sources of funds. However, large money center banks with ready access to the Eurodollar market frequently use Eurodollar borrowings for overnight and weekend funding arrangements. Unlike the CD market, the Eurodollar market is essentially an overnight market, with interest rates subject to bigger and more frequent changes.

Commercial Paper Sales of Bank Affiliates

Commercial paper is a short-term, unsecured, uncollateralized promissory note that corporations with solid credit ratings issue as a means of borrowing funds for a short time.

Banks are not permitted to issue commercial paper, but many banks are owned by holding companies that can issue it. Commercial paper issued by a bank holding company can benefit the bank in two ways:

❖ The holding company can deposit the proceeds from commercial paper sales in the bank, increasing the bank's funds.

❖ The holding company can use the proceeds from the commercial paper offering to purchase loans or investments from the bank, effectively improving the bank's overall earning-asset position.

Since a bank is usually a bank holding company's major investment or asset, commercial paper issued by the holding company generally is considered of high quality and perceived to be secured by the implicit backing (assets) of the bank itself.

In the 1960s, the nation's large banks used their holding company structure to obtain funds through commercial paper issues by their affiliates. Under this system, a subsidiary of the bank holding company would issue its own commercial paper. Because commercial paper was not subject to Regulation Q ceilings, the interest rate that the subsidiary could offer exceeded the rates that banks themselves could pay on time deposits. Thus, commercial paper instruments were highly competitive. Purchasers of the subsidiaries' paper knew that even though the paper was unsecured, the parent bank of the holding company implicitly stood behind the paper. The combination of implicit bank backing plus a competitive interest rate free from Regulation Q constraints made the commercial paper easily salable.

The money received from the subsidiary's commercial paper sales was then channeled back to the parent bank. However, since these funds were not deposits, they were not subject to reserve requirements—every dollar received could be used to support an additional dollar of new loans.

In response, the Federal Reserve modified its reserve requirement rules in 1970 to define as deposits the funds a bank receives from an affiliate's sale of commercial paper. This source of funds was then subject to reserve requirements, thereby closing a loophole in the regulations that the Federal Reserve contended had impaired its monetary policy control. The Monetary Control Act of 1980 ended the reserve requirement rule.

Repurchase Agreements

Under a repurchase agreement, or RP, a bank sells securities from its portfolio at an agreed price, with an understanding that it will repurchase them at a higher price within a specified time. (Specified times between sale and repurchase are usually a few days, so the value of the securities involved remains unchanged.) The repurchase agreement is effectively a collateralized loan to the bank by an external party or other bank.

Repos or RPs offer the lender an unusually secure loan and the bank a low-cost form of financing because of the security collateral. Generally, the securities themselves do not leave and re-enter the bank; rather, the repurchase agreement merely stipulates the lender's prior claim on the securities.

In 1969, the nation's large commercial banks introduced the repurchase agreement as a source of funds innovation. RPs, like demand deposits, were posted as a bank liability. The difference between repurchase agreements and demand deposits, however, was that the reserve requirement against repurchase agreements was zero until 1979, while the reserve requirement against demand deposits held by large banks could be as high as $16\frac{1}{4}$ percent.

This difference in reserve requirements was substantial enough for banks to pay an interest return to their own corporate demand depositors with whom they entered into RP arrangements, and still profit because they could convert newly freed reserves into earning assets. Today, the repurchase agreement has become an integral component of the cash management systems banks market to corporations and state and local governments. Corporations and municipalities with idle funds enter into continuing RP contracts with banks every day.

In 1979, the Federal Reserve imposed an 8 percent reserve requirement against repurchase agreements and certain other managed liabilities that exceeded a base amount. This move was designed to improve the Fed's control over the money supply by reducing banks' use of repurchase agreements and other nonreservable liabilities as reserve sources. The reserve requirement was imposed as part of a special credit restraint program, which was terminated in 1980.

Federal Funds

Federal funds are immediately available funds that banks borrow and lend to each other for one business day. Banks use the funds primarily for reserve adjustment transactions.

The term federal funds comes from the reserve account balances banks maintain at Federal Reserve banks. When the practice originated in the 1920s, New York City banks that were members of the Federal Reserve borrowed from one another by presenting checks drawn on their reserve accounts at the Federal Reserve Bank of New York. Today, banks use the Federal Reserve's wire transfer network (FedWire) to make instantaneous transfers of reserve account balances.

Money market banks rely on the daily purchase and sale of federal funds to adjust their reserves, so that they neither hold excess reserves—which carry a high cost in forgone earnings—nor incur penalties for reserve deficiencies. Most money market banks prepare early morning estimates of their expected reserve position for that day. Based on those estimates, they adjust their reserves with daily purchases or sales of federal funds.

Most of the federal funds market activity is based in the money market banks in New York City. These banks buy reserves from regional and small community-based banks that may not have a ready market for overnight loans, then channel those funds to their own brokers, dealers, or multinational corporate customers.

The federal funds market became the dominant market for obtaining reserves in the 1960s. The widespread use of federal funds in that decade—which grew even greater in the 1970s and 1980s—has been attributed to the following factors:

❖ In 1960, the Federal Reserve changed its reserve requirement rules to allow banks to count vault cash as part of their reserves. This addition increased the amount of reserves available that could be bought or sold.

❖ The Federal Reserve was reluctant to open its discount window to supply banks routinely with additional reserves.

❖ In 1963, the Comptroller of the Currency ruled that nationally chartered banks could post federal funds transactions as purchases and sales, not as borrowings and loans. The change in nomenclature removed federal funds transactions from federal restrictions on how much money one bank could lend to one borrower.

❖ Banks became more sophisticated throughout the decade in reducing the level of their excess reserve balances. In 1960, the amount of excess reserves Federal Reserve member banks held daily equaled 4 percent of required reserves. By the end of the decade, however, the daily average had fallen to less than 1 percent.

❖ The strong competition among money market banks for correspondent banking business encouraged money market banks to begin trading federal funds in order to provide a new service to respondent banks and corporate customers—buying and selling immediately available funds.

Some economists contend that the money center banks in New York play an important role in the banking system by redistributing reserves. This redistribution maximizes the use of the banking system's reserves by ensuring that banks with excess reserves can shift those reserves to banks with reserve deficiencies or banks that need reserves for investments or loans.

Other economists suggest that the growth in federal funds purchases by the New York City banks can result in situations where the funds bought greatly exceed required reserves. This carries grave risks. For example, in 1974, New York City's Franklin National Bank made a basic error that contributed to its failure; it relied on short-term federal funds borrowings as a source of funds to finance long-term loans. As federal funds rates rose, Franklin National Bank paid more for money to finance its assets than the return it was obtaining on those assets. This practice was partially responsible for the bank's illiquidity and insolvency. Ironically, the refusal of the New York City money market banks to sell Franklin National Bank any additional federal funds forced the bank to approach the Federal Reserve as the lender of last resort. It eventually merged with a healthier financial institution.

Because banks use the federal funds market so extensively as a source of funds for adjusting their reserve positions, conditions in this market are generally an accurate measure of monetary policy. The federal funds rate is so sensitive to shifts in the demand for and supply of reserves in the banking system that the Federal Reserve uses it as both a target and a monitor for its open market operations.

Other Managed Sources of Funds

Purchases of Term Federal Funds

Term federal funds are federal funds with a maturity of more than one day—usually two days to a year. In 1978, the Comptroller of the Currency ruled that because their maturity exceeded one day, the funds were subject to overall borrowing and lending limits to which nationally chartered banks must adhere.

Loans Sold under Repurchase Agreements

Banks first began to sell loans under agreements to repurchase in 1969. However, loan repurchase agreements never emerged as a significant source of reserves because

- ❖ they were not exempt from reserve requirements or Regulation Q ceilings because the Federal Reserve classified them as deposits
- ❖ they were (and still are) subject to overall borrowing limits to which nationally chartered banks must adhere

Borrowing from the Federal Reserve

Most banks do not borrow from Federal Reserve banks as a routine source of reserves. The Federal Reserve historically has viewed low-interest loans from its discount window as a safety valve to ease pressure on banks least able to cope with short-run asset or liability adjustments during tight money periods. Banks that rely too extensively on the Federal Reserve's discount window fall under administrative surveillance by the Federal Reserve, which can pose problems for the bank's management and board of directors. Also, banks have come to understand that frequent use of the discount window at any time reduces the Federal Reserve's willingness to accommodate future borrowing. Thus, most banks use the discount window sparingly.

Major Uses of Funds

Exhibit 9.2 profiles the major uses of bank funds, which include cash assets; government securities holdings; and business, consumer and real estate loans.

Exhibit 9.2 *Balance Sheet of the Commercial Banking System, 1990*

Assets		Percent	Liabilities and Capital		Percent
Cash assets		7	Demand deposits		14
Currency and coin	(15)				
Reserves with the Fed	(15)		NOW and ATS accounts		6
Balances with banks	(28)				
Cash items in process	(42)		Savings deposits		19
Securities		19	Time deposits		36
U.S. Treasury	(70)		CDs—large denomination	(53)	
State, local, and federal agency	(30)		MMDAs	(25)	
			Other time accounts	(22)	
Federal Funds sold and securities purchased under RPs		5	Federal funds purchased and securities sold under RPs		14
Loans		65			
Business	(30)				
Consumer	(20)				
Real estate	(40)		Other liabilities		4
Other	(10)				
			Capital		7
Other assets		4			
Total Assets		100%	Total Liabilities and Capital		100%

Note: Numbers represent percentage of total and are based on 1990 figures for 12,800 domestically chartered commercial banks. Total assets/total liabilities and capital were $2.9 trillion.

Source: Federal Reserve *Bulletin*, April 1991

Cash Assets

Vault cash, reserve deposits at the Federal Reserve, deposit balances at other banks, and cash items in the process of collection constitute a bank's cash assets. These assets are referred to as primary reserves because they represent a bank's first source of liquidity to meet demand claims.

Cash items in the process of collection and interbank balances or account balances at the Federal Reserve are beyond bank management's immediate control. Necessary for a bank's liquidity, for meeting reserve requirements, or for obtaining services from correspondent banks or the Federal Reserve, these assets must be forecast, but they cannot be managed. Large banks can predict daily or weekly changes in cash assets with a fair degree of accuracy, but bank management cannot normally manage the inflow and outflow of cash assets as it can that of other, less liquid, assets.

Cash assets generally do not earn an interest or investment return for a bank but may entitle it to some services. Many small banks pay for the check-clearing services provided them by their correspondent banks by maintaining an agreed daily compensating deposit balance. Banks held about 7 percent of their assets as cash assets in 1991.

Government Securities Holdings

U.S. Treasury, federal agency, and state and local government securities traditionally have not been subject to bank management control. Large portions of many banks' securities portfolios are used to meet pledging requirements against trust operations and to serve as collateral for government deposits. Until 1980, they were used to meet state reserve requirements. Increasingly, however, the securities that banks hold in excess of these needs are sold or used for repurchase agreements.

Many of the nation's largest banks have dealer departments that hold securities for trading purposes. These trading-account assets are subject to substantial management control because trading positions at most banks depend on the funds bank management is willing to allocate to its dealer department. (Banks carry the value of securities they hold for trading purposes at market value rather than at cost, as they do for securities they own for investment purposes.)[1]

Securities investments allow banks to diversify risks in lending funds. Banks can also promote stronger account and deposit relationships with local governments by purchasing their newly issued securities.

More than two-thirds of all bank investments are made in U.S. government obligations. Treasury bills are the shortest-term debt obligations of the U.S. government, with original maturities of three or six months. Treasury notes and bonds are longer-term debt obligations, with original maturities of one to

---

four years for notes and five years or more for bonds. Treasury securities offer banks an investment free of credit risk (risk of default); a large, immediate secondary market; and income exempt from state and local taxes. For this reason, banks use Treasury securities, primarily bills, as major short-term investments and as a backup source of liquidity for meeting seasonal demands for funds and unexpected drains of primary liquidity.

State and local obligations (municipal securities) consist of the short-term (one year or less) tax warrants and tax anticipation notes issued by states and municipalities and the long-term (one year or more) bonds issued by these governments. Many of the nation's 80,000 state and local governments finance short-term revenue needs by selling tax anticipation notes that mature within one year. These notes often are issued not only by the governments themselves, but also by their agencies, including local housing authorities, school districts, and drainage and sewer authorities. They are issued in anticipation of taxes, other revenues, or proceeds from the sale of long- term bonds that have been pledged to retire the notes.

Income earned on all state and local obligations is exempt from federal income tax, which offsets the lower interest returns paid on municipal obligations. For several decades, commercial banks have reduced their effective tax rates below those of other corporations by investing in municipal securities. A bank's ability to use tax-exempt sources of income is limited, however, by the level of its taxable income. In the 1980s, many banks reduced their effective tax rates to such a low level that heavy investments in tax-exempt obligations, which pay lower returns, were no longer profitable.

Banks' purchases of municipal securities declined in the early 1980s, mainly for this reason. Banks also had less profit to shelter with tax-exempt investments because their earnings declined in the 1980s. In addition, changes in tax regulations in 1982 and 1986 disallowed most of the interest deductions for municipal bond carrying costs, and many banks shifted to tax-sheltered leasing to minimize taxes. Banks also were discouraged from holding municipal securities because the risk of default of some issuers of state and local government securities increased in the 1980s. These trends have raised concerns among many financial market analysts that banks' incentives for holding municipal securities in the 1990s may be sharply reduced.

Federal agency obligations are securities issued by U.S. government-owned or government-sponsored corporations and agencies. These include the Federal Home Loan Mortgage Corporation (FHLMC); Federal National Mortgage Association (FNMA); Federal Housing Administration (FHA); and Government National Mortgage Association (GNMA). Banks hold certificates that represent participation in a portfolio of loans held by the agencies. The certificates count as investments rather than loans for the banks.

Business Loans

Business loans, also called commercial and industrial loans, are made for business and professional purposes and have traditionally been the largest single category of loans on most banks' books. The loans can be either single-payment or installment loans and can be secured or not secured. Most business loans banks make are short-term loans, typically with a 3- to 12-month maturity. Business loans usually carry comparatively low processing costs and low incidence of default. They are not subject to usury limits in most states, and there is considerable flexibility in their pricing.

Today, business loans account for only 30 percent of total bank lending. Profound changes in corporate borrowing practices and increased competition from thrifts and finance companies have taken a heavy toll on banks' business lending, particularly among large banks. In recent years, most major corporate borrowers have obtained substantial funds directly from the market by issuing commercial paper rather than borrowing from banks.

However, these loans are generally the lowest yielding of all bank loans. Normally, the profitability of business loans is enhanced by compensating balances (which banks can invest) and by commitment fees. Under a compensating balances loan arrangement, borrowers are required to maintain deposit balances equal to a fixed percentage of the loan value.

Some banks require a minimum daily balance, others an average daily balance during the term of the loan. In addition to enhancing the profitability of business loans, compensating balances provide a bank with added protection because the bank has priority over all other creditors with respect to the balances on deposit. If the borrower defaults on the loan, the bank can offset its outstanding loan balance with any existing deposit balance. The practice of requiring compensating balances, however, is far from universal. In the 1980s, banks and corporate borrowers opted increasingly for explicit fee charges to cover loan costs rather than compensating balances.

A loan commitment fee is a separate service charge a bank levies on a corporate borrower who arranges a loan for a future time. Banks increasingly relied on loan commitment fees in the 1980s to increase income on commercial and industrial loans. These fees eventually became a significant component of banks' noninterest earnings.

The practice of banks committing themselves for a fee to corporate customers for loans can reduce bank management's flexibility to manage the bank's loan portfolio. While a bank can hold down the dollar amount of loans it makes by changing the interest rates it charges and the noninterest terms it imposes on credit lines, loan commitment fees may lock the bank into future loan expansion. Banks frequently make loan commitments to corporate customers without knowing the exact amount the corporation will be borrowing or the date the funds will be borrowed. Most banks carefully monitor the dollar amounts of their loan commitments. Nonetheless, a bank that relies heavily on loan commitment fees can have a good idea of how much each borrower may want, but can never be sure that it will have sufficient reserves on any given day to honor all commitments that could be exercised. Thus, it may have to borrow to honor prepaid commitments and could find itself paying more for funds than the prearranged loan charge.

Consumer Loans

Consumer loans are made to individuals for personal expenditures. Most consumer loans are short-term installment loans that require repayment at predetermined intervals, often monthly. A considerable portion of bank consumer lending is in the form of credit extended on bank credit cards.

Consumer loans generate a predictable cash flow return to banks because repayment of the principal and interest is usually prescheduled. However, some banks book installment loans as discounts instead of loans to provide an immediate cash flow return. In a discount, the bank deducts the interest due on the loan in advance; the remainder goes to the borrower. By contrast, interest on a loan is paid at maturity or in installments during the life of the loan.

In the 1970s, market interest rates rose above the maximum rates banks could charge, because of state usury ceilings. Although ceilings were raised in many states during the 1970s, banks were generally unable to charge rates sufficiently high to provide a profitable return on consumer loans.

In the 1980s, market interest rates declined and banks' consumer lending increasingly shifted to credit extended on bank credit cards. However, beginning in 1986, bank loans for new automobile purchases, traditionally a major component of consumer loan demand, began to drop sharply as consumers switched to auto finance companies to borrow money. In an effort to sell bloated inventories, the nation's car manufacturers instituted below-market dealer financing rates on new car purchases. This practice has continued into the 1990s with devastating effects on banks' share of auto lending. Today, auto finance companies make three-quarters of all loans for new car purchases.

Consumer lending is subject to extensive regulations and entails greater credit risks than other loans. Loan-processing costs are also high relative to the small size of most consumer loans. Factors such as these have caused many banks to reevaluate their use of funds for consumer loans in the 1990s.

Real Estate Loans

State usury ceilings made real estate loans unattractive to banks in the late 1970s and early 1980s because high market interest rates exceeded the maximum rates banks could charge on residential mortgages. However, the sharp decline in market interest rates in the mid-1980s helped bring down residential mortgage rates to their lowest levels in a decade and triggered a spate of home buying and mortgage refinancings. In the late 1980s and early 1990s, banks' mortgage lending soared as banks increasingly filled the mortgage market void created by the closing of large numbers of insolvent S&Ls and the flight of anxious depositors from sound S&Ls. By 1990, real estate loans accounted for 40 percent of bank lending.

Real estate loans, like consumer loans, generate a predictable cash flow return for banks, but yields on these loans are lower than yields for most other loans. In the past, real estate loans were the lowest risk loans a bank could make because they were fully collateralized by property that appreciated while the principal was repaid, thus reducing the bank's credit exposure. Banks' experience with commercial real estate loans in the 1980s, however, has raised doubts about the validity of this long-standing banking premise. Many banks took losses on commercial real estate loans when borrowers defaulted and banks found that the market values of properties collateralizing the loans were less than the amount of the outstanding loans.

Summary

In the 1960s and 1970s, banks revolutionized the management of sources and uses of bank funds by focusing on liabilities—meeting demands for new loans by buying or borrowing needed funds. This approach, called liability management, required bankers to evaluate carefully and use a balanced blend of sources of funds over which they had complete control, such as federal funds, large-denomination corporate CDs, repurchase agreements, and Eurodollar borrowings.

The management of bank funds changed in the 1980s. The Monetary Control Act restructured and simplified reserve requirements early in the decade, and Regulation Q ceilings were eliminated in 1986.

At the same time, the introduction of interest-bearing transaction accounts altered the public's deposit preferences. Today, banks can no longer rely on stable demand deposits and consumer time and savings deposits as guaranteed sources of funds.

Banks developed new strategies in the 1980s and 1990s as the spread narrowed between the interest rate they pay for funds and the interest rate they receive on funds they lend or invest. These strategies include attempts to match assets and liabilities by maturity and duration, and attempts to maintain balanced or favorable repricing gaps in the timing of maturing assets and liabilities.

While banks are free to pursue individual strategies to obtain new funds, all banks are subject to the Federal Reserve's monetary policy and reserve requirement rules. These determine the growth of deposit balances in the banking system and the cost and return on banks' sources and uses of funds.

Questions

1. Cite three liability adjustment practices that banks developed in the 1970s to obtain reserves and expand their earning assets.

2. Banks can no longer count on demand deposits and consumer time and savings deposits as stable sources of funds. Why?

3. Why did the federal funds market become the dominant market for obtaining reserves in the nation's banking system?

4. What difficulties have banks found in following the matching strategies of funds management?

Endnote

1. In December 1991, the Financial Accounting Standards Board (FASB), the nation's rule-making body for accountants, issued a new rule that requires banks, beginning in 1992, to disclose the market value of all their assets in footnotes to their annual reports. Congress also passed legislation that requires bank regulators to develop, by 1993, a set of market value disclosure rules for banks when reporting their assets and liabilities.

BANK SERVICES

Objectives

After successfully completing this chapter, you will be able to

- ❖ identify the major cash management services banks offer and the kinds of customers that use these services
- ❖ describe how balance-reporting systems, lockbox arrangements, and controlled disbursement services work
- ❖ identify the major services bank holding company affiliates provide
- ❖ explain the Federal Reserve's criteria in evaluating whether to allow bank holding companies to provide a new service

Introduction

Providing cash management services has become an increasingly important and controversial aspect of banking. The nation's money center banks and large regional banks are the main providers of these services. They see cash management services as meeting a growing need of corporate customers for timely and accurate data on the status of their accounts and the options available for maximizing the return on their deposits. Many of the nation's smaller community-based banks see cash management services as a growing threat to their deposit base and a practice that could lead to a concentration of most bank deposits on the books of only a handful of the nation's biggest banks.

The regulatory agencies are ambivalent about cash management services. They recognize banks' legitimate need to offer services to corporations that maximize the company's funds. However, they are concerned about cash management services that exploit deficiencies in the U.S. payments mechanism or impair monetary policy control by evading reserve requirements.

Banks and Cash Management Services

Cash management services that banks provide to depositors—mostly business firms—usually entail informing depositors about the availability of funds in their accounts, consulting with depositors about their investment options, and consolidating a depositor's account balances to realize a maximum interest return. Major domestic firms, multinational corporations, government entities, and others want the services and are willing to pay for them because they can earn a considerable return from every invested dollar that previously sat idle in an account.

The increasing demand by corporate and government depositors for these services and their corresponding growth are largely a phenomenon of the past 20 years, a phenomenon generated by

- ❖ lack of interest payments on demand deposits and limitations on interest payments on time deposits imposed by Regulation Q, both of which held interest returns below those earned in the market

- ❖ growth in inflation and interest rates, which increased the cost of holding idle balances

- ❖ inefficiencies in the check collection process that causes float

- ❖ geographic restrictions on taking deposits and collecting checks, which create additional float time

Balance-Reporting Services

A daily balance-reporting service provides several benefits:

- ❖ Corporations can invest funds daily, thereby increasing earnings by reducing daily holdings of idle demand deposit funds.

- ❖ Corporations can monitor banks daily to assure that their transactions are being handled and posted correctly.

- ❖ Banks can locate excess deposits the corporation might have lost track of. By concentrating these deposits—transferring the funds into one central account—the company can invest the total amount of funds available at a more favorable rate than through separate smaller investments.

The primary users of bank balance-reporting services are companies that have accounts at many banks across the country. Their motivation is timing and convenience. Most of these companies can obtain the same information provided by a bank's daily balance report service if they phone all their local, regional, and money center banks each morning. But such activity would be too costly and time consuming. Also, corporate treasurers can obtain optimum yields on daily surplus funds invested if the investments are made early each morning.

Yields on instruments in the New York money market typically peak early each morning as brokers and dealers bid for funds to finance their inventories. As the day progresses and brokers and dealers obtain funds, yields typically decline. Thus corporate investors want daily balance information early.

By linking daily balance reports to concentration account services, a bank can invest the total amount of funds held by the corporation in all of its diverse accounts at a more favorable rate than through separate smaller investments from each account. Under a concentration service, a bank establishes a central intake account that allows the firm to pool the balances collected by, or deposited in, scores of local banks. Local banks automatically transfer deposited funds, usually by wire transfer, to the concentration account service bank. This process allows the firm to consolidate its cash balances, making it easier and less expensive to place idle funds in money market investments. It also reduces the amount of total cash balances that need to be held.

Most banks provide corporate customers with monthly, weekly, or daily paper reports on the status of their accounts. Major U.S. multinational business firms have had fairly advanced cash management systems of their own for some time. Even without the reports banks provide, these corporations would have little difficulty in placing surplus funds into the nation's money markets. However, it was not until banks began offering balance-reporting services that investment options were made available to smaller business depositors. Before banks offered cash management systems, most companies

---

waited until receiving their monthly bank statements before moving account balances.

Deposit Consolidation Service

A deposit consolidation service enables companies with offices in different locations to have these offices' daily check and cash deposits consolidated into a single corporate account without losing the identity of each deposit location. Supermarket chains, fast-food chains, and department stores are typical users of this service. Banks with extensive branch networks are typical providers of the service.

Banks initiate the service by giving each company office preprinted deposit slips that include an MICR-encoded identification number for that office. As deposits are made in different branches, they are posted to a single company account. The bank's accounting system, and subsequent reports or statements provided to the company, indicate the amounts deposited by each office. Many banks' deposit consolidation reports also indicate offices that did not deposit on a given day.

The value of the service is not only in concentrating daily funds for maximum earnings, but in providing corporate management with early identification of unexpected sales trends at specific offices.

Treasury Workstations

In the 1970s, several of the nation's biggest banks began to offer multinational corporations and major U.S. companies an automated report service, or treasury workstation. The workstation supplies, from one online source, immediate information on the availability of corporate funds in all accounts and at all banks throughout the country.

An initiating bank—usually a major correspondent bank—ties its head office, its branches, and its respondent banks into a time-sharing computer system. After the close of business each day, these offices phone in demand deposit information on subscribers' accounts to the computer. The initiating bank's computer processes this account information overnight. By the next morning, corporate treasurers can obtain, through minicomputers or terminals in their own offices, printouts with detailed information on the corporate account balances.

By comparing the actual balances held at all banks against required compensatory balances for services, corporate treasurers can determine whether excess funds are available for investment or where account balances may be deficient. Typically, the bank initiating the service provides wire transfer access to corporate accounts so that corporate treasurers can redress imbalances instantaneously. Corporate treasurers can transfer surplus funds to accounts against which disbursements have been made; they can avoid short-term borrowing costs to cover payments; and they can avoid selling short-term money market investments to build up account balances in anticipation of disbursements.

Many bankers expected the treasury workstation to become the leading cash management service of the 1980s. This expectation was based on corporate treasurer's increasing use of personal computers to access bank services. In 1984, about 90 percent of all large companies—those with more than $500 million in annual sales—and about two-thirds of all other companies were using microcomputers in their treasury management activities. The treasury workstation was seen as building on a trend toward service automation. However, the workstations were not as popular with corporations, or as profitable to banks, as originally anticipated.

The nature and cost of software to synthesize and analyze balance and transactions data may be responsible. Several money center banks have developed comprehensive software packages that they have sold to their corporate cash management customers for use with the workstations. Other money center banks have modified vendors' systems for resale. Regional banks offering workstations have tended toward purchasing vendor software packages and marketing them without customization.

Lockbox

A lockbox is a post office box that banks provide as a depository for corporate checks.

In a typical lockbox arrangement, customers send their check payments to post office boxes closest to major customer mailing addresses instead of to the corporation's headquarters or its main bank. The corporation arranges with local banks to empty the lockboxes several times each day.

Since the check writer sends payments to a local post office box, this reduces mail float, which allows the corporation to increase its earnings through earlier collection. Checks written on local bank accounts result in quicker credit to the corporation than interregional checks presented to one national site. The local account balances are then transferred to one money market bank for daily investment.

Many banks in suburban areas have found that they can successfully market a lockbox arrangement to regional or local companies whose operations are centered in nearby cities. Suburban lockbox arrangements are attractive because mail volume is often smaller in these areas and U.S. postal service is faster. A lockbox arrangement with a suburban bank allows a city-based corporation to reduce mail float by a day or more on check payments. On average, lockboxes reduce mail float from one to four days.

Since lockbox banks make frequent pickups at the post office box during the course of a day (including Saturday) and process the checks immediately, corporations receive quicker credit for checks than if the company received the checks directly and then deposited them at their local banks.

In the 1940s, RCA was the first major corporation to use the lockbox system. Today, thousands of corporations use lockboxes in their cash management programs.

The widespread use of lockboxes enabled the nation's regional banks to partially displace smaller, local banks as primary recipients of corporate demand deposits. Most national corporations use the services of about 20 to 50 different banks across the country. After the introduction of lockboxes, these companies continued to maintain account relationships with local banks but the corporation's branches and subsidiaries no longer made sizable deposits into all these banks. The deposits were typically placed in several key regional banks whose strategic locations made them ideal lockbox depositories.

Some banks charge explicit fees for lockbox services, while others require compensatory account balances, and others use a combination of both. Banks typically send invoices and the record of each day's lockbox deposits to the firm renting the box. Banks also send photocopies of checks. In many cases, lockbox deposit information is processed on magnetic tape that can be used with the firm's computerized accounting system.

Industry surveys indicate that the most frequently used lockbox sites are in Chicago, Los Angeles, Dallas, and Atlanta.

Lockbox Networks

In the 1980s, a number of large banks began to establish their own nationwide lockbox networks. In a conventional lockbox service, a corporation deals separately with each bank where it has a lockbox. Under a network service, a corporation deals with only one bank. All check deposits, invoice data, and account balance information related to the company's regional lockboxes are centralized through one bank.

Four general types of lockbox networks have emerged. Each arrangement has positive and negative features, in terms of the availability of deposited check funds to corporations and the cost effectiveness and ease of administration to banks.

Proprietary Network. In this network, a single bank owns and operates lockbox processing centers in locations remote from its home city. Proprietary networks offer optimal funds availability to corporations but are the most expensive for banks to establish and operate.

Remittance Intercept Network. This network uses multiple post office boxes from which banks ship remittances back to a central processing center.

The remittance intercept network is less expensive to operate than a proprietary network, but funds availability to corporate accounts is slower because of the transportation time involved in shipping remittances before processing them.

Bank Consortiums. Consortiums involve several banks in a collection network; however, each customer has only one main contact bank. A key problem for consortiums is that the main contact bank may not be able to service lockbox operations adequately at the other network banks.

Joint Ventures. Ventures between banks and nonbanks use excess processing capacity at the nonbank partner at several locations. Problems can arise when industry competitors of the nonbank partner oppose submitting sensitive customer-related remittance information to the nonbank partner for processing.

About 20 percent of the nation's large corporations now obtain lockbox services through a network arrangement. However, many bankers and industry analysts doubt whether broader corporate interest in network arrangements can be generated and whether profit returns for banks from the service can justify the considerable costs involved in establishing additional networks.

About 325 banks offer wholesale lockbox services—corporations send payments meant for other companies directly to the bank for processing. Of these banks, the 50 largest providers have automated systems—some are image-processing systems that forward digitized pictures of documents and checks by computer to corporate lockbox customers.

Most industry analysts say that image-processing systems have the potential for reducing the costs of providing lockbox services in the 1990s by speeding the data entry of lockbox receivables and by reducing labor costs.

Controlled Disbursement

A controlled disbursement service provides a corporation with more control over its day-to-day cash balances by positioning its account at a bank that receives only one shipment of checks for collection each morning. The bank then tells the firm the value of the checks drawn on its account so that the firm knows, usually before noon, how much of its balances on that day exceed the amount needed to cover the checks—and how much is available for investment.

Many banks offer a zero-balance account option for their controlled disbursement service. Under this option, the corporation is allowed to maintain its account at the controlled disbursement bank (or banks) with a zero balance. When the value of the checks presented against the firm's account is tabulated and the company receives the information, it wires to the bank the amount of funds necessary to cover the checks. This arrangement allows the firm to economize on daily transactions balances at each of its disbursing banks by eliminating the need for daily excess or precautionary balances. It also provides the firm with centralized data on its daily transactions.

Some banks allow corporate accounts to cover checks presented against zero-balance accounts with depository transfer checks. These preauthorized checks are maintained at the bank by the corporation and drawn on one of the corporation's local banks. Upon request for coverage, one of these checks is issued in the appropriate amount and deposited in the account. The deposit, although it is in uncollected funds, provides the coverage. Banks that allow corporations to cover checks presented against zero-balance controlled disbursement accounts with depository transfer checks, effectively grant those companies an interest-free loan for a day because it takes at least one day for transfer checks to clear.

Other funding options that banks offer include an overdraft credit line or a compensating balance for funding and drawing off interest-bearing accounts held at the bank by the corporation. A number of banks allow corporate cash management customers to forecast each day's expected disbursements and to fund their expected disbursements with a depository transfer check. The bank grants an earnings credit on any overage and imposes an overdraft charge on any underage.

Most large banks have computerized accounting and funds transfer systems that enable corporate cash managers to initiate wire transfers from computer terminals at the corporate site that are linked to the bank's computer. Often this service is tied to other computerized cash management services the bank provides, such as programs that forecast the company's daily cash flows.

The federal government has become a major user of controlled disbursement, as have many of the nation's leading corporations. The Medicare program, for example, began to issue checks on banks in regions distant from check recipients in the late 1970s. In doing so, the government realized many of the benefits corporations obtain from their own disbursement practices—the issuing agency had better control over its check payments and was able to invest its funds for a longer period. However, banks were not selected on the basis of increasing float time. The Medicare program's controlled disbursement is rooted in the government's practice of awarding service contracts to the lowest private sector bidders. Medicare's check-issuing and -processing services go to regional banks that have submitted the lowest contract bid. Many of these banks are in areas remote from Medicare check recipients.

When a Medicare check is presented for collection, the bank paying the check can automatically draw on Treasury funds through a letter of credit arrangement. Under that arrangement, paying banks present Treasury vouchers to the Federal Reserve for payment. Treasury funds are fully invested until the Fed draws down its account balance. Previously, Medicare maintained funds in its bank accounts to cover outstanding checks. Under the current program, if the recipients do not deposit their Medicare checks immediately, the Treasury profits from the float time. Under the previous system, Medicare would have transferred funds into its accounts to cover the checks, and banks would have been able to invest the undisbursed funds.

Payable-Through-Draft Service

A payable-through draft is a checklike instrument issued by a company, in conjunction with a bank, for use in controlling and disbursing funds. These drafts are not checks, because they are payable by the issuing company, not the company's bank.

Payable-through drafts are used by insurance companies where field personnel issue payments to policyholders and the endorsement of the draft constitutes a legal release of liability, as in the case of an auto damage settlement, or a claims settlement for fire damage to a house.

When the drafts are received by banks—after they are deposited by policyholders—they are accumulated and forwarded, usually once each day, to the company's central office for review. Company representatives validate each draft's signature, amount, and endorsement. The company also notes any drafts it wants to dishonor and returns them to the bank, usually on the same day they are received. The bank then debits the company's account for the total sum involved, in most instances after the company has transferred funds into its account to provide settlement coverage.

Account Reconcilement

A widespread and successful cash management service that banks generally offer to companies that issue hundreds or thousands of checks each month is an automated account reconciliation service. This service provides computerized monthly reports (on paper, magnetic tape, or computer disk) that list all the checks paid against the company's account during the previous month.

Companies that use an account reconciliation service typically provide the bank with a list of checks they issued the previous month. The report they receive from the bank shows, by date and amount, checks that have been paid and checks that are outstanding, and it does so in the sequence that corresponds to the company's list.

Companies avoid the time and expense that would be associated with manual reconcilement of monthly checks and they obtain a tracking device that enables them to efficiently monitor and control disbursements. Most banks retain and store the company's canceled checks.

Intra-Industry Cash Management Services

Several banks have developed cash management services to help companies in the same industry that do a lot of business with one another by reducing intraindustry transfers and payments. One example involves the oil industry. In the 1970s, the Bank of the Southwest in Houston established a clearing house for intraindustry payments the nation's oil companies made to one another. The arrangement, still in operation, is called Petro-clear.

In principle, the Petro-clear system works much like a local check-clearing arrangement among banks. Payment transactions among participants are netted out before settlement is made.

The nation's oil companies typically buy large amounts of crude oil from one another during the course of a month. This practice would ordinarily necessitate numerous check payments, bookkeeping costs, and substantial account balances to cover checks. However, under the Petro-clear arrangement, the oil companies do not send checks for purchased oil to one another. Two oil companies, after agreeing on net amounts involved between them during the month, notify the Bank of the Southwest, which is responsible for debiting and crediting each oil company's accounts. The bank receives net debit and credit data from all the two-party agreements made during the month and posts only the final net total of these amounts for the entire group. Generally, oil companies in a net debit position wire money to the bank the day before the prearranged monthly date of settlement.

A second example involves the airline industry. In the 1970s, New York's Chase Manhattan Bank developed a system for the airline industry that allows airlines to net intraindustry payments, much as oil companies do in the Petro-clear system.

When travelers book flights involving more than one airline, they typically pay one carrier, who then redistributes funds to the other carriers involved. Instead of exchanging checks for the gross amount of these intraindustry billings, airlines settle on a net basis through accounts on Chase's books.

Each airline prepares a monthly billing sheet that lists the amounts that other airlines owe it. The airlines wire these data to Chase, which nets the amounts due each airline to one another, then wires the settlement back to each airline. Chase debits the accounts of airlines in net deficit positions and credits the accounts of airlines with net surplus positions. As in all net settlement arrangements, the sum of the credits and debits nets to zero. If an airline has insufficient balances to cover a debit, it wires additional funds to Chase.

Currency Management

The management of coin and currency flows, essential in banking, is also basic to the profitable operations of a broad range of nonfinancial businesses.

Recognizing this precept, a few banks—the National State Bank of Elizabeth, New Jersey, being one of the first—began to offer a currency management service for business customers in the early 1960s. Since then, numerous regional banks have developed currency management programs for both business depositors and respondent banks.

In a currency management service, a bank picks up coin and currency from customers and transports the cash to a central processing site where it is sorted, counted, packaged, and credited to customers' accounts where it can be used for payments or investment purposes. In addition, major users of currency and coin, such as amusement parks and race tracks, often need a large number of rolls of specific coins and packaged currency. A bank's currency management service also provides these items.

Banks that offer currency management services generally market these services to the following types of businesses:

❖ retail stores that sell a large volume of low dollar-value merchandise

❖ financial institutions, including banks, that do not use Federal Reserve services

❖ government offices, such as bridge and turnpike authorities, state lottery commissions, and public transportation agencies

❖ service providers that engage in high-volume cash business, including race tracks and amusement parks

Many banks, particularly those in resort communities and agricultural regions where large numbers of transient workers reside, often experience sharp fluctuations in depositors' demands for cash. These banks often have quantities of cash on hand well above liquidity or reserve requirement needs, resulting in lost interest earnings and increased security costs. Banks in such circumstances often implement their own currency management systems or rely on services their correspondent banks provide.

The basis for all bank-oriented currency management services is comprehensive information reporting, which provides banks with data on the seasonal patterns of their currency flows. By taking into account seasonal patterns and adjusting for such short-term factors as holiday and weekend currency patterns and Social Security payment dates, a good internal currency management system can be devised. Such a system would also consider currency order and shipment practices and compare transportation charges offered by correspondent banks.

Some banks have developed sophisticated mathematical forecasting models that use both past and current data on cash-to-deposit ratios to help predict cash needs. By using these models, banks minimize cash on hand and convert idle cash into earning assets. In doing so, banks also cut internal costs on blanket insurance bonds because reduced cash on hand reduces risks.

Regulators and Cash Management Services

Noon Check Presentment

In 1984, the Federal Reserve extended its check presentment times from 10:00 a.m. to 12:00 p.m. in an effort to speed the check collection process and reduce Federal Reserve float in the banking system. Most of the nation's large banks saw this schedule change as a direct threat to the competitiveness of their controlled disbursement services and protested the action to the Federal Reserve.

Corporate disbursing accounts are typically maintained at banks outside Federal Reserve cities. Because of their relatively remote locations, these banks had received a single, early morning delivery of checks from Federal Reserve banks each day before the check presentment time extension. Early presentment allowed banks to process presented checks and notify corporate customers by midmorning of the exact amount required to fund their disbursing accounts. Banks argued that presentment at noon would prevent banks from processing checks and notifying corporate accounts of their balances until midafternoon, when money market interest rates are typically lower and corporate treasurers have fewer available investment options.

To assist banks with their controlled disbursement operations, the Federal Reserve began to offer payer bank services concurrent with its introduction of the later presentment schedule. These payer bank services summarize dollar totals and MICR line information for certain accounts specified by the payer bank and send the information immediately to the bank, well before the check is processed.

Reserve banks are required to provide the information to payer banks no later than 11:00 a.m. local time. The payer bank service enables a controlled disbursement bank to determine each day's available balance for its corporate disbursement accounts. It still has to verify the checks, which are presented later in the day. Because some of these checks could be returned unpaid, the actual available balance could differ from the balance the bank told the company earlier in the day. However, such discrepancies are infrequent.

Remote Disbursement

In the 1970s, some companies developed sophisticated computer programs that examined the mailing addresses of check recipients and then drew checks for them against balances at the most remote bank in which the company had an account to delay collection for as long as possible. Companies often established accounts at small, remote banks for this purpose. This practice, known as remote disbursement, became a widely used arrangement on which companies relied to maximize float and manage their cash positions.

For example, a New York corporation might draw a check on an account at a Fairbanks, Alaska, bank to pay a New York resident to whom it owes money. When the New Yorker deposits the check at a local bank, the local bank has to wait two days to get credit from the Federal Reserve for the amount of the check. It will, of course, take longer than that to collect the funds from the Alaska bank. The depositor would have had to wait until funds became available for the deposited check. Before the Expedited Funds Availability Act of 1987 established the current five-day maximum hold on interregional checks, the wait could have been as long as two weeks. However, the New York corporation would obtain several extra days or perhaps a week of float time in which to reinvest the check recipient's money.

In the late 1970s, the Federal Reserve called on banks to stop engaging in remote disbursement practices with corporate customers. The Federal Reserve said that banks could continue to provide controlled disbursement services, but outlawed remote disbursement because it exploited deficiencies in the check collection system and ran counter to public policy goals to improve the speed and efficiency of nationwide payments. The courts tended to agree. In one major class action suit on the remote disbursement practices of the Merrill Lynch brokerage firm, the firm agreed to stop sending checks drawn on banks in California to New York residents.

Reserve Avoidance Sweep Accounts

In 1991, the Federal Reserve found another cash management service that ran counter to public policy goals—a new sweep account service that exploited a loophole in the Fed's reserve requirements regulations. Under the new service, banks automatically transfer idle balances from corporate transaction accounts into seven-day CDs at the end of each day.

During any day, corporations can draw on their transaction accounts with checks from uncollected funds that become available that day and from the proceeds of one or more of the daily maturing CDs. Because there are no reserve requirements on time deposits (compared with a 12 percent reserve requirement on transaction accounts), the automatic sweep reduces banks' costs and allows banks to pay corporations a premium interest rate on their seven-day CDs.

The Fed saw the new sweep account not as a legitimate cash management service but as an effort by banks to evade reserve requirements, which would impair monetary policy control. The Federal Reserve proposed to close the loophole in its regulations by classifying these transactions and seven-day CD accounts as one linked account, subject to reserve requirements.

Changing Cash Management Service Strategies

The nation's major corporations began gradually to reduce their holdings of demand deposits at banks in the 1960s, as they became adept at shifting idle funds into Treasury bills, commercial paper, and CDs. In the 1970s, corporations pruned their demand deposits even further when banks began providing improved balance- reporting and money transfer service programs.

The widespread development and use of cash management services have changed some of the fundamental relationships between banks and their corporate customers. Corporations are now less dependent on their banks for their own sources and uses of funds. Because of this, they have become more discretionary in choosing bank management services, no longer feeling it necessary to buy the service offered by their lead bank.

Before 1977, few banks offered online cash management services. However, by the late 1970s, the willingness of corporations to shop for cash management services generated significant competition among banks to provide these services. Some banks responded by joining the cash management system networks of other banks. Others responded by linking into private networks, and some developed their own systems. Today, most of the nation's large banks provide similar online cash management and account information reporting services.

Although cash management services were initially oriented toward meeting the needs of large national corporate depositors, banks have marketed these services to small companies. In the 1960s, many small businesses were relatively indifferent to their daily cash positions and were content to leave occasional excess funds idle. However, that indifference changed with the escalation of interest rates in the 1970s and early 1980s and the development of new deposit types, money market instruments, and money market funds. Banks that experienced considerable declines in demand deposit balances began to recognize a need for cash management services oriented toward small business firms.

These cash management services have been directed specifically to small companies whose operations are widely dispersed. Companies such as retail stores and department store chains often run into temporary liquidity problems because they cannot manage their cash flows. They often have sufficient funds, but they do not know where the funds are or how they can be used to cover payments. Banks have recognized that small companies are attracted by marketing campaigns that promote a comprehensive balance-reporting and investment advisory service as a way of preventing illiquidity and, in extreme cases, insolvency.

The growing sophistication of corporate cash management has placed considerable pressure on banks to respond with services that will meet corporate needs in the 1990s. Those needs, as perceived by banks and supported by industry surveys of multinational corporations, are for float and investment information, international cash management services, and corporate trade payment services.

Float Analysis

Corporations want detailed daily breakdowns of both uncollected and available funds on hand in every account and information on the likely float time associated with check disbursements made the previous day. Most of the nation's large banks provide this service as part of their account information reporting program.

Investment Information

Corporations want timely information on investment options and automated overnight investment programs that obtain maximum yields.

International Cash Management Services

Multinational corporations want daily balance reports on their accounts in domestic and foreign banks—in their own currency and in a range of foreign currencies. Several of the nation's large banks have begun to offer multicurrency reporting systems that allow multinational corporations to manage foreign exchange cash flows centrally and in one common currency.

The nation's large banks have begun testing whether artificial intelligence computer technology can be profitably applied to international cash management services. Promising applications are foreign exchange trading systems that could help corporate treasurers make spot decisions on buying or selling foreign currencies. The systems identify pricing trends, incorporate judgments of foreign exchange experts, and recommend a course of action. They also provide corporations with information on the factors that led the computer to the recommendation, such as interest rate changes, a new assessment of market psychology, or newly available foreign country economic data.

Most industry analysts see enormous revenue potential for banks' use of foreign exchange cash management services in the 1990s because of the volume of foreign exchange transactions conducted in the U.S. and the volatility of foreign exchange rates.

About $425 billion in foreign exchange transactions were cleared each day through the nation's banks in 1991. It is not unusual for relative prices among the world's major currencies to change during the course of a day by as much as 2 to 3 percent, providing corporate treasurers opportunities for trading profits or more effectively managing their company's global funds position.

Corporate Trade Payments

An increasing number of banks and the U.S. Treasury are examining the feasibility of using corporate trade ACH payments as part of their cash management programs. Corporate trade payments in ACH form would contain addenda records allowing banks to forward invoice, purchase order, and other information along with the payment itself. A group of U.S. and Canadian banks is also testing a data interchange service for corporate trade payments that would be provided electronically through the S.W.I.F.T. network.

Corporate trade payments are widely used in Europe, but not in the United States, nor is there a common communications standard or format in this country governing the ways banks send and receive electronic data. Without a standard, electronic data interchange among U.S. banks is likely to be impractical and costly. For these reasons, most industry analysts see electronic data interchange as having little immediate market or profit potential in the United States.

The Outlook for Cash Management Services

In the 1970s, most banks based their decisions on whether to offer cash management services on broad business objectives. For some banks, those objectives did not include cash management services. Other banks were unwilling to commit the considerable economic resources required to provide these services. Many midsize banks provided selective cash management services only to specific customers that requested the service. Banks typically provided these services without a standardized service delivery system or a standardized pricing schedule. For the banks that opted to provide cash management services, the services were viewed as a way to attract and hold corporations as bank customers, rather than as profitable services in their own right.

In the 1980s, as banks' interest spreads on loans and investments narrowed, many banks turned to noninterest sources of income to maintain their profitability. Cash management services were seen as a potentially lucrative source of fee income.

Banks have faced a problem in focusing on cash management services as a source of profits. With the exception of the nation's largest banks, most banks do not have internal cost accounting systems capable of measuring the value of specific cash management services. Most banks that offer cash management services believe their services are generating profits. However, many industry analysts dispute this contention. They cite ACH services, consulting services, and lockbox network arrangements as cash management services that have not generated profits for most banks. Analysts contend that banks offering cash management services have incurred large capital costs to implement account information and communications systems and that these systems will not begin to pay their way until well into the 1990s.

Bank Holding Companies and Bank Services

Bank holding companies have changed the basic structure and service orientation of U.S. banking. A bank holding company is a corporation that owns or controls one or more banks. It is not a new corporate form—it has been around since the turn of the century—but it has had its greatest impact since the 1960s because

- ❖ The holding company structure provides banks with the means to circumvent restrictions on branching imposed by state and federal laws. Since the 1960s, the growth of bank holding companies has been greatest in states that are most restrictive. Branch banking prohibitions do not cover the activities of bank holding companies. A subsidiary of a bank holding company can enter a new geographic area, whereas a bank branch might be prevented from doing so.

- ❖ The holding company structure allows banks to engage in activities and offer new services through subsidiaries, activities that are forbidden to the bank itself. In fact, after Congress separated banking from other lines of commerce in the Banking Act of 1933, some banks used holding companies to evade the law and engage in commercial activities.

In the 1950s, concern over the potential for concentration in banking posed by bank holding companies and concern that bank holding company activities could lead to unsound banking practices, moved Congress to legislate federal control over bank holding companies. The Bank Holding Company Act of 1956 applied federal antitrust laws to the activities of multibank holding companies and gave the Federal Reserve power to approve or deny applications from multibank holding companies to acquire additional banks. The act also limited the nonbanking activities of multibank holding companies to activities that were directly related to banking.

The 1956 act did not cover companies that controlled only one bank, primarily because very few one-bank holding companies existed at that time. However, in the mid-1960s, many banks began to view the one-bank holding company structure as a means of escaping the tight money policies that the Federal Reserve was pursuing. For example, banks could obtain a new source of loanable funds by establishing a holding company structure and having a subsidiary of the company issue commercial paper.

The one-bank holding company movement accelerated as banks increasingly sought access to broader markets, new activities, and new locations. In 1970, Congress amended the Bank Holding Company Act to cover one-bank holding companies. Today, the 6,000 bank holding companies in the United States have subsidiary banks that hold more than 90 percent of all U.S. banking deposits, and about two-thirds of all banking offices in the nation are affiliated with bank holding companies.

Since the 1960s, the Fed has approved a broad range of separate activities for bank holding companies, including

- issuing credit cards
- providing trust services
- selling general and portfolio investment advice, economic information, and bookkeeping and data processing services
- providing courier services
- providing management consulting services
- issuing traveler's checks and money orders
- dealing in bankers' acceptances and brokering gold bullion
- providing services associated with mortgage banking, finance companies, factoring companies, trust companies, collection agencies, and credit bureaus
- servicing loans
- acting as insurance agent, broker, or underwriter for credit-related life, accident, and health insurance
- acting as a general insurance agent in towns with populations of less than 5,000
- leasing personal and real property and providing land escrow services
- sponsoring, organizing, or controlling a closed-end investment company
- providing investment services that promote the welfare of the community
- providing securities brokerage services
- selling property insurance of $10,000 or less through finance company subsidiaries
- providing advisory services for those seeking to buy commodities or foreign exchange
- acting as futures commission merchants
- selling financial counseling, tax planning, and tax preparation services to consumers
- underwriting and dealing in revenue bonds, commercial paper, mortgage-backed securities, and consumer-related receivables
- underwriting and dealing in corporate bonds and corporate stock as long as the revenue from these activities does not exceed 10 percent of the subsidiary's total revenue.

Federal Reserve Criteria for Bank Holding Companies

Activities or acquisitions of bank holding companies must be "closely and properly related to banking," according to the basic criteria the Federal Reserve Board uses when it evaluates applications from bank holding companies to engage in a new activity. In determining whether a proposed activity is closely related to banking, the Federal Reserve must examine whether the activity is

- ❖ one in which banks have traditionally engaged
- ❖ so closely related to traditional banking activities that banks would be well equipped to engage in the activity
- ❖ integrally related to permissible banking activities.

If any of these criteria apply, the proposed activity is deemed closely related to banking.

The Federal Reserve must then determine whether the proposed activity is properly related to banking by evaluating the public benefits and costs likely to be associated with the activity.

If, in the Fed's judgment, the holding company's activity would clearly lead to substantial market concentration, decreased or unfair competition, conflicts of interest, or unsound banking practices, it denies the request.

To approve an activity, the Board must be convinced that the activity meets a public need or provides a clear social benefit. In effect, the holding company must present a strong, documented case that shows the Board how the holding company's provision of the new service would generate benefits to the public—such as greater convenience, greater service selection, lower price or more efficiency.

In many applications, the Federal Reserve finds evidence that the proposed activity works both for and against the public good. In those cases, the Federal Reserve Board decides on the basis of net public benefits—that is, it weighs the benefits that would likely accrue against the potential social costs. Land development and commodity trading are two activities that bank holding companies have been prohibited from engaging in because the Board decided that these activities were not closely or properly related to banking—in effect, they failed the net public benefits test.

Under the complex U.S. bank regulatory and supervisory structure, national banks are subject to the rulings of the Office of the Comptroller of the Currency (OCC), their prime regulator. Over the past three decades, the OCC has authorized national banks to provide the same services granted by the Federal Reserve to bank holding companies. However, there have been some anomalies. In the 1970s, the Federal Reserve Board would not allow bank holding companies to operate travel agencies, a service that about 150 banks—some state chartered, some nationally chartered—were providing at that time.

The OCC ruled that this activity was permissible for nationally chartered banks. This gave rise to a situation in which a bank holding company could not operate a travel agency directly, but could provide the service through its nationally chartered bank subsidiary. In a similar anomaly, the Federal Reserve denied real estate brokerage to bank holding companies, but the OCC granted it to nationally chartered banks.

In the 1980s, the Federal Reserve reassessed some of its net public benefits criteria. For example, bank holding companies were allowed to acquire thrift institutions if the thrift could not otherwise remain in business. The severe deposit losses thrift institutions experienced in the 1980s and the Fed's concern for the future viability of the thrift industry prompted this policy change. However, the Federal Reserve deliberately slowed its granting of new powers to holding companies, contending that the banking system and bank regulators needed time to evaluate the changes bank holding companies were bringing to the nation's financial system and the competitive and public benefit effects these changes might have. But bankers contended that this policy slowdown impaired banks' ability to compete with brokerage firms, life insurance companies, and other nonbank institutions that had begun to offer banking services.

In the mid-1980s, the banking industry sought to convince Congress that federal legislation allowing banks to provide insurance, underwriting, and brokerage services was needed to maintain competitive equality among financial institutions. By the late 1980s, however, Congress had not acted and the banking industry shifted its efforts to state legislatures, the courts, and the regulatory agencies. These efforts helped banks achieve limited underwriting powers for their holding company affiliates in many states and expanded powers in others. Almost half the states authorized state-chartered banks to provide insurance, real estate, brokerage and/or underwriting services in the 1980s. Some states also permitted banks to invest in corporate stock and real estate development projects.

In 1992, Congress was considering several bills that would permit banks in all states to affiliate with brokerage and dealer firms, to underwrite and sell corporate stocks and bonds without limitations, to permit bank holding company affiliates to sell insurance and mutual funds, and to allow commercial and industrial companies to own bank holding companies.

Source of Strength Doctrine

In regulating bank holding companies, the Federal Reserve has long relied on the source of strength doctrine which says that bank holding companies must serve as a source of strength for their subsidiary banks, providing them with capital and other assistance if they run into difficulties. The policy was established to ensure that bank holding companies would support weak subsidiary banks rather than letting them become insolvent, thereby shifting the cost of their failures from their parent holding companies to the FDIC.

The source of strength doctrine was not at issue in the 1960s and 1970s because bank holding companies were not pervasive and only 120 banks had failed during both decades. In the 1980s, however, the doctrine became a point of contention between bankers and the Federal Reserve—two-thirds of all banks had become subsidiaries of holding companies and close to 1,000 banks had failed. In 1989, the Federal Reserve initiated a civil suit against Mcorp, which was the second largest bank holding company in Texas before it declared bankruptcy that year. The Federal Reserve maintained that Mcorp had failed to act as a source of strength for its subsidiary banks. Before Mcorp filed for bankruptcy, the OCC had declared 20 of its 25 subsidiary banks insolvent. Closing these banks and paying off depositors cost the FDIC about $2 billion.

Mcorp challenged the Federal Reserve's suit, arguing that the Fed had no legal basis for imposing the source of strength doctrine on bank holding companies. The federal court agreed and noted that if holding companies were required to provide funds to troubled subsidiary banks, they would be wasting their assets, impairing their creditworthiness, and violating their duties to their stockholders. However, the Federal Reserve appealed the ruling to the U.S. Supreme Court, maintaining that nullification of the doctrine would create a regulatory vacuum that could pose substantial risks to the banking system.

In December 1991, the Supreme Court ruled in favor of the Federal Reserve, although it did not directly address the legality of the source of strength doctrine. That issue, however, is no longer in dispute. Congress enacted legislation authorizing the Federal Reserve to impose the source of strength doctrine on bank holding companies. The 1991 law that bolstered the deposit insurance fund also requires undercapitalized banks to provide regulators with a plan for selling stock, reducing assets, and/or borrowing funds to rebuild capital. Bank holding companies not only have to guarantee that undercapitalized bank subsidiaries follow their plans but can be required by the Federal Reserve to provide needed capital that is not otherwise obtained. A holding company's maximum capital contribution would be limited, however, to an amount equal to 5 percent of the holding company's total assets.

Deposit Concentration and the Future of Cash Management Services

Concentration of the nation's banking deposits on the books of fewer and fewer banks is a trend that grew slowly in the late 1940s, and accelerated with the holding company movement of the 1960s and 1970s. Today, many of the nation's small and medium-sized banks feel that the introduction of such cash management services as automated daily balance reporting will quicken the pace of deposit concentration. The transfer of a corporation's excess deposits from dozens of regional and local banks to one money market bank in a city such as New York City, Chicago, or San Francisco is a key feature of the cash management services the nation's major banks provide. The nation's smaller banks fear that the movement toward centralization of deposits will reduce a major source of deposits and earnings.

However, banks of all sizes have experienced a loss of corporate deposits as a source of earnings. All banks saw higher turnover rates on deposits in the 1980s and lower average balances as both corporate and individual depositors increasingly shifted funds into high-yield, short-term money market instruments. The higher service fees imposed by all banks for payment as well as cash management services were an attempt to offset the growing loss of corporate funds as a source of earnings.

Corporate cash management service needs also have changed—changes that have reduced potential profits for those regional and money center banks that actively market their cash management services to major corporations. In 1990, most of the nation's large companies—those with annual revenues in excess of $500 million—were using only seven banks each for their cash management services, down from a nine bank average in 1986. Industry surveys suggest that not only are nationwide companies relying on fewer banks for cash management services, but that companies are selecting banks primarily on the basis of the lowest service price.

The decreasing demand for cash management services has forced banks to reduce profit margins, improve operating efficiency, reduce operating costs, and tailor services to specific corporate needs to remain service competitive. Some banks have withdrawn from cash management services that they could not competitively price. For example, several large New York City banks no longer provide a retail lockbox service because operating the service proved too costly.

In the 1990s, banking industry analysts expect the focus of banks' cash management services to shift from speeding check collection, concentrating funds, and controlling disbursements to managing information. They expect this shift because the conditions that stimulated the growth of the check-oriented cash management services in the 1970s and 1980s, such as high inflation and interest rates, are not expected to prevail in the 1990s. These conditions increased the opportunity cost and time value of idle funds and supported a rising level of Federal Reserve float. Time delays in processing and presenting checks also were factors, as were restrictions on banks' ability to offer corporations interest-bearing accounts and limited interstate branching.

In the 1980s, Regulation Q ceilings ended, inflation slowed, and the Federal Reserve reduced the level of float while speeding up check processing and presentments. Many analysts believe that in the 1990s the prohibition on interest payments on demand deposits will be removed and restrictions on interstate branching will be eliminated.

These changes may be the death knell to cash management services in the 1990s. Bankers believe that broad technological developments and bank regulatory changes will work against cash management services because corporations will be able to transact all their domestic and global banking business through one institution, regardless of location. In that environment, there would be little need for account consolidation services and few markets for sophisticated balance-reporting services, the two mainstays of most banks' cash management offerings.

Other bankers feel that cash management services will survive and prosper in the 1990s as long as they adapt to changing market needs. These bankers see a financial market that will still offer a wide range of investment returns and risks. They feel there will still be a significant number of corporate depositors willing to pay for investment and advisory services to maximize returns and minimize risks.

Corporate needs for elaborate balance-reporting systems and collection arrangements, such as lockboxes, may be reduced in the 1990s. However, corporate treasurers will need more timely and automated financial and accounting statements and reports and more information and assistance in managing the corporation's total global asset and liability position.

Summary

Cash management services seek to maximize every available dollar in a corporation's account by speeding up the collection of checks payable, slowing down disbursements, and/or consolidating all corporate account balances each day. By receiving timely information about the availability of consolidated funds, corporations can make investment decisions that maximize daily earnings on these balances. Users of cash management services—major domestic firms, multinational corporations, government entities—want and are willing to pay for these services because they can

❖ increase their earnings by using check funds sooner

❖ hold funds earmarked for payments longer

❖ use every available dollar previously held idle

Many banks offer balance-reporting systems, lockbox network arrangements, account reconciliation services, and controlled disbursement services.

However, concerns have been raised within the banking industry about the growing concentration of deposits in banking caused by cash management. Concerns have also been raised about whether cash management services are as profitable to banks as believed.

Bank holding companies also have had a major impact on bank service offerings. As bank holding companies obtain new service powers in insurance, brokerage, and real estate, bank services of all kinds are likely to emerge as an even bigger source of bank earnings and the focus of bank management attention.

Questions

1. What four factors have stimulated demand for cash management services from banks in the past two decades?

2. What are the benefits to corporations of a lockbox service?

3. What are the characteristics of a competitive controlled disbursement service?

4. Why have so many banks adopted the holding company as their corporate structure?

THE EVOLVING
BANKING SYSTEM

Objectives

After successfully completing this chapter, you will be able to

- ❖ identify the major changes that have occurred in banking over the past two decades
- ❖ discuss the significance of current trends in banking and their probable impact on the future of banking
- ❖ explain the importance of productivity in banking, the problems banks face in addressing productivity, and actions banks might take to increase productivity

Changes in Banking

Banking has changed dramatically over the past two decades; three of those changes are particularly noteworthy:

❖ The dominant position of commercial banks in the United States and world financial markets has declined.

In the 1950s, commercial banks were the nation's sole providers of payment and deposit services and were the primary repositories of the country's financial wealth. This is no longer true. In the 1950s, banks held more than 55 percent of the nation's financial assets. Today they hold less than 35 percent. In the 1970s, U.S. banks held 30 percent of the world's banking assets; today they hold less than 10 percent. Twenty years ago, 6 of the 10 largest banks in the world were U.S. banks; today no U.S. bank ranks among the world's 10 largest and only 2 U.S. banks rank among the world's 50 largest. In 1991, Japanese banks held about 40 percent of the world's banking assets and Japanese and other foreign banks accounted for nearly one-third of all business loans made in the United States.

Now banks must rely on deposits with interest rates tied to money market rates rather than on demand and savings deposits, which historically represented a low-cost, stable source of funds. On balance, interest expenses rose faster than interest earnings since the deregulation of interest rates in 1980, which narrowed interest spreads and eroded banks' profitability. The profitability of the banking industry steadily declined in the 1980s and from 1984 to year-end 1991, more than 1,300 banks failed. In 1991, about 1 in 10 U.S. banks registered a loss and 10 of the nation's 48 banks with assets of $10 billion or more were unprofitable. Also, as exhibit 11.1 shows, the outlook for the survival of more than 400 banks in 1992 and 1993 is not promising.

The position of the nation's commercial banks declined, not only because they lost some markets to foreign banks and domestic non-bank financial institutions but because these institutions took a larger share of a vastly bigger domestic and global financial market.

❖ Banks introduced electronic technology to their internal operations and to the delivery of payment services.

Virtually all banks today rely on computers and computer-related equipment for check processing, internal recordkeeping and accounting, and interbank transfers of funds. More and more banks are turning to electronic funds transfer systems in their retail operations.

❖ In the past 20 years, innovations in banking services and practices, and modifications in banking law and regulation have accelerated changes in banking. Commercial banks have lost their near-monopoly in providing demand deposits and checking account services. The business of banking has become more competitive and more consumer-oriented.

Exhibit 11.1 *Commercial Bank Failures (average number per year)*

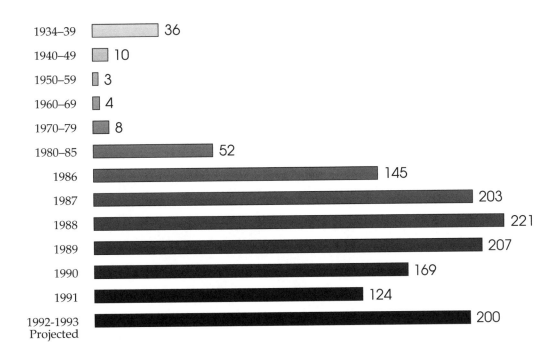

1934–39	36
1940–49	10
1950–59	3
1960–69	4
1970–79	8
1980–85	52
1986	145
1987	203
1988	221
1989	207
1990	169
1991	124
1992-1993 Projected	200

Note: The FDIC was established in 1934.

Sources: **Federal Deposit Insurance Corporation; Congressional Budget Office;** *Washington Post*, **January 2, 1991, and December 8, 1991;** *American Banker*, **January 3, 1992.**

Predicting the Future

Studies of banking trends over the past two decades and examinations of emerging developments offer some insight into how banking might develop in the next two decades.

This method of prediction, called extrapolation, is not foolproof. Sometimes, simple mathematical projections of trends can be misleading because it is hard to judge how long trends will continue. For example, if the rate of bank mergers from 1981 to 1991 continued until the year 2011, only 200 banks would remain. While virtually all banking industry analysts project continued bank mergers and a sharp decline in the number of banks over the next two decades, few see the 1980s pace of mergers continuing unabated over the next 20 years.

Extrapolation of trends also cannot predict banking innovations, new payment practices, or specific banking laws or regulations that will alter the course of banking's development. Nor can it foresee the course of banking developments. For example, bankers were told in the early 1960s that the payments mechanism of the 1980s would be checkless or even cashless, based on expectations that newly emerging electronic payments technology would transform banking over the next 20 years. This extrapolation could not foresee the public resistance to change and the regulatory constraints that prevented the transformation.

Similarly, few bankers, even those who expected significant regulatory and legal change in the 1970s and 1980s, could have anticipated the fundamental restructuring of banking and banking regulation that Congress advanced in the 1980 Monetary Control Act and the 1989 Financial Institutions Reform, Recovery and Enforcement Act.

Nonetheless, projecting the future on the basis of current trends is an important exercise for banks. It provides a basis for banks to initiate programs and strategies for successfully dealing with the future. By identifying trends that may be harmful to their long-term interests, banks can act to forestall the projected effects. And banks can begin to adapt their operations, technology, business strategies, personnel practices, and interbank relationships to position themselves so that they can garner increased profits and bigger market shares.

Changes in the Payments Mechanism

There will be many changes in the payments mechanism over the next two decades. Foremost will be advances in payments technology: improvements in wire transfer systems, further automation of retail banking services, extension of electronic payments systems to retail outlets, and continued development of network payments systems.

Payments Technology

Advances in payments technology changed banking in the 1970s and 1980s, and will continue to act as a catalyst for change in the 1990s and beyond. However, the U.S. payments mechanism in the year 2012 will probably not differ significantly from the one that exists today.

Coin and currency will continue to play a small but important role in the day-to-day convenience transactions of consumers and retailers. Paper payments made against transactions deposits will continue to be the primary consumer and business payment method. And banks will continue to devote considerable resources and management attention to check processing and collection. What is likely to change by the year 2012, however, is the proportion of paper payments relative to electronic payments. The next two decades will see a much greater proportion of consumer, business, and government payments made electronically.

Wire Transfer Systems

The wire transfer systems that banks and the Federal Reserve installed in the 1960s and 1970s to move interbank balances increased the speed and efficiency of moving money and made it possible for a broad range of banks to offer wire transfer services to corporate and individual customers. These wire transfer systems, primarily FedWire and CHIPS, also allowed banks to increase their volume of payments and make transactions flow through a narrower base of demand deposits and reserves. However, these two factors substantially increased banks' risks in using wire transfer systems.

Over the next two decades, improvements in wire transfer technology will allow banks to manage payments risk while handling a greater volume of electronic information related to payment transactions. Broad use of payment netting arrangements will blunt the accelerating growth of interbank electronic transfers, while new technology will encourage banks to develop specialized electronic payment services for corporate and individual accounts, supported by smaller, more powerful and less expensive computers. Virtually all depositories will have direct computer-to-computer or terminal-to-computer links to national wire transfer systems.

Retail Banking Services

Retail banking services as well as internal bank operations will become increasingly more automated. New technology will allow high-volume banks to provide more sophisticated payment and cash management services to customers at lower unit costs. The costs of new technology in the 1980s were more than most small and mid-sized banks could afford. As a result, these banks were unable to provide electronic payment services equal to those of the nation's big banks. However, over the next two decades, the availability of less expensive computers will enable even small, community-based depositories to offer elaborate cash management services and allow virtually all small business and individual account holders to obtain returns on temporarily idle cash balances. Also, many small and mid-sized banks will merge, seek holding company affiliations, or establish service companies under cooperative arrangements, which will enable them to broaden their services.

Service Delivery

Providers of banking services already include nontraditional participants such as department stores, brokerage firms, and telephone companies. The options for delivering banking services to consumer and corporate customers by these nontraditional sources will be greater in 10 years than they are now. More business will be transacted between terminals in retail stores and phones in homes, and cable television and telephone links will allow virtually all banking to be conducted in homes and offices. However, Americans will still prefer to visit banks to conduct most of their banking business.

Network Payment Systems

Banks will increasingly rely on networks of ATMs and POS terminals to deliver nationwide retail banking services. Consumers will perform more retail banking activities with credit and debit cards and increase the use of ATMs, POS terminals, and television and telephone transactions. However, the volume of personal cash and check transactions involving banks will likely be no lower in the year 2012 than it is today.

Changes in Banking Structure

The next two decades also will be a period of change in banking structure. These changes will be prompted by

- ❖ the increasing elimination of legal and regulatory differences between banks and other financial institutions
- ❖ the development of more extensive interstate banking as electronic payments technology proliferates and nationwide branching is authorized
- ❖ bank consolidations
- ❖ increasing emphasis on new banking services
- ❖ increasing emphasis on reducing operating costs

Legal and Regulatory Differences

The legal and regulatory differences among savings banks, savings and loan associations, and commercial banks have all but disappeared. Over the next 20 years, other financial institutions, such as credit unions, finance companies, insurance companies, pension funds, money market funds, and brokerage firms will be offering banking and payment services similar to those offered by banks. In fact, it is likely that large companies, such as IBM and General Motors, will provide banking services through subsidiaries.

In the early 1990s, Congress was considering several bills that would allow financial institutions and commercial business firms to establish financial service holding companies that would be allowed to own banks. Interstate branching restrictions will likely be removed by federal legislation, and the financial services that can be provided by bank holding companies will likely be broadened. These changes will lead Congress to restructure the powers and responsibilities of the federal bank regulatory agencies.

Congress has been considering a functional approach to regulating financial service holding companies. Under functional regulation, each agency responsible for a specific financial activity—such as insurance, brokerage, or banking—would be responsible for regulating the subsidiary engaged in that activity irrespective of the origin of the holding company. However, some analysts forecast that by the year 2000, the bank supervisory and regulatory functions of the Federal Deposit Insurance Corporation, Comptroller of the Currency, and Federal Reserve Board will be combined into a single agency.

In the early 1990s, it is most likely that Congress will restructure the federal deposit insurance system to strengthen the depleted deposit insurance fund and to reduce banks' risk taking. Several bills to limit insurance coverage and to change the way banks' insurance premiums are assessed (from the total amount of the bank's insured deposits to the risk rating of the insured bank) were debated by Congress in 1991. Although the bank regulatory structure is likely to change, chartering, insurance, and examinations will remain the primary focus of the federal regulatory oversight of bank. Increased regulation may even emerge in the area of bank management controls on information privacy and communications security in EFT systems.

The prevailing viewpoint, however, is that regulatory responsibilities will be reallocated among the federal agencies as banks expand more extensively outside their home states and begin providing insurance, real estate, and mutual fund investment services.

Interstate Banking

In the 1970s, electronic payments technology helped banks circumvent the geographic barriers limiting their market activities. In the 1980s, most of the geographic barriers fell. Almost all states enacted laws that permit out-of-state bank holding companies to acquire or establish subsidiary banks in their state if the holding company's state reciprocates. These state laws have already enabled banks to expand their activities within multistate regions and, by the early 1990s, will enable banks to expand nationwide.

In 1992, Congress was considering legislation that would permit banks themselves, not only their holding companies, to branch nationwide. If Congress authorizes nationwide branching in the 1990s, as most industry analysts forecast, interstate banking will be given a powerful stimulus. Interstate branch offices do not require separate boards of directors, management teams, payments processing systems, or accounting systems. Thus, they would be much less costly for a holding company to operate than a separate subsidiary bank.

The expansion of interstate banking in the 1990s does not mean that the nation's money center banks will establish branches in small towns across the country. Instead, interstate banking for the nation's large banks will more likely involve opening selected offices in major markets and linking EFT terminals to the telephone or television hookups of depositors throughout the country. Small and mid-sized banks also will participate in interstate banking through shared national payments systems.

Changes in Bank Consolidation

Low profitability and eroding competitiveness will force many banks and thrift institutions to seek affiliation with other depositories during the next two decades. The 1990s will be a period of substantial consolidation. Thousands of depositories will become absorbed into the nationwide organizations of larger institutions. However, thousands of strong, community-based banks will survive and profit as independent institutions by serving their local markets through affiliations with national payment networks, such as Visa, MasterCard and/or interstate ATM systems.

By the year 2000, the number of banks in the United States is likely to decline to about 8,000 from today's 12,000 plus, as banks continue to merge in an effort to reduce operating costs, increase capital, and retain competitive market shares of key banking products. However, bank customers are not likely to notice much difference. While merged banks will combine management and back office operations, relatively few branches are likely to be closed. The trends of the 1980s suggest that as the number of banks decline in the 1990s, the number of bank branches will continue to increase (see exhibit 11.2), perhaps to 60,000. Trends also suggest that a large share of new bank branches in the 1990s will be housed in supermarkets.

Branch offices in supermarkets increased from 200 in 1985 to 1,200 in 1991. Most of these branches were established by banks in the nation's southern and southwestern states. Industry analysts project that by 1994, 300 to 600 additional branches will be housed in supermarkets, most of them established by banks in the northeastern states. Many bankers see in these branches a way to reach and serve a broader base of customers in the 1990s at low cost. Supermarket branches are typically staffed by two to five people, equipped with one or more ATMs, and cost about one-third less to build and maintain than conventional stand-alone offices.

Exhibit 11.2 *Number of U.S. Banks and Branches*

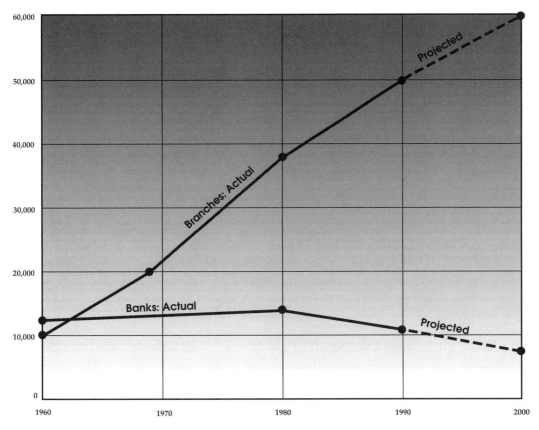

Source: *American Banker*, April 16, 1991

Projections differ regarding the degree of consolidation that will take place after 2000. But consolidation patterns in other industries have led many analysts to project that by the year 2012 the structure of the U.S. banking industry will consist of the following four tiers:

Global banks. The first tier will comprise a select group of full service financial institutions that operate in both U.S. and overseas banking markets. Not all these banks are expected to be the same as the dominant commercial banks of the 1990s. It is likely that several foreign-owned banks and several nonbanking institutions will be in this tier. The global banks—about 20 to 30—will offer a full range of domestic financial services while playing a major role in international trade and finance. Several Japanese conglomerates will probably dominate this tier with assets approaching $500 billion each; most global banks, however, will probably have assets in the $100 billion range.

The Evolving Banking System   295

Superregional banks. The second tier will consist of 40 to 60 major regional banks that will provide consumer and business banking products and services—and such specialized international products as foreign exchange and letters of credit—over much larger geographic markets than most regional banks now have. They will each hold $30-$50 billion in assets and will dominate their regions' midsize business and consumer markets.

Specialized banks. Several thousand banks probably will occupy the third banking tier. These banks will be distinguished by their commitment to a single product line, a specific group of customers, or a select segment of the banking market. The specialized banks will provide customized service in, for example, mortgage lending, short-term business financing, brokerage, or insurance. Residential mortgages probably will be arranged by specialized mortgage banks operating through real estate brokers with funds supplied in the nation's bond markets. Most personal loans probably will be made on credit cards through banks that specialize in installment credit, and small businesses will likely do most of their borrowing from specialized finance companies. A significant portion of these banks' retail transactions probably will be through electronic terminals linked to stores. The specialized banks will remain competitive with the total service global and superregional banks by offering customized services.

Community-based banks. Most of the banking industry will comprise the fourth tier. These banks will provide a broad range of financial services, but will focus only on local markets and customers. The competitive environment in 2012 for third and fourth tier banks will be much more intense than it is today, with department store chains, brokerage houses, and finance companies firmly entrenched as active bank competitors.

Banking Strategies

As fees for banking services exceed interest income as the primary source of bank earnings, the provision of bank services to individual and corporate customers will become increasingly more important. The traditional business of banking—taking in demand deposits and making loans—will shrink in importance during the 1990s as competition increasingly cuts profit margins in these activities.

Lending funds to major corporations will continue to decline as the primary use of banks' funds, although lending to small and midsize companies will continue to be lucrative. Banks' fundamental relationships with major corporations also will likely change. In the early 1990s, corporations were increasingly shifting their banking relationships to more conservatively managed banks. Most analysts contend that if bank failures continue at a high level, the deposit insurance system remains underfunded, and bank profitability remains low, corporations' shift to the highest quality banks could increase sharply by the mid-1990s, causing the merger pace to quicken among banks and leading to a greater concentration of deposits.

As commercial lending becomes progressively less profitable for banks, insurance, mutual funds, and other consumer investment products are likely to become increasingly more profitable. This projection, which assumes that banks' product powers will be expanded in the 1990s, is based on demographic trends that show that the U.S. population will be growing older over the next 10 to 15 years. Forecasters project that most bank customers will be beyond their peak borrowing years and into the wealth accumulation stage of their lives. Thus, consumer borrowing demands are likely to slacken, while consumer demands for diversified savings and investment products are likely to intensify. To meet these new demands, banks will have to become expert at selling mutual fund and annuity products together with traditional banking products. This task will be difficult and costly because bank personnel will have to be trained to sell the broad range of savings and investment products that banks may have available in the 1990s.

Reducing Operating Costs

Reducing operating costs became a prevalent bank management practice in the 1980s; this practice is seen by most industry analysts as continuing well into the 1990s as banks institute strategies to restore profitability.

In the 1980s, bank profitability, particularly for the nation's largest banks, was jolted by an explosion in noninterest expense; banks saw their operating costs skyrocket by 50 percent from 1980 to 1985. (See exhibit 11.3.) Operating expense growth slowed somewhat in the last half of the 1980s, in response to banks' cost-cutting initiatives, but still registered a 30 percent increase, bringing the industry's total noninterest expenses to more than $100 billion, almost double banks' operating costs at the beginning of the decade.

Most banks focused their cost reduction strategies on the noninterest expense category that increased the fastest in the 1980s—employee benefits costs—and salaries, the core component of bank operating costs. For example, most banks changed their health insurance programs to require employees to pay a share of the costs of medical insurance coverage for dependents and tightened other fringe benefits. Nonetheless, today, employee health insurance coverage, pension benefits, and other salary-related costs still add 25 to 40 percent for every salary dollar spent by a bank. Many banks also instituted one or more of the following staff reduction measures, all of which are likely to be periodically applied in the 1990s.

Layoffs. Many of the nation's largest banks resorted to layoffs in the 1980s and early 1990s in an effort to prune their size and reduce operating costs. However, analysts see a potential danger in the broad application of this expense reduction tactic. They contend that bankwide layoffs can often spread uncertainty and lower morale among surviving staff on whom the

---

Exhibit 11.3 *Noninterest Expense Growth at the 10 Largest U.S. Banking Companies*

	Gross Expenses Average Annual Growth Rate (percentage)	Overhead Costs (noninterest expense as a percentage of interest income)		
	1981-1986	1984	1985	1986
Citicorp	19	49	46	45
Chase Manhattan Corp.	15	54	52	55
Bank America Corp.	11	63	66	66
Chemical New York Corp.	13	50	49	47
J.P. Morgan & Co.	18	17	10	11
Manufacturers Hanover	15	50	46	46
Security Pacific Corp.	18	52	49	51
Bankers Trust N.Y. Corp.	11	27	23	8
First Interstate Bancorp.	13	59	57	54
Wells Fargo & Co.	12	55	50	52
Average	**15**	**48**	**45**	**44**

bank must depend for higher productivity. Unless layoffs are targeted to specific areas in which the bank is reducing its involvement—closing branches or phasing out cash management services—some work processes may be impaired, reducing the bank's efficiency and, ultimately, increasing its operating costs.

Early retirement. In the 1980s, most large banks offered employees nearing retirement age financial inducements to retire early. Banks generated savings by replacing older workers who were earning high salaries with younger workers at lower salaries and not replacing every retiree. This strategy succeeded, in part, because the nation's labor force was growing rapidly in the 1980s and young workers were readily available. However, projections show that fewer workers will be entering the labor force in the 1990s than in the 1980s and by the year 2000, one-third of the labor force will be over age 45. Thus, banks' reliance on early retirement programs as a cost reduction strategy may not be effective in the 1990s. Some industry analysts project that banks may have to pay increasingly higher wages in the 1990s to attract and retain essential personnel. As banks recognize this trend, industry analysts forecast that banks will increasingly invest in labor-saving technology and intensify efforts to institute more productivity-generating management and work practices.

Reorganization and consolidation. Many banks have reorganized their internal management structures to parallel changes in business strategies, and regrouped various line and staff departments to match market conditions and service offerings, and consolidated branch offices to reduce costs. For example, by combining related departments and broadening middle-management spans of control over employees, large banks have found that fewer managers, supervisors, and secretarial staff are needed. Also, banks with branch operations have found that a small staff can turn out the same volume of work as a large one by consolidating certain back office operations, such as data processing, accounting, and funds transfer.

In the 1980s, the focus of most bank reorganizations and consolidations was on back office and operating departments where, despite automation, staff growth had increased steadily since the early 1960s. Many banks that automated in the 1960s and 1970s found that automation did not bring lower operating costs or smaller staffs. In many instances, reductions in low-salaried clerical personnel were more than offset by increases in high-salaried data-processing and other computer-related technical personnel. Banks' efforts in the 1980s to reduce operating costs sought to solve this problem.

Over the next decade, it is likely that fewer back office staff will be needed by banks of all sizes. Many banks will reduce their need for operating staff by buying their data-processing, check-processing, and accounting services from nonbank companies. Other banks are likely to reduce operating staffs by consolidating more of their branch operations and computer systems at central sites, which will provide all offices with access to computer services through terminals and leased telephone lines.

In the 1980s, several major New York City banks used their back office consolidations as an opportunity to transfer some or all of their major operations out of the city into nearby suburban areas or, in some instances, to other regions of the country. New York bankers contend that such geographic reorganizations have not only provided their banks with essential back-up processing capabilities, but will reduce costs through lower real estate and occupancy expenses, and lower labor, transportation, and utility costs. Industry analysts project that increasing numbers of large urban-based banks in other regions of the country are likely to shift operations to suburban locations in the 1990s to achieve such savings.

Hiring workers over 65 as part-time tellers and clerical workers. Today, most banks rely on part-time staff for covering peak periods in branches and in back office operations. Many banks have found that they can reduce salary and benefits costs by hiring senior citizens, especially their own retirees, as part-time workers. As hourly wage employees, these workers are paid no fringe benefits, and in the case of retirees, there are no agency fees. Agency

---

fees can raise the hourly cost of a temporary employee about 50 percent above that of a regular employee in the same job. Banks also avoid extensive training costs with retirees who bring their knowledge of the bank and bank operations to their part-time job.

Many retirees, however, are reluctant to earn more than $4,000 annually in order not to jeopardize their full Social Security benefits. Thus, they tend to be willing to work only a limited number of hours.

Hiring contract personnel. Some banks have reduced costs by hiring personnel on contract as consultants, rather than as employees, in areas where discrete projects or tasks are involved. For example, some banks have disbanded their marketing or data-processing units and contracted their former

Exhibit 11.4 *Bank Employment in the 1980s by Major Job Category*

Job Category	Average Number of Jobs
Bank tellers	343,000
Bank managers	280,000
General office clerks	110,000
Secretaries	74,000
Bookkeeping and billing operators	61,000
Clerical supervisors	59,000
Proofreading machine operators	46,000
Computer operators	35,000
Bank statement clerks	29,000
Building custodians	22,000
Typists	20,000
Loan closing clerks	19,000
Banking and insurance credit clerks	19,000
File clerks	18,000
Bill collectors	17,000
Accountants and auditors	16,000
Messengers	14,000
Top 17 Job Categories	1,182,000
Total Banking Employment	1,500,000

Source: **Bureau of Labor Statistics; New York Stock Exchange;** *American Banker*, **April 16, 1991**

employees, as individuals or as a group, to perform specific tasks, such as conducting a market survey or installing and testing new computer software. The contract guarantees the former employees a certain amount of business (and income) but gives them the freedom to work at other jobs. Banks save because they do not have to pay Social Security taxes or fringe benefits for consultants on contract.

Use of this strategy in the 1990s, however, may be limited by new IRS regulations. The IRS will apply strict criteria to determine whether a worker is really a self-employed consultant or an employee under the guise of a consultant. The purpose of the criteria is to prevent tax avoidance by both employers and employees.

Bank Employment

Bank employment is projected to decline in the 1990s from 1.5 million in 1990 to about 1.3 million by the year 2000, with the bulk of the reduction coming from the nation's larger banks. Industry analysts base this projection on three consensus expectations for the 1990s:

❖ Banks will continue to use strategies designed to reduce operating costs.

❖ The number and size of bank mergers will continue to grow.

❖ Banks will continue to automate.

Few analysts see bank employment declining by more than 20 percent (200,000 jobs) over the next 10 years because basic growth in the volume of deposits, check processing, and other payments-related work done by banks' back office personnel will prevent large staff reductions. Some analysts suggest that the decline in bank employment in the 1990s could be as few as 100,000 jobs, noting that, despite massive layoffs at the nation's leading money center banks, total employment at the 100 largest bank holding companies (adjusted for mergers) actually increased in 1990 by 1.5 percent over 1989 levels to 1.1 million.

In 1960, commercial banks employed about 650,000 people. By 1985, the total banking workforce had grown to more than 1.5 million, then bank employment levels began to decline as banks began to retrench in response to escalating operating costs and declining profits. However, automation played a major role. By the mid-1980s, the productivity-generating effects of increased automation in such areas as check processing, funds transfer, and cash management operations made large-scale clerical and operating staff reductions possible. Most of the banking jobs eliminated in the 1980s were in back office clerical and data-processing areas.

Banking employment is highly concentrated, with the nation's 20 largest bank holding companies accounting for about one-third of all bank employees. Bank employment is also heavily weighted toward teller and clerical jobs.

Exhibit 11.4 shows that the top 17 job categories in banking (out of 258 occupation categories) account for nearly 80 percent of all banking jobs; most are bank teller or clerical positions, such as typists, secretaries, and clerks.

Industry analysts forecast that banks will continue to rely on computer technology in the 1990s to reduce their overall employment needs. Many bankers expect that continuing automation over the next two decades will significantly reduce the need for tellers, the largest job category of bank personnel. However, there is no evidence to date that increased automation or ATM deployment has displaced tellers. Automation often requires more bank personnel to maintain computers and software, to supply ATMs with cash, to prepare and tally ATM tapes, and to address consumer inquiries and complaints.

Most banking analysts believe that the application of computer technology in the next 20 years will lead to staff reductions in back office operations. For example, the use of image-processing systems, which send digitized images of checks and other documents electronically, eliminates the need for many key-punch operations. Some studies suggest that as much as 40 percent of most banks' data-processing staffs could be reduced if the industry adopted image technology. Analysts also project that many banks will reduce back office employment needs by ending their in-house processing of checks and accounts-related data. These banks will purchase necessary computer, accounting, and data processing services from other companies.

The national trend toward applying computer technology to office activities and secretarial operations will be particularly strong in banking, but this application is not likely to generate substantial staffing reductions. Instead, the nature of clerical, executive, and professional functions in banking will change. Personal computers and desktop terminals will give bankers instant access to files and data, and teletype-telephones and interactive television will increase the efficiency of conference calls and meetings. A considerable share of work also will be performed at operations centers remote from banks' head offices, or at home via terminal access to bank computers.

Banking Workforce

Banks will face new challenges in recruiting, training, managing, and motivating employees over the next decade because of profound changes in the workforce. Demographic trends in the 1980s and early 1990s suggest that by the year 2000 the workforce will be older and will be comprised of more women and minorities than it is today.

These trends suggest that over the next 10 years there will be a disproportionate increase in the number of women and minorities employed in banks and in the number of bank employees in the 30-50 age group. There will also be a shift from the employment of primarily clerical and technical personnel toward the employment of more professional and customer-contact personnel.

These changes will have a major impact on the personnel policies and practices of banks. Many banks have already modified personnel policies to accommodate the needs and concerns of the changing workforce. These modifications, which are likely to become pervasive in banking in the 1990s, include

- ❖ health benefits that cover employees' parents as well as dependent children
- ❖ both paid and unpaid leave for employees to care for a newborn
- ❖ job sharing, in which two employees share one full-time position
- ❖ work at home arrangements, in which part of the work is done at home
- ❖ flextime opportunities that allow employees to work 35 to 40 hours in less than 5 days
- ❖ flexible benefit programs that allow employees to select the benefits that best meet their personal and family needs

The introduction of new products and services by banks, and banks' continuing adoption of new technology to process data and information also will require bank management to devote increased resources to employee education and training in the 1990s.

Productivity Issues

The need to increase productivity—to generate more output per worker—is a critical, operational issue facing banks in the 1990s. One measure of bankers' concern with productivity is that an increasing number of banks have appointed officers specifically to oversee their banks' efforts to improve productivity.

When productivity does not increase, rising operating costs invariably lead to rising prices or declining profits. For banks, static productivity poses a particular problem. Banking is essentially a labor-intensive business; labor costs constitute the largest single component of noninterest expense of most banks. However, banks cannot easily pass on rising labor costs to consumer and corporate depositors. For one thing, banks are limited by law to maximum interest rates they can charge on a considerable portion of their earning assets—consumer loans and real estate loans. Also, the market for banking products and services is highly competitive. When a bank's loan rates or service charges rise too rapidly, customer demand for services can shift to nonbank financial institutions that provide similar services and offer similar products.

Since competitive forces place interest expense largely beyond banks' control, much of bank management's focus in the 1980s fell on short-run measures to control and reduce labor costs in order to restore profitability. However, the focus of bank management in the 1990s has broadened to include measures that can improve worker productivity as a long-term solution.

Measuring Productivity

The precise reason why workers become more or less productive is not known. Some economists contend that productivity increases and decreases may not be attributable to any one major reason, but rather are related to broad changes in the economy.

For example, in the 1950s and 1960s, the continuing shift of workers from farming occupations to manufacturing jobs contributed significantly to growing national productivity because industrial jobs typically generate higher productivity than do farm jobs. In the 1970s and 1980s, however, the increasing shift of workers from manufacturing jobs to service employment contributed to a slowing of national productivity because service jobs typically generate lower productivity than manufacturing jobs.

Other reasons include the level of education, skill, and experience of the workforce, and the amount of capital and quality of technology that companies use in production. New workers who lack skills require more time and resources for training, leaving less time to produce. Banks are likely to face such labor market conditions for key entry-level workers in the 1990s. Firms that do not add new capital or technology to their work processes do not provide the support necessary to generate sharp increases in productivity. Most banks have recognized this traditional source of productivity.

In the late 1980s, banks were spending $12 billion annually on computer software and telecommunications equipment, almost three times the annual amount spent on this technology in the early 1980s.

External factors can affect productivity as well. For example, many bankers contend that consumer protection regulations issued in the 1970s and 1980s were unduly complex and absorbed increasing amounts of management time and expenditures for legal resources that could have been more profitably used to increase output.

The composition of the nation's economy has shifted toward the production of more services—whether governmental, financial, legal, medical, or recreational—and the production of fewer goods. However, productivity in the service industries is difficult to measure. In banking, as in all service industries, there are few production lines against which easy measures of output per hour or output per worker can be made. The government's productivity measures count such activities as the number of checks cleared and loans made per employee. However, most of banking involves clerical, analytical, administrative, and managerial work. The productivity of these kinds of work cannot be readily identified. Furthermore, the quality of a product or service cannot be evaluated easily.

Many banks rely on productivity proxies to measure their own performance within the industry. One such proxy subtracts a bank's interest expense on deposits and borrowings from its total operating revenues to obtain a profit margin figure. The bank's personnel expenses, including salaries, bonuses, fringe benefits, and payroll taxes, are then divided into that figure to give bank management a measure of how many dollars of profit are being generated for each dollar spent. A measure like this enables a bank to track its own performance against other banks of like size, but it is not a good measure of the productivity of the bank's workforce.

Many banks also have their own measures of efficiency. Some banks evaluate employee performance in operations that are quantifiable, such as the number of hourly transactions a teller handles or the number of checking account statements a clerk reconciles each day. Measures like these help banks to determine their productivity for some activities, but they fall short in measuring the quality of the work performed over time. Also, these measures have limited application in the professional, technical, and managerial activities of most banks, where the quality of the work is essentially the product.

Improving Productivity

From 1979 to 1988, productivity in the industrial sector of the U.S. economy increased at an average annual rate of 3.9 percent, while productivity in the service sector increased at an average annual rate of only 0.4 percent. However, the productivity of commercial banks substantially exceeded the service sector average, increasing at a 2.3 percent annual rate for the entire decade. Banks' annual output per worker increased because extensive staff reductions were made from the mid-to -late 1980s while the volume of work thoughout the decade sharply increased. What cannot be discerned from the productivity statistics is whether the quality, timeliness, and efficiency of bank services improved and whether customers' convenience and satisfaction with bank services increased.

In the 1980s, bank management focused on improving productivity in the back office—that is, upgrading internal operating efficiency. The focus in the 1990s will likely be on improving productivity in the front office by promoting efficiency in the delivery of services directly to customers.

Most banks have made significant productivity gains by increasing productivity in their back offices and data-processing centers. Technological improvements have increased the volume of paper checks handled and enabled fewer people to perform larger and more complex transactions.

On balance, technology improved the speed and accuracy with which money and data were transferred between banks and among different units within a bank. For some banks, however, technology and data processing have not been the answer to increasing productivity. Automation has enabled some banks to process a greater number and variety of transactions more quickly, but the overall quality of their deposit-related services has declined. Also, the costs for some banks of increased technical staff and computer consultants have outweighed the savings. Not all banks were able to adapt their organizational structures and management processes to the automated environment of the 1980s.

Many banks, however, developed a measurement of productivity of their computer-related operations. This allowed management to track the efficiency and output of these operations over time. However, little attention was paid to increasing the productivity of front office operations.

In the 1990s, banks will be faced with two broad, but not mutually exclusive, options:

❖ reduce the labor-intensive costs of providing services directly to customers by developing new ways to do more with fewer tellers, clerks, or other bank personnel

❖ get bank customers to do more for themselves—bank by telephone; make payments by cable television; use ATMs and POS terminals

If bank customers are willing to give up personal banking, which is largely dependent on costly labor-intensive service, banks may, in the long run, be able to reduce the ratio of cost to each unit of service provided.

The latter option is similar to what the nation's telephone companies faced in the 1970s. By sharing technology and systems and getting customers to accept direct dialing, the nation's telephone companies were able to reduce labor-intensive costs and meet growing service demand. The grocery industry, facing a similar challenge in the 1940s, successfully introduced the self-service supermarket.

Productivity Programs

Traditional theories on productivity attribute gains in output per worker in any industry to economic fundamentals—the amount of capital (machines) employers use to assist workers, the technology of the machines, the way workers are organized, and the inventions and innovations that improve the way products are made or services are delivered.

Modern theories on productivity have tended to focus on worker attitudes and factors in the work environment that appear to stimulate or constrain worker output. Among the factors that economists have identified are the following:

❖ the level of a worker's pay, the degree of employer recognition for the work performed, and the way the company's compensation is allocated among different units and groups of employees

❖ the degree of individual autonomy and discretion the worker has in performing tasks, and the nature of those tasks

❖ the amount of cross-training an employee receives in other related jobs that broaden career paths

❖ the amount of information, feedback, and support a worker receives from other departments and from management, and the interpersonal interaction between and among employees and management

❖ the establishment of a management structure that has few levels of hierarchy and promotes a decent physical working environment

Some modern productivity theorists contend that the way a bank's workforce is used, the philosophy and approach of a bank's senior management to bank employees, and a bank's personnel practices are as important in generating front office productivity as investment in technology. The front office and support operations of most banks largely involve clerical, analytical, administrative, and professional activities, as well as ongoing personal interactions of bank employees with depositors, potential customers, and one another. Productivity gains in these activities are typically a result of employee and management motivation and initiative.

Quality of Work Life

Work attitude and motivation studies in the United States have shown that educated employees are motivated more by the quality of their life at work than by salaries. Among the factors in a job that motivate employees are the following:

❖ participation in management decisions that affect their jobs

❖ challenging tasks and assignments that have a clear purpose

❖ potential for personal growth and development of skills and abilities

❖ compensation that is closely tied to accomplishment

❖ recognition by management for work that is done well

❖ ongoing communication from management about what is going on in the company

Banks that do not satisfy these wants for their employees tend to produce a low quality of work life at the bank and a high level of employee dissatisfaction, often reflected in a high turnover rate, high rate of absenteeism, high error rates, and low morale. Banks with these internal conditions do not typically generate ongoing increases in productivity. By contrast, banks that raise the level of their employees' job satisfaction can increase productivity. A bank with a contented workforce that feels self-fulfilled will have a low rate of absenteeism and turnover, which will keep labor costs low. This bank will also typically have a lower rate of errors, which will improve the quality of its service and increase productivity.

Quality Circles

In addressing these work-related factors, one program that has been successfully employed in several major banks is the quality circle.

A quality circle is a highly structured program in which employees brainstorm. Through periodic quality circle sessions, management uses the expertise of employees to solve work or quality problems and improve the bank's performance.

The Japanese developed the quality circle concept in the early 1960s by applying the theories of U.S. behavioral scientists Abraham Maslow, Frederick Herzberg, and Thomas McGregor. In the late 1970s, many of the nation's large banks sought to apply quality circles to improve their productivity performance.

The quality circle program involves a structured process in which problems must be specifically identified. Problems within the area of responsibility of employees are analyzed based on proposals, discussions, and recommendations for alternative solutions. After participants in the quality circle agree to one recommendation or solution, a presentation is made to senior bank management. Because the quality circle sessions are designed to be structured, management must provide training and must actively participate in the sessions, as well as agree to accept recommendations from the employee groups.

Production-oriented departments, such as check-processing and wire transfer departments, have been the starting points for most bank quality circle programs. As routine operations were improved and productivity increased, quality circle programs were expanded to the front office and to professional and staff departments. In the 1980s, many banks were successfully using quality circles to

- ❖ rearrange teller lines to speed up customer service and more evenly distribute work
- ❖ establish express teller lines
- ❖ improve security at teller windows

However, bankers who have worked with quality circles in front office areas have found that productivity improvements are often small and take time to develop. They have also found that a quality circle program cannot be readily introduced to front office operations in the absence of a total management commitment to quality control efforts.

Other Approaches to Productivity

Some banks have opted for flexible salary structures, more bonuses and recognition programs, broader employee career paths, and job enrichment for clerical employees to cut turnover rates and thereby improve productivity.

Other banks have sought to develop criteria for measuring the productivity of bank professionals and staff. In the 1980s, many banks expanded their staff operations, adding to existing departments and creating new ones in such areas as marketing, planning, data processing, and employee training. These departments, highly labor intensive and costly, typically do not lend themselves to easy productivity measurement and evaluation.

The Task Ahead

Increasing productivity throughout the banking industry will not be easy. Both management and employees will have to be better trained in the process and concepts of productivity; devise better criteria for measuring productivity; develop new tools and techniques for improving productivity and share the rewards for those improvements. Many banks see human resource management as an important means to control labor costs and increase productivity. Industry studies suggest that by focusing management attention on the quality of work life, improvements in employee morale and the quality of bank services can be attained. This would increase productivity and generate cost savings by reducing absenteeism, on-the-job accidents, and error rates. Operating management will have to continue to shift its focus toward improving the quality of work life in the bank. Projections in the 1990s are that cost cutting alone will not likely be sufficient to restore profitability and maintain competitiveness in the environment facing banks over the next 20 years.

Summary

Banking is in the midst of profound change. Since 1980, banks have seen the rise and fall of S&Ls as major competitors and the entry of nonbank financial institutions into the banking business. Banks also have seen the opening of Federal Reserve services to all depositories at explicit prices, the elimination of Regulation Q ceilings, and an explosion in interest expense as new deposit products have come to dominate balance sheets. The relative position of commercial banks in United States and world financial markets has declined, bank interest rate spreads have narrowed, and profitability for the nation's largest banks has eroded. However, most banks have shown remarkable adaptability to change.

In the 1990s, it is likely that the federal regulatory agencies will be restructured, and interstate branching and new service powers for banks in insurance, mutual fund investments, and real estate will be authorized.

Projections of present trends in the banking environment over the next two decades suggest advances in payments technology but no revolutionary changes in public payment or banking practices. Substantial consolidation among banks and thrifts through mergers and holding company affiliations is also projected. Trends suggest that bank operating costs and more intense competition will be key problems confronting banks. A major concern of banks today is increasing bank productivity to meet these problems. While banks face difficulties in measuring the productivity of many of their operations, some promising possibilities for increasing productivity, such as quality circles, have already generated benefits for many banks.

Questions

1. List three significant changes that have occurred in banking over the past two decades.

2. Based on current trends, cite three likely changes that will occur in banking or the U.S. payments mechanism by the year 2012.

3. What two options do banks face in addressing the issue of front office productivity?

4. What measures or programs have some banks adopted to increase productivity?

Glossary

ACH credit float Reserves that the Federal Reserve inadvertently withdraws from the banking system when, in processing ACH payments, it debits accounts of sending banks, but delays prevent the simultaneous crediting of the accounts of banks expecting the funds.

ACH debit float Extra reserves that the Federal Reserve creates in processing ACH payments when it credits the accounts of receiving banks before collecting payment from paying banks.

Altered check A check on which the date, name, or amount has been changed or erased. A bank is responsible for paying checks as originally written and it can refuse to pay a check that has been altered.

Asset allocation A bank funds management strategy in which funds are assigned to securities and loan asset categories and then reallocated as loan demand changes.

ATM network Linked ATMs that allow depositors to access their accounts for cash or account balance information through the ATMs of any participating bank.

ATS account An account arrangement in which funds from a time account are automatically transferred into a checking account to cover presented checks.

Audit trail A printed record of transactions created as a by-product of a bank's data processing or accounting operations. It enables an auditor to trace an activity, such as the processing of a check, on a step-by-step basis.

Automated clearing house (ACH) A clearing facility operated for the convenience of the banks in a particular region, generally through the regional Federal Reserve bank. Automated clearing houses electronically process interbank credits and debits. They may also handle the electronic transfer of government securities and customer services, such as the automatic deposit of customers' wages, direct deposit of Social Security payments, and preauthorized payments of bills by banks.

Automated teller machine (ATM) Unmanned terminal that allows customers to handle routine banking transactions such as cash withdrawals, deposits, and funds transfers.

Availability schedule Credit for cash letters (checks) deposited with correspondent banks or with Federal Reserve banks, granted in accordance with an availability schedule that gives banks immediate, one-day, or two-day deferred credit, depending on the location of the banks on which the checks are drawn. The availability schedule is constructed to reflect the approximate amount of time it should take to collect the check. However, credit availability is granted regardless of the amount of time it takes to collect an individual check.

Available funds Check deposits that are considered collected and available for use by the depositor.

Bad check A check returned to the payee from the depositor's bank marked unpaid because of insufficient funds in the depositor's account.

Bank credit card A form of consumer credit known as open-end credit (for example, MasterCard and Visa) that allows cardholders to make purchases from merchants and pay for the purchases by making installment payments to a bank.

Bank float Deposits credited to a depositor's account in one bank but not yet collected from the bank on which the items were drawn.

Bank Insurance Fund (BIF) The deposit insurance fund for commercial banks administered by the FDIC.

Bank panic Fear or anxiety that drives depositors to hastily withdraw funds from banks, other financial institutions, and financial markets. Bank panics have forced banks into collapse because they were unable to meet depositors' claims.

Bank regulation Implementation of banking laws through government-issued rules and directives.

Bank supervision The enforcement of banking regulations through continuous onsite examinations.

Bankers' acceptance A type of credit instrument similar to a money order drawn on and accepted by a bank to finance the export, import, shipment, or storage of goods. The term "accepted" means that the bank agrees to pay the money order at its maturity on behalf of its customer, who is obligated to pay the bank the amount being financed.

Bank check A bank's check drawn on itself and signed by an authorized bank official.

Bilateral credit limits Limits that banks impose on one another for the maximum amount of CHIPS provisional funds they are willing to receive from one another over CHIPS.

Board of Governors The seven-member supervisory body of the Federal Reserve System. Each member is appointed by the president for 14 years, with the Senate's consent. *Also referred to as* Federal Reserve Board.

Book-entry security A Treasury or U.S. government agency security for which ownership information is held on computerized records at a Federal Reserve bank. This form of security protects against loss or theft and reduces processing costs by eliminating the need for physical transfers.

Branch bank   A multioffice banking facility whose ability to branch is controlled by state law.

Brokerage firm   A company that buys and sells securities on behalf of customers for a fee.

Canceled check   A check that has been paid and charged to the depositor's account, then imprinted with the date of the payment and the name of the presenting bank. These checks are generally retained in the bank's files until they are sent to the check writer with a statement of account transactions, usually monthly.

Cap   A limit on the maximum amount of overdrafts a bank can generate with all other participants in CHIPS and FedWire.

Capital requirement   The amount of capital (funds paid in by stockholders) necessary for a bank to receive a charter. The capital adequacy standard for most banks is 6 percent (capital funds as a percentage of a bank's total assets); the standard for large banks involved in international banking is 8 percent.

Cash item   Any item immediately convertible into cash.

Cash items in the process of collection   The asset posting that a bank makes on its balance sheet for checks received from depositors for which payment has not been received.

Cash letter   An interbank transmittal form that accompanies cash items sent from one bank to another. The form contains the date, the banks involved, the total dollar amount of the checks, and the type of credit availability associated with the checks—immediate, or one-day or two-day deferred.

Cash management   Services banks provide to corporate customers to speed collection of checks, control disbursements, and provide timely account balance information, so that corporations can maximize their available funds.

Cashier's check   A bank's check drawn on itself and signed by an authorized bank official.

Central bank   A bank responsible for controlling a nation's monetary policy, and serving as its lender of last resort. The Federal Reserve is the central bank of the United States.

Certificate of deposit (CD)   A receipt for time funds deposited with a bank. CDs are widely used for investment purposes and are traded as short-term paper in the money markets.

Certified check   A check for which payment has been guaranteed (or certified) by the bank on which it is drawn. A certified check becomes an obligation of the bank. For this reason, banks are required to charge the depositor's account immediately for the amount of the certified check.

CHAPS   An acronym for Clearing House Automated Payments System, an interbank wire transfer system operated by the London clearing house for use by banks in the London area. Participants guarantee funds sent over CHAPS.

Charge-off   An outstanding loan balance that a bank writes off as a bad debt loss because it no longer expects to be repaid.

Check   A written order to a bank instructing it to pay on demand a sum of money on deposit to the party whose name appears on the order.

Check clearing   The process by which banks that receive deposited checks obtain payment from the banks on which the checks are drawn.

Check guarantee service   A bank service that guarantees payment of a check to merchants and other banks.

Check presentment   The physical delivery of a check to the bank on which the check is drawn. The law requires such presentment before a check can be paid.

Check reconcilement   A banking service that itemizes, in serial order, all checks received, paid, and outstanding during the statement period. The service also provides corresponding account balance information.

Check routing symbol   A numerical code that facilitates the handling and routing of checks for collection. The code is the denominator of the fractional number located in the upper right-hand corner of a check; it is reproduced in MICR symbols at the bottom of the check. The first two digits identify the Federal Reserve district in which the drawee bank is located. The third digit designates through whom the check will be cleared and the fourth indicates whether the check will be credited with immediate or deferred funds.

Check truncation   The elimination of the physical handling and/or storage of checks.

Checking account   *See* demand deposit.

Circuitous routing   A nineteenth-century banking practice of sending checks on long, circuitous collection routes across the country to avoid having to pay exchange charges.

City check   A check drawn on a bank located in the same city as the Federal Reserve office. Immediate credit is given to city checks cleared through a Federal Reserve bank.

Clearing   The interbank presentation of checks and settlement of resulting balances.

Clearing balance   An account that a depository institution holds at a Federal Reserve bank in lieu of or in addition to, required reserve balances to facilitate transactions involving Federal Reserve services, and to avoid daylight and overnight overdrafts.

Clearing House Interbank Payments System (CHIPS) An electronic funds transfer system operated by the New York Clearing House Association that enables participating banks to make domestic and international interbank payments.

Collateral Something of value, such as a car or a house, that a borrower pledges as backing for a loan.

Collected funds Checks for which the bank has received payment.

Commercial bank A privately owned financial institution that makes business loans, accepts demand deposits, and provides a variety of other financial services.

Commercial paper A negotiable, short-term, unsecured promissory note in bearer form, issued by well-regarded businesses. Commercial paper is generally sold at a discount and has a maximum maturity of nine months. *Also called* paper.

Compensating balance The funds that a business firm or respondent bank must leave on deposit with a bank to obtain services.

Comptroller of the Currency The official of the U.S. government, appointed by the president and confirmed by the Senate, who is responsible for chartering, examining, supervising, and, if necessary, liquidating national banks.

Consumer bank *See* nonbank bank.

Consumer float The extra use of funds consumers obtain during the time interval between creation of a check and its ultimate payment by the bank on which it is drawn.

Controlled disbursement A cash management service designed to maximize available balances for a corporation. It is offered by banks that receive only one early-morning presentment of checks. After the bank makes postings to the corporate account, the corporation can use all remaining funds without concern for further postings during the day.

Core deposits Deposit balances that are relatively stable, are unlikely to be withdrawn, and carry predictable costs.

Corporate trade payment An electronic transaction between corporations that transfers funds and payments-related information.

Correspondent bank A bank that holds account balances of smaller banks and provides services to those banks, primarily through those accounts.

Country check A check drawn on a bank located in the same Federal Reserve district, but outside a metropolitan or suburban area. Federal Reserve banks give one- or two-day deferred credit on such checks.

Credit Acceptance of an agreement to repay a loan of money in the future.

Credit policies A bank's internal policies regarding loans. These policies

---

generally establish the degree of risk the bank will take in making loans, the type of loans it is prepared to make, the maturity and other terms of its loans, and the authorization limits of its loan officers.

Credit unions Cooperative organizations of individuals with a common affiliation—such as employment. Credit unions are owned by their members and accept deposits of members in the form of share purchases, pay interest on the shares out of earnings, and primarily provide consumer installment credit to members.

Creditworthiness A borrower's ability to obtain credit from lenders, usually based on the amount and quality of the borrower's assets and repayment history.

Dealer firm A company that buys and sells securities for its own account.

Debit card A plastic card that serves as an access device to an EFT terminal. When used for payments, it immediately transfers funds from the user's account (a debit) to another party.

Deferred availability schedule The time schedule the Federal Reserve uses in crediting banks for checks presented for collection. The schedule either grants credit on the same day or defers credit for one or two days, depending on the proximity to Federal Reserve offices of the banks on which the checks are drawn.

Delayed availability Banks' practice of deferring credit for several days on checks deposited by customers to ensure that the checks are not returned unpaid by the banks on which they are drawn.

Demand deposit A noninterest-bearing deposit or account that is payable on demand. The account holder can make payments by writing checks against the deposit or can withdraw cash from the bank on demand.

Demand deposit accounting (DDA) The automated demand deposit book-keeping function in banks.

Depository transfer check A preauthorized, presigned check drawn on another bank that a corporation gives to a bank to provide funds coverage if, on any given day, its account would otherwise be in overdraft.

Depository Trust Company (DTC) A private New York bank that serves as a settlement agent for institutional participants in the securities market, such as banks, insurance companies, and brokerage and securities dealer firms.

Direct deposit account Automatic deposit of funds from a paying source to a checking or savings account.

Direct send The method of check collection in which deposited checks are presented directly to their drawee banks for settlement.

Discount rate The interest rate that Reserve banks charge depositories for loans.

Discount window   The figurative expression for the Federal Reserve facility for lending reserves to depositories.

Disintermediation   The public's mass withdrawal of deposit balances from banks and thrifts for direct placement into money market investments, such as Treasury bills and mutual funds. This is a reversal of the traditional flow of consumers' funds into financial intermediaries. Disintermediation occurred in the 1960s and 1970s when interest-rate ceilings prevented depositories from matching prevailing rates.

Dollar-amount encoding   To imprint the dollar amount of a check in magnetic ink characters on the bottom of the check so that computerized machines can process it.

Dual banking   The regulatory system in the United States that permits a bank to obtain a charter from either the state or the federal government.

Electronic check presentment   Transfering funds electronically by transmitting payment instructions contained on paper checks.

Electronic Funds Transfer System (EFT)   A system or technology for transferring funds electronically.

Endorsement   The signature, placed on the back of a negotiable instrument or in an accompanying power, that transfers the instrument to another party and legally implies that the endorser has the right to transfer the instrument. Endorsement enables the bank to transfer checking account funds between accounts and to other banks.

Eurodollar borrowings   A bank's borrowings of dollar-denominated funds on the books of banking offices outside the United States.

Exception item   A check that a bank cannot honor for one reason or another, such as a stop payment order or insufficient funds.

Excess reserves   Reserve balances that depository institutions maintain beyond those required.

Exchange charge   A service charge made by a drawee bank for paying checks and other instruments presented to it.

Expedited Funds Availability Act (EFAA)   A law passed by Congress in 1987 that requires financial institutions to make deposited items available for withdrawal on an expedited basis. The hold limits in 1991 were two days for local checks and five days for nonlocal checks.

Federal Deposit Insurance Corporation (FDIC)   The agency of the federal government that provides deposit insurance to commercial banks through the Bank Insurance Fund (BIF) and to savings and loan associations through the Savings Association Insurance Fund (SAIF). The FDIC also has primary federal examinations responsibility over insured state banks that are not members of the Federal Reserve system.

Federal funds The reserve balances that banks borrow from each other, usually on an overnight basis.

Federal funds rate The interest rate that banks charge one another for overnight loans of reserve funds.

Federal Reserve float The difference between uncollected cash items in the process of collection by Federal Reserve banks and the deferred availability credits made by the Federal Reserve. The Fed credits banks for cash items on a deferred availability schedule based on average collection times, but it receives payment for the cash items only after they have been presented to the bank on which they were drawn. Federal Reserve float occurs in the time interval after the sending bank has been credited until the time funds are received from the paying bank.

Federal Reserve notes Nearly all the nation's circulating paper currency consists of Federal Reserve notes printed by the Treasury Department and issued to the Federal Reserve, which puts them into circulation through the commercial banking system.

Federal Reserve System The central bank of the United States, unique because it is quasigovernmental and decentralized. The Federal Reserve System consists of 12 Reserve banks, supervised by a Board of Governors in Washington, D.C., and 5,600 commercial banks.

FedWire The Federal Reserve's electronic funds transfer and communications network, which depositories use to transfer reserve balances and government securities.

Financial institution An institution that uses its funds chiefly to purchase financial assets (loans, securities) as opposed to tangible property. Financial institutions can be classified as nondeposit or depository institutions according to the nature of the principal claims they issue. Nondeposit institutions, such as life insurance companies and pension funds, issue claims in the form of the policies they sell or the promise they make to provide income after retirement. Depository institutions obtain funds mainly by accepting deposits from the public.

Financial Institutions Reform, Recovery and Enforcement Act (FIRREA)
This 1989 act sought to resolve the problem of insolvent S&Ls by creating a new agency—the Resolution Trust Corporation (RTC)—to take over insolvent S&Ls and find buyers for them or liquidate their assets and reimburse insured depositors. FIRREA also established a new deposit insurance fund for S&Ls, to be administered by the FDIC, tightened S&L capital requirements, and rescinded some lending and investment powers that had been granted S&Ls in the early 1980s, such as investment in junk bonds and real estate development projects.

Fit currency Circulated currency that has been returned to the Federal Reserve but is not too wrinkled or dirty to recirculate.

Float Money balances that for a period of time appear on the books of both the check writer and the check receiver, because of the lag in the check collection process.

Foreign exchange The currency of another nation. Trading in or exchange of foreign currencies for U.S. funds or other foreign currencies.

Fractional reserves A banking principle under which banks maintain reserves equal to a fraction of their outstanding deposits, which enables them to create a multiple of new deposit balances.

Functional regulation Regulating banks and other institutions according to the activities they are engaged in rather than what they are.

Gap The difference between maturing assets and maturing liabilities in a given time period.

Gap management The control of maturities of assets and liabilities to maintain the desired relationship between them. Although objectives can change over time, gap management may involve gapping or attempting to maintain a balanced maturity position.

Giro Retail EFT systems used in Europe that provide nationwide funds transfer coverage by linking banks and post offices with EFT terminals.

Hedging Controlling the risk of one transaction by engaging in an offsetting transaction. For example, a bank that wants to protect a segment of its securities portfolio from a rise in interest rates can hedge by selling the same amount of securities for future delivery at a current price.

Hold The restriction of payment of all or part of the funds in an account.

Holding company (one-bank or multibank) A corporation or bank that owns or controls one or more banks.

Home banking A banking service that enables bank customers to make payments, transfer funds between accounts, or communicate with their bank from a personal computer at home.

Image processing The electronic transfer of the digitized image of a check or other paper document.

Individual retirement account (IRA) A tax-deferred account that allows a customer to deposit a stipulated amount and to earn interest. Tax on the account is deferred until retirement, when it presumably will be taxable at a lower rate.

Inflation An economic condition characterized by rising prices with a corresponding drop in money's purchasing power or value.

Insolvency (bank) A condition in which the accounting value of a bank's assets are less than the value of its liabilities.

Insufficient funds A condition in which a depositor's account balance is inadequate for the bank to honor a check.

Interbank wire transfer   An electronic transfer of funds through an account balance at the Federal Reserve or an account balance maintained at a correspondent bank.

Interchange charge   A transactions fee arrangement that the national credit card companies use. Under this arrangement, the bank that holds the account of a merchant depositing a credit card slip pays a fee to the bank that issued a credit card to the merchant's customer.

Interdistrict settlement account   An account that each Reserve bank maintains on the books of the Interdistrict Settlement Fund, established in Washington, D.C., to handle check settlements among Reserve banks. A check presented to one Reserve bank that is drawn on a bank in another Federal Reserve district results in a transfer of interdistrict settlement account balances from one Reserve bank to another.

Intraday overdraft   An account whose balance during the course of a day is negative because charges (debits) momentarily exceed credits. Intraday or daylight overdrafts occur because banks are unable precisely to match funds transfer payments and receipts over the interbank EFT systems for their corporate accounts or for their own accounts.

Lifeline banking services   Basic checking and savings account services that banks would provide at low cost or free of service charges, so that low-income individuals could have access to banking services.

Line of credit   A specified amount of money that a customer may borrow without filing a new loan application.

Liquidity   The degree to which an asset can be readily converted into money.

Loan commitment fee   A fee banks charge corporate customers for a prearranged loan to be used at a future date. The fee compensates the bank for committing its money in advance and assures the borrower that credit will be available.

Loan loss reserve   A reserve account that covers expected losses on loans. As losses are incurred, they are charged against the account.

Local clearing house   A central site where banks in one locality present checks drawn on one another for collection and exchange. Each participating bank's balance at the clearing house is adjusted on a net basis to reflect the difference between the value of checks paid and the value of checks collected to and from other banks in the collection arrangement.

Lockbox   A banking service provided for the rapid collection of a customer's receivables and rapid credit to the customer's account. The service includes collecting the mail from the company's post office box; sorting, totaling, and recording the payments; processing the items; and making the necessary bank deposits.

Managed liabilities Those sources of funds that bank management can control through purchase or borrowing actions, such as corporate CDs, Euro-dollar borrowings, and federal funds purchases.

Maturity The date upon which a security, loan, or other financial instrument becomes due and payable.

Merchant discount charge A fee that banks charge merchants for processing and accepting the credit risks on the merchant's credit card sales.

MICR—magnetic ink character recognition The symbols on the bottom of the face of a check that enable banks' check reader-sorter computers to read the information on a check electronically. MICR encoding can include the amount of the check, the account number, the bank's number, and the serial number of the check.

Mixed cash letter A package of checks containing a mix of city, RCPC (regional check processing center), and country checks that the presenting bank has not sorted into these separate categories.

Monetary Control Act of 1980 This act established new reserve requirements for all depository institutions, extended access to Federal Reserve borrowing privileges and other services to all depositories, required the Federal Reserve to charge explicit prices for its payments services, provided for the phaseout of deposit interest-rate ceilings by 1986, and granted broader powers for thrift institutions.

Monetary policy The Federal Reserve's actions that influence the cost of money (interest rates) and the availability of money (the growth rate of the money supply).

Monetization of gold The Treasury's issuance of gold certificates to the Federal Reserve in return for an equal dollar credit to the Treasury's account at the Federal Reserve.

Money Any item that serves as a generally accepted medium of exchange. A medium of exchange allows people to compare the value of goods and services (standard of value) and store generalized purchasing power for future use (store of value).

Money creation Commercial banks create money by granting loans, which add new deposit dollars to the checking account balances of businesses and individuals. When a bank grants a loan, it receives a borrower's promise to repay, which is an asset (something of value) that increases the bank's worth. The bank simultaneously adds new bookkeeping entries to the borrower's checking account, thus increasing its liabilities (something owed).

Money market deposit account An account that Congress authorized in 1982 that carries a market interest rate and allows the depositor limited check-writing privileges (three checks per month).

Money market fund   A company that pools investors' funds for placement in money market instruments, stocks, and bonds.

Money order   Checks that are purchased for a fee from a bank, drawn either on the bank or its correspondent.

Money supply   The amount of money the public has immediately available for spending.

Mutual fund   A diversified portfolio of securities from which investors can buy shares.

Mutual savings bank   An institution mutually owned by depositors that offers transaction and savings accounts and makes the bulk of its loans as mortgages.

National bank   A bank whose charter is granted by the Comptroller of the Currency. It must belong to the Federal Reserve System and the FDIC.

Negotiability   The ability to transfer ownership of a check or other financial instrument by endorsement.

Net settlement   Settlement of payments among participants in check-clearing or similar arrangements by netting the claims participants present against one another and posting only the resulting credit or debit differences. In a net settlement, all accounting entries for the day's transactions net to zero among the group of participants (that is, the debits offset the credits).

Netting   An arrangement in which multiple payments due to and due from specific parties to one another are not sent but are combined and netted into single payments due or owed and then sent.

Nonbank bank   A bank that has been divested of its commercial loan portfolio or checking accounts by its parent holding company, so that it no longer meets the legal definition of a commercial bank under the Bank Holding Company Act of 1956. This legal loophole, which was closed by a 1987 amendment to the Bank Holding Company Act, enabled major retailers, insurance companies and finance companies to enter the banking business in the 1980s.

Noninterest expenses   The expenses a bank incurs as a result of its on-going operations—salaries and fringe benefits, building upkeep, equipment, and depreciation expenses.

Nonpar checking   An out-of-town check credited to a depositor's account at less than par (face) value.

Nonsettling bank   A participant in CHIPS that uses the account of another bank to settle its CHIPS payments.

NOW account   Acronym for negotiable order of withdrawal. The account provides the demand features of a checking account and also pays interest.

Office of Thrift Supervision The federal regulatory agency responsible for chartering and supervising savings and loan associations.

Off-line bank A bank that does not have a terminal connected to the FedWire system. It has to initiate wire transfers of funds through the Federal Reserve by telephone.

Online bank A bank that has a terminal connected to the FedWire system, which enables it to initiate and receive wire transfers of funds and securities directly through the Federal Reserve.

On-us item A check deposited in the bank on which it is drawn and collected through internal adjustments on the bank's books.

Open-market operations The purchase and sale of U.S. obligations, munici-pal obligations, other money market instruments, and foreign exchange by the Federal Reserve. These operations influence the growth of the nation's money supply and are the principal means by which monetary policy is imple-mented.

Operational controls The internal systems, procedures, and policies a bank has in place to ensure that its electronic funds transfer, check collection, and other deposit operations are performed efficiently.

Operational risk The risk a bank incurs if, during the day, it cannot send or receive electronic funds, or settle its position, because of a computer failure.

Overdraft A situation that occurs when the closing balance in a depositor's account for a particular day is negative. This results when charges (debits) exceed the sum of the previous day's balance and credits for the current business day.

Overdraft account A checking account with a line of credit that allows the account holder to write checks for funds in excess of balances. Upon present-ment of such checks, the bank credits the account with the amount of a loan drawn off the credit line, which can be repaid at a later time.

Package sort checks Checks drawn on one bank only and packaged for delivery to that bank.

Packet switch system An EFT system that routes funds transfers through a linked network of self-contained processing and message-switching centers, rather than through a central computer.

Par or par value The nominal or face value of a stock or bond certificate, expressed as a specific amount marked on the fact of the security. Par value is not related to market value, which is the amount a buyer is willing to pay for an item. No premiums or discounts from the face value will be made.

Passbook savings A savings account that uses a passbook in which the bank records transactions.

Pass-through account The reserve account of a bank or thrift that chooses not to deposit reserves directly at a Reserve bank but rather at a correspondent bank, which must redeposit the funds at the Federal Reserve. This pass-through reserve account arrangement was established in 1980 to enable non-member banks and thrifts to meet Federal Reserve reserve requirements within the context of their correspondent banking relationships.

Payable-through-drafts Checklike instruments written on a corporation rather than on a bank but payable through a bank; such drafts are recognized as checks only after funding coverage is provided for their clearance rather than when they are written.

Payments mechanism Payment devices and institutions used to move funds, make payments, and settle balances due between individuals. The Federal Reserve plays a major role in the U.S. payments mechanism through its distribution of currency and coin, check processing, and provision of wire transfer and automated clearing house services.

Payer bank The bank responsible for paying the check, typically the bank on which the check is drawn.

PIN Acronym for personal identification number, a multidigit code that each customer must enter in an ATM or POS terminal to activate transactions.

Point-of-sale (POS) terminal The in-store computer terminal that transfers information on the books of participating banks or funds between purchasers and merchants.

Postdated check A check that bears a future date.

Premium credit card A credit card that provides the holder with additional benefits and a higher credit line.

Presentment fee A fee banks charge other banks that present checks directly to them for same-day payment.

Primary reserves The sum of all of a bank's liquid assets—cash, deposit balances held at a correspondent bank, its reserve account at the Federal Reserve, and cash items in the process of collection. These assets are a bank's primary source of liquidity to meet demand claims.

Private Sector Adjustment Factor (PSAF) The markup the Federal Reserve adds to its service prices to reflect profit, taxes, and costs that would have been incurred if the services were provided by a commercial bank.

Profitability The efficiency rate at which a bank is employing and managing its assets and generating an investment or profit return on its owners' equity.

Proof department The bank department that sorts, distributes, and verifies all transactions arising from the bank's deposit operations.

Provisional funds Funds received in payment that have not yet been settled.

Receiver risk   The possibility that provisional funds received through CHIPS will not be settled at the end of the day.

Recession   An economy characterized by declining national output of goods and services for at least six months, coupled with rising unemployment.

Regional check-processing center (RCPC)   A Federal Reserve check-processing operation that expedites the collection of checks drawn on depository institutions located within specified (usually suburban) areas.

Regional reserve bank   One of the 12 Federal Reserve banks responsible for providing banking services to depositories in its district. Reserve banks issue the nation's currency—Federal Reserve notes—and hold most of the reserves that depositories are legally required to maintain against deposits.

Regulation CC   The Federal Reserve regulation that governs bank's delayed availability and return items practices.

Regulation D   The Federal Reserve regulation that establishes depositories' reserve requirements and delineates related reserve maintenance rules.

Regulation E   The Federal Reserve regulation that governs bank's and consumers' rights, liabilities, and responsibilities in EFT systems.

Regulation J   The Federal Reserve regulation that governs banks' check collection and wire transfer activities.

Regulation Q   The Federal Reserve regulation that prohibits the payment of interest on demand deposits, differentiates between demand and time deposits, and, until 1986, specified the maximum rates a bank could pay on time deposits.

Remote disbursement   A practice designed to slow the collection of checks and provide maximum float time. For example, a corporation establishes a zero-balance account at a bank located in a remote geographic area, writes all its checks against that account, and covers the checks when they are presented for payment with funds transferred from other banks.

Repurchase agreement   The purchase of a security, usually a three-month Treasury bill, under an agreement that the seller will buy back the security within a specified time (usually a day or two) at an agreed price.

Required reserves   Funds that banks must keep by law as a kind of backing against their customers' deposits. To create more money a bank must have more reserves (excess reserves) than required by law.

Reserve balance   A balance maintained at a Federal Reserve bank or a qualifying correspondent institution to satisfy the financial institution's reserve requirements. *See also* pass-through account.

Reserve checking/overdraft checking   A combination of a checking account and a preauthorized personal loan; also called cash reserve, check credit, or personal line of credit.

Reserve deficiency   A situation that occurs when a bank's daily average reserve balance is less than the daily average required reserve balance during a given reserve maintenance period (the period during which required reserves must be maintained). Institutions are permitted to carry over a deficiency of up to 2 percent into the next maintenance period without penalty.

Reserve requirements   The percentage of reserves banks must hold against deposits.

Reserves   Bank assets that are eligible for meeting legal reserve requirements, specifically, cash on hand or funds deposited at the district Reserve Bank.

Resolution Trust Corporation (RTC)   A government-sponsored corporation created by Congress in 1989 to take over insolvent S&Ls and find buyers for them or liquidate their assets and pay off insured depositors.

Return item   A check that is returned unpaid by the bank to which it was presented.

Risk   The degree of uncertainty that a loss will be sustained in a loan, investment, or payment transaction.

Savings and Loan Association (S&L)   A depository institution that offers transaction and time deposit services and makes the bulk of its loans as mortgages.

Savings Association Insurance Fund (SAIF)   The deposit insurance fund for savings and loan associations administered by the FDIC.

Scrip   A temporary document that entitles the holder to receive money or another item of value at a future date.

Secondary market   A market, such as the government securities dealer market, where ownership of financial assets is transferred from one party to another.

Secondary reserves   A bank's securities portfolio. Because a bank's securities assets can be sold easily for liquid assets to meet demand claims, these assets are considered the second source of a bank's reserves. A bank's primary source of reserves is its liquid assets.

Securitization   The practice of packaging a portfolio of specific loans, such as auto loans, mortgages or credit card loans, into a single financial instrument and selling the instrument in the secondary market as if it were a security.

Sender risk   The risk a bank incurs if it electronically transfers funds in excess of available balances.

Settlement   The irrevocable transfer of value in a payment transaction.

Settling bank   A participant in CHIPS that is authorized to settle payments for other participants.

Share draft   An interest-bearing checking account that credit unions offer. Congress authorized share drafts in the Monetary Control Act of 1980.

Source of strength doctrine A Federal Reserve policy that bank holding companies must provide subsidiary banks with financial assistance when necessary to avert the banks' insolvency.

Special Drawing Rights (SDRs) International money balances created by the International Monetary Fund and allocated to its member nations. SDRs can be used only by governments to settle international debts.

Spread The difference between a bank's return on assets and its cost of liabilities.

Staledated check A check six months old or older received by a bank for payment. The bank can return such an item unpaid because the check has not been presented for payment within a reasonable time.

State bank A bank chartered by state banking authorities. A state bank may or may not be a Federal Reserve member and may or may not belong to the Federal Deposit Insurance Corporation.

Statement savings A savings account in which a periodic statement replaces the passbook.

Stop payment order An order by a customer to his or her bank not to negotiate a previously issued check.

Store and forward capability The capability of a funds transfer system to accumulate transfer requests for future release, store transactions information on file, and forward stored transfers on command.

S.W.I.F.T. An acronym for Society for Worldwide Interbank Financial Telecommunication. S.W.I.F.T. is an international message system that banks use when transferring funds. Most S.W.I.F.T. messages are interbank instructions related to third-party foreign trade payments.

Systemic risk The risk that the failure of a major bank to settle its CHIPS payments at the end of the day will lead to a sequential collapse of other banks and CHIPS itself.

Third-party format standard A banking industry standard for the position and placement of account-related information in wire transfer messages that banks send for their corporate accounts.

Third-party payment An electronic funds transfer that a bank makes on behalf of a depositor to an account holder at another bank.

Thrift institutions Mutual savings banks, savings and loan associations, and credit unions.

Time deposit Any deposit in a bank account that cannot be withdrawn before a specified date or without advance notice. Examples include savings deposits, time certificates of deposit, and time deposits (open account).

Transaction account A deposit or account from which the holder can withdraw money to make a payment or a transfer to another party through such means as a check, draft, payment order of withdrawal, or telephone transfer. Examples of transaction accounts include demand deposits, NOW accounts, savings deposits subject to automatic transfer, share draft accounts, deposits that can be accessed through an automated teller machine, and deposits from which payments can be made with a debit card.

Transit item   A check drawn on an out-of-town bank.

Transit number   A numerical coding system originated by the American Bankers Association to facilitate the sorting and processing of checks. Each bank is assigned a unique number, made of two parts separated by a hyphen. The first part of the number identifies the state, city, or territory in which the bank is located, and the second part identifies the bank itself.

Traveler's check   A special fixed-amount check issued by a bank or other institution and sold at many franchise locations. The purchaser of these checks pays a fee for the convenience of guaranteed rapid replacement in the event of loss or theft.

Treasury bill   A marketable U.S. Treasury security with a life of one year or less, sold to the public at weekly auctions on a discount basis in minimum denominations of $10,000 and in book-entry only form. *Also called* T-bill.

Two-party payment   An electronic funds transfer made by one bank to another bank, usually in payment for federal funds purchases or as a settlement for third-party CHIPS payments made during the day.

Unbundled service   A bank service that is not linked to any other service or service package and, thus, can be obtained separately. An unbundled service usually carries an explicit fee.

Uncollected funds   Check deposits that the bank has not yet collected.

Underwriting   The purchase of new offerings of corporate stock or the debt securities of a corporation or government entity for resale in the secondary market.

Unfit currency   Currency of such poor quality that it cannot be recirculated.

Uniform Commercial Code   General body of commercial law that governs the sale of goods, the use of commercial paper and checks, check collection, and personal property transactions. Most states' banking laws encompass the Uniform Commercial Code.

Value dating   A funds transfer instruction that designates the date on which the transferred funds are to be made available to the recipient.

Wire transfer   An electronic transfer of funds.

Yield   The rate of return on an investment.

Index

❖

❖

Magnetic ink character recognition (MICR)
>data to prepare magnetic tape, 99, 227
>encoding, 99
>instructions, 98
>processing of checks, 98, 213
>standardization, 16, 98

Mail float. *See also* Consumer float
>definition, 27
>reduction by lockbox, 267

Managed funds. *See* Bank funds

Managed liabilities. *See* Liability management

Mandatory sharing of EFT technology, 29

Marketing strategies, 228-29

Market value disclosure rules, 262

Maslow, Abraham, 308

Maturity matching, 241

Mcorp
>and source of strength suit, 283

McFadden Act (1927), 60, 154-55

McGregor, Thomas, 308

Medicare controlled disbursement program, 270-71

Medium of exchange, 2

Merrill Lynch
>customer services, 50
>and remote disbursement practices, 275

Mismatching of assets and liabilities, 243

Mixed cash letters
>float elimination, 122
>packages of checks, 105, 112
>unencoded, 112

Modems, for home banking, 151

Monetary Control Act (1980), 35, 38-41, 290
>and fund management, 240, 247-48
>reserve requirement rules, 75
>and savings and loan associations, 44

Monetary policy
>and federal funds market, 255
>goal of Federal Reserve, 197

Monetizing of gold by U.S. Treasury, 207

Money creation
>how banks multiply deposits, 192-96

Money market banks
>centralization of deposits, 284
>reliance on federal funds, 254

Money market deposit account (MMDA), 36-37, 47-48

Money market funds, 47-48

Money panics, 94

Money supply

❖

Risk reduction, 184-86
    continuing payment contracts, 186
    intraday overdraft credit plan, 184-85
    netting systems, 185-86
Rule 13, 176

Same-day presentment fees, 114-15
Savings and loan associations (S&Ls), depositories in housing finance, 44-45
Savings Association Insurance Fund (SAIF), 45, 65
Savings banks, 43-44
Savings certificates
    definition, 55
Savings deposits
    definition, 52
Scrip, 62, 90
Sears, 48-50
Secondary reserves, 239
Securities. *See also* Futures contract; Government securities holdings
    service fees, 233
Securitization, 244
Sender net-debit cap, 181
Sender risk, for CHIPS participants, 176
Settlement
    definition, 106
    in EFT payments, 163-64
    failures, collateral for, 179-80
Settlement risk, 174-78
Share accounts, 46
Share drafts, 46
Sharing losses, 179-80
Simplified employee pension (SEP) accounts, 55
Smart card, introduction and feasibility, 10
Society for Worldwide Interbank Financial Telecommunications (S.W.I.F.T.)
    membership and operations, 170-71
    system of payment, 172
    transaction volumes, 171
Source of strength doctrine, 282-83
Special drawing rights (SDRs), U.S. Treasury, 207
Specialized banks, 296
Spread, 240
Spread management, 238, 240-41
Staledated checks, payment on, 214-15
State banking departments, 65
State-chartered banks
    check clearing, 63
    responsibilities, 65
    rules and regulations, 63
    rules on sharing EFT services, 29

Two-party payment, 164

Unbundled service, 113
Uncollected funds
        to cover check, 216
        crediting respondents' account, 15
        distinguished from unavailable funds, 212
Underground economy, 95
Unfit currency replacement, 97
Uniform Commercial Code (UCC)
        article 4A, 80
        checking and banking provisions, 79, 124-25
        depositors statements, 226
        section 3-506(2), 79
        section 4-402,
        treatment of checks, 123, 124-25, 212-16
U.S. Treasury
        cash holdings, 208
        currency issuance, 93, 207
        currency outstanding, 207
        deposits with Federal Reserve banks, 208
        monetization of gold and special drawing rights (SDRs), 207
        securities, 166-67
Usury
        ceilings on consumer loans, 247
        ceilings on real estate loans, 247
        state laws, 260, 261

Vault cash, 96-98, 257

Wire transfer
        definition, 163
Wire transfer systems. *See also* Interbank funds transfer systems
        direct computer-to-computer links, 291
        in next two decades, 291
        operational vulnerabilities, 176-78
        and Regulation J, 80
        speed and efficiency of moving money, 80, 291
        Zengin system, 22
Workforce. *See* Personnel

Yield, market interest rise, 265

Zengin system, 22
Zero-balance accounts, 269